FORT WORTH PUBLIC LIBRARY

P9-CDA-207

345.7302523 WILLIAMS
Williams, Daniel R.
Executing justice

Central

JUN 3 0 2001

CENTRAL LIBRARY

EXECUTING JUSTICE

ST. MARTIN'S PRESS
NEW YORK

EXECUTING JUSTICE

AN INSIDE ACCOUNT OF THE CASE OF MUMIA ABU-JAMAL

DANIEL R. WILLIAMS

EXECUTING JUSTICE: AN INSIDE ACCOUNT OF THE CASE OF
MUMIA ABU-JAMAL. Copyright © 2001 by Daniel R. Williams. All
rights reserved. Printed in the United States of America. No part of
this book may be used or reproduced in any manner whatsoever
without written permission except in the case of brief quotations
embodied in critical articles or reviews. For information, address
St. Martin's Press, 175 Fifth Avenue, New York, N.Y. 10010.

www.stmartins.com

Title page photograph © Jennifer Beach / Prison Radio 92 & 93

Book design by Claire Vaccaro

Library of Congress Cataloging-in-Publication Data

Williams, Daniel R.
    Executing justice : an inside account of the case of Mumia
Abu-Jamal / Daniel R. Williams.
        p. cm.
    ISBN 0-312-27666-4
    1. Abu-Jamal, Mumia—Trials, litigation, etc. 2. Trials
(Murder)—Pennsylvania—Philadelphia. 3. Police murders—
Pennsylvania—Philadelphia.
    I. Title.

KF224.A354 W55 2001
345.73'02523—dc21
                                                    2001018567

First Edition: May 2001

1   3   5   7   9   10   8   6   4   2

TO MY MOTHER,
WHO TRAVELED A ROUGH ROAD
SO THAT I MIGHT HAVE
A SMOOTHER RIDE

CONTENTS

FOREWORD

As I write, Mumia Abu-Jamal is in his eighteenth year of solitary confinement on death row in Pennsylvania's State Correctional Institute. He was tried, convicted, and sentenced to death for the shooting murder of Philadelphia police officer Daniel Faulkner. His appeals have all been rejected by the Pennsylvania state court system. His lawyers are now engaged in a last attempt to overturn the conviction by bringing their case to Federal Court in Philadelphia.

The trial of this black journalist and activist has attracted worldwide attention. The thirty-eight members of the Congressional Black Caucus have called for a new trial, as have several European governments, political figures such as the Reverend Jesse Jackson, labor unions, and ad hoc committees of writers, performers, and university professors. The scrupulous human rights organization Amnesty International has described Mumia's trial as a travesty and listed him in their registry as a political prisoner. There are so many issues of dubious police behavior, judicial impropriety, and apparent prosecutorial misconduct attached to this case as to have established a clear moral imperative to reconsider the entire basis of the case against Mumia. Yet the Philadelphia Brotherhood of Police, elements of the local press, and what appears to be the entire political establishment of Pennsylvania is unrelenting in its insistence that he be executed as a proven cop killer.

Mumia Abu-Jamal was defended by a court-appointed lawyer who did not wish to defend him and was unprepared to do so: Mumia was denied the right to defend himself and excluded from the court-room for crucial portions of his trial; a jury was picked with blatant efforts to eliminate blacks from the panel; the pivotal prosecution witnesses, one a paroled offender, the other a prostitute with bench warrants against her, and thus subject to police intimidation, offered damning testimony at the trial that contradicted what they had said the night of the officer's death; second-thought testimony by a patrol officer friend of the victim offered months after he made his original statement was admitted in evidence; a crucial defense witness, another policeman, was made unavailable for the trial; and the trajectory of Mumia's own bullet wound from Officer Faulkner's gun did not ac-cord with the prosecution's scenario of where he was standing when he and the police officer were supposed to have exchanged fire.

As a black radio journalist critical of the police and sympathetic to the beleaguered black MOVE communalists subsequently bombed out of their Philadelphia enclave, Mumia was not unknown to the le-gal establishment. He had belonged to the Black Panther Party as a teenager, a fact duly recorded by law enforcement and used by the prosecution to represent that this man who had never been known to commit an act of violence in his life was motivated to murder police-men by virtue of his radical beliefs. Two more contextual matters must be noted: that the trial judge, Albert Sabo, had sentenced more convicted defendants to death—most of them black men—than any other judge in the country; and that there existed at that time in the Philadelphia Police Department a culture of racist brutality and cor-ruption, since documented by the district attorney's office, which found, among other lawless activities, the routine subornation of per-jury to secure conviction of defendants whom the police knew to be innocent.

None of this, of course, is proof of Mumia's innocence. Yet it does suggest the need for careful examination of the trial and post-trial record in the presumption that a capital case above all others must be made with the most painstaking attention to the highest standards of American law. I believe the present work by Daniel R.

Williams, an attorney and a member of the defense team attempting to win Mumia a new trial, offers both those who believe in Mumia's innocence, and those who are just as passionately convinced that he is guilty, the opportunity to test their beliefs against the thorough account of the whole sad story, presented in these pages, beginning on that terrible December night in Philadelphia when, at 4:00 A.M., a young and conscientious police officer was mercilessly gunned down in the street.

One would expect a defense attorney to tilt his story in his client's favor. While there is no doubt in Mr. Williams's mind that his client is innocent, what he is concerned to show here is not one man's innocence of the charge against him, but, in all its details, the nature of a juridical event. The surprise here is how honest, how forthcoming, and at points how confessional this account is as it takes us step by step through the original trial and the appellate procedures since then. We are shown once again the painful truth that the magisterial body of law central to our national identity can be brought to its knees by the demon inadequacies of human character. All trials generate competing narratives that are in many respects extra-legal. The case is made from evidence, yes, but also from interpretive ascription, the prevailing politics of the legal establishment, tabloid sociology, the jury's inferences from courtroom behavior, and the performance powers of attorneys. Trials can be marred by stereotypical thinking; they can be shaped by the careerist self-interest of prosecutors and a defendant's lack of financial resources; they can fall prey to the intellectual insufficiency of judges—they are vulnerable to every one of the monumental number of failings of our human nature that regularly satirize the idea of justice.

The thrust of Mr. Williams's book is judicious. He can be as critical of his client's courtroom conduct as he can of the behavior of the judge. He is as honest in his opinions of his colleagues at the defense table as he is of the state's attorneys. He is as sensitive to the terrible years of pain and anguish suffered by the slain officer's family members as he is to a man's state of mind who has lived alone in a cell under a death warrant for eighteen years.

During the course of those eighteen years the passions of Mumia's supporters and his detractors have only increased in intensity. On both sides the rhetoric is enraged, the "paid-for" ads hyperbolic, the rallies loud and defiant. The cause in the name of Mumia's innocence has attracted organizations from the margins of American politics. Establishment media derive from this fact the likelihood of his guilt; he is discredited by the people who support him, even as they are discredited by whom they support. The cause in behalf of Mumia's guilt and the need to execute him and bring closure to the case is spearheaded by the Philadelphia Brotherhood of Police, and has generated advertising income from police associations across the country. At neither extreme can there be a legal certainty to match the righteousness. It has been difficult to articulate the unresolved prior issue, which is not this defendant's innocence or guilt but whether the trial that put him on death row rose to the level of basic standards of American justice.

That is the issue this book addresses. I hope it will attract enough honest readers from both sides of the dispute, those who have not taken the trouble before this to acquaint themselves with the legalities, the personalities, and the crucial turnings of the case. Even the bereaved family of the slain officer has to understand that unless a man is found guilty beyond a shadow of a doubt, there can be no true closure. And we all have to understand that every time a judge enters the courtroom and calls for a capital case to be heard, the law as well as the defendant is put on trial.

—E. L. DOCTOROW

INTRODUCTION

The Problem of Ambiguity

During the past ten years, Mumia Abu-Jamal has become the most recognized—dare I say, celebrated—death row inmate in the world. His incarceration on Pennsylvania's death row, since his conviction in 1982 for the shooting death of a young Philadelphia police officer, has become a flashpoint for a revived and flourishing death penalty debate in this country. The *New York Times* recently called him "the new face of the death penalty debate." He is for many progressives, political radicals, and students worldwide something much more potent—a symbol of, among other things, a disturbing phenomenon: the metastasizing prison–industrial complex that reminds us that an omnipresent racial polarization still grips our society. Songs, poems, and stories have been written about, or have been inspired by, him. He has spawned sundry tabletop merchandise: tote bags, whistles, candles, mouse pads, T-shirts, compact discs, etc. He has become the latest incarcerated cause celebre among the artistic, intellectual, and chattering classes in our media-crazed society. Some claim, with both delight and dismay, that he is a product of the burgeoning Internet— the first Internet political prisoner.

No doubt Mumia has done much to attract attention to himself. He has done so, not by cheap theatrics but by the sheer force of his intellect and his passion to speak for those who are largely ignored in the tumult of our "wired" culture. He has written three heartfelt, and critically well received, books. He has issued biting commentaries in numerous publications (including the *Yale Law Journal,* one of the most selective venues in academe). His trenchant oral recordings about living a life on death row, awaiting state-sanctioned death, were approved for airing on National Public Radio, until outcry among law enforcement groups and conservative politicians intimidated NPR into changing its mind. Television programs, airing on such national venues as HBO, the A&E Network, and ABC, have offered various analyses of the case.

The attention on Mumia's case will only intensify as it moves further down the corridors of the judicial system. Either he will be executed or he will be given a new trial. Either way, there will be much noise and clamor.

I am one of Mumia's attorneys, and I have been involved in the case since 1992, a full decade after his conviction. When I agreed to join the defense team, at the request of my mentor and friend, Leonard Weinglass, I had no idea that Mumia's case would become what it is today: a lightning rod of controversy amidst a broader controversy that is escalating (and will continue to escalate) over the use of the death penalty as a so-called "law and order" tool. Len and I, with the aid of other lawyers, law students, and activists, have dissected the prosecution's case against this famed death row inmate to perform a legal autopsy of sorts. We were not involved in the trial or original appeal of Mumia's conviction. The case was over, as far as the authorities in Pennsylvania were concerned, when we stepped in a decade after the trial to perform that autopsy—that is, to determine whether Mumia's guilt and punishment had been appropriately and justly adjudicated. What we found is laid bare in the pages that follow.

■ Cornel West, a leading public intellectual (a rare breed today), has asserted without equivocation that Mumia is "unjustly imprisoned for a crime he did not commit." One can only be struck by the boldness of those words from an academic not otherwise prone to political sloganeering. West's bold proclamation of Mumia's innocence may be among the most audible, by virtue of his stature as a credible and respected public intellectual, within a chorus of similar proclamations by many other notables (such as Alice Walker, Ossie Davis, and Angela Davis). But it is part of a chorus nonetheless.

There are others, however, who proclaim with equal adamancy that Mumia is a cop killer—and an unrepentant one at that. They have the argumentative upper hand insofar as he has been found guilty by a jury, a verdict twice upheld by the Pennsylvania Supreme Court. The strength of the anti-Mumia position rests on the presumption, which most Americans accept as akin to religious dogma, that our judicial system is the envy of the world. That presumption comes under scrutiny in this book, but for the moment I want to say that it would be unfair to dismiss those who seek Mumia's execution as evil persons who secretly desire the killing of an innocent man. Rightly or wrongly, informed or not, those pushing for execution genuinely believe Mumia is a cop killer.

And then there are those in the middle: agnostics in what has rapidly grown into a holy war. Actors Ed Asner, Mike Farrell, and Alec Baldwin are the most visible exemplifications of this position. Mumia may very well be guilty, the agnostics argue, but who is to say? There has been no legitimately fair proceeding to adjudicate his guilt. His trial was a travesty, a besmirchment and stain on "American justice." He deserves a new trial.

Because I am a lawyer for the defendant, it would be expected that I would proclaim my client's innocence, and I do. But a lawyer's proclamation of his client's innocence is understandably met with skepticism. The interesting question, to me, is not whether I or any lawyer or celebrity believes in Mumia's innocence. It is the proclamation itself that intrigues me. After all, people proclaim Mumia's innocence at the same time that they (rightly, in my view) denounce his trial as a farce and demand a new one. But without a genuinely fair trial where *all* of the evidence is presented *and* tested, what substance is there to a proclamation of innocence—or of guilt, for that matter?

Cornel West's assertion, like the assertions by others, that Mumia is innocent of the shooting death of a police officer back in December 1981, it seems to me, reflects both an ideological stance and an expression of faith. It is an ideological stance insofar as those who are willing to embrace Mumia as a factually innocent man are, by and large, persons with a certain (but not necessarily homogenous) political outlook who view Mumia's case as part of a larger ideological struggle. It is an expression of faith, at its core, because it derives from the belief that a man as articulate, as compassionate, as committed as Mumia is to the lost and forgotten souls in the world cannot be guilty of a cold-blooded murder. It is an assertion that seemingly precludes even the notion that life and human beings are complicated enough to allow that Mumia's guilt can coexist with his sincere and deeply committed allegiance to social justice.

The agnostics in this jihad over Mumia's fate add a sobering message: we who believe in Mumia's innocence can only insist upon a process that allows for our faith to be tested. If it can be proven that Mumia has not been accorded a trial process that inspires confidence in the jury's verdict, then the pro-Mumia forces will have the moral authority to insist that those who seek his execution be equally courageous and put their faith in that same crucible of adversarial testing—a crucible we conventionally call a fair trial. Remember: it is the crucible itself, and not what we put in it, that expresses most fully our societal values.

■ In the end, it seems to me that the polar extremes shouting at each other in this raging battle speak from deep reservoirs of pain, anger, and fear. The widow of the slain officer understandably insists that the original jury verdict in 1982 should be respected and carried out, as she no doubt needs to believe that it conclusively resolved the issues relating to her husband's untimely and violent death. It is worth taking a moment to reflect on her pain, and to be sensitive to how the intensity of interest in Mumia's case must hurt her, as well as the other family members and friends of the slain officer.

Convictions assuage the hurt of crime victims and those close to them. Ambiguities, unresolved crimes, however, act as anticoagulants, interfering with the healing of open psychological and emotional wounds. People who find themes of "law and order" more compelling than calls for social justice have their own fears, born of insecurities that their values and hard-earned possessions are threatened by those who have different visions of what is socially and economically possible in America. Those fears find expression in angry calls for harsh punishment and state-sponsored killing; the venom of "Let Mumia Fry" must be understood as anger concealing fear. The eye-opening truth is that America is filled to the brim with such fearful people. Just listen to the anti-crime, pro-death penalty rhetoric of politicians. I defy anyone to demonstrate that political discourse on crime and punishment, especially discourse on the death penalty, is anything but histrionic, demagogic, and fear driven.

Those who proclaim Mumia's innocence, many of whom are members of historically oppressed groups or are politically allied with such groups, also speak from pain found deep in the wells of their experiences. Cornel West, Alice Walker, and other progressive intellectuals and writers rightly admire Mumia for his ability to draw such groups and people together. He is able to do this in part because of his enormous vocal and literary gifts. But he builds bridges and forges bonds among people from within death row primarily because his writings are dedicated to the pains and sufferings of the struggling poor and dispossessed who are ever-increasingly becoming downtrodden in this world of escalating stock values and Internet millionaires. The struggle waged on Mumia's behalf, though on the surface prompted by strong feelings that his trial was unfair or that he is innocent, is perhaps more profound than most other struggles waged for the unjustly convicted. This is true, in my estimation, because this struggle to "Free Mumia" seemingly allows for the ventilation of the pain and suffering of the struggling poor and dispossessed—the voiceless, as Mumia's supporters would say.

It is precisely this—Mumia's heartfelt allegiance to social justice, genuine human connectedness, and fundamental morality—that calls attention to something more intriguing in West's proclamation of innocence. He makes it in the context of praising Mumia as a man with an intact, evolved, and flourishing soul living in a place that human beings have constructed to starve and ultimately destroy the soul. Mumia is a voice, West observes, that forces us to confront the demons immanent within "our capitalist 'civilization' [which] is killing our minds, bodies and souls in the name of the American Dream." What is intriguing is that Mumia, with his indestructible soul, represents the dark side of the American Dream for those who look to him as a symbol in the struggle for political and social justice, just as he is such for those who want him dead. That's the ambiguity of Mumia Abu-Jamal.

Ah, *ambiguity*. West's proclamation begs the question: is Mumia's stature as a writer, the "truth" of his message, unworthy of attention if he is guilty of firing a bullet into the brain of a young police officer? Does guilt for such an act necessarily muffle this voice for social justice? Or can such a guilty man nonetheless still speak to us, clearly and credibly? Indeed, even if his guilt somehow justifies extinguishing his right to remain alive, does it extinguish the worth of his message? In short, does Mumia's worthiness as a voice for the voiceless depend upon his innocence? If so, why?

These are questions that no one, so far as I can tell, bothers to ask. So the answers lie hidden somewhere in the universe, probably to be discovered when historical distance permits greater objectivity. In a narrow, legalistic sense, these questions are irrelevant to the arduous task that I and others have before us in our quest to win Mumia a new trial. But it is fair to consider, given that Mumia's case confronts the inscrutable connection between life and death, what Mumia's predicament might say to us about our human existence. I wrote this book in that spirit.

—DANIEL R. WILLIAMS
DECEMBER 2000

To assert in any case that a man must be absolutely cut off from society because he is absolutely evil amounts to saying that society is absolutely good, and no one in his right mind will believe this today.

ALBERT CAMUS

ONE

GOOD VERSUS EVIL

Once again, the venom of hatred and
disdain for the law enforcement profession
has vented its ugly anger on one of
Philadelphia's finest.

STATEMENT BY THE PHILADELPHIA
CHAPTER OF THE FRATERNAL
ORDER OF POLICE, DECEMBER 9, 1981

1. THE KILLING

A body in a blue police uniform lay still on the sidewalk. A few feet away, slouched on the curb near the front bumper of a parked car, was a black man with dreadlocks, bleeding with a gunshot wound to his chest, his right arm stretched across his torso, his legs protruding into the street but lazily bent at the knees, his whole body listless. An empty .38 revolver with a two-inch muzzle was just beyond his reach to his left. The body in the blue uniform had belonged to twenty-five-year-old police officer Daniel Faulkner, or just plain Danny, as his friends and family knew him.

Earlier that morning, on December 9, 1981, a minute or two shy of 4:00 A.M., someone fired a bullet into Officer Faulkner, striking him between the eyes as he lay helpless on the cold pavement. For some, the crime never was a mystery. The twenty-seven-year-old dreadlocked black man, Mumia Abu-Jamal, found at the crime scene wearing a gun holster and sitting on the curb within inches of the alleged murder weapon, was not simply an obvious suspect; he seemed to be the only one who could have committed the crime. But for others who knew the young and talented journalist, the de facto spokesperson for Philadelphia's disenfranchised minorities, it was incomprehensible that Mumia—that is what most people called him, just Mumia—would even be capable of perpetrating such a monstrous act. The crime was more than just a murder mystery; it was an opportunity to silence the man people had begun to dub the voice of the voiceless.

■ Thirteenth and Locust Street was, at the time of this crime, part of Philadelphia's red-light district, a neighborhood that came alive after midnight with prostitutes, lost souls, and nighttime carousers. At 3:54 A.M., patrol car 612, with its twirling red dome light, was parked at a curb on Locust Street about a quarter of a block east of the Thirteenth Street intersection. An old beat-up blue Volkswagen, license plate dangling, was parked at the curb in front of the police car, in full view of Officer Faulkner as he sat peering through the windshield, the hand-held police radio up near his mouth. Two cars on a city street, one suggesting disorderliness situated in front of another that spoke bluntly of "law and order." By the looks of it, Officer Faulkner was in the midst of an ordinary traffic stop.

The central dispatcher heard Officer Faulkner's routine notification over the police radio—"This is patrol six-twelve. I have a car stopped at Twelfth, uh, Thirteenth and Locust"—and dutifully put out the call for a backup. Officer Faulkner was about to step out when he looked around to gauge what risks were involved. He didn't have a partner cruising patrol with him, so he was particularly cautious about his actions. Something—it is unclear what—told him that a backup unit was not enough. He contacted central dispatch again.

Officer Faulkner, tall with dark hair and eyes and a slap-your-back friendly disposition, was five years into his work as a Philadelphia police officer. He had joined the force after a brief stint in the army upon graduating high school. He left his modest row house in the Eastwick section of southwest Philadelphia to begin his night shift at 11:30 P.M., after having spent some time at his dining room table paying bills. His house was in the midst of renovations and the bills were mounting. Money was tight, but he and his young wife, Maureen, didn't have any children—not yet, at least. Maureen knew that when they did, Danny would be a good father. She could tell by the way he loved to play baseball with the neighborhood kids during the summer. But why rush? They were still young and happy to enjoy life alone together for a while. They had a ski trip lined up for after Christmas, and a cruise to Bermuda in the spring.

One of seven children born into a working-class family, Faulkner was going to celebrate his twenty-sixth birthday on December 21, twelve days away. He was planning on taking the detectives exam over the upcoming weekend and was confident he would score well. He seemed to have a knack for police exams and had a penchant for discipline. He was proud of the fact that he had finished second in his class at the police academy. He was also intent on finishing up the last few credits for his associates degree at Philadelphia Community College. It wouldn't be exactly right to say that Danny Faulkner was ambitious. His life had always been lived on a small canvas. It's just that he was committed to making the most of it. Maureen loved that about him.

It was approaching 4:00 A.M., and Officer Faulkner spoke into the radio for the last time. He usually wore a bulletproof vest underneath his perfectly pressed uniform, but Maureen noticed that he hadn't put it on that night. Strange, she thought momentarily, before falling asleep. "On second thought, send me a wagon at Thirteenth and Locust," Faulkner muttered quickly. The request for a "wagon" meant he was intent on making an arrest, and he didn't want to be alone—not at this hour of the night, and not in this part of town.

Officer Faulkner stepped out of the patrol car, scanned the area again, and put his hat on. No one would have faulted him if he hadn't put his hat on. Many, maybe even most, Philadelphia patrol officers, deep into their night shift, dispense with the formality. But not Officer Faulkner. He insisted on the hat, just as much as he insisted on polished shoes and a pressed uniform.

Danny Faulkner had less than two minutes left in his life. Soon he would be lying face up on that cold, dingy pavement, lifeless, with a bullet in his brain.

■ It didn't take long for Locust Street to be bristling with activity. The night had been punctured with short, crackling, violent bursts of sound. Those who heard the crisp explosions—was it four, maybe five jolts of sound? bystanders just couldn't seem to remember—knew instantly it was gunfire. Homicide detectives, crime scene investigators, patrol officers, police photographers, curious onlookers, and several witnesses to various aspects of the "incident," hovered around the bloodstained asphalt. The dead police officer, found lying on the sidewalk, was immediately taken away to nearby Jefferson University Hospital, with the hope that somehow he could be revived. It wasn't until all the commotion died down that someone picked up Faulkner's hat from the street. The hat, unlike everything else, was still in perfect condition—and it remained so for a jury to see seven months later.

Mumia Abu-Jamal, too, was taken to Jefferson University Hospital, but not before, according to court witnesses, his head was rammed into a light pole and his body kicked and punched by infuriated police officers summoned to the scene. Mumia could never have guessed that the evening would devolve into this. He had had an enjoyable dinner with friends, among them a journalism colleague and a local politician, before getting into his cab to earn some badly needed money. His journalism career was at a crossroads, and he was moonlighting as a cab driver to support himself and his wife and children while trying to reassert—perhaps rediscover—his identity as a journalist. Some reporters on the city hall beat had been whispering that Mumia's marriage was on the skids and that he had begun to lose his objectivity as a reporter. But now, his entire life was derailed, as he lay on the hospital bed, handcuffed to the railing, looking up at his older sister, Lydia.

Mumia had refused medical treatment when the police, as they put it, "deposited" him on the emergency room floor. When family members appeared at the hospital, they urged him to accept treatment while trying, amidst the bedlam, to grasp what had happened. Mumia finally agreed. Emergency room surgeons operated for two and a half hours to repair damage caused by a bullet later discovered to have been discharged from Officer Faulkner's police-issued revolver. The police simply "knew" that Mumia had shot the officer. But how had Mumia been shot? None of the witnesses on the scene could say.

The question of how Mumia had been shot—at what point during the few seconds of the incident—would be a mystery that would plague the entire case, and in the end, may hold the key to his exoneration.

Lydia was with him when the anesthesia wore off. Mumia motioned for her to come nearer. His voice had always bespoken his strength, even in childhood; but now it was only a whisper. Come nearer, he gestured again. "I didn't have anything to do with it. I'm innocent." Lydia nodded and squeezed his hand.

Maureen never had a chance to exchange whispered words with her husband at the Jefferson emergency room. Danny Faulkner was pronounced dead at about 5:00 A.M., but in reality, he died instantly once the bullet struck him between the eyes, penetrated his skull, and then obliterated his brain.

The new mayor, William J. Green III, and other city dignitaries would come to the hospital later in the morning, designated by the Commonwealth to vent the city's anger over a senseless attack on that thin blue line that separates law from disorder. They would join Danny Faulkner's young widow at the hospital as she attempted to grasp what had happened.

The president of Lodge No. 5 of the Fraternal Order of Police quickly issued a statement: "Once again, the venom of hatred and disdain for the law enforcement profession has vented its ugly anger on one of Philadelphia's finest." Mayor Green ordered the city to lower flags at half-staff for thirty days, as "Philly's finest" wore black ribbons on their badges. Faulkner was the second cop killed in the line of duty that year. More than five thousand people, including the mayor and virtually every municipal leader, turned out for the memorial service at St. Barnabas Roman Catholic Church in southwest

Philadelphia. Even the voluble and controversial ex-mayor, Frank Rizzo, appeared, but remained uncharacteristically silent in the face of news cameras and a phalanx of journalists beckoning him to give one of his trademark invectives.

Danny was supposed to go deer hunting the day he was buried, a friend of his reflected, eyes moistened with emotion as the two hundred cars in the motorcade passed by.

For the next seven months, the killing of Officer Daniel Faulkner, and the life and times of the presumed killer, would be fixtures in the local papers and television news broadcasts. There would be much hand-wringing over how it could be that a gifted journalist, a passionate spokesperson for the poor, with no criminal past and a reputation as a gentle man, could find himself accused of such a vicious murder.

In racially polarized Philadelphia in 1981, a black man with dreadlocks was immediately looked upon as an enemy of the police. Philadelphia was the home of the radical MOVE organization, a group evoking bemusement among many, but vitriol among police officers who still remembered a killing of one of their own in a police siege upon a MOVE compound in 1978. Mumia had been raising eyebrows for the past three years among journalism colleagues, the public, *and the police,* because of his outspoken support for MOVE members, whom he felt were the latest victims of police brutality in a city that Mayor Rizzo had nourished with police-state methods. Mumia had never kept to himself his affinity for MOVE's spiritually based back-to-nature tenets. It was obvious to the arriving police officers, even before an investigation was launched, that Mumia had vented his rage, which was MOVE's rage, against authority by mercilessly killing Officer Daniel Faulkner.

There would be a trial. But for the police that night, a trial was nothing more than an unpleasant detour on the way to extracting the ultimate revenge for this malicious cop-killing. Executing justice was all that remained.

This was a clear-cut case . . . the strongest I've
ever prosecuted.

PROSECUTOR JOSEPH McGILL

2. AN OPEN-AND-SHUT CASE

Mumia Abu-Jamal was indicted for the shooting death of P.O.
Daniel Faulkner, and arraigned within a week of the crime on
the charge of murder in the first degree (along with a weapons possession count) from his hospital bed, where he was recuperating from
the gunshot wound received from the slain officer's revolver. With no
clear idea how Mumia was shot, investigators would endeavor to develop a theory to explain it. By the time of the arraignment, the
Philadelphia court system had appointed Anthony Jackson, a solo
criminal defense practitioner, to represent the "indigent defendant."

If Jackson thought that this high-profile murder case would be a
career maker for him, he couldn't have been more wrong. Prosecuting
the case was Assistant District Attorney Joseph McGill, an experienced, aggressive and highly skilled prosecutor who knew how to bring
back death verdicts. He was one of District Attorney Ed Rendell's
golden boys in the office. Furthermore, Jackson's every decision and
judgment would be second-guessed by the legion of supporters for
Mumia who attended every court session. He would have to chart a

difficult course to get the case ready for trial, and he would have to do so with very little money. He was court-appointed, so he was beholden to the penny-pinching Philadelphia criminal justice system for the funds necessary to defend his client. As if that were not enough, the trial would take place in Courtroom 253—the well-known way station to Pennsylvania's death row. Judge Albert F. Sabo, a small-minded, mean-spirited judge, but a darling of the prosecutors, would preside over yet another death penalty trial.

This, however, was not going to be an ordinary criminal trial.

It began in early June 1982 and ended on July 3, with a decision by a jury of twelve to "impose death." The prosecution presented four "eyewitnesses" who, with their testimony packaged together, provided a straightforward account of what happened on the night of the killing. Officer Faulkner had made a routine traffic stop; the Volkswagen driven by Billy Cook, Mumia's brother, apparently had turned toward oncoming traffic on a one-way street. Cook walked toward the front hood of the patrol car and words were exchanged. Faulkner then attempted to put handcuffs on him, when Cook suddenly struck the officer in the face. In response, Faulkner pulled out his heavy-duty flashlight and hit Cook in the head. During this scuffle, a man launched into a run from across the street toward the scene. No one has ever disputed that the man who ran across Locust Street toward Faulkner and Cook was Mumia Abu-Jamal.

The entire dispute in the trial centered upon what happened in the next few seconds. According to the prosecution, the man running across the street brandished a gun and fired into the back of Officer Faulkner at close range. The wounded officer staggered from the curb to the middle of the sidewalk. Faulkner then fell to the ground as the shooter hovered over him, the revolver pointing downward. After firing several shots, Mumia Abu-Jamal trudged over to the curb, near the front bumper of the Volkswagen, and sat down. Within a few minutes, police officers arrived on the scene and found Mumia slouched on the curb, and the supposed murder weapon, with five empty shells, lying nearby.

The prosecution had more than just eyewitness testimony pointing to Mumia's guilt. It also had two witnesses who claimed that he shouted out a profanity-laden confession. And as for the gun found within inches of Mumia's reach, the prosecution couldn't definitively prove that it had fired the bullet retrieved from the slain officer's brain; but it did claim that the ballistics analysis strongly indicated that it was the murder weapon.

It was an impressive case. The evidence needed to be answered.

■ CYNTHIA WHITE'S STORY

Cynthia White was standing on the corner of Locust and Thirteenth Street. She had been working the streets that night, one of several black prostitutes congregating on Locust. As the time approached 4:00 A.M., and the bars and nightclubs prepared to close, White expected that a new spate of customers would soon bargain for her services. She saw the patrol car parked behind the Volkswagen, but didn't pay it any attention. A patrol car in the neighborhood was no big deal to Cynthia White.

The police were always a heavy presence in this part of Philadelphia, and they were a fixture in the lives of Philadelphia prostitutes. A federal investigation would later expose a sophisticated network of police corruption, involving high-ranking cops enmeshed in a scheme to extort money from prostitutes, pimps, and bar owners. White had always had a good relationship with the cops—a good relationship, in fact, was essential to her business. Of course, she had no way of knowing, as she advertised herself in the cold, that she was about to become the key witness in one of the most explosive murder cases in Philadelphia history.

On June 21, 1982, Cynthia White sat in a witness chair in Courtroom 253, located in historic city hall, a majestic century-old building in the heart of Philadelphia, with a statue of William Penn situated atop a slender dome on the roof. The courtroom itself gestured at the majesty of the law, with its high ceilings, oak trimmings, and French

Renaissance-style decor. In the natural light of the courtroom, White looked older than her twenty-four years—more depleted than haggard. Because she rarely smiled when not working, her face sagged, giving her a wearied appearance. As she squirmed a bit in her seat, she put her hands on the inside of her thighs and jutted her shoulders forward as she waited for the prosecutor to get on with it. She looked small on the witness stand. In fact, she was a small woman without her high heels.

The jurors stared at her, struggling to hear her whispered answers. "I'm going to ask you to speak very loudly," McGill directed as he pointed toward the microphone. He wanted the jury to hear what she had to say—*every word of it.*

Mumia sat at the defense table as White sat poised to bury him with her testimony. When she first sat down in the witness chair, she was anxious to get the whole thing over with. But as she descended deeper into her story, she became more at ease. At ease not so much from enjoyment but apparently from that unique thrill, for the time being at least, of feeling important.

Joe McGill was going to make his case with Cynthia White. Slowly and deliberately. Important testimony in a death penalty trial must be drawn out slowly and deliberately. Slowly and deliberately, because important facts must be nurtured. They must be displayed, then absorbed by the mind, and then woven into a story that evokes a web of feelings. The men and women on the jury would have a weighty decision at the end of this trial. They would have to decide whether Mumia should walk again among the free or become, through deliberate state action, an inert mass of human flesh returned to the earth. McGill understood well that facts were not enough. There would have to be that web of feelings pulsating inside these jurors to countenance another killing. Transforming facts into feelings is a slow and deliberate process.

White claimed she saw Officer Faulkner pull the Volkswagen to the curb, emerge from his vehicle, and then walk toward the driver's-side window. The driver stepped out before he arrived, and the two walked back toward the police car and then up onto the sidewalk, talking or arguing along the way. Shortly after they reached the sidewalk, White told the jury, the man suddenly struck Officer Faulkner "with a closed fist to the cheek."

Faulkner whirled the man around. White explained that the officer then pulled back the assailant's arm as if to place him in handcuffs. She was quite familiar with handcuffing, having been arrested about thirty-eight times, according to official documentation; probably more, in reality. She claimed not to see Officer Faulkner unleash an assault of his own in retaliation. That was an odd omission on her part. Few things arouse more anger than an audacious act of violence directed at a police officer.

McGill asked White to step down and demonstrate what she was describing. The request was, strictly speaking, unnecessary because her verbal description was perfectly clear. But necessity is a relative notion: he wanted the scene to be replayed again so the "facts" could be absorbed by the jury this time through their eyes, not just their ears.

White stepped down from the box and moved toward the well of the courtroom. Her initial nervousness had withered away completely by now. The jury watched the show, for that is what it was, by prosecutorial design, as she demonstrated how Faulkner pulled the driver's hands behind his back, wrists crossing, when the latter whirled around to hit the officer.

"Now, Miss White, when did you first see the man running across the street? At what point?"

White paused, as if to re-create the scene in her head. Her lips jutted out, not quite pursed, giving the impression she was reaching back into her memory for the truth. Consciously or not, she was effective in conveying credibility. "When the police had the driver in a position to handcuff him, that's when the man came running," White explained.

Before Mumia had caught Cynthia White's eye, he had been in the driver's seat of his own cab, anticipating another fare from among the many patrons of the numerous night spots nearby. From his cab situated in a parking lot across the street from where Officer Faulkner was struggling with the driver of the Volkswagen, he noticed the red turret light atop the patrol car. He then saw the Volkswagen, and his body stiffened. In one motion he opened the door and glided out of the cab. He looked again just to be sure. Yes, it was his brother's Volkswagen. Was that his brother with the cop, or was it his brother's business partner, Ken Freeman, a frequent passenger in the Volkswagen? He strode briskly through the commercial lot and reached the street. He didn't notice Cynthia White, and he had no cause to. His attention was on the cop and the other man. He then broke into a run. Yes, it was his brother, Billy Cook. And his brother was bleeding.

White claimed that Mumia went from a walk to a run about midway across Locust Street. She claimed to have noticed that he was brandishing a gun. Mumia fired twice at the officer's back at point-blank range, White insisted under friendly questioning. "Come down again," McGill summoned, "and show us once more what it is you saw."

McGill knew that White's testimony on this point would be critical—perhaps the most critical in the whole trial. He asked her to demonstrate what happened in that moment just before the officer hit the ground, not for show but to hammer in a point that he needed the jury to accept. Somehow, White explained, Officer Faulkner spun himself around to face Mumia and began to fall to the pavement. White was certain that the officer was grabbing for something as he was falling. McGill looked over at his jury. He felt, as a good trial lawyer ought to feel, that this was *his* jury, and *his* jury was paying attention.

What was it that Faulkner was grabbing for? White couldn't say. "Will you demonstrate to the jury, Miss White, when you said the police officer fell and you said he grabbed something? . . . Stand here. You don't have to fall all the way. Just, you know, give us a general idea how it happened."

White complied, twisting around and leaning back as if to fall to the ground.

The prosecutor would never get White to say that the officer had succeeded in pulling out his gun. But he felt he had enough from White's account to resolve the nagging mystery of how Mumia received his near-fatal gunshot wound to the chest. He theorized that Officer Faulkner managed to fire his service revolver once, striking Mumia in the chest, as he was falling to the sidewalk. What White had observed, McGill would later suggest to the jury, was Officer Faulkner reaching for his service revolver. McGill again asked her to demonstrate in front of the jury box.

"He came over and he stood on top of him. . . . He came over and was doing like this here with the gun."

Wounded, Mumia allegedly stood over the terrified young man and emptied his revolver. White stood in front of the jury, with her right arm outstretched and her hand positioned like a simulated gun. She jerked her hand back three times, simulating the recoil of a firearm, as she told the jury that Mumia "was doing like this here with the gun."

She stood for a moment, waiting for the director to give her the next cue to the performance, but the prosecutor just pointed toward the witness chair. She walked back to her seat and crossed her legs, waiting for the next question.

"Would you point him out, Miss White?" Her right hand was pressed against her lip, her elbow on her knee, when she suddenly thrust her index finger toward Mumia, her arm rigid for several seconds.

"Any doubt in your mind, Miss White?" The abrupt finger stab already revealed the answer, but she verbalized one anyway. Viewing the scene from about three car lengths away, White was sure that it was the defendant, now seated at a table some twenty feet away, who killed the officer.

White then explained to the jury that, after the shooting, Mumia had stumbled over to the curb and sat down. And indeed, when police arrived at the scene, less than two minutes thereafter, they saw Mumia slumped on the curb near the front bumper of the Volkswagen, his chin bobbing slightly on his heaving chest.

As far as the prosecutor was concerned, Cynthia White was all the prosecution needed to make out its case against the defendant.

ROBERT CHOBERT'S STORY

McGill, of course, was delighted that he had more eyewitness testimony, as it is a mistake to take anything for granted in a jury trial. He called to the stand a cabdriver who saw the shooting from within his cab moments after discharging a passenger onto the sidewalk on the southeast corner of Locust and Thirteenth Street. Robert Chobert, a troubled twenty-two-year-old white man serving out a probationary sentence for committing arson for pay at a school, was logging his last fare in his notebook when he heard a single shot.

"I looked up, I saw the cop fall to the ground, and then I saw Jamal standing over him and firing some more shots into him." Chobert was the kind of witness a trial lawyer loves. No ambiguities, just a straightforward answer.

He had the look of a youthful beer drinker, pale with dull eyes and unruly hair, all of which suggested he didn't welcome conversation from strangers. Something about the way he tightened his face when prompted to talk gave the impression that he just wasn't into small talk. When he entered the courtroom to testify, it looked as if he were going to break into a run down the aisle and jump over the railing. As he walked between the prosecution and defense tables, he shot a quick glance over at Anthony Jackson, perhaps already thinking about the inevitable cross-examination.

He had been staying at a local hotel, for his own protection, according to the detective who was sitting next to the prosecutor in the courtroom. Chobert didn't seem to mind it, so long as he wasn't paying the bill. He thought it was all kind of ridiculous, putting him in a hotel for a couple of weeks. He couldn't imagine that his life was in danger because he was a witness in this case. After all, it wasn't a mob hit. Chobert figured that the MOVE organization—the black radical group that had taken root in Philadelphia—might be involved in some way, but the MOVE members seemed to be too hung up on "the system" to be bothered with him.

McGill wanted to break the scene down into little snippets. So he asked Chobert to explain exactly what he saw when he looked up from his notepad. "I saw the officer fall," Chobert explained, with the terse precision that pleased the prosecutor.

"And then, tell us again, what did you see happen?"

"I saw him shoot again several more times."

"Now, what then did you see the shooter do?"

"Then I saw him walking back about ten feet and he just fell by the curb." No running, no fleeing, just *walking* the few feet to the curb—the curb where Mumia was ultimately found.

Hadn't he told the police that the shooter "ran away?" Jackson would press later on in his cross-examination. That was a "mistake," Chobert responded. Jackson had little ammunition with which to attack Chobert's retreat from his initial police statement. Chobert had indeed told investigators at the crime scene that the shooter "ran away," but he also claimed that the police apprehended him. Now, on the witness stand, Chobert insisted that the shooter never ran at all, but only traversed the few feet to the curb, thus mapping the testimony of Cynthia White.

McGill didn't even attempt to get Chobert to explain how Mumia had been shot. He evidently knew from the prep sessions that Chobert couldn't say, despite his claim that he watched, uninterrupted, the events unfold between the shooter and Officer Faulkner. After the shooting ended, but before the police arrived, Chobert stepped out of his cab and walked toward the body on the sidewalk. Jackson never seized on the puzzling aspect of this testimony. If Chobert walked toward the slain officer, then doesn't that indicate the shooter had fled the scene? Isn't that what Chobert, in essence, told the police that night—that the shooter "ran away"? Does it make sense that Chobert would walk in the direction of the crime scene, seconds after a man had just brutally executed a police officer, if that executioner remained there, as he was now suggesting?

The arriving police ordered him back to his cab. They soon came back to him after they had whisked Officer Faulkner away and had thrown Mumia into the police van.

Like White, Chobert gave a statement to interviewing detectives at the scene, describing what he had seen and the physical attributes of the shooter. Homicide detectives, figuring that a cab driver's on-the-scene identification would be more solid—less impeachable, in the argot of litigators—than that of a prostitute, escorted him to the police van where Mumia lay. Chobert knew that the man sitting on the curb was now in the police van because he had seen the police put him there.

"And then what?" the prosecutor prompted the witness.

"They took me over to the wagon, like I said, and they asked me, 'Is that the guy?' I said, 'Yes, it is.' " He identified Mumia as the shooter.

"Do you recall telling the police the type of hair that the shooter had?"

Chobert nodded and it looked as if he were going to crack a smile, but he caught himself. "Yeah, he had long matted hair . . . like a MOVE member."

Jackson tried to shake Chobert from his certainty that Mumia was the *one*. The attack only caused Chobert to harden as a witness. "I know who shot the cop, and I ain't never gonna forget it." You're sure? the defense attorney asked again. "Pretty damn right I am."

The prosecution was in good shape with Chobert's on-the-scene identification. Although Chobert couldn't provide the seamless narrative that White offered the jury—especially in his inability to account for Mumia's gunshot wound—he took the sting out of the fact that White's credibility could always be questioned by virtue of how she made her living. Chobert also corroborated a key aspect of White's account: he, too, told the jury that he had seen the shooter stumble over to the curb at the front of the Volkswagen after firing point-blank at the fallen officer. Regardless of how Chobert and White may have described the shooter—and their descriptions differed between them and did not match Mumia's physical attributes—the fact that they both claimed to see the shooter finally situate himself in the very place that the police found Mumia less than two minutes later was powerful enough to substantiate that Mumia was the killer. Chobert's on-the-scene identification of Mumia in the police van was just icing on the cake.

■ MICHAEL SCANLAN AND ALBERT MAGILTON

Two other eyewitnesses were called by the prosecution. While neither could definitively say who was the shooter, their observations strongly suggested that the shooter was the man who had run across Locust Street. Since there was no dispute that that man was Mumia, Scanlan and Magilton, as far as McGill was concerned, further corroborated the theory that Mumia was the shooter.

Scanlan, a young well-dressed white man who had just dropped off his date, was driving alone in his Ford Thunderbird east on Locust. He admitted to having had "a few cocktails . . . a couple hours before." He brought his vehicle to a stop in the left-hand lane at the traffic light on Locust just west of the intersection with Thirteenth Street, a distance he estimated to be "several car lengths" behind the police car, but which was actually nearly one hundred feet. He remained at the intersection until after the shooting, facing the rear of the police car.

Scanlan looked as if he had experience in testifying, though he claimed he didn't. He seemed to know how to connect with his audience by brushing his eyes across the panel of jurors angled to his left. He kept a respectful posture throughout his testimony—something that neither Chobert nor White could do—and wasn't afraid to smile. There never was much to smile about during the trial, but Scanlan, more than the others, seemed willing to open up. He could be a very dangerous witness, Jackson must have thought to himself as he sat coiled like a cat ready to bounce into action, his chair turned in the direction of the witness box.

Scanlan's observations differed markedly from those of Cynthia White. Whereas White had the scuffle between Officer Faulkner and Billy Cook taking place on the sidewalk, Scanlan testified he first saw the two men in the street in front of the police car. According to Scanlan, Officer Faulkner had Billy Cook spread-eagled over the hood of the police car and was beating him with what appeared to be a flashlight or billy club after Cook had swung around and struck him in the face. Scanlan's observations were confirmed by the fact that Faulkner's seventeen-inch flashlight was found at the scene with a broken lens. Moreover, the officers who took Cook into custody immediately after the shooting reported seeing fresh blood running down his neck and from the left side of his face, a fact confirmed by photographs taken of Cook. Cynthia White's version, unlike Scanlan's, omitted any mention of Faulkner hitting Cook. Whether that fact would hold any significance for the jury remained to be seen, but it certainly raised a question about White's seamless account of what happened.

The important fact for McGill was that Scanlan saw a man running across Locust Street toward the two scuffling men. Although he testified that this man brandished a gun, he later modified that claim with the admission that it was simply an assumption on his part. When he saw the shooting through the flashing red turret light atop the patrol car, he *assumed* that the shooter was the man who had run across the street. That's why he just *assumed* the man running across the street had brandished a gun. Jackson could understand how Scanlan, an apparently honest man with no real ax to grind, could assert something as an observed fact when, in reality, it was nothing more than an assumption. Experienced criminal defense lawyers acutely understand how the human mind pieces together bits and pieces of an observed event, stitching them together with assumptions to create an uninterrupted mental film of what supposedly happened. It is in the stitching where mistakes are often made.

Of all the witnesses, Scanlan was the only one who candidly admitted that there was "confusion when all three of them were in front of the car."

The most articulate and engaging of the eyewitnesses, Scanlan was the most potent. The jury winced at hearing Scanlan's depiction of Officer Faulkner's execution: "The man walked over and was standing at [Officer Faulkner's] feet and shot him twice. I saw two flashes. I could see the one that hit the officer in the face. . . . His body jerked. His whole body jerked."

McGill was pleased with Scanlan as a witness, but he wished that he could have provided more. McGill never asked him to identify the defendant in the courtroom as the shooter, because he knew that he couldn't make the identification. Detectives had tried to get him to identify Mumia at the crime scene. With another identification, they thought, perhaps the prostitute witness would not even be necessary. But that was not to be. Scanlan's confusion over what he had seen manifested itself in his identification. He followed the homicide detectives over to the police van and obediently peered inside. He saw a man laying inside, not quite in a fetal position, but curled up nonetheless. The detectives told Scanlan to look carefully—was this the man who shot the cop? The urge to say yes was compelling, with all of the police activity around him and the urgency evident in the voices of the detectives. He couldn't help but notice that this man had flowing dreadlocks. Wasn't it the driver who had the dreadlocks? Scanlan wondered. He tried to reconstruct the sequence of events in his mind as he stood in the cold night air, looking inside the van. He looked over toward the buildings where Billy Cook was in the company of police officers. He compressed his lips as he tried to figure out which man did what. Is he the one? the detectives wanted to know. Scanlan looked hard again inside the van. He noticed Mumia's labored breathing. "No," he finally told them, "he was the driver."

"Fuck," one of the detectives groused.

Albert Magilton was on and off the witness stand before anyone could realize that he didn't offer much at all. He couldn't describe the shooter. He didn't even see the shooting. He was in the west crosswalk of the intersection, heading north across Locust. He reported seeing Officer Faulkner's vehicle "put on the lights" at the intersection of Locust and Thirteenth while both vehicles were proceeding east on Locust. He saw the officer and the driver "walk onto the pavement" between the cars. Magilton then turned away from the scene to cross Locust in the midst of traffic. Although he noticed a man run across Locust, he didn't look in the direction of the crime scene until he heard gunshots. Police never even tried to have Magilton attempt an identification.

Scanlan and Magilton were valuable witnesses, not in their own right but as bolstering witnesses for White and Chobert. White and Chobert claimed that it was Mumia who had the gun in his hand as the bullet exploded out of the chamber and struck the officer. Scanlan and Magilton reinforced the point that Mumia had, just seconds earlier, run across Locust Street toward the scene; and Scanlan contended that it was the man who ran across the street—whatever he looked like—who shot the officer.

■ THE CONFESSION

Prosecutors love confessions. It makes their job so much easier. They don't need to bolster the credibility of their witnesses; they don't need to make sure that scientific tests were done correctly; they don't need to worry about the integrity of the physical evidence. The defendant convicts himself through his own words.

Juries feel good about confessions too. Jurors don't want to convict innocent people. They want to make sure that their verdicts of guilt don't compound a tragedy with an equally horrific tragedy of sending an innocent man to death at the hands of the law. So when they hear evidence that a defendant confessed to the crime, their job is made that much easier also, and their consciences are not racked with nagging questions about whether they had done the right thing.

Defense lawyers are fond of playing on that human frailty—the human tendency to wake up nights wondering if you had made a mistake on a gravely important matter. Defense lawyers, hoping to frighten jurors into finding reasonable doubt, often remind them that, at some point in their lives, they will have thoughts intrude on their sleep, asking whether the man they convicted was *really* guilty. The hope, of course, is that the jury will take a risk-averse approach to the case—as the Constitution demands—and find that the prosecution simply cannot prove its case beyond a reasonable doubt. But where the prosecution has evidence of a confession, such pleas and reminders to a jury ring hollow.

A defense lawyer cannot, under any circumstances, let evidence of a confession enter into a case without challenging it vigorously. In a death penalty trial, challenging the confession is a life-or-death task. The prosecution claimed that Mumia confessed to the killing of Officer Faulkner, and the defense had to answer that claim.

Both Officer Faulkner and Mumia were removed by the police from the scene of the shooting and taken to Jefferson Hospital, three blocks away. Mumia was taken from the police van and dumped violently onto the emergency room floor near the entranceway. Fortunately for Mumia, he didn't stay there long, as he was seen by an emergency room crew within ten minutes of his arrival. Doctor Anthony V. Coletta, a surgical resident on call, responded immediately to a trauma code on his beeper. When he reached Mumia he found him to be "weak . . . on the verge of fainting . . . if you tried to stand him up, he would not have been able to stand." Although he was on the floor for about ten minutes, according to two prosecution witnesses, Mumia sealed his fate while he lay there awaiting a doctor to tend to him.

A hospital security guard named Priscilla Durham told the jury that Mumia shouted out to the fifteen to twenty police officers hovering around him, "I shot the motherfucker, and I hope the motherfucker dies." When she heard the remark, she figured out, as she tells it, "what was going on." Mumia was the arrestee who shot the other patient in the emergency room; he was the cause for the mass influx of police officers into Jefferson's emergency room. A little while later, according to Durham, Mumia shouted out the confession again, phrased in exactly the same way. Through it all, Durham told the jury, Mumia was "screamin' and hollerin'."

Jackson challenged Durham's account of hearing this confession. He had no choice. If the jury believed that Mumia bragged about the killing in such a coldhearted way, the jurors would not only convict for sure but would probably want to flip the electrocution switch themselves. Jackson brought out the fact that Durham didn't mention the confession to law enforcement personnel for approximately three months.

Durham was ready with an answer, obviously expecting that the defense would make that point in cross-examination. She turned to the jury, gave a slight nod, and explained that she had, in fact, reported hearing the confession the very next day, to her supervisor. She went on to explain that her supervisor hand-wrote her statement, memorializing the fact that she had, indeed, heard the confession. Jackson was stunned. If Durham had reported hearing the confession on the following day, then it would be impossible to undercut the confession in any realistic way.

Jackson understood that Mumia's life hung in the balance. He demanded to see this hand-written statement.

McGill claimed never to have seen the statement, which in itself was a remarkable fact, but suspiciously told the judge that he "would be very glad to have it brought over." If McGill had never seen the document, how did he know it was readily retrievable? Surely he had to have known that Durham was going to say on the witness stand that she reported the confession to her supervisor on the following day. It was a devastating claim to the defense—too devastating for this highly aggressive prosecutor not to have known about it, as he was suggesting. Something was up, but Jackson just didn't know what it was.

"Cross-examine her about something else," the judge advised. "You can call her later on."

When the cross-examination was over, the jury was left with Durham's testimony, but no hand-written statement. But, like manna from heaven, a detective assisting the prosecutor during the trial marched down the center aisle and entered the well of the courtroom during a brief recess. He was carrying a piece of paper, and he seemed to be holding it with reverence, making sure that its edges didn't get wrinkled. He handed the document to McGill, who took a moment to read it through.

Bingo! The detective was able to retrieve a typewritten statement purporting to be a memorialization of Durham's report of the confession to her supervisor. He was able to retrieve it before Durham was excused from the stand. It couldn't have been scripted any better for the prosecutor. McGill pompously walked the treasured document over to the defense table, fully aware that the drama would only bolster his case. He rested it in front of Jackson, without a word, but his mannerism suggested that he was telling Jackson to "give it his best shot."

Jackson barely looked at the document before he showed it to Durham. It didn't have a signature—not hers, not anyone's. Jackson detected that Durham appeared to be surprised by the document as well. He pressed her about it, not knowing what she would say. Trial lawyers hate asking questions without knowing the answer in advance. They're taught to do it only in the most desperate situations, and even then to err on the side of holding back. Durham said she had never seen it, but claimed that it looked like a typewritten version of the hand-written account.

McGill wanted to put that document into evidence. But he had a problem: how could he justify its admission into evidence if Durham didn't actually draft it? The rules of evidence are quite strict about the admission of documents that can't be authenticated by a witness. After all, an unauthenticated document, such as this one, could have been generated at any time. But this problem was easily surmountable, not by dint of effort or crafty lawyering. There was, in fact, no problem at all, because sitting on the bench was Judge Albert F. Sabo, a Philadelphia prosecutor's best friend. Judge Sabo seemingly operated on a simple rule: if a document or testimony helps the prosecution, it comes into evidence. It's not an evidence rule that law professors teach their students, but then again, law professors know little about the law as it is deployed in a real courtroom in a real case. Judge Sabo applied that rule in this case and allowed the typewritten document into evidence for the jury to analyze for itself.

Jackson was deflated. His questioning from then on subtly but unmistakably took on a different complexion. The questions now were phrased as if he had to accept as fact that Mumia had stupidly shouted out a confession. Jackson even suggested in his closing argument, preposterously, that Mumia shouted the confession to deflect attention from the real perpetrator—his brother. Could there be any doubt what the jury was going to do now?

Mumia understood, probably more acutely than anyone else, that

Durham had done considerable damage. He had been insisting on his right to represent himself from the very moment that the trial began, but that right had been taken from him—for disruptive behavior, according to the judge; for no good reason other than concern that he would be too effective, according to Mumia and his supporters. Mumia stood to question this security guard, and he threw out a question to her. A few jurors shook their heads disapprovingly. Judge Sabo gave the command to remove the jury from the courtroom and they were hustled out.

"You realize if you interrupt in front of this jury I'm going to have to remove you again," Judge Sabo warned.

Mumia hadn't been intimidated by the warnings before, and he wasn't intimidated now. "Judge, you can remove me again and again and again and again. I am going to point out to you what is important to me; that this is *my* trial; that this man [gesturing toward Jackson] is *your* employee, not mine; that he is functioning for the court system, not for me; he is not doing what I am telling him and directing him to do but what you are ordering him to do. . . . I am protesting his appointment, his continuing functioning here. I wish for him to be withdrawn immediately."

"Are you going to make some statements in front of the jury?" the judge asked.

"Well, I had planned to defend my life in front of the jury. I plan to represent myself in front of the jury. I plan to cross-examine witnesses in front of the jury. I plan to make a closing statement and argument in front of the jury. But obviously you have other plans."

"In other words, you're telling me if I bring the jury in, you're going to stand up and start making statements in front of the jury?"

Mumia knew exactly what Judge Sabo was doing: he was "making a record" to justify his banishment once again from the courtroom. "I didn't say that at all, Judge. I told you what I plan to do."

"Okay. We'll bring the jury in and we'll play it by ear. Like I told you before, if you act up—"

"Judge, I'm not acting up," Mumia protested. "I'm not acting at all. I'm telling you the truth."

The jury was brought back into the courtroom, and Mumia rose again to question Durham. The jury turned and shuffled out of the courtroom again. It had become a virtual daily routine for the jury.

"Okay, Mr. Jamal, it is obvious to the court that you intend to disrupt the proceedings in front of the jury."

"I am not disrupting. It's obvious I intend to defend myself."

"Well, once again I am removing you from the courtroom."

As had happened many times before in this wild spectacle of a trial, an armed court officer, prompted by Judge Sabo's directive, took Mumia out of the courtroom and relegated him to a holding cell as the trial proceedings continued.

McGill wasn't going to take any chances with the jury when it came to the confession. He called another witness, Police Officer Garry Bell, Faulkner's onetime partner. Bell went to the hospital immediately after hearing news that Danny had been shot. He was standing at the nurse's station when a corps of officers dropped Mumia onto the emergency room floor. He looked over and saw a dreadlocked black male lying there and he concluded that his fellow officers had just brought in the killer. White-hot with anger, Bell went over to Mumia, knelt down to look into his eyes. According to Bell, Mumia looked at him and uttered the exact words that Durham had recounted for the jury. In response, Bell told Mumia, "If he dies, you die."

In his opening remarks to the jury, McGill promised that they would hear evidence of a confession that revealed a "picture of extreme arrogance, defiance, even a strange boastfulness. . . ." The prosecutor fulfilled that promise.

■ THE BALLISTICS AND MEDICAL EVIDENCE

Two guns were recovered from the crime scene. Officer Faulkner's gun, a police-issued .38 Smith and Wesson, contained six Remington .38 special cartridges, one of which had been fired. The projectile from the spent shell was later retrieved from Mumia's lower vertebra. The other gun, found within inches of Mumia's outstretched hand at the crime scene, was also a .38—a five-shot Charter Arms revolver with a two-inch barrel. The Charter Arms revolver contained five cartridges, all of which had been fired.

There was no doubt that the Charter Arms belonged to Mumia. He had bought it eighteen months earlier and registered it in his name after having been victimized by robbers in his cab. In fact, the operator of the sporting goods shop that sold Mumia the gun distinctly remembered him. Asked why he remembered him, the witness testified that "he was very well-spoken and well dressed." Folks who buy guns, this gunshop proprietor seemed to be saying, aren't typically well dressed or well-spoken. Or was it the combination of Mumia being black with dreadlocks *and* "very well-spoken and well dressed" that made such an imprint on his mind?

McGill made a point of letting the jury absorb fully the fact that Mumia's revolver contained "plus P" high-velocity bullets. The witness explained that the plus-P bullet is known in the gun trade as a "devastating bullet."

Devastating? "When it hits the target, it just almost explodes," the firearms expert explained.

The prosecutor's message to the jury was disturbing: Mumia was not only pleased by what he had done, to the point of bragging about it; he had envisioned the need to lay waste another human being when he bought this gun loaded with "devastating" bullets, months before he ever encountered Danny Faulkner.

Prosecutors like to bring in medical evidence, even when it is incidental to the guilt/innocence calculus. Clinical talk of how a bullet pierces through skin and punctures vital organs has a certain attraction and power. It conveys humanity's fragility in the face of evil. An angry black man, poised with a gun containing exploding bullets, can snuff out the life of a young police officer in an instant, and there is nothing one can do to stop it from happening . . . except to take revenge through the force of the law and hope that it somehow deters others. That is what a prosecutor wants a jury to *feel*.

So McGill let the trial linger for a while on clinical and scientific discussions about how Officer Faulkner died. The state's pathologist was called to the stand, and he described how he had removed a bullet from the officer's head. It was too deformed, so he said, to be ballistically matched to a particular gun. McGill underscored the fact that the deformed bullet fragment was a .38 caliber with rifling characteristics "consistent" with Mumia's Charter Arms revolver, thus narrowing the range of firearms that could have expelled the deadly bullet. It was certainly of little use to simply conclude that the fragment was a .38: how many .38 caliber weapons existed on the streets of Philadelphia? Too many, by anyone's count.

The prosecution had alleged that Mumia fired several shots, at point-blank range, at Officer Faulkner as he lay helpless on the sidewalk. Only one struck him. Why? Although McGill didn't harp on the point, the picture for the jury was that Danny Faulkner desperately rolled his body from side to side to avoid being killed. He succeeded in causing the shooter to miss twice. The shooter then bent down closer, all the better to ensure that the final bullet would reach its intended destination.

■ AN OPEN-AND-SHUT CASE?

The prosecution had a compelling case. Some say the trial record proves without doubt Mumia Abu-Jamal brutally killed Officer Danny Faulkner. Joseph McGill is fond of telling the public that he's never had a stronger murder case in his successful and high-profile career as a Philadelphia prosecutor. The Fraternal Order of Police, campaigning nationwide to battle the forces favoring Mumia, call it a "clear-cut case" and accuse Hollywood celebrities of being "fools" for joining forces with "anti-death penalty groups, left-wing extremists, and misguided academics." The Philadelphia district attorney's office even dispatched an angry letter to Hollywood celebrities supporting Mumia, like Ed Asner and Whoopi Goldberg, extending McGill's claim to say that it was "one of the strongest" cases ever prosecuted in that office. To reach an even wider audience, District Attorney Lynne Abraham (who was actually the municipal court judge presiding over Mumia's arraignment) penned an op-ed piece in the *New York Times*, entitled "Mumia Abu-Jamal, Celebrity Cop Killer," questioning how anyone could be seduced by this cold-blooded killer.

Such seemingly overwhelming evidence—four eyewitnesses (including two prompt on-the-scene identifications), a highly memorable confession by an angry black radical with a perceived affiliation with an antiestablishment organization, an alleged murder weapon found at the scene with rifling characteristics consistent with the bullet that drilled through Officer Faulkner's brain, and a suspect found within feet of the deceased officer and within reachable distance to the gun: it all begs the question, why is there a fuss over Mumia's case? Why have Hollywood celebrities, authors, academics, political notables, college students, and progressive activists around the world seized upon this man's predicament when, it would seem, his predicament is one of his own making?

There is not perhaps anywhere to be found a city in
which prejudice against color is more rampant than in
Philadelphia.

FREDERICK DOUGLASS

Philadelphia is bleeding to death because of the MOVE
tragedy.

PHILADELPHIA JUDGE STANLEY KUBACKI

3. THE SOURCE OF GOOD AND EVIL

Racial polarization is a defining feature of Philadelphia, as it has been since the mid-1800s when Frederick Douglass visited the city and decried the subjugation of blacks. Warnings from nineteenth-century intellectuals of an awakened and angered underclass became a reality in the 1960s, as the Black Panther Party, Huey Newton's radical black empowerment group, gained a strong foothold in Philadelphia's minority communities (40 percent of its population), and the municipal and federal governments took note. The FBI in August 1967 launched a surreptitious offensive against so-called "Black Nationalist Hate Groups" (BNHG) nationwide as part of its overall domestic surveillance program known as COINTELPRO, short for "counterintelligence programs."

The FBI, popularly regarded as a premier crime-fighting agency, was in the '60s and '70s a political police force engaged in extralegal activities calculated to contain, and if possible destroy, left-wing political dissent of all types. Slowly emerging in the public record is a more complete accounting of this domestic counterinsurgency campaign. Hoover's obsession with Martin Luther King, Jr., which extended to psychological warfare calculated to induce King to commit suicide, is now a matter of public record.[1] Thomas I. Emerson, the late Yale law professor, remarked that the FBI's COINTELPRO operations "jeopardized the whole system of freedom of expression which is the cornerstone of an open society. . . . At worst it raises the specter of a police state . . . [where] in essence the FBI conceives of itself as an instrument to prevent radical social change in America. . . . [T]he Bureau's view of its function leads it beyond data collection and into political warfare."[2]

In fact, J. Edgar Hoover's obsession with black nationalism stretched back to the days of Marcus Garvey (1917–18), one of the first black nationalists to receive widespread attention in the United States. When the National Association for the Advancement of Colored People (NAACP) was formed in 1940, principally in response to widespread lynchings, the FBI quickly penetrated that staunchly anticommunist organization to look nonetheless, and without success, for communist "contamination and manipulation."

During the 1960s, as spontaneous and uncoordinated rebellions flared up in various cities, Hoover became increasingly concerned that the formation of black organizational leadership would lead to the harnessing of black rage, which in turn would threaten "law and order"—a coded expression for protecting the status quo. To Hoover and others in the Bureau, the solution was obvious: destroy even the possibility that blacks could become organized. They used whatever means were at hand to achieve that end.

The Black Panther Party was originally established in Oakland, in the fall of 1966. Shortly after Labor Day 1968, Hoover publicly announced that "the greatest threat to the internal security of the country" was the Black Panther Party.[3] Justifying aggressive FBI tactics on claims that the Panthers were nothing more than violent thugs, Hoover completely whitewashed the fact that the "ten-point program" of the Black Panther Party was inspired with themes of direct community political control over, and economic self-sufficiency within, the black communities. In late 1967, the Panthers initiated free breakfast programs for black children, and offered free health care to blighted communities.[4] A year later, the Black Panther Party expanded its efforts into community education and antidrug programs. The success of the Panthers in attracting allegiance within black communities sparked concerns within the FBI, with one senior agent noting in a memo that membership was "multiplying rapidly."[5]

Indeed it had. By 1968, there were as many as five thousand members in the Black Panther Party, with chapters in over a dozen cities. The FBI itself admits to 295 distinct COINTELPRO operations against black nationalist groups; of these, 233 were aimed at the Black Panther Party specifically.[6] Shootouts between police and the Panthers stoked the prejudices of the white population just as it further radicalized many student leftists. New Left leader Tom Hayden advocated and organized target practice for young political radicals, black and white, so alarmed was he over the rash of shootouts involving the Panthers.[7] "The total number of fatalities resulting from these brutally illegal activities on the part of the nation's 'top law enforcement agency,'" one knowledgeable observer laments, "will probably never be known, nor will the number of years spent by innocent people railroaded into prison cells or the number of lives wrecked in somewhat more subtle ways."[8]

■ Justified on dubious security grounds, COINTELPRO tactics provided the green light for municipal police agencies to engage in police-state activities. Philadelphia became the preeminent example, if not the paradigm, of police-state governance in urban America in the activist era of the '60s and '70s. Frank L. Rizzo, Philadelphia's mayor from 1972 to 1980, exemplified the image of the tough-talking brute who ran a town with unquestioned authority. As the onetime head of its police department, Rizzo transformed the Philadelphia police force into a political weapon targeted at left-wing organizations, all in the name of law and order. Philadelphia was over 40 percent black and it was a breeding ground for radical politics in the heady days of the '60s and early '70s. Aware that they were governing a city containing a large minority community under the thumb of an unresponsive white power structure, Rizzo and other power brokers in Philadelphia feared that themes of black nationalism and empowerment would resonate with, and hence radicalize, what had long been a rather quiescent underclass. Rizzo wanted to keep it that way, and the property-owning and middle-class whites of Philadelphia were solidly in accord. There was an implicit pact between Rizzo and the business community in Philadelphia: the police could do whatever they must to keep their boots on the throats of the underclass, so long as the crime rate was kept under control, left-wing political activism neutered, and the business climate cultivated.

Rizzo, the son of a police sergeant, had served in the Philadelphia police department for forty-five years. He was, no doubt about it, a larger-than-life figure. Although he rose through the ranks to become mayor in 1972, he never quit being a police officer in terms of his political disposition and outlook. As a cop, Rizzo prided himself on the liberal use of brute force. He encouraged it in other cops, giving it a wink and a nod even when he was mayor. Rizzo's police-can-do-no-wrong credo pervaded the collective consciousness of the police department, and to a disturbing extent the public at large.

To consolidate power as mayor, and thus to further imbue police officers with a feeling of invincibility, Rizzo worked hard to place loyalists in critical positions of power within the municipality. The main line of defense against governmental abuse, the state judiciary, was brought into line with crude political tactics. Judges who looked askance at police heavy-handedness found themselves off the bench after lost reelection bids. Strategic leaks of embarrassing and sensitive private information targeted at political enemies created a climate of fear among those who otherwise could have challenged Rizzo's obsession with political activists and organizations seeking meaningful social change in Philadelphia.

Rizzo first honed his aggressive police tactics on bohemian counterculture hangouts that sprouted in various parts of the city in the mid- to late '60s. Rizzo took it as a crusade to rid Philadelphia of counterculture kids and freethinking young people by demolishing the commercial establishments that were created to cater to them. There would be no Haight-Ashbury or Greenwich Village in Philly. Police raids of head shops, funky cafés and bars made the cost of doing business virtually prohibitive. Rizzo the Raider, as he became known, reasoned, quite rightly, that hippies and pot-smoking youngsters from outside Philadelphia would be disinclined to flock to the city if the urban environment provided no safe havens for their activities.

Homegrown political radicalism was the next target. The most glaring example of Rizzo's fixation on squelching potentially radical political activity occurred in November 1967. Rizzo authorized a "riot-plan" intervention into a demonstration outside a school meeting where high school students were negotiating with school officials over implementation of a black studies program. The demonstrators numbered in the several thousands, voicing their support for the students. In classic Rizzo style, police officers wearing motorcycle boots and leather jackets encircled the demonstrators. Rather than give space to the demonstrators, the police gradually tightened the perimeter, provoking the demonstrators. It is unclear what prompted the announcement, but it was inexorable that the announcement would come: "Get their black asses!" Rizzo shouted. The jittery cops collapsed the leather-clad perimeter onto the demonstrators, engulfing them in a swirl of violence. The Philadelphia director of the ACLU, attending the demonstration to monitor police brutality, reported that Rizzo's cops beat the demonstrators "unmercifully with clubs."

Rizzo's fear of cultural and political subversion became hauntingly fanatic when it came to more organized left-wing political activism. Philadelphia developed a premier special police unit, known as the Civil Defense squad, to surveil and ultimately subvert the subversives. Modeled after similar units within the FBI, the CD squad used all of the domestic counterinsurgency tactics that were in play against national figures on the left. Infiltration with snitches and undercover operatives into progressive and left-wing political organizations was routine. Bulging files containing photographic surveillance and observation notes rested in file cabinets down the hall from the records room containing files on criminals and open criminal investigations.

"We keep a record in the file of all demonstrators we cover," one CD squad officer stated in court testimony during the trial of well-known peace activist Philip Berrigan.

At the height of '60s activism, the Panthers in Philadelphia stood out (as they did in other U.S. cities). How could they not, with their military bearing and discipline, and their tough-talking, no-bullshit rhetoric. There was no doubt the Panthers and Rizzo were destined to collide, but not before they engaged in a toxic catch-me-if-you-can surveillance game. In mid-September 1969, a bugging device was discovered in the Panther headquarters in Philadelphia. Later that month, the Panther office was looted and internal documents illegally seized, including, ironically, signed petitions gathered by Panther members in its campaign for community control of the police.

In March 1970, CD squads, with the help of FBI agents, raided another Panther office in north Philadelphia and arrested eleven people believed to be Panther members. Five months later, very early one August morning, CD squad units simultaneously raided Panther offices at three Philadelphia locations, with television news cameras in tow—another classic Rizzo move, as he was consumed by the desire to manipulate public perception through carefully orchestrated media events. With stunning speed, CD squad officers and federal agents, protected by bulletproof vests and chosen for their expertise with firearms, aggressively subdued Panther members, who actually never put up any genuine resistance. They then proceeded to loot and destroy the offices.

To say that Rizzo had a monstrous dislike for the Panthers is an understatement. He relished belittling them in the press, hoping to provoke their ire and thus induce bloodshed, which could then be used to justify even more repressive police tactics. After the August 1970 raids, Rizzo taunted the Panthers as "yellow" because the arrestees had complied immediately with law enforcement directives to drop their weapons. Rizzo suggested that the Panthers were all bark and no bite because they didn't engage the raiding cops in a shootout. The arrestees were also humiliated, upon Rizzo's orders, by having to stand naked for prolonged periods of time, awaiting to be strip searched. News photos depicted naked Panther members, with uniformed white police officers standing next to them with shotguns, chins up, chest out, and obviously satisfied—photos disgustingly suggestive of an African safari. Rizzo loved the photos and the imagery of police domination. "Imagine," he gloated, "the big Black Panthers with their pants down."

In the immediate aftermath of the August raids, news reporters confirmed complaints by Panther leaders that files and office equipment were stolen and the physical plant of the offices destroyed. When reporters confronted Rizzo with this, he grew even more defiant, with vintage Rizzo-like panache: "We're dealing with a group of fanatics, yellow dogs. . . . We are dealing with psychotics and we must be in a position to take them on. These imbeciles and yellow dogs . . . we'd be glad to meet them on their own terms. Just let them tell us when and where."

It would never be a fair fight, of course. Rizzo had the guns, the numbers, the judges, and "the law" on his side. Especially "the law."

■ It was in this climate that Mumia gained political consciousness as a young teenage Black Panther Party member. Mumia credits a kick in the face he received from a Philadelphia cop when he was fourteen years old for his membership in the Party. In fact, he became one of the founding members of the Philadelphia chapter at the age of fifteen. As Mumia tells it, he and three other "Afro-headed" youngsters went to a George Wallace rally, insanely yelling "black power" amidst a sea of rednecks. Attacked by upward of ten burly men, Mumia and his ebullient friends tried to summon help from the police. Here's how Mumia describes what happened next: "[A] cop saw me on the ground being beaten to a pulp; [he] marched over briskly—and kicked me in the face. I have been thankful to that faceless cop ever since, for he kicked me straight into the Black Panther Party."

Mumia was precisely the type of black youth that the Panthers sought in their efforts to erect a militant left-wing organization. The Panthers were unabashedly Marxist, blending the revolutionary zeal of

Franz Fanon with the communist doctrines of Mao Tze-tung. In the years leading up to Mumia's entry into the Black Panther Party, black radicals were presented with two paths to black empowerment: one provided by the Student Nonviolent Coordinating Committee (under the leadership of Stokely Carmichael) and the other by Huey Newton's Panthers. SNCC veered in the direction of black separatism, rooted in the belief that black empowerment could only thrive outside the hegemony of white influence. On the other hand, Newton rejected the whole notion of separatism; instead, he felt that the Panthers would become a vanguard of the left generally, and as such, they could lead oppressed people of all stripes to genuine revolutionary socialism. Whereas Carmichael aroused crowds with the chant "Black Power!" the Panthers invoked the slogan "All Power to the People"—meaning, power to oppressed people everywhere. SNCC and Carmichael appealed to the college crowd; Huey and the Panthers appealed to the urban ghetto youths.

Mumia (along with his twin brother Wayne) was born in Philadelphia on April 24, 1954. By Mumia's own account, his pre-Panther years were "absolutely unremarkable." He grew up poor in a housing project in north Philly, one of five boys and one girl born to Edith Cook. His father died when he was twelve, but his mother—who by all accounts was a remarkably strong woman—maintained a tight-knit, loving, and spiritually nurturing household. Mumia took to religion as a youngster, becoming a student of religious texts while others read comic books. In fact, people who remember Mumia as a child uniformly characterize him as a lover of books and gifted with words. The poet Wordsworth observed that "the child is the father to the man." Mumia the man is very much the offspring of Mumia the child.

Edith named her son Wesley. Wesley Cook took on the more evocative name Mumia Abu-Jamal not so much in a moment of epiphany but over time during the self-exploratory years of adolescence. In many ways, Wesley Cook grew into Mumia Abu-Jamal, with the change in name reflecting a change, a birthing, of a new consciousness. It started in a high school class taught by a teacher from Kenya. In a modest effort to broaden the horizons of the students beyond the suffocating confinement of urban existence in the projects, this teacher gave Swahili names to his students. Somehow, whether by happenstance or design, Wesley Cook was dubbed Mumia. Free spirited by temperament and captivated by the notion that he could be liberated from the name given to him at birth (actually a difficult thing to do, psychologically and emotionally), Wesley Cook took a liking to the name, not coincidentally at a time when he took a liking to the liberation themes of black empowerment rhetoric.

The name Abu-Jamal came about later. Mumia's firstborn son was named Jamal. *Abu-Jamal* is Arabic for "father of Jamal." Hence, Mumia Abu-Jamal, a Swahili and Arabic combination.

Joining the Black Panther Party in May 1969, Mumia quickly impressed with his intelligence and his instinctive need to communicate. At fifteen, he became the Philadelphia chapter's minister of information. It was his job to issue written status reports on the Philadelphia chapter to the Oakland headquarters, which would then be published in edited form in the national Panther journal, *Black Panther–Black Community News Service*. Mumia dove into the assignment, and took enormous pride (which he still carries to this day) in the journal's wide international circulation. It seemed to him that journalism was in his genetic makeup, something that he had no choice but to do. Mumia was so taken by his foray into journalism that he increasingly resented conventional schooling as an encroachment upon what he regarded as the truly transcendent work of the Panthers. He dropped out of high school, briefly it turns out, to work full-time as a journalist. The precocious teenager soaked in the experience, traveling and working in New York and the Bay Area when not typing away in the Panther offices in Philadelphia.

Mumia, of course, didn't know it at the time, but considerable COINTELPRO attention was focused on the *Black Panther–Black Community News Service*. FBI headquarters in 1970 observed that "the BPP newspaper has a circulation of . . . 139,000. It is the voice of the BPP and if it could be effectively hindered, it would result in helping to cripple the BPP."[9] The New York FBI office endorsed the sentiment: "[the FBI] realizes the financial benefits coming to the BPP through the sale of this newspaper. Continued efforts will [therefore] be made to derive logical and practical plans to thwart this crucial BPP operation."[10]

FBI files, almost a thousand heavily redacted pages of which have thus far been disclosed, indicate that Philadelphia and federal authorities took an interest in Mumia even before he officially became a member of the Panthers. Reflective of the thoroughness of law enforcement's surveillance of political activists, the name Wesley Cook appeared in a 1968 surveillance report, documenting Mumia's arrest at the pro-George Wallace rally mentioned earlier. The interest intensified, of course, when this young, impassioned high school kid assumed a prominent role in the Philadelphia chapter of the Black Panther Party. Perhaps comparing Mumia to typical suburban adolescents, surveillance officers didn't know quite what to make of this young teenager's commitment to radical politics. It was enough, however, to provoke security concerns, as this entry in an FBI document illustrates:

> In spite of the subject's age (fifteen years) Philadelphia feels that his continued participation in BPP activities in the Philadelphia Division, his position in the Philadelphia Branch of the BPP, and his past inclination to appear and speak at public gatherings, the subject should be included in the Security Index.

Mumia's writings, his whereabouts, his interpersonal relationships, his speeches—all became part of the security databank of the municipal and federal government. Law enforcement agencies never detected any criminal activity on Mumia's part, only a dedication to the Panther's goals, which essentially boiled down to black empowerment. But he was never far from the minds of those responsible for "domestic security" (the justificatory language of COINTELPRO). Indeed, on at least two occasions, Mumia, without his knowledge, came under quick suspicion for involvement in at least two homicides (though never arrested), later attributed to the overtly violent Black Liberation Army, only to be removed from suspicion upon ironclad proof that he could not have been involved.

Mumia reduced his involvement with the Black Panther Party in 1970 to return to Benjamin Franklin High School. Confident and thoroughly politicized, Mumia quickly led a student movement to change the school's name to Malcolm X High School. School officials balked at the demand, but Mumia acquired a grudging respect among the adults as an articulate and charismatic leader.

Mumia's experience in the Black Panther Party planted the seeds of activist journalism that have flourished ever since. Mumia began his broadcasting career, after attending Goddard College, at a Temple University radio station, WRTI-FM, where he did a commentary show on black affairs until 1973. Two years later, Mumia became a popular presence on station WHAT, airing broadcasts on a coveted morning show spot. Politics was always a part of Mumia's journalism, just as it was an integral part of his work ethic. So it is not surprising that Mumia left WHAT after he led an employment grievance–related walkout with other station employees.

Mumia then briefly went to WPEN, only to move over to WUHY as a reporter and a commentator in July of 1979. It was as a WUHY reporter that people began to take notice of Mumia as a fixture at city hall. Mumia understood what Rizzo was all about, and he understood the dynamics of racial oppression in Philadelphia. His news reports typically focused on the victims of that oppression, highlighting stories dealing with housing, prisons, education, and poverty. But what set Mumia apart was not so much the subject matter of his journalism, or even the passion he brought to his craft. His news pieces were not grandiose diatribes against the white power establishment, or embellished left-wing critiques on municipal politics. They dealt, more often than not, with small stories involving real people with real pain within a real city with a really nasty government. It was the small stories that illuminated the bigger picture of Philadelphia's racial polarization. People in the marginalized communities listened to Mumia because his stories lent a dignity to their lives by giving voice to their frustrations and by simply acknowledging that they existed. Mumia had a keen understanding that indifference suffocated the human spirit. Feelings of isolation among disenfranchised poor people demoralized them and etched a path to alcohol and drug abuse, violence, and crime. Human connectedness, to this day, is a recurring theme in his writings. It didn't take sitting in a tiny cell on death row, twenty-three hours a day, for Mumia to appreciate the importance of human contact.

His journalism colleagues listened admiringly because he had a resplendent gift to enliven a story with drama and vividness, and did so with seeming effortlessness. He had the rare ability to draw pictures with words and evoke emotions with his voice. Mumia had a way of speaking that cut through cognitive barriers, disengaged intellectualisms that stood in the way of true understanding, and induced people to *feel*. A Bob Marley song says, "He who feels it, knows it." Mumia's gift as a journalist operated on that insight.

Mumia's ability to tease out the drama in a story with remarkable prehensile sensibility, and then to weave the facts together with his mellifluous voice, led to the now-famous encomium "voice of the voiceless." His journalism led to numerous awards and citations, including one from the Society of Professional Journalists. He became president of Philadelphia's Association of Black Journalists in 1980, and in January 1981, he was identified by the *Philadelphia Inquirer* as one Philadelphian to watch, because his "eloquent, often passionate, and always insightful interviews bring a special dimension to radio reporting."

Yet as Mumia sat there in the predawn hours of December 9, 1981, slumped on the curb next to the front right bumper of his brother's beat-up Volkswagen, blood oozing out of his chest and soaking his shirt, he was a criminal suspect in a brutally vicious murder of a cop; a man who arrived in that seedy side of Philadelphia at an hour when most respectable folks are tucked away in bed because he was moonlighting as a cab driver; a man who drove a cab because his career as a journalist, a remarkably promising career, was at a crossroads. Fired at radio station WDAS because his journalism was perceived to be growing more tendentious and biased, Mumia began driving a cab to support his family. Beset by marital difficulties and financial strains, Mumia grew more distant from his professional colleagues. They knew that Mumia had taken on the dreadlocked hair-style associated with the much-maligned and much-misunderstood Philadelphia black radical group MOVE, but they didn't know *why*. They knew that Mumia wrote stories about MOVE with heartfelt sympathy and with an increasingly overt alliance to its tenets, but they didn't understand *why*. They didn't understand, and certainly didn't approve of, Mumia's selling of MOVE-published newspapers in the city hall pressroom. People began to wonder: What's up, Mumia?

■ The MOVE organization—the name shortened from Christian Life Movement—surfaced in Philadelphia during the early 1970s. It arose largely through the teachings of an enigmatic, self-taught carpenter named Vincent Leaphart. Inspired by the spiritual precepts and dietary regimen of a religious sect known as the Kingdom of Yahweh, Lea-phart developed a worldview that, at first blush, seemed innocuous. Immediately identified by their dreadlocks and their adopted surname, Africa (Leaphart became John Africa), MOVE members quickly went from items of curiosity to curious threats to the status quo. MOVE was described by most so-called mainstream journalists as a back-to-nature cult, a terse description that captures a certain essence to the group, as it billed itself as devotees of a simplified, more life-affirming mode of living. According to a MOVE statement,

> *MOVE's work is to stop industry from poisoning the air, the water, the soil, and to put an end to the enslavement of life— people, animals, any form of life. The purpose of John Africa's revolution is to show people through John Africa's teaching, the truth, that this system is the cause of all their problems (alcoholism, drug addiction, unemployment, wife abuse, child pornography, every problem in the world) and to set the example of revolution for people to follow when they realize how they've been oppressed, repressed, duped, tricked by this system, this government and see the need to rid themselves of this cancerous system as MOVE does.*

John Africa's devotion to simplicity and his deep skepticism of science and technology had a certain seductive charm. "Science is a trick," he intones in his tract, *The Teachings of John Africa*, which MOVE members regard as a sacred text. "Man will see the air and build a fan, see the sun and invent a light bulb, see a bird and build a plane. He will duplicate, copy the principle of life rather than DO AS, be like the principle of life." This advocacy of touching Mother Nature in the raw, unmediated by "duplicate" devices, translated, in practice, into eating only raw foods, eschewing even the extermination of cockroaches and urban vermin, and disavowing the use of soap and modern-day plumbing. Others in the Powelton Village community where MOVE took root, not surprisingly, were hardly enchanted with this back-to-nature ideology.

In a 1996 interview, Mumia described MOVE as a "family of revolutionaries, of naturalist revolutionaries . . . who oppose all that this system represents." Just as his journalism colleagues back in the late '70s didn't understand his affinity for MOVE, Mumia didn't understand the generalized and intense antipathy felt by most Philadelphians toward its members. "They are the beginning of a movement," Mumia announced to colleagues in 1979, "anyone with eyes and perception can see that."

"What I found," Mumia explained in that 1996 interview, "were idealistic, committed, strong, unshakable men and women who had a deep spirit-level aversion to everything this system represents. To them, this system was a death system involved in a deathly war. To them, everything this system radiated was poison—from its technological waste to its destruction of the earth, to its destruction of the air and water, to its destruction of the very genetic pool of human life and animal life and all life."[11]

Mumia's sympathies for MOVE reflected not only his affinity for its underlying doctrines of simplicity and spiritual awakening but also sprang from Mumia's awareness of Rizzo's iron-fisted racist rule over Philadelphia. Mumia's disgust over Rizzo's infectious racism was shared by a growing segment of Philadelphia as early as 1978. Rizzo ran a blatantly racist reelection campaign in 1978 ("Vote White" was one campaign slogan), which failed to resonate as forcefully as it once had with the white citizenry. Philadelphians grew impatient with Rizzo, as his heavy-handed tactics, which were once grudgingly tolerated by many well-to-do citizens, did not lead to significant reductions in the crime rate, as he had promised. Moreover, the indiscriminate use of deadly force and lesser forms of police abuse against minorities began to disturb many Philadelphians.

In fact, revelations of police abuse even caught the attention of the Department of Justice. Hearings were held in 1979, an unprecedented occurrence, where witnesses described rampant brutality, massive cover-ups, and suppression of evidence of police abuses. Business leaders testified that they had entered into a Faustian pact with Rizzo: police abuses would be tolerated on the promise that the business climate would improve by virtue of a declining crime rate and a subjugated minority community.

The federal government hearings substantiated and reinforced the view of many in Philadelphia that the city had become a virtual police state, which had led to dangerous levels of racial polarization. The escalation of racial tensions provoked ever greater demands by progressive political groups for social justice, which in turn prompted Philadelphia cops to resort to even more draconian police methods. It was a vicious cycle that the Department of Justice sought to break.

On August 13, 1979, the Justice Department filed a lawsuit against the city of Philadelphia, Mayor Rizzo, and over a dozen top city and police officials. The essence of the suit was the charge that the city and its municipal leaders condoned systematic police brutality. Never before in U.S. history had an entire city police department been accused of violating civil rights of its residents, not only through outright physical brutality but by the crudest of Orwellian methods of surveillance as well. The suit was never litigated, however. A federal judge dismissed it, not because evidence was lacking but because the federal government lacked the authority (the legal concept is termed "standing") to institute such a suit. The outcome, however, was, in a significant sense, beside the point. The actual point was made loudly and clearly by the mere filing of the suit. Philadelphians took notice.

■ True to form, Philadelphia law enforcement couldn't avoid conflict with the MOVE organization. From 1974 to 1976, Philadelphia police arrested MOVE members some four hundred times for offenses ranging from disturbing the peace to illegal weapons possession. The police had an "unconcealed disgust and contempt" for MOVE members.[12] According to journalists John Anderson and Hilary Hevenor:

> *By September of 1976, there were reports that John Africa had decided to abandon the course of peaceful resistance. Leaphart, one newspaper article noted, had 'told his followers to prepare for a showdown with police.' And so it was about this time that MOVE members began doing calisthenics, practicing boxing and martial arts, and most ominous of all, stockpiling weapons and ammunition.*[13]

Things began to come to a head in May 1977, arising from the city's desire to rid itself of MOVE. According to city officials, people living in the Powelton Village section of west Philadelphia, a middle-class black neighborhood of row houses, complained about the sanitary conditions of the MOVE compound and the noise coming from MOVE members' use of a bullhorn to disseminate their diatribes against "the system."

When verbal threats and warnings did nothing to frighten them into submission, the police department, on August 8, 1978, resorted to a bulldozer. They tore down the barricades and knocked out the windows of the MOVE headquarters. About twenty officers then rushed into the tattered communal residence, ready to open fire. They found the first floor empty of people. They soon discovered that the MOVE members, disoriented and fearful for their own lives and the lives of their children and their animals, had taken refuge in the basement. Firemen unleashed their hoses in an attempt to flood the basement with water; smoke was also blasted into the confined space. The Stakeout officers then opened fire on the trapped MOVE members.

News photographers captured images of desperate women trying to climb out through a basement window with children in their arms. With bullets whizzing, compounded by the ricochet of the bullets emanating from uncontrolled gunfire, the police assault on the compound never acquired any semblance of order or logic. It descended into chaos virtually at the moment heavily armed Stakeout cops entered the building.

Authorities claimed that the wild shootout had been started by violence-prone MOVE members, which resulted in the death of one police officer and the injury of a dozen others. Police Officer James J. Ramp, fifty-two years old and one of the "old men" of the Stakeout Unit, received a single gunshot wound (exactly where was a subject of intense dispute), killing him.

Ramp had earned the right to end his career sitting behind a desk, but he had been drafted into the MOVE assignment. Ten years removed from actual street police duty, Ramp didn't even know how to put on his blue riot helmet when he was dispatched to Powelton Village. "I've been off the street so long, I don't know what to do anymore," he joked as his helmet rested backward on his head.

Enraged by Ramp's death and convinced that the bullet came from a MOVE gun, Stakeout cops seized MOVE leader Delbert Africa as he tried to surrender and beat him unmercifully. Their frenzied rage left them unconcerned over the fact that news photographers captured the brutality on film.

After the dust settled, eleven MOVE members were arrested. A press conference in city hall later that afternoon provided the platform for Police Commissioner Joseph O'Neill to excoriate MOVE for the Ramp killing. Mayor Rizzo then cursed reporters, blaming the *Philadelphia Inquirer* in particular for helping to create a climate for this sort of disaster. "Every week in your goddamn newspaper, every weekend, they have headlines in your paper about policemen did this, did that, murder, murder, murder. . . . That's what's wrong with this city. . . . You're destroying it. The people you represent are destroying it." Pointing to the death of Officer Ramp, Rizzo exclaimed that it showed the need to restore the death penalty in Philadelphia. "Put them in the electric chair," Rizzo hollered, "and I'll pull the switch!"

It wasn't only the top brass who expressed outrage over Ramp's death. The prevailing sentiment among officers, as one police officer described it, was that the Stakeout Unit "should have killed all of them." Another officer told a reporter that MOVE members wanted violence so that "those animals will become martyrs." The malevolence lingered for years, as the Ramp killing became a rallying cry for Philadelphia cops in their vendetta against MOVE and their distrust of blacks generally. The tragic and highly publicized 1985 bombing of the relocated MOVE compound on Osage Avenue, leading to the death of John Africa and ten other MOVE men, women, and children, can only be understood against the backdrop of the 1978 siege on MOVE's Powelton Village compound. Many of the older cops involved in the police action in 1985 distinguished themselves from other younger cops with the title " '78 veterans." The war against MOVE continues to this day.

In the trial of the MOVE Nine, the arrested MOVE members were convicted in the shooting death of Officer Ramp and sentenced to prison for thirty to one hundred years (two others were separately tried—one was convicted, the other acquitted after renouncing her MOVE affiliation). The trial was an ordeal—a harbinger of Mumia's trial—with acrimonious exchanges between judge and defendants leading to frequent expulsions from the proceedings. The trial judge, sixty-eight-year-old Edwin S. Malmed, a conservative white man with a penchant for gentlemanly rectitude, loathed the convicted defendants. "In my opinion," he said before pronouncing sentence, "any thought of rehabilitation of these defendants would be absurd. They have persisted in setting their own bizarre codes of conduct without regard for the laws of the Commonwealth or the rights of others, and I don't think their attitudes will change."

As an aside, three Stakeout Unit officers who beat Delbert Africa in front of television cameras and still photographers were also put on trial. Judge Stanley Kubacki dismissed the charges at the close of the prosecution's case. "Philadelphia is bleeding to death because of the MOVE tragedy," he said.

One of the reporters covering the MOVE Nine trial was Mumia Abu-Jamal. A day after the sentences were handed down, the trial judge appeared on a local radio talk show. A caller came on the line and asked the judge, "Who shot James Ramp?" The judge admitted that he had no idea. That caller was Mumia.

Mumia had no way of knowing that his frequent attendance at the MOVE Nine trial, and his manifest sympathy for the group (graphically demonstrated by his new dreadlocks), would come into play a few years later in his own legal predicament. The courtroom for the MOVE Nine trial was always filled with cops, as the trial moved along from December 1979 to May 1980, with overt hostilities expressed against those attending in sympathy with the defendants. Mumia was among those repeatedly harassed by police inside the courtroom and out in the corridors of that temple of justice.*

■ The first officers at the scene of the Faulkner shooting, a year and a half after the conclusion of the emotionally heated trial of the MOVE Nine, were two Stakeout Unit cops. Mumia was a well-known ally of MOVE to police officers and officials who were '78 veterans still angered by the Ramp shooting. Witnesses observed officers beating Mumia at the scene before putting him into a police van. With law enforcement officers predisposed to believing that Mumia, a perceived member and/or ally of MOVE, had just killed a brother officer in cold blood, the question naturally arises: What were they capable of doing to make sure that evidence at Mumia's trial would exist to ensure that "justice for Danny" would be done? What would angry cops do to execute justice?

*For complete accounts of the MOVE tragedy in Philadelphia, *see* Boyette, *Let It Burn! The Philadelphia Tragedy* (New York: Contemporary Books, 1989); Paolantinio, *Frank Rizzo, The Last Big Man in Big City America* (New York: Camino Books, 1993); Harry, *Attention, MOVE! This is America!*; Anderson and Hevenor, *Burning Down the House: MOVE and the Tragedy of Philadelphia* (New York: W. W. Norton, 1987).

I know there are certain cases that have
explosive tendencies in the community. And
this is one of them.

JUDGE PAUL RIBNER

4. CONSTRUCTING GOOD VERSUS EVIL

A trial is a frightening event.

Those who have never experienced courtroom combat tend to view trials as nothing more than a highly structured mechanism to resolve conflict. Resolving conflict undoubtedly expresses the *function* of a trial—the imposition of order on conflict, the chaining down of passions with reason, the rectification of legal wrongs. But to a dedicated trial lawyer, a trial is always a battle between good and evil fought on a terrain of bleak emotions. The trial lawyer must tap into the harsh emotional core of a case, find its deepest *human* elements, and then construct a strategy to place his client's cause on the side of good, or at least, in opposition to evil. In a criminal case, the prosecution comes into the process presumptively on the side of good and the defense lawyer on the side of evil. A major hurdle for the defense is turning the tables.

Tapping into the emotional core of a case necessarily involves getting inside the emotional universe of one's client, and to the extent possible, that of the other major players in a case. In so doing, the trial lawyer risks exposing the deepest regions of his own dark side, of his own sorrow, distress, and anger, because these and other emotions are the human elements of virtually every criminal trial. To do a trial right, a trial lawyer must have the courage to explore his own innermost being in order to truly understand, and then to effectively communicate to the audience of twelve, the forces at work in the human drama that led up to the dispute being litigated in the courtroom. Because when it comes time to represent the client in this civilized form of combat, the trial lawyer must communicate to the jury in an authentic way, from a vantage point of genuine understanding and empathy. If the jury sees the trial lawyer as nothing more than a mouthpiece, a person who will use words only to manipulate rather than to reveal deeper truths, then the jury will never trust that lawyer; and without trust, there can be no truthful communication; and without truthful communication, there can be no persuasion. Moreover, when the trial lawyer engages the trial process as an authentic person, when he presents his case as if it somehow is an exercise in his own self-awareness, a project of self-knowledge, the jury cannot help but become enraptured by the drama that underlies the dispute. Every trial, because it is rooted in conflict, is a drama that has the ingredients to captivate. And all good drama is self-revelatory.

The process of getting inside the emotional core of a case so as to transform it into your own client's battle of good against evil, and of arriving at that crucial point of authenticity in a trial, begins the moment the client enters the trial lawyer's life.

■ Unfortunately, capital defendants are often defended by shockingly incompetent lawyers. Some have been known to sleep through parts of the trial; some have showed up drunk, high, or hungover; some have spoken ill of their clients, virtually inviting the jury to execute them; some don't even speak on their behalf at all. Few try to understand the client. In Texas, a model jurisdiction for advocates of government-run death machinery, lawyers jokingly refer to the "mirror test" as the barometer for determining whether a defendant has been denied constitutionally adequate counsel. If you put a mirror underneath the nose of the attorney and it fogs up, the constitutional requirement of effective assistance of counsel has been satisfied.

Anthony Jackson, Mumia's court-appointed lawyer, was far from the bottom of the barrel. He was admitted to the bar in July 1974, after graduating from Temple University's law school. Before law school, he had worked in the Philadelphia police department as an evidence technician, storing crime scene evidence for possible use at trial, photographing crime scenes, and conducting fingerprint tests. He also spent a few years working as an investigator for the public defender's office and for private criminal law practitioners. At the urging of a local criminal defense lawyer (who, by coincidence, handled Mumia's appeal after his trial), Jackson applied to law school. He entered into his legal training well suited to the rough-hewn world of criminal law.

One of the few black law school graduates in Philadelphia at the time, Jackson took his first job as a prosecutor with the Philadelphia district attorney's office. He became a prosecutor somewhat reluctantly. While in law school he took a criminal law seminar taught by Arlen Specter (later to become a U.S. senator), and he submitted a paper dealing with the scarcity of black prosecutors in the United States. As a result of that paper, Specter invited him to join the district attorney's office in Philadelphia. According to Jackson, "it was probably the last place I thought of working, but I guess to some extent I was a little bit embarrassed about it so I did take the job." Jackson's heart, however, was never in the work. He didn't have the prosecutorial mind-set that admires orderliness over compassion, accountability over empathy. Prosecutors disdain excuses, scoff at human weaknesses, and treasure the slippery notion of individual responsibility. Jackson naturally leaned toward the underdog and empathized with the frailties of the human heart. He was compassionate by nature, given to exhibitions of emotion at the drop of a hat—not qualities a district attorney wants in young prosecutors. "I didn't like prosecutors," Jackson bluntly admits. He was a prosecutor for only six months.

After a few years working to reform the Philadelphia prison system, Jackson took a job in 1978 with the Public Interest Law Center of Philadelphia (PILCOP), an organization dealing with, among other things, police brutality in Rizzo's Philadelphia. "It was funded by the Law Enforcement Assistance Administration," Jackson explained in court testimony in 1995. "It was specifically funded to explore avenues of increasing police-community relations; . . . we were trying to create an avenue for citizens here in Philadelphia to file complaints and have them meritoriously examined." In fact, Jackson, who became the director of PILCOP, was actively involved in the grassroots work behind the Justice Department lawsuit filed against the city of Philadelphia, Mayor Rizzo, and others.

Well-known as an active player in the fight against police abuses in Rizzo's Philadelphia, Jackson had been approached by concerned friends of Mumia to visit him while he was recuperating in the hospital. He didn't know if the visit would lead to an attorney-client relationship; he didn't actually consider it seriously, as he was still with PILCOP and had not yet set up an office for private practice. As it turned out, because Mumia was in no condition to seek out a lawyer himself, and because the arraignment on the murder charge was to happen within a day or so, Jackson accepted an appointment from the court to handle the case.

There was no mistaking it: Jackson was overwhelmed with burdens when he took on Mumia's case on December 12, 1981. Having been out of private practice for three years, he didn't have file cabinets filled with case files. In fact, Mumia's slim file was one of the first cases he acquired, and he had a "Mumia" file even before he had an actual office. It took Jackson over a month after taking on the appointment to set up an office. With no money coming in, no office support, and unaware of what he was getting into, Jackson was destined to hit stormy weather right from the beginning.

■ Jackson straightened his tie as the elevator made its way to the sixth floor of the city hall building. There would be television cameras in the hallway, he figured, and he wanted to look presentable. He had not dived into the case as of yet—too busy setting up an office and scrambling for new business—and his client was still recuperating from his injuries. A month had not yet passed since the killing of Officer Faulkner. Jackson was not without a plan for the morning's court appearance, however. He had a client who claimed he was brutalized by police; the first order of business, he concluded, was to document those injuries in the court record.

He stepped out of the elevator, walked down the hall, turned the corner and headed toward Courtroom 613. The camera lights beamed in his direction as he moved closer to the entrance door, but he waved the reporters away. There would be time enough for talking with them later. The court clerk had been waiting for him. The prosecutor, Joseph McGill, was already present, sitting at the prosecutor's table thumbing through a sheaf of papers. Jackson greeted his adversary in his customary friendly fashion, and the two talked briefly at the railing separating the spectator section from the well of the courtroom where the combatants duel over truth and justice. McGill was considerably taller than Jackson, with gray hair, a penetrating stare, and an aristocratic bearing. His salt-and-pepper mustache dominated his long, narrow face, giving him a severe look. He casually remarked that, for the time being at least, Mumia's brother would be a codefendant in the case, although he was not charged with the homicide. Jackson had not known that.

"Step up, Mr. Jackson," the judge said in a friendly tone. He then directed his clerk to call the case.

"This is the Commonwealth versus Wesley Cook, aka Mumia Abu-Jamal," the clerk announced, placing an exaggerated accent on the second syllable to Mumia's name.*

"Good morning, Your Honor," Jackson said. "I'm appearing for the defendant, Wesley Cook."

"Your Honor, we're prepared to proceed with the preliminary hearing," McGill quickly announced. A preliminary hearing is a pro-

---

*People often pronounce the name with the accent on the second syllable, thus, 'MuMEEa'. Mumia himself puts the accent on the first syllable.

ceeding where the prosecution presents evidence to show that it has sufficient evidence (probable cause) to detain the defendant for trial.

Jackson did a double-take. What preliminary hearing? He quickly stammered through an explanation that his client remained in the hospital, having sustained, aside from a gunshot wound, "injuries all about the body," including contusions and lacerations. He told the judge he wanted photos to document those injuries.

Judge Paul Ribner, a rugged, tough-talking criminal court jurist, wasn't interested in exploring Jackson's request. He wanted to know if Jackson was ready for the preliminary hearing. Usually the preliminary hearing is a routine matter, with the defense attorney playing little or no role other than to gather as much information as possible for eventual use at trial or as an aid to conduct an investigation. Jackson was, nonetheless, not prepared to handle a preliminary hearing. It was a Tuesday. He had mistakenly thought that the preliminary hearing was scheduled for that Friday, January 8. On top of that, he told Judge Ribner that he wouldn't be ready on that day either, because he had scheduled another matter to attend to in Manhattan.

After having spent the past three years doing civil litigation, Jackson had forgotten about the rigors and pacing of criminal defense practice. In civil litigation, a month is a blip in time; in capital litigation, where immediate investigation is key to putting together a defense, a month of inactivity, especially if it is the first month after the commission of the crime, can be cataclysmic. Witnesses can be lost, stories begin to harden, crime scene evidence is used up in laboratory testing. Homicide investigators are already deep into the investigation well before a criminal defense lawyer even meets his client. The first month in a murder case for a defense lawyer is catch-up time.

"Well, this is the kind of case you want to keep on top of," Ribner cautioned. Not at all pleased with Jackson's ill-preparedness, Ribner insisted upon proceeding on the eighth.

Expecting that the judge would accommodate his scheduling conflict, Jackson was caught flatfooted. "I'm now finding out that this matter is listed for the eighth and I am now told today for the first time, for the very first time, that there's a codefendant in the case."

"You are a smart defense lawyer, Mr. Jackson," Ribner chided. "But when you tell me that you didn't know there was a codefendant in this matter—well, all I can say to you is you'll have to spend a little more time on this case. Check it out, before you get to a hearing in this matter." The judge leaned forward and looked squarely at Jackson. "You have a big murder case here, and you'll have to keep on top of it. Because this case is going to get a lot of exposure in the community." Ribner could see that the courtroom was divided down the middle, white faces on one side of the aisle, and black faces on the other. "I know there are certain cases that have explosive tendencies in the community. And this is one of them." He had no idea how prescient those words would become.

On Friday morning, Jackson rushed out of his house to get to court on time, not wanting to irritate Judge Ribner further. He arrived in Courtroom 613 and discovered that his rushing was in vain because Ribner wasn't presiding over the preliminary hearing. It would be Judge Edward Mekel, a far more laid-back jurist. That wasn't the only surprise for the morning. He went into the lockup to talk with Mumia and found him dressed in a white hospital gown. Mumia had fallen ill the night before and had to be taken to the hospital. He was brought to city hall directly from the hospital. Jackson knew that Mumia would not be forced into appearing in open court wearing only the gown. He was about to get his first lesson about his client.

Mumia had been offered prison clothes to permit him to appear in open court. Mumia was adamant: no prison clothes in court. Prison guards informed Judge Mekel of Mumia's refusal to accept prison garments. Agitated, Judge Mekel nonetheless avoided a power struggle with Mumia. Instead of suspending the proceedings for the day or forcing Mumia to make the choice of foregoing attendance at the preliminary hearing or acquiescing on the issue of prison garb, he sent the sheriff to a local store to buy clothes for him so the proceedings could begin without unnecessary acrimony. Rumors circulated among the reporters that McGill gave money to the sheriff for this unusual shopping spree.

Four hours later, Mumia entered the courtroom wearing brown

pants and a brown plaid shirt. It wasn't his style of clothing, but the sheriff wasn't interested in fashion when he bought them. Mumia took a seat next to his brother. It would be the last time the two brothers would ever sit next to each other. Billy Cook adored his older brother, looking upon him with a fond reverence because Mumia, unlike himself, seemingly had a bottomless reservoir of God-given talent and a trajectory to his life. Cook discarded his first name and began calling himself Wesley after Mumia ceased using the name. Cook told his lawyer that he used the name Wesley out of love and admiration for his brother.

Cook stared blankly at the wall behind the judge. Mumia sat with his usual posture, slightly bent forward and chin resting against clasped hands, as if listening to an interesting story. But the story was not one that pleased Mumia, or his brother for that matter. Cynthia White was on the stand—the first witness called by the prosecution in the preliminary hearing.

Maureen Faulkner sat in the front row, crying, as White began her testimony.

Her testimony was brief—typical for a preliminary hearing. Prosecutors are reluctant to have witnesses put their stories on the record before trial. The more times a witness provides details of an incident, the greater the likelihood that an inconsistency will surface, and inconsistencies are the lifeblood of criminal defense work. Criminal defense lawyers seize upon inconsistencies, twirling them in the light like a jagged crystal to find that perfectly beautiful refraction of light that might induce the jury to find reasonable doubt.

White's story at the preliminary hearing was, in its broad outlines, the story she was to give to the jury six months later. She spoke of the Volkswagen being pulled over; Billy Cook and Officer Faulkner walking over to the front of the patrol car; Cook hitting the officer; and most crucially, Mumia darting from across the street to shoot at the officer, several times, with the coup de grace as the officer lay helpless facing the dark December heavens. She claimed never to have seen any violence inflicted upon Cook, a claim she was to adhere to at the trial.

Jackson began his cross-examination with the expected goal of trying to tease out as much detail from White as the judge would allow. Cross-examination in a preliminary hearing is not really cross-examination as trial lawyers conceive of it. It is usually a cat-and-mouse game with a judge: the defense lawyer trying to ask as many questions about the details of a witness's story (that is, to "discover" information), and the trial judge, prompted by objections from the prosecutor, looking to keep the questioning confined (that is, to block discovery). Suggestive of Jackson's early lack of preparation, he mistakenly referred to Cynthia White as Miss Washington until she summoned the courage to correct him. "Excuse me, it's Miss White," she said meekly. Jackson sheepishly apologized.

The preliminary hearing generated one inconsistency that illustrated the malleability of White as a witness, which was to become a major aspect of Mumia's legal struggles later on. White insisted that Mumia had a gun in his left hand as he scurried across Locust Street toward his brother. McGill was probably displeased with this description, as Mumia had a holster on his left side, which would suggest that he would have grabbed his gun with his right hand (Mumia is also right-handed). It appears that the difficulty was ironed out, as White testified at trial that Mumia had the gun in his right hand, not his left.

When White finished testifying, Maureen slipped out of the courtroom, still crying.

McGill then called a law enforcement witness to testify, and what he had to say was undoubtedly significant. Inspector Alphonse Giordano, a veteran officer in the Rizzo mold who, as a onetime commander of the Stakeout Unit, despised everything about MOVE, lumbered up to the witness chair and rested his full frame comfortably as he waited for the first question. McGill called Giordano to the stand to establish that Mumia had admitted to the shooting. But Giordano's testimony about a confession was not the confession that the jury was to hear about at the trial. Giordano explained that he entered the police wagon where police officers had placed Mumia. "I asked him if he was hurt," Giordano explained. "As I opened his coat up I noticed a shoulder holster under his left armpit that was empty. I asked him where's the gun from the shoulder holster."

"What did he say?" McGill prompted.

"His response, 'I dropped it beside the car *after I shot him.*' "

It would be a fair question to ask why Giordano's "confession" testimony was not later presented to the jury. Prosecutors don't forgo such damning evidence unless its costs seriously outweigh its enormous and obvious benefits. The answer to this mystery was to be answered on the first business day after the trial concluded. On that day, Giordano was relieved of his duties in the police department, disgraced by suspicions of corruption. Giordano was later indicted on corruption charges arising from a highly publicized scandal involving extortion and financial kickbacks received from prostitutes, pimps, sleazy bar owners and the like that rocked the Philadelphia Police Department. The federal investigation revealed he had been receiving upward of $3,000 a month in illegal payoffs. He ultimately pled guilty to tax fraud based upon his receipt of these payoffs. Giordano was tainted goods; McGill evidently couldn't use him at trial.

With these two witnesses establishing probable cause, McGill rested his case. The defense was under no illusions about the judge's decision: Mumia would be held over for trial. The next issue was to be bail.

That bail was even an open question is remarkable. Capital defendants don't secure bail—at least, they're not supposed to. Jackson called two witnesses at the bail hearing. Mumia's mother, Edith Cook, testified that her son would be staying with her if he could secure his pretrial release. The other witness was a journalism colleague, Timothy St. Hill. St. Hill had known Mumia for fifteen years and was the one who nominated him to be president of the Association of Black Journalists, a position Mumia held in 1981. Thinking bail was out of the question, McGill didn't feel the need to challenge their testimony.

Judge Mekel thought otherwise. He set bail at $250,000.

There was no way the district attorney's office was going to let the bail order stand, as miraculous as it was. McGill immediately went back to his office and slapped together a motion to revoke the bail order; he then arranged for the placement of the case on the Monday calendar.

Jackson and Mumia were back in court on Monday, this time before Judge Ribner. Whatever prompted Judge Mekel to look favorably upon Mumia would not have that effect upon Judge Ribner, and McGill knew it. McGill had no doubt that bail would be revoked completely by Ribner, and by the end of the day, it was. But one judge will not simply override another of his colleagues; there has to be some face-saving rationale to smooth over the bruised egos that inevitably flow from one judge's encroachment upon another judge's exercise of discretion. Understanding this, McGill and Jackson had witnessed lined up to testify. Judge Ribner made the point very clear as well: "I am not going to change another judge's order without a full hearing, that's definite." A hearing, with new witnesses, would provide the cover needed to override another judge's decision, giving the whole process a patina of legitimacy.

The district attorney's office was not the only entity bent on getting the bail revoked. In its first of many acts taken against Mumia over many years, the Fraternal Order of Police—the FOP for short—dispatched a telegram to Judge Ribner. The telegram urged him to revoke Mumia's bail, a highly improper move for obvious reasons. McGill claimed to know nothing about this communiqué. Judge Ribner, for his part, tried to assure the defense that the telegram should not provoke alarm. "It doesn't affect me," he pledged. "It doesn't prejudice me toward the sender, will have no effect on anything I do here."

McGill chimed in: "I'm sure it will have no effect, Your Honor."

That Jackson had the wherewithal to call witnesses supporting Mumia's right to bail, when it was patently clear that it was a futile exercise, was, in retrospect, an oddity in the case. Jackson would hardly exhibit a fraction of that sort of vigilance later in the trial when it would have mattered much more. The witnesses Jackson did call were not typical of defendants accused of killing cops. But Mumia was no ordinary defendant, that much was clear.

Jackson called several prominent Philadelphians to the stand. State

Senator Milton Street had known Mumia for over ten years when he was called upon to tell Judge Ribner about his friend's commitment to social justice and community renewal. Mumia was highly sensitive to Philadelphia's delicate racial affairs, Senator Street explained, and he was one of the few young black men in the city willing to make race a topic of public debate. The senator testified that he had "never known Mr. Jamal to be a violent person."

Jackson called another local politician to vouch for Mumia. Like Senator Street, State Representative David Richardson was confident that Mumia would honor his commitment to appear for trial. He had known him for seven years, often working with him on matters of community affairs. Representative Richardson echoed Senator Street's testimony that Mumia was not a violent man.

Although McGill knew that the bail hearing was but a formalistic prelude to the revocation of bail, he still took the opportunity to cross-examine the two politicians. McGill's approach to these witnesses provided a glimpse into his thinking about the motive behind the shooting of Officer Faulkner, and it foreshadowed how he would pitch the case to a jury—to the right kind of jury, that is.

McGill wanted to know whether they had read or heard Mumia make statements indicating hostility toward the police. They hadn't. McGill broadened the inquiry: had they known that Mumia was a onetime member of the Black Panther Party? Were they aware of statements he made while associated with that organization? Had they ever discussed with him his affiliation with, or sympathy toward, the MOVE organization? At one point in the questioning of Representative Richardson, McGill tried to confront him with a quotation attributed to Mumia contained in a newspaper article. Judge Ribner cut McGill off. McGill would try again later . . . much later. He was going to use this newspaper article; he was sure of it.

McGill cared little about the answers these witnesses gave; he couldn't resist making a point, and he didn't want to wait until trial to make it. According to McGill's way of thinking, Mumia was a political radical with ties to what he regarded as dangerous black nationalist groups who had no qualms about gunning down the guardians of a hated "system" that supposedly oppressed people of color throughout the world. Officer Faulkner was a victim of radical race politics, no less than was Officer James Ramp. McGill, unlike Jackson, was getting to the core of the case early, fleshing out the good-versus-evil story he would later tell the jury. He just needed to make sure that he was going to get the right kind of jury to accept his story line. Getting the right kind of jury was important, probably the most important thing McGill had to do to secure Mumia's conviction and put him on Pennsylvania's death row.

■ The media took a keen interest in the case, unsurprisingly, and that concerned Mumia. He understood instinctively that jury selection would be critical. Concerned with having a panel of whites with preconceived ideas about his dreadlocked appearance, Mumia urged Jackson to do something to protect the jury pool. In a court appearance on February 22, Jackson told Judge Ribner that there was a "practical problem" that had to be dealt with: Mumia didn't want to be photographed each time he was escorted down the corridor to appear in court. A onetime courthouse journalist, Mumia understood the power of those images of him in handcuffs. It would be tough to select an impartial jury with that image splashed on newspapers and beamed into the television sets of a curious Philadelphia citizenry.

"It's a circus-type atmosphere," Jackson complained, "and I don't think it's necessary." If only Jackson knew what was in store.

Jury selection was still months away. A lot had to be done in the meantime, but those things would have to wait. Like many overburdened solo practitioners, Jackson had a myopic outlook on his practice: cases that were months away from trial sat tucked away in a file cabinet while tasks that should have been completed last week took up his full attention. He would come up with a defense before trial; he was sure of it.

To the extent that Jackson ruminated about his strong-willed client, he thought about prosecution witness Cynthia White. How was he going to deal with her eyewitness account? Jackson knew there were other eyewitnesses, but he only thought of White because she was the only one, as of the winter of 1982, to have taken the stand and put on the record what she had supposedly seen.

Jackson was appropriately suspicious of White, as he knew from experience that Philadelphia law enforcement had a history of manipulating prostitutes. He was aware of the talk about police corruption involving extortion and kickbacks from prostitutes and pimps. In May 1981, the Federal Bureau of Investigation began an undercover investigation of the interconnection between Philadelphia police and the city's prostitutes. The investigation, which was highly publicized, focused on the Sixth District, where the Faulkner shooting took place. It produced a mountain of evidence revealing deep-seated corruption; numerous officers (including Inspector Giordano) were indicted, and many of them convicted. Jackson had no way of knowing for sure whether White was somehow ensnared in this web of corruption.

Jackson certainly allowed for the possibility that White, being a vulnerable young prostitute, had been manipulated to supply damning testimony, and surmised that she might not be able to identify Mumia in a lineup. He had decided to file a motion seeking to compel her to make that attempt. Searching for some legal hook to justify a lineup, he argued that this identification procedure was necessary because White initially described the man darting across Locust as having dreadlocks and the shooter having a hat on. According to Jackson this suggested that another person was at the scene, aside from the officer, Mumia, and his brother. McGill protested. A lineup was unwarranted, he countered, because the defense could cross-examine White at trial. Judge Ribner then interjected with a curious remark: White wasn't a pivotal witness, but only "a link in a chain of evidence." McGill said nothing to correct Ribner, even though, in fact, White was to be the most pivotal prosecution eyewitness at the trial. The prosecutor didn't want his witness subjected to a lineup, and that's usually enough for a criminal court judge. Jackson's motion was denied.

Mumia took notice.

There can be no equal justice where the kind of trial a man gets depends on the amount of money he has.

Justice Hugo Black, *GRIFFIN V. ILLINOIS*

People with a lot of money are always going to get better services. But we aren't in the business of correcting every social problem.

Philadelphia judge David Savitt

5. THE STRUGGLE FOR MONEY

Of the nearly 3,700 inmates on death row today, most were represented by lawyers with deficient skills in capital litigation and handicapped by limited resources—a truly deadly combination.

The problem of inadequate resources and counsel in capital litigation has always coexisted with capital punishment in this country, first coming into sharp focus in the famous 1932 Scottsboro Boys case. The American Bar Association conducted an exhaustive study, published in 1990, of the impact of underfunded counsel on the application of the death penalty. It concluded, in the cautionary language customary of elite members of the bar, that "the inadequacy and inadequate compensation of counsel at trial" was one of the "principal failings of the capital punishment systems in the states today."[1]

The heart of the problem is money. Prosecutors have it, capital defense lawyers don't. District attorneys' offices are funded with public money, and no one bats an eye. Too often defense lawyers with clients facing death do not even seek out money for experts, either because they're ignorant of the process or because they have become too jaded to try. Judges, ordered to be budget conscious and thus looking for any excuse *not* to authorize the release of funds, consistently demand that the defense lawyer explain precisely why an expert is needed. The defense lawyer, caught in a catch-22, often cannot articulate the need because he doesn't have the money to consult with an expert to learn *if* expert consultation and testimony will be useful in a case. And then there is the situation where the court grants the defense a sum of money, but it turns out to be such a pittance that no expert wants to get involved. God forbid that a lawyer ask for appointment of another lawyer to help in the preparation of a defense. As death penalty expert Stephen Bright noted: "Although it is widely acknowledged that at least two lawyers, supported by investigative and expert assistance, are required to defend a capital case, some of the jurisdictions with the largest number of death sentences are still asking only one lawyer to defend a capital case."[2]

Who gets assigned to handle capital cases is often determined with money in mind. In death penalty jurisdictions where fairness has not completely been dispensed with, the state legislature allots funds for the creation of an indigent defense program equipped to handle capital cases. New York and California are two such jurisdictions with admirable staffs of committed and extremely talented lawyers, investigators, and mitigation specialists. But in too many jurisdictions, and Philadelphia was one of them at the time of Mumia's trial, judges simply appoint private practitioners to take on capital cases, regardless of competence and training. Because the pay is atrocious, and delayed in coming, typically only the least talented members of the trial bar make themselves available for capital cases. The court-appointment method is favored by some jurisdictions because the costs of sustaining an ongoing office committed to excellent representation is far more expensive than the episodic payment to private, financially strapped lawyers.

Judges often look to the least qualified members of the trial bar to take capital cases—the so-called courthouse hacks who hang out daily at the criminal courts building. They often shun calling upon other members of the bar, because they don't want to impose on their busy lives dedicated to making money. In any event, the reasoning goes, why not appoint a lawyer who is more than happy to take an assignment for want of any other legal business?

Anthony Jackson was a quintessential candidate for court appointment on a capital case. He needed clients *and* he needed to be a team player within the Philadelphia criminal justice system in order to survive economically as a defense lawyer.

■ It was inevitable that Jackson would plead for money. *Plead* is the right word. In Philadelphia, like the worst jurisdictions in the South, money for justice was scarce. Jackson needed to hire an investigator, a ballistician, and a pathologist, but he could do so only through the beneficence of stingy, budget-conscious judges working within a municipality starved for revenues. At the time, the practice in the Philadelphia courts was to allocate a fee of $150 per expert or investigator, doling out slightly more on an ad hoc, unpredictable basis. Under this system, either the defense lawyer had to convince experts and investigators to provide their services and risk never being paid a full fee, or the lawyer himself would pay for their services out of his own pocket and assume the risk that he would never receive full reimbursement.

Jackson cynically regarded the whole process as a sham, and with good reason. One Philadelphia trial judge, David Savitt, crystallized the judicial attitude at the courthouse: "People with a lot of money are always going to get better services. But we aren't in the business of correcting every social problem." Administrators in city hall made it clear to Philadelphia judges that money was scarce. Judge William Manfredi, the onetime presiding judge of the Philadelphia Homicide Calendar who allocated resources in death penalty trials, described the judges' job as balancing "the competing interests of quality representation with the economic situation of Philadelphia." Given Philadelphia's dire economic straits, the scales were heavily tilted away from capital defendants, a constituency with no political clout.

■ Jackson's problem with money at this juncture in the case, however, wasn't only whether he would get paid; it was also a matter of *when*. He understood from the complaints within the local defense bar that, in Philadelphia, court-appointed lawyers often wait two years before their fee petitions are acted upon; and too often their requested fees are slashed by judges who care little about the economics of law practice. The same was true for experts and investigators. Word spread rapidly among forensic specialists that itemized bills collected dust in judges' chambers for years before a fraction of the total was paid out. Few experts accepted court appointments in Philadelphia under these conditions. That was Jackson's problem: he couldn't get any experts to help him without payment up front, and he certainly was in no position to pay for the experts himself.

On March 18, 1982—some ninety days after his appointment as Mumia's lawyer—Jackson approached Judge Ribner for funds to hire an investigator. Calls were coming in to his office from people who claimed to have information about the shooting. Jackson claimed that the calls were too numerous for him to handle. An investigator would help, if only he could assure payment. Judge Ribner wasn't about to open up the coffers for Mumia's defense, but he did obliquely assure Jackson that additional funds would be released after services had been performed and itemized bills submitted. Jackson never took up the court's suggestion to get itemized bills because no one was willing to take the risk of not getting paid.

On April 29, Jackson was back in court pleading again with Judge Ribner for release of funds so that he could *retain* an expert, but the results were the same. Trial was now around the corner, a little over a month away. It began to dawn on Jackson that he had not prepared as diligently as he should have. Panic had not yet infiltrated his consciousness, but that peculiar dread only a trial lawyer understands began to usurp his mood. There is no place for a trial lawyer to hide in a courtroom; as with an athletic competition, he triumphs or fails in the open, and that fact alone is enough to provoke dread over an upcoming courtroom battle. But here, Jackson also had a man's life in his hands, a vocal group of Mumia supporters eyeing his performance, calls coming in from people who claimed to have seen the shooting, and now, time was becoming a precious commodity. Jackson needed another attorney appointed to assist him.

"There is a problem in organizing the materials that I have before me, as well as preparing the appropriate research," he confessed. "There is a great deal of work to be done, a great deal of information to be developed, and I have some reservations as to whether or not I can properly be prepared to go to trial within the next three weeks, or three to four weeks."

Mumia sat stoically, taking in the fact that *his* lawyer was asking for a life raft to keep from drowning.

"Well, you'll have to work harder," Ribner advised.

"I have reams and reams of material to go through," Jackson continued, bypassing the judge's useless advice. "And that's my problem. Physically, Your Honor, I can do only so much. As Your Honor well knows, I do have other trials."

Ribner told Jackson that he would have to juggle his schedule because Mumia's case would not be delayed. It became apparent that Jackson's openness about his state of unpreparedness did not prompt the judge to look for ways to ensure that the upcoming trial would be fair; rather, it only emboldened him to push for the trial to begin as quickly as possible, the better to ensure that "justice" would be done.

"I am in the process of reducing my trial load, Your Honor, to allow me to prepare effectively for this matter." Jackson didn't want McGill to walk away with the impression that securing a conviction was going to be easy.

It is virtual malpractice for a lawyer to handle a capital case alone. "Two lawyers should always work on every capital case," Pittsburgh's director of the public defender's office testified before the Pennsylvania State Judiciary Committee. The American Bar Association standards for capital litigation call for two lawyers in recognition of the unique demands of a capital case. No corporate law firm representing a fee-

paying corporate client, where mere money is at stake, would countenance only a single lawyer on any case of magnitude. In fact, a
corporate litigator, even on a modestly complex project, would be
aided by a slew of Ivy League graduates who have taken a scorched-
earth approach to the litigation.

Judge Ribner, however, was not sympathetic. "Well, I don't recall,
in recent years, ever granting additional counsel in a murder case.
Years ago we did. But later on, because of *budget problems*, we adopted
the procedure of appointing one attorney." The scales, once again,
tilted toward preserving the budget. "So unless there's something startling about a case, I'm not inclined to grant additional counsel," Judge
Ribner explained.

Startling? Jackson wanted to know what kind of case would fit
within that category, if not this one. Wasn't it enough that the State
wanted to kill his client? Ribner quickly changed the subject, assuring
Jackson that he would be paid for his time: "Keep a careful list of
how many hours you put in, Mr. Jackson."

Ribner either was plain ignorant or simply not listening. Jackson
wasn't talking about getting paid; he was talking about getting help.
He needed help because he faced a seemingly open-and-shut case and
he hadn't interviewed any witnesses personally. With no investigator
working full-time on the case, Jackson was unable to contact the witnesses identified in the hundreds of pages of police reports. Their
addresses and phone numbers had been redacted and McGill refused
to disclose that information.

McGill wasn't doing anything underhanded in keeping this vital information from Jackson. He was merely taking advantage of a Philadelphia criminal justice policy. Jackson complained to Judge Ribner about
it: "The situation is that by virtue of your policy, Your Honor, of not
providing me with addresses, I have a difficult time in locating many of
these witnesses." Jackson also complained about McGill's insistence
that witnesses didn't want to talk to him in any event. By McGill's logic,
Jackson really didn't need the addresses and didn't need to talk to the
witnesses, because they wouldn't give him the time of day.

Prosecutors generally don't see the value in an investigation by the defense—at best, it's an annoyance; at worst, it creates the possibility of frightening off witnesses. Their attitude is, wait for the witnesses to testify and then cross-examine them; no need to go out and interview them ahead of time. To prosecutors, who rarely hone their cross-examination skills (because they are rarely called upon to cross-examine), pretrial interviews are only calculated to defeat justice by allowing the defense attorney to get a preview of what the witness will ultimately say on the witness stand, thereby improving the defense attorney's chances of twisting the witness's words to suit his client's ends.

Defense attorneys, by contrast, make their living through cross-examination, and they know that a good cross-examination hinges on preparation. The idea of a defense lawyer demolishing a witness before a mesmerized jury with a spontaneous flurry of questions is the stuff of fiction. Cross-examination is the defense attorney's treasured opportunity to tell the jury aspects of the story that make up the client's case. It is absolutely wrong—in fact, it courts disaster—to view it as an opportunity to ask questions in search of information. A good cross-examiner will look upon the witness as a mere prop to tell the story, not as a fount of information. Consequently, pretrial preparation—which means the acquisition of information—is the key to an effective cross-examination.

Jackson had a specific reason for wanting to interview the fact witnesses, aside from its value as a preparatory tool. "In my view there has already been some intimidation or misleading of the witnesses," he announced provocatively. McGill let the statement pass without rejoinder when he realized Jackson would not amplify on the accusation.

■ For forty minutes on April 29, Mumia stewed as the judge and his lawyer talked past each other. Mumia was no novice to courtroom procedure. He had covered the MOVE Nine trial fifteen months earlier as a sympathetic journalist. He had reported on other court proceedings. He knew that the Philadelphia justice system was not committed to ensuring that he would receive the minimal resources to mount a defense. Judge Ribner's reference to "budget problems" didn't surprise him. At the same time, he also knew that a trial lawyer is no magician. He needs information—from investigators and experts—to attack a prosecutor's case. He'd seen enough to know he was being railroaded.

"You ought to try the goddamned case," Mumia yelled to Judge Ribner, perforating the delusion that this particular defendant was going to acquiesce in an absurd charade. Jolted by the unexpected verbal eruption, Jackson whispered aggressively to his client, "Mumia!"

Judge Ribner responded quickly, firmly, and in the only way he knew how: "Sheriff, put handcuffs on him."

Mumia's patience, eroding throughout the morning, had now given way to a barrage of frustrated outbursts: "That's right, put the cuffs on. What are you afraid of, Ribner?" The judge ordered the sheriff to remove Mumia from the courtroom. "You go to hell!" he blurted out defiantly. "What the hell are you afraid of?"

Supporters who filled the small sixth-floor courtroom joined in. One of the spectators stood up and walked into the aisle, yelling that the court system was "trying to railroad the man, there ain't no justice!" Meanwhile, Judge Ribner, safely elevated on the bench and protected by armed court personnel, responded to Mumia, "I'm not afraid of you!" The sheriff's officers quickly ushered the supporters out of the courtroom as they too taunted the judge. Shouts from the corridor could be heard within the courtroom as Ribner, his face reddened with anger, tried to resume the session.

Mumia didn't offer physical resistance as he was escorted out of the courtroom. Judge Ribner tried in vain to act composed as if nothing had happened. "It was not your fault," he assured Jackson. "I will not let this affect my conduct of the case."

Jackson left the courtroom emotionally sapped. The morning's fracas was, he feared, just a harbinger of what was to come. On the one hand, a trial with elements of MOVE politics could never be smooth sailing. On the other hand, he shared his client's frustration. He too felt the urge to curse the judge and the whole tightfisted judicial system. The system would not allow for a fair fight, but it would cynically gesture at the notion of due process so that the jurors, who would be nothing more than temporary guests in the dirty world of criminal law, would come to believe that what they were witnessing was American justice, the finest in the world, operating in the name of law and order.

Reporters beckoned Jackson for a comment. Mumia's outburst was a reaction to the "cavalier attitude" that he felt pervaded the way the case was being handled, he explained. "There's a tremendous amount of work that still has to be done. My client is upset because he sees an attitude on the part of some others that it's no big thing. . . . His life is at stake."

With rebellion, awareness is born.

ALBERT CAMUS

6. SEEDS OF REBELLION

Go into a criminal courthouse and observe the process—not the trial process but the routinized pretrial process. Trials are a rarity. The criminal justice system cannot be judged—ought not be judged—solely by that extraordinarily rare event. To judge the criminal justice system through observations of celebrated trials is akin to claiming that you know all about the movie-making business because you like to go to movies, or that you understand football because you've seen the Super Bowl.

Sit in the spectator section of the courtroom and watch the pretrial process unfold with deadening monotony. I remember someone once describing the process as being like a package express terminal. A case is called out by a court officer and the file is handed up to the judge, who is much like a dispatcher routing the packages to their destinations. Two shipping clerks—the prosecutor and the defense lawyer—bicker over what to do with the package, which sits inert awaiting resolution of its fate. The bickering typically leads to a plea of guilty, and the package is routed to some far-off destination. "Next case," the judge declares, and another package is brought in.

Every so often—and it doesn't happen much, to be sure—a package reveals itself as a human being, and a rebellious one at that. This human being protests the package routing system. He announces that he wants to take control over his fate within a rigid routing system where obedience and silence prevail. He punctures the delusion of the dispatcher and the shipping clerks that what they are doing constitutes the law in action. "Sit down and be quiet," the judge/dispatcher will demand, offended by the awakening of the package. "This is a court of *law*!"

■ On May 13, 1982, with pretrial hearings two weeks away, Mumia resolved in his own mind that he would not allow himself to be a package in a bureaucratic routing system.

The state of Pennsylvania had earmarked his life, one so full of promise, for extermination, and as the seasons changed from winter to spring, Mumia hurled closer to touching the raw nerves of existence—that moment in life, which so few of us ever experience and thus may never understand, where decisions and actions directly and concretely affect whether one lives or dies. Whether from desperation, stress, or epiphany, Mumia drew closer to MOVE and took to heart the "teachings of John Africa." He would put his faith in those teachings, and the first public display of that faith would take place that morning.

Mumia stood before Judge Ribner and let the silence settle in before speaking. He appreciated the power of silence, that moment of anticipation before filling the room with the sounds of one's voice. Silence rivets the mind. A coterie of MOVE members sat in the audience awaiting the announcement. Unlike the MOVE members, the news reporters had no clue that Mumia was going to pull the case into a different direction. John Africa taught his followers that the "system" has its own laws, but that nature's laws have a force all their own. When you acquiesce to the laws and legal procedures that serve the "system," he taught, you relinquish the power within you. The teachings of John Africa dictate self-representation in a court of law.

Mumia announced that morning, in his honeyed baritone voice, that he would, from that moment forward, handle his own case and dispense with Jackson's services. Judge Ribner hadn't expected that such a request would be made, and he seemed to be caught off guard. This was, after all, a capital case, and it was no time for an attorney to have a "fool for a client"—the worn-out opprobrium invoked when a defendant seeks to represent himself. He asked the defendant standing before him if he understood what that meant. The Constitution required that Judge Ribner ask a litany of questions: Do you understand that you have to follow the rules and procedures of this court? Do you understand that you will not be able to complain later that a lawyer could have done a better job? Do you understand that this trial will proceed without regard to your lack of legal training? All of the caveats and warnings didn't dissuade Mumia from his decision. It was his life on the line; he'd see to it that it would be defended appropriately.

Mumia's decision would have huge repercussions on the trial proceedings. The Sixth Amendment to the United States Constitution guarantees a defendant the right to represent himself. But constitutional rights are often grudgingly recognized, and the right to self-representation is no exception. Judges hate it when a defendant invokes that right, because it bogs down the system. Attorneys, beholden to the operation of the court system, can be counted on to keep the case moving along, a preeminent goal of a judge. An untutored defendant representing himself is only interested in his own fate; he could care less about efficiency and has no need to be a team player in the criminal justice game. Judge Ribner wasn't pleased with what he was hearing, but he had no choice other than to honor Mumia's request.

Jackson wasn't cut loose, however, much to his chagrin. He thought, when he heard the announcement, that this ordeal would be over for him. Mumia wasn't a client who stood by silently as his lawyer (mis)handled the case. He was a demanding client, the type that prompts shudders in a criminal defense lawyer. They joke at conferences with other colleagues about the difficulties of having a demanding client and daydream about how much easier the practice of law would be if their clients weren't so damn demanding.

Mumia was more than a demanding client. He brought to the table a blending of intelligence and skepticism. He asked questions, and if the answers didn't make sense, he said so. He wanted to see all of the police reports, and he wanted to know why certain things were done, and why other things weren't done. He didn't trust law enforcement to disclose *all* of the evidence, and he knew better than to assume that the district attorney's office would play fair. Mumia's experiences as a journalist, and even his experiences with the Black Panther Party, had taught him to be skeptical.

Jackson's difficulties extended beyond client relations. The MOVE organization, still embittered over the conviction and incarceration of the MOVE Nine, rallied to Mumia's defense. Their members were conspicuously present at each and every court session in large numbers. Several MOVE members watching Mumia declare his intention to represent himself pursuant to the teachings of John Africa would perish, three years later to the very day, in a police firebomb attack on their home on Osage Avenue, resulting in the horrific deaths of six adults and five children. But for the time being, they, too, scrutinized Jackson's performance, and, by his lights, made ridiculous demands upon him. Additionally, the media was still going crazy over the case. Television cameras and reporters stood outside the entranceway to the courtroom at every appearance. It was all wearing him down, and he wanted out.

Jackson made a motion to Judge Ribner asking that he be freed of his professional obligations to Mumia. The judge flatly rejected the motion, knowing that it would only inject more chaos and delay into the case—the twin evils in the criminal justice system from a judge's perspective. He ordered Jackson to remain as backup counsel. The notion of backup counsel is not taught in law school or in continuing legal education seminars. No one really has a clear notion of what it means. It suggests that the lawyer is there to help the untrained (and foolish?) client sidestep the legal landmines that populate the terrain of a trial. But how that assistance is to be given is largely a matter left for the defendant and his backup counsel. One thing is certain: being backup counsel is a terribly frustrating experience for a trial lawyer. Trial lawyers, almost by instinct, critique other trial lawyers in action, often quickly jumping to the conclusion that they could do it better. So the frustration is all the more acute when the "lawyer" conducting the trial is an untrained lay person.

Mumia understood fully that Jackson wanted to be removed from the case, and that troubled him. He wouldn't go to a doctor who expressed reservations over providing treatment; he wouldn't even allow an unwilling mechanic to fix his car. He surely wasn't inclined to let a lawyer who virtually begged to be relieved from the case to remain by his side when the State was trying to take his life. "I am faced with an attorney who has said in full court that he is not functioning as backup counsel," Mumia explained to Judge Ribner.

"So?" the judge replied.

For an instant, Mumia was puzzled. "I need an attorney who's comfortable doing that," he continued. "As I expressed, I worked very closely with Mr. Jackson but I feel it is now time for me to defend myself." Ribner remained silent. "My point is that if I have a court-appointed counsel assigned as backup counsel who has expressed his inability to function in that role, then our relationship is compromised. My ability to depend on his resources is compromised."

The judge was not impressed. Jackson had been on the case for over five months; the machinery of death would not be stopped to allow another lawyer to come on board, with all of the associated delays, simply because the defendant was not satisfied with having a lawyer who wanted out of the case. He was stuck with Jackson, and Jackson was stuck with him. Neither was happy.

■ While Jackson was still fuming over being backup counsel, McGill couldn't have been more pleased. After the May 13 court appearance, the case was transferred for trial to the Honorable Albert F. Sabo.

Prosecutors in the Philadelphia district attorney's office loved to hear those two syllables, "Sa-bo." As one former prosecutor remarked to an investigative journalist looking into Sabo's record as a judge, "getting sent to Sabo is like a vacation for prosecutors." Philadelphia defense lawyer Mark E. Gottlieb characterized Judge Sabo as a favorite among prosecutors, saying, "I don't think there was anyone you would be happier with [as a prosecutor]." Gottlieb was in a good position to know: he once served as head of homicide prosecutors in the Philadelphia district attorney's office.

The son of immigrants and the first judge of Slovak heritage to ascend to the bench in Philadelphia, Albert Sabo initially wanted to be an FBI agent, but at five feet four, he was too short. For sixteen years before becoming a judge, he served as legal advisor to the sheriff's office. Sitting as a homicide judge for two decades—he was forced into retirement against his will in January 1998, for budgetary reasons—he had sentenced thirty-two people to death, far more than any other judge in the country. Forty percent of all death sentences in Philadelphia were meted out by Judge Sabo. One-fifth of all death row inmates in Pennsylvania stood in Judge Sabo's courtroom when they heard their fate. Ninety-two percent were black men. What makes this all the more remarkable is that Judge Sabo had heard fewer homicide cases than many of his colleagues. No one familiar with the Philadelphia court system ever wondered why Judge Sabo was called the king of death row.

"I've never lost sleep over sentencing defendants to death," Judge Sabo told one reporter. "I sentence 'em and I forget about 'em."

Defenders of Judge Sabo, such as Philadelphia district attorney Lynne Abraham, are fond of pointing out that in Philadelphia, as in most jurisdictions, it is the jury that ultimately decides whether a defendant should be sentenced to death. Judge Sabo merely carries out the will of the jury, the argument goes. This argument overlooks the enormous impact of a judge on the outcome of a case. There is a myth that "truth" filters to the top through the adversarial battle between litigants, and the judge merely referees the contest. The judge, according to this myth, keeps the contestants in line with his fidelity to the "law." The "law," of course, is perfectly neutral in this mythic conception of the judicial system.

This myth acquires its force in the public consciousness, in part, through the symbols that dominate a courtroom. The judge sits above the fray, looking down upon the trial lawyers as they supposedly battle over their contested versions of the "truth." The judge wears the black robes, with the United States flag on one side and the state flag on the other. On the wall above his head read the words, "In God We Trust," or some such slogan. When the judge rules upon a question of law, he does so with an aura of detachment.

The defenders of Judge Sabo who claim that the aspersions thrown his way are unfair rest their argument upon this myth of neutrality and detachment. Criminal defense lawyers who have appeared before Judge Sabo know better. One local lawyer told a *Los Angeles Times* reporter, "When you are a defense lawyer and you are in Sabo's courtroom, you are playing an away game. You are not with the home team."

The *Philadelphia Inquirer* conducted a study of Judge Sabo's trials. Published in a Sunday edition on September 13, 1992, the piece noted that in "case after case . . . the judge, through his comments, his rulings and his instructions to the jury, has favored prosecutors." The study indicated that Sabo would not shy away from providing advice to a prosecutor to enhance the chances of a conviction. Prosecutors, the study noted, often had to restrain Judge Sabo, for fear that he would go overboard and jeopardize a conviction, something that McGill would do several times during the trial. Such concern was amply justified: no judge in the United States competed with Judge Sabo in the percentage of capital cases reversed on appeal.

Judge Sabo's record as a jurist has also provoked consternation for its palpable racial overtones. Duquesne University law professor Bruce Ledewitz studied Judge Sabo's record as a presiding jurist over capital cases through the prism of race and concluded that it would be "unacceptable in the worst Southern death-belt states. . . ." In its publication, *Justice on the Cheap: The Philadelphia Story,* the Washington-based Death Penalty Information Center highlights Judge Sabo's death-penalty record to exemplify the destructive influence of race in the implementation of Pennsylvania's death penalty.

The *Philadelphia Inquirer* ran another story, approximately a year after Mumia's trial, indicating that one-third of the attorneys who participated in a survey rated Judge Sabo as "unqualified" to be a judge. The relevance of this anecdote, however, is not only in the survey results but also in Judge Sabo's unguarded response to them. He remarked, upon hearing of the results, that if he were a defense attorney, "I wouldn't vote for me either."

■ As the reality of the trial loomed, Jackson's displeasure over being backup counsel gradually took root in his anxieties over money. He had too many other commitments—such as making money to fund his law practice and pay his personal bills—to sit through a trial. He couldn't tell the judge that money was the reason he wanted out. He argued instead that he didn't know *how* to be backup counsel. He spoke in his customary rapid spurts, but with a noticeable edge of desperation in his voice.

"I have not been trained as backup counsel," Jackson warned. "Your Honor would be placing me in a situation I am unfamiliar with. I have never done this before and I am not sure, feeling that I would be effective in providing—"

"Whoa, there," Judge Sabo interrupted. "It isn't a very difficult job. It doesn't require too much to represent someone as backup counsel."

Sabo had a point, which Jackson couldn't deny. He would only have to sit at the defense table and provide advice episodically, if Mumia was amenable to soliciting it—and that was *his* choice. But it wasn't the intrinsic difficulties with dispensing advice, of course, that prompted Jackson's desperate plea. It was *this* case, with the pressures attendant on it, especially the inordinate attention it was receiving.

He knew where the case was heading: it would be a circus, filled with diatribes and ranting from the spectators. It was destined to be a vitriolic contest between defendant and judge, and McGill would stand poised to skewer whatever defense Mumia could muster. Jackson kept pleading with Sabo: "I would request that either additional or other counsel be provided as backup for Mr. Jamal. . . . I would not feel comfortable being Mr. Jamal's backup counsel. . . . Most respectfully, I would like the record to show as well that I would refuse to be backup counsel."

Jackson had become emboldened without realizing it. It was not his prerogative to refuse the assignment at this late stage of the proceedings. Jackson shifted the focus slightly, suggesting that the judge would be dooming the legitimacy of the trial from the very start if he didn't cut him loose. "I am suggesting that without due process Your Honor is requiring me to perform a function I have never performed in a matter where a man's life is at risk. . . . What I'm saying, Your Honor, is that I have never, never, since I have been practicing law, been backup counsel, and I am saying that I do not know how I would function and I feel uncomfortable that indeed I might be ineffective."

Sabo repeated again that it was no big deal to be backup counsel. Jackson would have to grit his teeth and endure an unpleasant duty. Sabo's motives were unstated but transparent: he wanted the trial to move at a rocket pace, and Jackson was expected to use his role as backup counsel to keep Mumia in line to accomplish that goal. More out of spite than anything else, Jackson took Judge Sabo's remarks to heart. During the period of time that virtually all competent trial lawyers dedicate themselves to preparing for trial, Jackson had done nothing on Mumia's behalf—or as he put it years later, "I just sat back with my hands folded. I wasn't doing him any good."

■ In early June, pretrial hearings began. The issues to be resolved were routine for a busy criminal justice system. Jackson had filed motions to suppress evidence—identification evidence, physical evidence, and, of course, evidence of Mumia's own alleged statements. Hearings were scheduled to determine whether those items of evidence should be suppressed—that is, disallowed for use at trial. The hearings were really pro forma—actually, an exercise in futility, because motions to suppress evidence are rarely granted, notwithstanding the false but alluring picture foisted upon a gullible public of judges allowing brutal murderers to go free on trivial technicalities.

Acting as his own lawyer, Mumia questioned witnesses at the pretrial hearings with surprising deftness. He stumbled on occasion, but so do the most seasoned trial lawyers. He certainly performed better than the judge and prosecutor expected. McGill called him the "smartest" defendant he had ever prosecuted. Mumia's most impressive work as a lay lawyer came about during his cross-examination of Cynthia White and Robert Chobert, two eyewitnesses who the prosecution called to testify at the pretrial hearings to substantiate that their identifications were legally proper. Although constantly interrupted by objections, Mumia kept his focus, and his cool, as he methodically exposed discrepancies in their testimony. Later, Mumia's cross-examinations of White and Chobert would be the template for the trial cross-examinations.

But it wouldn't be Mumia doing the questioning in front of the jury. McGill and Judge Sabo would see to that.

> [L]et's face it, again, there's the blacks from the low-income areas. . . . You don't want those people on your jury.
>
> [Y]ou know, in selecting blacks, you don't want the real educated ones. . . .

TRAINING TAPE ON JURY SELECTION FROM THE
PHILADELPHIA DISTRICT ATTORNEY'S OFFICE

7. JURY SELECTION

Pretrial publicity and race are the wild cards in the criminal justice game. Each affects the outlook of potential jurors, and thus each alters how the trial evidence will be received and weighed. The outcome in the battle over whose good-versus-evil narrative will prevail with the jury may be largely determined before the first words of testimony are even spoken.

When pretrial publicity focuses on the killing of a white police officer by a black radical, especially one associated in the public mind with a particularly misunderstood and maligned black group like MOVE, the judicial climate is poisoned against the defense right from the outset. Judge Ribner's observation that Jackson had a "big" case on his hands that would have "explosive tendencies in this community" was best interpreted as a warning.

While Officer Faulkner's death made the front pages of the after-noon papers on December 9, 1981, it was Mumia's ideology and political activities that gave the story its particular intrigue and bite. The *Philadelphia Inquirer* headlined: "Jamal: An eloquent activist not afraid to raise his voice." The *Philadelphia Daily News* was quick to point out that Mumia ". . . wears his hair in dreadlocks and was associated with several black activist causes. . . . [H]e was a leader of the local Black Panther Party while still a teenager." The media gravitated toward a particular remark by Mumia, made when he was an ebullient fifteen-year-old member of the Black Panther Party—"Black people are facing the reality that the Black Panther Party has been facing: political power grows out of the barrel of a gun."

To many middle-class whites in Philadelphia, Mumia's involvement in the Black Panther Party was of a piece with his sympathies for MOVE. Media profiles of Mumia lumped MOVE in with his teenage membership in the Black Panther Party, dodging discussion of the details of either organization or of Mumia's particular involvement in them. It was enough simply to mention the two organizations, allowing them to intersect in the personage of the arrested journalist so as to propagate an alluring portrait of a dangerous black radical fully capable of attacking a foot soldier of the status quo.

Inevitably, therefore, the killing and the arrest would be seen through the prism of Philadelphia's racial polarization. One *Philadelphia Inquirer* commentator stated that "radio talk shows were full of people calling in to say exactly what ought to be done about the killing of Police Officer Daniel Faulkner on the Locust Street strip in the early hours of Wednesday morning. Some of them, predictably, want to *lynch* the man who calls himself Mumia Abu-Jamal as soon as he recovers from the bullet wound placed in his gut by the dying cop."

At the height of the news blitz *Philadelphia Bulletin* columnist Claude Lewis took his fellow journalists to task for "straying from their purported posture of 'objectivity.' " Wrote Lewis: "They repeatedly attributed to Abu-Jamal a penchant for radicalism and militancy. Their characterizations sparkled with prejudicial passion, reducing in the public mind any possibility of innocence on the part of the suspect." Guilt or innocence was no longer the issue within the public discourse. It was all about explication, penetrating the inner meaning of the hideous crime. Mumia's radical politics, and Philadelphia's lingering torment over MOVE, were more than the backdrop to a crime story; they bestowed upon the entire affair a collective psychological anchor, as if Faulkner's death was the fruition of all that had come before in Philadelphia's history of race relations.

What was up for grabs in the approaching trial was whether these things amounted to an explanation for Mumia's otherwise inexplicable act of murder, or to an explanation for why the police and the court system was hell-bent on securing a conviction and death sentence, regardless of his actual guilt. Either the police were good and Mumia was evil, or vice versa.

McGill, for his part, understood immediately the death potential of these ingredients in the case. Within weeks of the crime, he had captured within his own mind an image of who this defendant was, and he began cultivating a story line that would infuse the killing with an emotionally charged meaning for his specially selected jury. It would not be difficult to fashion a good-versus-evil drama with Mumia Abu-Jamal wearing the proverbial black hat.

■ After three months on the case, Jackson had yet to penetrate beneath the surface of his case. As each day passed, he was increasing the likelihood that he would relegate himself to a reactive role in the trial, desperately trying to hold off the evidentiary onslaught by a highly aggressive and skilled prosecutor. He had not talked with any witnesses; he had consulted with no experts concerning the ballistics and medical evidence; nor had he even developed a plan on how to prepare an attack on the prosecution's case. He was far from grasping the defense's emotional core of the case.

As a black man, however, Jackson knew all too well the toxic effects of racism on the trial process. No set of advocacy skills can cleanse a trial atmosphere already polluted with racism. He first raised the issue of race on March 18, less than three months before the start of jury selection. He wanted the court to authorize the distribution of a jury questionnaire to those people who would be receiving a jury summons for possible service on the case of *Commonwealth v. Wesley Cook, aka Mumia Abu-Jamal.* Jury questionnaires are not uncommon in capital cases—they are routine in many states—as they help in selecting an impartial jury. Jackson wanted the distribution of questionnaires to help in stopping the prosecution from eliminating blacks from the jury pool. He had complained to courthouse journalists that the prosecutors in Philadelphia were notorious for "whitewashing" the juries, especially in death penalty cases.

"It has been the custom and the tradition of the district attorney's office to strike each and every black juror that comes up peremptorily," Jackson argued to Ribner. He was referring to the prosecution's use of peremptory strikes against prospective jurors, an allotment of challenges for which no reason need be given. "That has been my experience since I have been practicing law, as well as the experience of the defense bar; the majority of the defense bar knows that that occurs."

McGill didn't like what he was hearing. Slouched in his chair quietly twirling the edge of his mustache, he jumped abruptly out of his seat once Jackson raised the specter that race would play a role in the litigation. "Excuse me, Your Honor—I don't want to interrupt, but I want to make an objection."

Judge Ribner, reclining in his high-backed leather chair, knew exactly what McGill was going to say. "You are going to categorically deny that?" the judge asked incredulously.

Jackson didn't let McGill answer. "They always do," he interjected. "They always do."

Jackson, of course, was right. Defense lawyers *and* prosecutors are acutely sensitive to race, and that sensitivity gets funneled into strategies over jury selection. But Jackson's accusations were not based on hard evidence, only anecdotal data that defense attorneys across the nation store daily in their collective memory. What Jackson didn't know was that Philadelphia prosecutors were actually trained to race-sanitize the jury in order to maximize the chances of securing a conviction.

Sadly, judges are often not sensitive to the issue of race, taking on the narrowest understanding of how race and racism come into play in a criminal trial. They routinely balk at the idea that a murder case could have racial overtones unless the alleged killer openly declares his motive to be racial. Judge Ribner, in this respect, was a typical criminal court judge. Jackson's concern over the exclusion of blacks from the jury did not resonate with the judge, which is why the judge was not inclined to use public funds to distribute a questionnaire to ferret out latent racial attitudes and prejudices.

"This is a murder case," Ribner declared, now leaning forward and chopping the air with both hands. "I haven't seen any evidence that anybody has turned this into a racial incident."

Jackson understood that white judges rarely appreciate the influence of race in the criminal process. He tried, nonetheless, to explain that race seeps into the process more insidiously, particularly with jurors harboring preconceptions, stereotypes, and fears that undercut a black defendant's ability to defend against charges of killing a white person. Judge Ribner listened, but didn't care enough to understand. He was more concerned with the budget. As Judge Ribner put it: "It's never been done before, Mr. Jackson. At any rate, we're not going to pay for that. The county is *not* going to pay for that."

■ Until 1986, the judiciary was simply indifferent to the widespread practice of excluding minorities from criminal juries. That year the Supreme Court in a case called *Batson v. Kentucky* erected a three-tiered process for examining whether a prosecutor is improperly excluding minorities from a jury.* First, a defendant must challenge a prosecutor's exclusion of a juror with a plausible claim that race consciousness is playing a role. If a judge agrees that race might be playing a role, then the prosecutor must provide "race-neutral reasons" for the peremptory strikes. The third step permits the defendant to show that the race-neutral reasons are but a pretext for race-conscious selection methods (usually with proof that a minority is eliminated when a white, with similar characteristics, is not).

---

*To be sure, a lawyer for either side of a dispute may challenge his adversary's jury selection process under *Batson*.

Batson was a step in the right direction, but it in no way remedied the problem. Judges too often rubber-stamp prosecutorial explanations for striking blacks, even when those explanations are utterly preposterous. For example, in a 1987 Georgia case, the prosecutor used all ten of his peremptory strikes to remove all ten blacks from the jury panel. When the prosecutor was called upon to provide a race-neutral explanation for one of his strikes as required by *Batson,* he explained that one juror looked as "dumb as a fence post." For another black prospective juror, the prosecutor justified the strike because he "resembled the defendant." The judge found such explanations sufficient.[1] Another Georgia prosecutor justified an exclusion of a black prospective juror because she worked in a video store and therefore would not be "good with people." The trial judge found this explanation acceptable.[2] An Alabama prosecutor, with the trial court's imprimatur, justified his strikes of several blacks from a jury panel because they were affiliated with Alabama State University—a predominantly black institution.[3] In one instance, the court found the prosecutor kept a chart of the prospective jurors with the following categories: "strong," "medium," "weak," and "black." The prosecutor struck every black person from the panel, with the endorsement of the Alabama courts.[4] A Florida prosecutor in a death case eliminated ten black jurors from the panel, explaining that they were "inappropriately dressed," and with respect to one prospective juror, claiming he wore "pointy New York shoes." This prosecutor rejected a black woman because she was unemployed, but had accepted an unemployed white woman. The trial judge found no problem with these explanations.[5]

■ Evidence confirming Jackson's experiential intuition that race consciousness played a decisive role in jury selection by Philadelphia prosecutors came in the form of a videotape that surfaced during a 1997 election campaign for the office of district attorney in Philadelphia. This videotape was prepared ten years earlier by the Philadelphia district attorney's office expressly for the purpose of training prosecutors in the craft of race-conscious jury selection. The videotape shows a senior prosecutor named Jack McMahon standing before a crowd of young assistant district attorneys eager to learn how to be trial prosecutors. This training videotape was made under the auspices of then district attorney Ronald Castille. Castille now sits on the Pennsylvania Supreme Court, and he had refused to recuse himself from considering Mumia's second round of appeals in 1998, even though the issue of race-based jury selection in the Philadelphia district attorney's office would be a major point of contention.

In the training session, McMahon, a colleague and contemporary of Joe McGill, appropriately emphasized that "jury selection is the most important part of the trial." The most well-fashioned trial strategy is for naught if the audience is not receptive to the advocate's message. McMahon and the other senior prosecutors in the district attorney's office understood quite well that, in a city with a history of racial tensions and Rizzo-style brutality, a case built upon law enforcement testimony is not as well received by an audience of African-Americans as it is by an audience of Caucasians. "The blacks from the low-income areas are less likely to convict," McMahon asserts on the videotape. "There's a resentment for law enforcement and a resentment for authority." Themes of law and order sell better with middle-class whites, McMahon was preaching; and they are aroused to anger much more readily in a case of black-on-white crime, particularly where the crime is the killing of a white police officer. The key to success, McMahon taught his young audience with shocking bluntness, is keeping blacks off the jury. This was no easy task in a city with a population consisting of 40 percent African-Americans.

"People from Mayfair are good," McMahon notes on the videotape, referring to a white neighborhood, "and people from Thirty-third and Diamond [a poor black community] stink. . . . You don't want any jurors from Thirty-third and Diamond." He reinforces the message with the warning that "there's the blacks from the low-income areas . . . you don't want those people on your jury, let's face it." Later in the videotape, McMahon says: "In my experience, black women, young black women, are very bad"; and "You know, in selecting blacks, you don't want the real educated ones. . . ."

McMahon further advocated keeping a running tally of the racial composition of the jury pool, an irrefutable indication that race would play a key role in the exercise of peremptory challenges. "Another thing to do, little tips, too, when a jury comes in the room, the forty people come in the room, count them. Count the blacks and whites. You want to know at every point in that case where you are. In other words, the forty come in—you'll never get it just right. You don't want to look there or go, 'Is there a black back there?' "

Keeping tabs on the race of the jury pool was so important to the district attorney's office that McMahon advised young prosecutors to invent reasons to leave the courtroom, if necessary, to ascertain the racial composition of upcoming prospective jurors. "If you lose track or you're not sure of what's going on, you can always take a recess," McMahon advises. "Because a lot of times what they do is they'll like have the next group . . . sitting right out there in order. So you can say, 'Judge, I have to go to the bathroom.' You can go out and see what's left and check out what's left."*

No lesson on race-based jury selection is complete without a tutorial on how to avoid the strictures of *Batson*. "In the future, we're going to have to be aware of *Batson*, and the best way to avoid any problems with it is to protect yourself," McMahon cautions. "And my advice would be in that situation is when you do have a black juror, you question them at length. And on this little sheet that you have, mark something down that you can articulate later if something happens. . . . So if—let's say you strike three blacks to start with, the first

*This practice of tallying the race of each prospective juror was not only captured on videotape, it was also noted by several courts. In one case, the former chief of the Homicide Unit in the Philadelphia district attorney's office was caught red-handed. A federal judge noted: "The record demonstrates conclusively that, at each trial, the prosecutor [the chief of the Homicide Unit] kept careful records of the race of each prospective juror, and a running tally of how many persons of each race remained on the venire for possible selection." In another case, a federal magistrate found that a prosecutor's jury selection notes in a case tried in November 1981 "provide a contemporaneous chronicle of the spurious strikes for each black juror." That prosecutor, the magistrate further observed, "maintained . . . painstaking notes which revealed upon examination a running tabulation of the number of blacks left on the jury after each challenge was exercised."

three people. And then it's like the defense attorney makes an objection saying that you're striking blacks. Well, you're not going to be able to go back and say, oh—and make up something about why you did it. Write it down right then and there. . . . And then you can say, 'Well, the woman had a kid about the same age as the defendant and I thought she'd be sympathetic to him' or 'She's unemployed and I just don't like unemployed people. . . . ' So sometimes under that line you may want to ask more questions of *those people* so it gives you more ammunition to make an articulable reason as to why you are striking them, not for race."

Perhaps most brazen is McMahon's explicit instruction to disregard the prosecutor's duty to be fair. The U.S. Supreme Court has long made clear that the State's "interest . . . in a criminal prosecution is not that it shall win a case, but that justice shall be done. . . . It is as much [the prosecutor's] duty to refrain from improper methods calculated to produce a wrongful conviction as it is to use every legitimate means to bring about a just one."[6] The Court has also clearly stated that "the only legitimate interest [the State] could possibly have in the exercise of its peremptory challenges is securing a fair and impartial jury. . . . The State's interest in every trial is to see that the proceedings are carried out in a fair, impartial, and nondiscriminatory manner."[7]

McMahon has this to say about securing a fair and impartial jury: "The case law says that the object of getting a jury is to get—I wrote it down. I looked in the cases. I had to look this up because I didn't know this was the purpose of a jury. The law says, 'Voir dire is to get a competent, fair, and impartial jury.' *Well, that's ridiculous. You're not trying to get that.*"

Indeed, McMahon suggested to the young prosecutors that *they would lose their jobs* if they attempted to follow the law and choose fair jurors: "And if you go in there and any one of you think you're going to be some noble civil libertarian and try to get jurors, 'Well, he says he can be fair; I'll go with him,' that's ridiculous. *You'll lose and you'll be out of the office;* you'll be doing corporate law. Because that's what will happen. You're there to win. . . . And the only way you're going to do your best is to *get jurors that are as unfair and more likely to convict than anybody else in that room.*"*

■ Exacerbating the race problem in jury selection is the fact that, in a capital case, jurors who are resolutely opposed to the death penalty are not eligible to serve on a capital case. The process of eliminating from a jury pool those persons opposed to the death penalty is called death-qualifying a jury (or *Witherspoon*ing, a shorthand expression derived from the U.S. Supreme Court case *Witherspoon v. Illinois*). Death-qualifying a jury is a nightmare for defendants. After a jury pool has undergone a *Witherspoon*ing process, those remaining tend to be more of the law-and-order types, more prone to believe authority figures such as police officers, and more prone to convict. Criminologists virtually all agree that death-qualifying a jury renders it death-penalty prone. People opposed to the death penalty who are ineligible to sit on a capital case tend to be more liberal, more skeptical of authority, and more sensitive to human frailties. The *Witherspoon*ing process also results in a bias favoring white juries because a significantly higher percentage of blacks oppose the death penalty compared to the general public. Judges are not oblivious to the distorting effects of *Witherspoon*. Judge Savitt, a Philadelphia judge, noted that "the tendency has been for prosecutors to death-qualify the jury even when they have no intention to seek the death penalty, because they know that a death-qualified jury is a guilt-prone jury."

*McGill's race-conscious jury selection methods were, at the time of Mumia's trial, not illegal, which only underscores the fact that he engaged in the nefarious practice. The Pennsylvania Supreme Court, in *Commonwealth v. Henderson*, 497 Pa. 23, 29 (1979), stated:

> Put another way, it is not constitutional error for a prosecutor to challenge a black juror for the reason that the prosecutor believes—validly or invalidly—that a black venireman, because of the facts of the case, is less likely to be impartial than a white venireman. Put still more reductively, the race, creed, national origin, sex or other similar characteristics of a venireman may be proper considerations in exercising peremptory challenges when issues relevant to these qualities are present in the case.

■ An experienced death penalty prosecutor, McGill extracted what he wanted out of *Witherspoon*, largely without resistance from Jackson and Mumia, neither of whom had the experience and skill to counter McGill's maneuvering. At the end of the jury selection process, more than half of the blacks in the jury pool were immediately disqualified because they said that they could never vote for the death penalty. The beauty of it, for McGill, was that he wouldn't have to use his limited peremptory challenges on these undesirables. Frustrated, Jackson went on a radio program and complained about the racial effects of death-qualifying the jury. He later stated, in court testimony in 1995: "Trying cases in city hall, I know most DAs, in most homicide cases, will get rid of as many blacks as they possibly can, first through the death qualification and then through peremptory strikes."

As the selection process began, both Jackson and McGill, each in his own way, had to confront the inevitable fact that the citizenry in Philadelphia was acutely aware of the Faulkner shooting. With the courtroom filled with prospective jurors, Judge Sabo had to weed out those who had become too saturated with media accounts of the crime and the case generally. "Does anyone know anything about that incident, whether through television, radio, or the news media, the press?" the judge asked the assembled group. "If anyone knows anything about this incident, would you please rise and give your name to the court officer." Judge Sabo immediately realized that he should have phrased the question in the negative, because nearly everyone in the audience had stood up. "Since most of you have risen, I think it may be easier if you sit down and I rephrase the question. Is there anyone on this panel who does *not* know anything or has *not* read or heard or seen anything on television about this incident?" No one moved. Judge Sabo aptly observed, "Everybody here has read about him."

■ "Good morning, ma'am, my name is Mumia Abu-Jamal."

Juror number eighty-nine, an elderly black woman named Jennie

Dawley, viewed the tall defendant with the musical voice much as the other people on the jury selection panel did—as an oddity, not so much because of his dreadlocked hairstyle but because he was the *defendant*. The defendant is supposed to sit quietly at the defense table while his lawyer does all of the talking. The prospective jurors had not expected that Mumia would be handling his own case. It took time for them to come to grips with the fact that Mumia would be questioning them directly during the voir dire—a process of interacting with prospective jurors to assist the trial participants in selecting which of them to eliminate from service.

Although she had lived in southwest Philadelphia for over twenty years when she was summoned for jury duty, Dawley had never served before. She told Mumia that she was a retired common laborer who had no fixed opinion about what had happened on December 9. Mumia liked her. She seemed to be the kind of authentic person that he could relate to.

"Is there anything about how I look to you that offends you or turns you off?" Mumia asked.

"No, you look like people to me, that's all," Dawley answered in a heartbeat.

Mumia detected a certain feistiness in Dawley, a willingness to hold her ground. He asked her what her husband had done for a living. "Well," she said with a nod, "let's not bring him in. Okay. Let it rest like that. He's not here." She stood up to him, gently but firmly. Mumia liked that as well. She would stand up to the white folks hellbent on coming back with a guilty verdict, Mumia figured.

When McGill asked Dawley if she had any moral, religious, or philosophical scruples which would prevent her from sitting in judgment of another human being, Dawley put it simply: "No, I'm just plain old me."

After questioning scores of other people before her, Mumia knew that Dawley had to be on this jury. He didn't want to signal to McGill his strong feelings about her, so he took his time in letting the judge know that she was acceptable. He asked Judge Sabo for permission to ask some more questions. He probed a little more about her attitude regarding the notion that a defendant has no obligation to present a defense—a probing that masked his desire to select her.

It worked. McGill refrained from striking her with a peremptory challenge, primarily because he viewed her as elderly (and thus, likely to be hostile to radical politics) and would probably be ill at ease with Mumia's supposed arrogance. "You have been selected as juror number one," Judge Sabo informed Dawley. Mumia and the prosecutor, for the first and last time, agreed on something. But even that would not last long.

As pleased as Mumia was with Dawley, he could not have been more distressed about a juror than he was with Edward Courchain. A fiftyish white man, Courchain never disguised his inability to keep an open mind, admitting that he had developed a bias for the prosecution. He candidly disclosed to McGill that he could not accord Mumia a fair trial and that he would find it "a little difficult" to follow the law as given by the court. As the questioning progressed, it became evident that Courchain's inability to be fair to both sides resulted from his exposure to the media coverage of the case. He told McGill that he was "swayed a little bit" by the newspaper and television coverage.

Jackson had a single goal as he moved to the front of the defense table: nail down Courchain's answers about his partiality. "Mr. Courchain, you've indicated that you may have some difficulty serving in this case; is that correct?"

Courchain bobbed his head a few times. "That's right."

Jackson gently probed further. "And you further indicated that this difficulty arises from your exposure to the news media; is that correct?"

"Right." Courchain's terse reply signaled his suspicion over Jackson's probing.

Jackson, sensing Courchain's uneasiness, put to him the most pointed questions that could be asked of a prospective juror: "Now, as difficult as it may be to answer my question, and of course the questions of Mr. McGill, we unfortunately have to back you to the wall to get an answer from you. So, please, consider that when I'm asking you these questions. What we need to do is to determine your qualifications as a juror. The questions I'm asking you—although I know you can't predict with any absolute certainty what you're going to do in the future—we need to know now in your best judgment, whether or not you could be objective in this matter, stay in the middle, don't lean towards the prosecution, don't lean towards the defense, whether or not you could objectively determine the facts in this case?"

"Do you want an honest opinion?" Courchain asked.

"Yes, sir," Jackson responded.

"No."

Jackson was taken aback by the bluntness of the answer, but happy with it nonetheless. He couldn't resist asking Courchain to confirm the answer. "You cannot do that?"

"No."

Jackson could have stopped at that point. He had enough to justify removing Courchain, but he sensed that he could secure more answers to solidify the motion that he would soon make to remove this prospective juror as unfit to serve. "Sir, if I were to tell you that the law requires that if you were to serve as a juror you are to set that aside, could you do that?"

"I would try, but I don't know. Consciously, I don't know."

" 'Consciously—' " Jackson parroted.

"Unconsciously, it would still be there," Courchain explained.

"I understand that. And I don't mean to argue with you, sir. I'm just trying to get it as best as I possibly can, because you also said that you didn't think that you could be fair to both sides. Did I hear you correctly?"

Courchain became testy over the dissection of his words. "I said unconsciously I don't think I could be fair to both sides."

"*I don't think I could be fair to both sides*"—an answer like that pretty much assures a criminal defense lawyer that a prospective juror will get knocked off the panel on a cause challenge (a challenge based upon bias, favoritism, or other impediment to jury service). Jackson moved for Courchain's removal. "Denied," Judge Sabo ruled.

Perplexed by the ruling, Jackson realized he was now in a bind. He had no more peremptory challenges left to remove Courchain. He argued further with the judge, explaining that the law mandated that Courchain be removed. Judge Sabo turned to Courchain and asked him some more questions about whether he could be fair. All he could say was that he "would try." Jackson moved for his removal again. "Denied." Courchain was there to stay.

The only saving grace was that Courchain was an alternate and not on the actual panel of twelve. Not yet, anyway.

■ There is a reason why Jackson, rather than Mumia, was questioning Courchain. At the start of the third day of jury selection, Judge Sabo precipitously ruled that Mumia had to turn the jury questioning over to Jackson, despite the fact that he was doing very well in bringing out the feelings and attitudes of the prospective jurors. The desire to silence Mumia was disclosed to the press the day before. McGill told reporters that he would ask Judge Sabo to stop Mumia from further questioning the panel, claiming that several prospective jurors left the courtroom saying that they were too upset and afraid to serve.

When reporters found Jackson outside the courthouse, they asked him for his reaction to McGill's anticipated maneuver. Appalled that McGill was playing his hand in the court of public opinion, Jackson said that Mumia was doing a better job than anyone expected. "The prosecutor is just trying to minimize the effectiveness that Mumia is having in bringing out the true feelings of the jurors," Jackson said. "Legally, he's done a more than adequate job, and there's no good reason to stop him." Reporters observing the proceedings noted that Mumia's "demeanor during the selection process has been subdued."

On the following day, McGill let the morning session pass without making a move. Like any good lawyer, he was waiting for the right moment—a moment that everyone knew would come. In the afternoon, he found the prospective juror he thought would give him the answers he needed. The questioning of juror number 360 had just ended when McGill stood up to ask some follow-up questions, even though he was not going to challenge the defense's request for her removal.

McGill asked, "Before you answered these questions here and having Mr. Jamal ask you questions, that makes you feel very, very unsettled, doesn't it?" Juror number 360, a bookkeeper who exhibited nervousness from the moment she underwent questioning, answered, "Yes, it does."

"As a matter of fact, it scares you, doesn't it?" McGill continued, putting words in her mouth, an effective technique in jury selection when used sparingly to accomplish a clearly defined goal.

"Yes. It scares me to death."

That's what McGill needed, even though it remained unclear what the "it" was that scared this particular juror. Was it Mumia in particular, or was it having to sit for questioning on a death penalty case generally? McGill knew that in the skewed universe of Judge Sabo's courtroom, he didn't need to tease out such nuances. If McGill insisted that something be done, chances were that Judge Sabo would accommodate him.

McGill asked Judge Sabo to entertain his motion to reconfigure the jury selection process so that Mumia would no longer question prospective jurors. Mumia expected this maneuver before the trial even began. He knew that the daily practitioners in the criminal justice system expect to see a fumbling effort by an untutored criminal defendant. They don't bargain for an articulate and probing exploration by a defendant that actually induces people to speak their mind.

The art of jury selection is simple, but few lawyers know how to do it, because the process of legal education actually throttles the ability to communicate spontaneously and authentically with real people. They inherit from law professors a liking for word games and rigid logic, and they develop a discomfort with the free-flowing give-and-take of genuine communication. Consequently, most lawyers ask mind-numbing questions, peppered with multisyllabic, sterile words delivered stiffly— hardly an invitation to openness and honesty. They are too often afraid of relinquishing control and letting people speak their mind, afraid that someone on the panel will say something negative or controversial. Their fears cause them unwittingly to stifle those human beings from whom it is most important to hear, oblivious to the fact that their openness and honesty is a gift. It is a gift because when it comes time for deliberations, jurors will be in a back room speaking their mind, and the trial lawyer is not invited, thus negating his power to diminish the impact of negative remarks and unstated hostility that might affect the outcome of the case. It's best to hear what a person has to say about various issues in the case *during jury selection,* where the damaging remarks and clues to hostile attitudes are made visible. At least during the jury selection process, the trial lawyer has some ability to keep the hostile ones out of the deliberations.

Mumia had always been a natural and fearless communicator, and he had honed that craft during his years as a radio commentator and journalist. But more importantly, he loved people and was unafraid to be vulnerable. As a result, he was open to hearing the good and the bad. He wanted to know if the prospective jurors didn't like his hair, if they were afraid of him, if they came into the city hall building already feeling that he was probably a cop killer. His own willingness to be open and vulnerable induced communicative reciprocity in many of those whom he questioned.

McGill didn't like that, so he wanted Judge Sabo to do something to put a stop to it.

Judge Sabo did not disappoint. Although McGill wanted him to take over the questioning, Judge Sabo preferred not to. He offered a compromise: he proposed that Jackson take over the questioning. Mumia wasn't going for it, seeing it as the first step toward stripping him completely of his right to represent himself. "I object totally. I object totally to that so-called compromise."

"Well, that's fine, then. I'll take over the voir dire," the judge threatened.

"I'm not surprised. I said you would do it yesterday," Mumia retorted.

"The rules allow me to do it, and I will do it in the interest of justice."

"That's not in the interest of justice; it's in the interest of a conviction," Mumia protested.

Jackson thought it was shortsighted of Mumia to stand on principle at a time like this and reject the compromise. It would be disastrous to allow Judge Sabo—or any judge, for that matter—to conduct the questioning, because he would engage in purely perfunctory inquiries without the keen ear of an advocate. Jury selection is far too important to relinquish to judges. If judges could conduct an effective voir dire, they wouldn't be judges; they would be trial lawyers. Jackson explained to Mumia that he could do the questioning far more skillfully than the judge and that he had no interest in taking over the case. He promised Mumia that he would retreat into the backup role once the jury selection was over. "Hey, I know you don't want it," he whispered to Mumia. "I don't want to be in this position, either; but in my opinion it would be better for me to participate in the voir dire than to leave it to him [gesturing toward the bench]." Mumia reflected for a moment, a glacial anger welling inside him. He then waved his hand to indicate that Jackson should take over. Jackson handled the questioning for the four remaining days of jury selection.

When the selection process was over, a mostly white and mostly male panel was selected (nine white, eight male). Four of the twelve were retired, two were unemployed, and, with one exception, the others blue-collar laborers. The *Philadelphia Inquirer* made a point in noting that "prosecutor Joseph McGill used most of his twenty peremptory challenges to turn down blacks and younger people." From a statistical point of view, black jurors faced odds of being struck by McGill that were over sixteen times greater than for other jurors.

It is tempting to pretend that minorities on death row
share a fate in no way connected to our own, that our
treatment of them sounds no echoes beyond the
chambers in which they die. Such an illusion is
ultimately corrosive, for the reverberations of injustice
are not so easily confined.

JUSTICE WILLIAM BRENNAN, *MCCLESKEY V. KEMP*

8. RACE AND THE DEATH PENALTY

Racism, while most visible in the jury selection process, is a
virus that permeates the entire machinery of death. It feeds on
discretion.

The essential dilemma in death penalty jurisprudence is applying
discretion in a nonarbitrary and nondiscriminatory manner while allowing it to exist within the criminal justice system. Discretion permits
the system to take into account the individualized circumstances of a
capital defendant and of the crime itself. The system of capital punishment in this country strives to include everyone within the ambit
of the death penalty who supposedly deserves that punishment, while
excluding everyone who, for reasons of innocence or particular circumstance, even if guilty, should not be put to death. This effort to
avoid over- and underinclusion necessarily mandates that some degree
of discretion be permitted in the criminal justice process when it
comes to applying the death penalty.

Therein lies the problem. While discretion exists within the death
penalty process in order to humanize it, discretion creates space for

the evils of racism. Racism has always existed in nineteenth- and twentieth-century death penalty jurisprudence in the United States. In fact, the death penalty, many scholars have noted, is a relic of slavery and racial violence in the United States. Supreme Court justice Thurgood Marshall expressed precisely this thesis in one of his capital punishment opinions: "The criminal law expressly differentiated between crimes committed by and against blacks and whites, distinctions whose lineage traced back to the time of slavery."

Undeniable racial disparity in the application of the death penalty has been a key piece of ammunition in the abolitionist's rhetorical armory. When the Supreme Court struck down the death penalty in the United States in 1972, racial disparities in defendants sentenced to death was a decisive impetus for some of the justices on the Supreme Court to rule the death penalty unconstitutional. But when the Supreme Court approved in 1976 new death penalty statutes that seemingly corrected the problems of discrimination and arbitrariness, capital punishment litigators renewed their watchful eye on how the death penalty was being applied, assured that it was just a matter of time before statistical evidence would confirm that capital punishment is a fundamentally racist institution that has no place in a civilized society.

In the mid-'80s, the NAACP Legal Defense Fund concluded that the time had come for a powerful challenge to the death penalty with the statistics it had been waiting for. Warren McCleskey was, in 1978, just another black man in Fulton County Superior Court in Georgia sentenced to die for killing a white police officer. After several unsuccessful appeals to the Georgia Supreme Court, lawyers from the Legal Defense Fund presented evidence in federal court on McCleskey's behalf that had the potential to end capital punishment in this country once and for all. Lawyers for McCleskey presented statistical evidence, packaged in a study conducted by Professors David Baldus and George Woodworth in which over two thousand murder cases in Georgia were examined, that showed that the death penalty was imposed in a racially discriminatory manner. The study demonstrated that in Georgia, between 1976 and 1980, defendants charged with killing whites were

4.3 times more likely to receive the death penalty than those charged with killing blacks. It concluded that black defendants charged with killing whites were more likely to receive a death sentence than any other racial combination. The study also found that prosecutors would more frequently seek the death penalty when the victim was white and the defendant was black.

When the case was accepted for review by the U.S. Supreme Court, hopes among many ran high that *this* would be the case that delivered the knockout blow to the death penalty. I was a law student in the spring of 1986 and I was taking a capital punishment seminar taught by the lead lawyer in the *McCleskey* case, Jack Boger of the NAACP Legal Defense Fund. Jack recruited me to work on the statistical issues in the case, and during that spring and early summer I contributed what little I could as a law student. Naive as I was, I couldn't imagine the Court not being bowled over by the statistical evidence. But in a highly controversial 5–4 decision issued in 1987, the Supreme Court rejected McCleskey's claim that the death penalty was unconstitutional under the Equal Protection Clause of the Fourteenth Amendment to the Constitution because of its discriminatory nature. It was my first real lesson in the realities of lawyering: law is not like buying a refrigerator—there are no guarantees.

Justice Lewis Powell authored the majority decision, arguing that McCleskey had failed to show that the decision makers in his particular case acted with a discriminatory purpose. A mere showing of discriminatory *impact*, which was undeniable in the Baldus study, was insufficient to infer discriminatory purpose, and therefore, insufficient to prove a constitutional violation. The majority also rejected the claim that the death penalty violated the Eighth Amendment (the amendment that outlaws cruel and unusual punishment) because it was applied in an arbitrary manner in which racial prejudices influenced whether prosecutors seek the death penalty and whether juries impose it. The majority acknowledged that racial prejudice may influence a jury's decision. But in a conclusion that was very much a throwback to the infamous *Dred Scott* decision in which the Supreme Court stated that a black person does not have rights that a white person is bound to respect, the majority found that the documented virus of racism within the death penalty machinery was constitutionally acceptable. Indeed, the Court ruled that statistical disparities would inevitably result from the necessary discretion given to prosecutors and juries, and that the Constitution does not "place totally unrealistic conditions" on the use of the death penalty—as if expecting our criminal justice system to be free of the taint of racism is a totally unrealistic condition.

Four justices dissented (Brennan, Marshall, Blackmun, and Stevens), issuing strongly worded opinions attacking the insensitivity of the majority. "We as a people ignore [Warren McCleskey] and what his case stands for at our peril," Justice Blackmun cautioned. "We remain imprisoned by the past as long as we deny its influence on the present. The destinies of the two races in this country are indissolubly linked together. The way in which we choose those who will die reveals the depth of moral commitment to the living."

Justice Brennan, the studious conscience of the Court, correctly observed that the majority was afraid to accept the implications of the Baldus study. There was no reason to expect that racial disparities in the criminal justice system *only* existed in death penalty jurisprudence; ruling in favor of McCleskey would put the Court on a slippery slope where the entire criminal justice edifice could collapse under the weight of racism. Indeed, the majority opinion itself suggested that a finding in favor of McCleskey could throw "into serious question the principles that underlie our entire criminal justice system." Accepting the Baldus study as a predicate for constitutional analysis would, Justice Brennan said, "open the door to all aspects of criminal sentencing." Stripped to its core, Brennan said, the *McCleskey* case reflects a fear of "too much justice."

In 1994, Justice Blackmun revisited the travesty of the *McCleskey* decision with a personal account of his deep disaffection with the death penalty. He underscored the fact that the Baldus study provided "staggering evidence of racial prejudice," which the Court turned its back on, and that "race continues to play a major role in determining who shall live and who shall die." He then struck the most disturbing note of all. Georgia, Blackmun noted, had done more than most other states to erect a nondiscriminatory system, yet it "was still unable to stamp out the virus of racism."[1] Justice Antonin Scalia, the most staunchly pro-death penalty justice on the Court, wrote that race discrimination is "real, acknowledged in the decisions of this court, and ineradicable."[2] This single fact, which the Court submerged from view in its opinion, suggested that the Court was willing to accept the inevitability of racism within capital punishment because, when it came to a choice between accepting racism as inevitable within capital punishment and jettisoning the death penalty, the Court opted for the former.

A few years after the *McCleskey* decision, another justice spoke of the decision. Justice Lewis Powell—the one who cast the swing vote and wrote the majority decision—revealed to his biographer that he had changed his mind about *McCleskey*, regretted that he had voted as he had, and had come to believe that "capital punishment should be abolished."[3] If anything should demystify the law, this revelation should. The death penalty survives today, as flawed as it is, not because the majesty of the law, as some reified entity existing apart from the vagaries of the human condition, decrees that it be so; it survives only because a slim, *momentary* majority voted against Warren McCleskey.

The majority decision in *McCleskey* ended its constitutional analysis with this simple piece of advice: take it to the legislatures. Statistical evidence of racial discrimination is not a constitutional matter, the majority reasoned, but a legislative matter that is best considered in the political arena. *McCleskey* exemplifies what has been happening with death penalty jurisprudence over the past three decades. The United States Supreme Court has gradually shifted to a hands-off approach to death penalty jurisprudence—a shift toward the "deregulation of death" as court-watchers and death penalty scholars have dubbed it. The case of *McCleskey v. Kemp*, with its final advice to abolitionists to seek relief in the legislature, is now a landmark of willful judicial blindness.

Efforts to arouse legislative sympathies over racial disparities have been largely fruitless. The Racial Justice Act, a modest piece of legislation that would empower federal courts to review capital cases for possible racial bias, has bounced around the halls of Congress but has never been passed. Between 1988 and 1994, increasingly watered-down versions of the Racial Justice Act were formulated to ease the queasiness felt by Republicans. During the summer of 1994, the Racial Justice Act (packaged with the title, Fairness in Sentencing Act) nearly made it to the House and Senate floor for a vote, but was dropped from the Omnibus Crime Control bill in the House-Senate conference committee. Throughout it all, the Department of Justice, with vigorous encouragement from prosecutors nationwide, robustly argued against its adoption.

The Justice Department's spirited opposition to the Racial Justice Act was not based upon governmental doubts that racism infects the application of the death penalty. After the Supreme Court issued the *McCleskey* decision, the United States General Accounting Office (GAO) published a report in 1990 that concluded that the race of the defendant and the race of the victim demonstrably influence whether the death penalty is imposed in the United States. The GAO examined twenty-eight studies conducted by twenty-one sets of researchers investigating racial disparities in the imposition of the death penalty and found them to be valid. The GAO report concluded that in 82 percent of the studies, race of the victim was found to influence the likelihood of being charged with capital murder or receiving the death penalty. "This finding was remarkably consistent across data sets, states, data collection methods, and analytic techniques," the report indicated. The GAO report went on to find that "more than three-fourths of the studies that identified a 'race of defendant' effect found that black defendants were more likely to receive the death penalty."

One way to appreciate the statistical analyses connecting race to the death penalty is to transform our vantage point: race is more likely to affect death sentencing than smoking affects the likelihood of dying from heart disease. The United States government has taken no action in one instance; swift action in the other.

The international community has not let *McCleskey* go unnoticed. The United Nations Special Rapporteur on Extrajudicial, Summary or Arbitrary Executions issued a report in January 1998, indicating that the death penalty was imposed in a discriminatory and arbitrary manner in this country: "Race, ethnic origin and economic status appear to be key determinants of who will, and will not, receive a sentence of death." It further noted that the *McCleskey* decision permits United States courts to tolerate racial bias in death penalty cases. Eighteen months earlier, in July 1996, the Geneva-based International Commission of Jurists, which consists of respected judges from around the world, released a 260-page report on racism in this country's death penalty, finding that it is administered in such a way that it "cannot be assured" that defendants receive a fair hearing. "The Commission is of the opinion that . . . the administration of capital punishment in the United States continues to be discriminatory and unjust—and hence 'arbitrary'—and thus not in consonance with Articles 6 and 14 of the Political Covenant and Article 2(c) of the Race Convention."

■ What about Philadelphia?

In 1998, Professor Baldus and his colleagues published a highly detailed study of the death penalty in Philadelphia. This study revealed that the death penalty in Philadelphia poses a "problem of arbitrariness and discrimination . . . [that] is a matter of continuing concern." The "problem" detected by Baldus and his colleagues is that the odds of receiving a death sentence are nearly four times higher if the defendant is black.

Of course, there are crimes that are so horrendous—serial killing comes to mind—that they eclipse race. White or black, some defendants are found to have committed acts so gruesome and abominable that a jury imposes death without regard to race. At the other end of the spectrum, a killing may evoke less horror and shock, such as a killing done in the heat of passion or under the influence of intoxication. There, too, race may play no role. The true test of race as a factor in the death penalty is how it weighs in on "judgment call" cases—those where a jury could go either way. In cases of midrange severity, prosecutors have tremendous discretion not to seek the death penalty, and juries have meaningful discretion not to impose death. Thus, the most probative examination of racism in the application of the death penalty would focus on the midrange cases.

Baldus and his colleagues attempted precisely that. They broke down the severity of the crime into eight categories, numbering one through eight with one being the least severe and eight the most severe. Where the crime falls within category five (midrange severity), race plays a strong role in the decision making: a quarter of all blacks receive death in this category, compared to 5 percent for other defendants. For severity ranges of six and seven, black defendants are sentenced to death at rates 15 percent higher than for other defendants. For ranges three and four, the percentage differential is 8 and 11 percent, respectively. These statistical results confirm the public's already-aroused suspicion that a black is more likely to receive the death penalty than a white person for the same crime, according to a June 16, 1997 *Newsweek* magazine poll.

In *McCleskey*, the Baldus study focused on the race of the victim. Baldus and his colleagues also looked at the race-of-victim effect in Philadelphia as well. The study, not surprisingly, showed that a black defendant and white victim (Mumia's case, of course, fits this category) is a deadly combination for defendants.

Armed with Baldus's data and research, and emboldened by expressions of concern over the death penalty from other jurisdictions, the Philadelphia City Council, on February 10, 2000, voted 12–4 for a resolution calling for a moratorium on executions in Pennsylvania. Philadelphia is the largest of a growing number of municipalities in the United States urging a halt to executions.

Philadelphia and Georgia are not the only locales with racial disparities in the death penalty. Baldus and his colleagues examined data in three-quarters of the states with prisoners on death row. In 93 percent of those states with available data, there is evidence of race-of-victim disparities. In half of those states, the race of the defendant served as a predictor of who received a death sentence. In Florida, a defendant is 4.8 times more likely to get death if the victim was white than if the victim was black. In Illinois, which is currently under a death penalty moratorium, the chances increase 4 times; in Oklahoma, 4.3 times; in North Carolina, 4.4 times; and in Mississippi, 5.5 times. In Kentucky, the 1996 death row population consisted only of defendants convicted of killing whites.[4] In 1998, Kentucky became the *only* jurisdiction to pass a Racial Justice Act bill which permits race-based challenges to prosecutorial decisions to seek a death sentence.

The legacy of *McCleskey* has proven to be more powerful than the damning and pervasive statistical evidence of racism within the criminal justice system. The federal courts have not granted relief based on a racial application of the death penalty in any case. The reason is obvious: *McCleskey*'s requirement that the defendant show purposeful discrimination by the prosecutor or the jury in the defendant's particular case—that is to say, to "get inside" the mind of the prosecutor or jury—is virtually impossible. No one within the criminal justice process will openly declare that the death penalty is being imposed on a particular defendant because he or she is black or brown. Statistical evidence is the only viable evidence that could be presented. Because statistical evidence is deemed irrelevant under *McCleskey*, litigating a race discrimination challenge to the death penalty is, for all practical purposes, a monumental waste of time.

This is *my* trial; this is *my* life on the line.

MUMIA ABU-JAMAL TO JUDGE SABO

Mr. Jamal is, if not the most, then one of the most intelligent defendants by far that I have ever run across.

PROSECUTOR JOSEPH McGILL TO JUDGE SABO

9. FLOWERING OF REBELLION

Mumia entered the courtroom with two armed deputies trailing behind, one carrying a stack of files clutched against his chest. The deputy plopped the stack on the defense table in front of the designated chair for the defendant while the other removed the handcuffs from Mumia's wrists. Hands liberated, Mumia pumped his fist energetically and smiled broadly at the spectators, and many of them reciprocated with encouraging words. He then turned his attention to the papers stuffed in the file folders in front of him in preparation for the first day of testimony. He said nothing to his attorney already seated next to him.

The court crier pounded three times on the table to signal that everyone was to come to order for the start of the court session. With the announcement, "God save this Honorable Court," Judge Sabo, decked out in his black robes, bounded up the steps and mounted the bench, elevated well above everyone else. He scanned the room and then looked to see if the court reporter was ready to transcribe the proceedings. McGill, too, was looking expectantly over at the court reporter. When she nodded, indicating that she was ready to take down every single word that would be said during that day's proceeding, McGill rose to his feet.

"I would ask the court to instruct Mr. Jamal to stick with evidence or what he intends to show or whatever during the opening statement." Although Mumia did not have legal training, McGill had no intention of cutting him any slack. In fact, he wasn't taking Mumia's lack of legal acumen for granted. He wanted Judge Sabo to keep a tight rein on him, because he knew Mumia had a gift for words and a proven ability to enrapture an audience. But most critically, Mumia's decision to represent himself also gave him one major advantage that concerned McGill: he could communicate his version of events without taking the witness stand, and thus avoid the unpleasantness of cross-examination. McGill didn't want to accord Mumia that kind of latitude in the trial; he wanted him on that witness stand.

McGill was convinced that cross-examining Mumia would lead to his unraveling. It is preferable to cross-examine educated witnesses, especially those who have inflated self-images, over questioning simple, vulnerable persons who are unaccustomed to manipulating words. If cross-examination is a duel between the witness and the trial lawyer, which it surely is, then it must be a duel fairly fought. A demolishing cross-examination of an unassuming and unpretentious witness rarely scores big points with a jury. In all likelihood, the jury will identify more readily with the besieged witness than with the slick and crafty lawyer. The jury sees the examination for what it is: an unfair fight; and the jury sees the trial lawyer for what he or she is: a bully. McGill was convinced that the jury would give him permission to attack his prey, and he felt assured that he would attack skillfully. He looked upon Mumia as an arrogant revolutionary incapable of keeping a lid on his radical political views, which this particular jury, picked from within a community saturated with anti-MOVE media coverage over the past several years, would find repulsive. It would be a fair duel, because Mumia would be a worthy opponent; and most importantly, the jury would enjoy witnessing it.

But there would be a whole trial to undergo, a virtual journey to experience, before Mumia would be given the opportunity to take the witness stand. The first order of business was the delivery of the opening statements. The opening statement would be Mumia's singular moment to bring the jury to his side. It was his opportunity, uninterrupted and uncross-examined, to tell the jury, from his point of view, what happened just before 4:00 A.M. on December 9, 1981, as he ran across Locust Street toward Officer Faulkner and his brother.

An opening statement is no luxury, and it is certainly more than just a synopsis of the case. It is, perhaps, the most vital moment in trial advocacy—a moment that must be entwined with the jury selection process. This process, when done correctly, primes jurors for the theories and themes that will be communicated in the opening statement. Research powerfully suggests that jurors begin to develop their outlook on a case upon hearing the opening statements. What they hear at the beginning of the trial, if compelling, becomes the mental scaffolding upon which the case is constructed. It guides the jury to construe the testimony in a way that is favorable to the advocate's side.

Although the essence of advocacy is communication, the trial process provides an inhospitable way to communicate. Witnesses get on the stand and the story dribbles out in little bits and pieces. A witness is not given carte blanche to launch into an uninterrupted narrative about events he or she may think is important. Little nuggets of information are extracted from the witness, question by question, punctuated by irrelevant detours and interrupted by objections, sidebars, and breaks in the proceedings. On top of that, a jury is entirely passive, barred by rules of procedure from asking questions of its own. This passivity inevitably leads to periods where jurors "zone out" for varying periods of time, thus resulting in testimony (sometimes crucial testimony) being missed. A good opening statement gives the jury a picture of the case as a whole—like a painting that is about to be cut up into little pieces, only to be reassembled slowly over time. The reassembling process is the trial itself, and the mental picture of the painting facilitates the placement of each piece into the proper place. Even if some pieces are missing, either because a juror has zoned out or because the evidence wasn't presented, the juror will fill in the resulting gaps with the full-blown image image provided by the trial lawyer in the opening statement. No competent trial lawyer forgoes the opportunity to give an opening statement; and very, very few skilled trial lawyers, if any at all, delay giving the opening statement. A skilled trial lawyer takes her case to the jury as soon as possible, and as often as possible.

■ McGill pushed his chair back and moved quickly toward the jury as if adrenalin was causing his blood to stampede through his veins. He was obviously anxious to tell his audience *his* story of good versus evil.

Mumia immediately took to his feet. "Judge, I have a statement."

Judge Sabo ordered Mumia and the lawyers up to the bench for a sidebar conference. Sidebar conferences, as anyone who has served on a jury knows, are meetings off to the side of the judge's elevated bench where matters can be discussed beyond earshot of the jury. As frustrating as a sidebar conference is for the excluded jurors, it pales in comparison to the agony for a lawyer in being excluded from the private sanctum of a jury deliberation room.

Judge Sabo wasn't going to take any chances with Mumia. Anything Mumia wanted to say would have to be said at sidebar, and not in front of the jury.

"I need a microphone at the table," Mumia whispered.

"I don't have one," Judge Sabo answered, a confused look on his face. The only microphone in the courtroom was the one for the witness. It wasn't customary for lawyers to have microphones, at least not in Courtroom 253.

Mumia glared at the judge. "You get one," he demanded as the judge shook his head briskly.

To Judge Sabo, this was akin to a child brashly talking back to a parent. He angrily called out to the clerk and ordered the jury removed from the courtroom while he restored the fragile balance of justice within his judicial domain. Figuring that he could accomplish this in a matter of minutes, he told the clerk to keep the jurors assembled so that the proceedings could begin in haste. But, as he was to do on several occasions in the trial, Judge Sabo underestimated Mumia's resolve.

The two sparred for what seemed like hours over the trivial issue of a microphone. Judge Sabo, notorious for his quick temper and his penchant for using contempt citations as a club to keep lawyers in line, threatened Mumia with contempt. "Judge, that warning doesn't mean anything to me," Mumia asserted. "If you want to find me in contempt, go ahead—I'm on this trial for my life. You know those warnings mean nothing to me." Judge Sabo couldn't deny that Mumia had a point.

Somehow the arguments over the microphone transformed themselves into arguments over whether Mumia could have the assistance of MOVE founder John Africa at the trial. John Africa was charismatic, perceptive, and verbally skillful. He communicated through aphorisms, analogies, and stories—keys to communicating effectively. He had used that skill to secure an acquittal for himself from serious weapons charges in a federal trial the previous summer, single-handedly defeating two highly trained federal prosecutors in a case that seemed to be a lock for the prosecution. Attending that trial as a journalist, Mumia was impressed with John Africa as he watched him in action representing himself. "I'm an innocent man," John Africa told the jury in his closing argument. "I didn't come here to make trouble or to bring trouble, but to bring the truth. And goddamn it, that's what I'm going to do! I'm fighting for air that you've got to breathe. I'm fighting for water that you've got to drink, and if it gets any worse, you're not going to be drinking that water. I'm fighting for food that you've got to eat. And, you know, you've got to eat it, and if it gets any worse, you're not going to be eating that food." When the jury announced its not-guilty verdict, John Africa had one thing to say: "The power of truth is final."

Mumia wanted some of that "power of truth." He had actually been clamoring for John Africa's assistance for weeks, but Judge Sabo never took the request seriously. John Africa is not a lawyer, Sabo reasoned, so he can't appear in court in any representational capacity. But Mumia wasn't demanding that John Africa represent him as a lawyer. He wanted John Africa to *assist* him. Sabo reconstructed the request in order to delegitimize it; and if he'd had a defendant who was less intellectually agile, he probably would have been able to get away with it. Mumia, however, was incensed over the tactic. In another courtroom several flights above Courtroom 253, a police officer was permitted to sit at the defense table with his son who had been charged with a homicide offense. Why, Mumia wanted to know, was he not accorded the same right?

Judge Sabo was an old-school judge: if he said no, then that's it—no more arguments. Mumia would have to accept the services of Anthony Jackson, a man trained in legal procedure.

"I don't want that man [Jackson] as my defense attorney," Mumia responded.

"I don't care what you want," Judge Sabo angrily retorted.

"Damn what you want. This is *my* trial. It's *my* life on the line." Mumia shot his fist into the air in a "black power" salute.

McGill figured he knew what was going on: Mumia wanted to make the trial political theater, and by doing so, engineer a mistrial. Mumia surely knew about Bobby Seale's conduct in the famous Chicago Eight trial in Chicago, which dominated the news in 1969. Probably the most famous political trial in United States history, the trial of the Chicago Eight, which amused many and disconcerted many more, involved conspiracy-to-riot allegations arising from the unrest at the 1968 Democratic Convention in Chicago. The charges were brought against the key leaders of various left-wing contingents struggling for social change: Abbie Hoffman and Jerry Rubin represented the Yippies (that is, the counterculture); David Dellinger represented the pacifist strain of the antiwar movement; Rennie Davis and Tom Hayden were leaders in the left-wing student movement (the "New Left"); Lee Weiner and John Froines were exemplars of left-wing academics; and Bobby G. Seale was the designated black man, the cofounder of the Black Panther Party. Seale wanted legendary attorney Charles Garry to represent him, but Garry fell ill shortly before trial. Judge Julius Hoffman refused Seale's request that his case be postponed while Garry recuperated. Seale then demanded to represent himself. This too Judge Hoffman refused. With each demand from Judge Hoffman that he accept the representation of William Kunstler, Bobby Seale responded with the same defiance, adamancy, and fearlessness as Mumia thirteen years later: "He is not representing me. I am entitled to represent myself." Seale, like Mumia, simply refused to acquiesce, which ultimately led to Judge Hoffman's infamous order to the courtroom marshals: "Take the defendant into the room in there and deal with him as he should be dealt with in this circumstance." A short while later, Seale was carried back into the courtroom, gagged, handcuffed, and bound to a metal chair. When Seale was able to rattle the handcuffs against the metal, the judge ordered the marshals, in his customary Victorian locution, to "make that contrivance more secure." Ultimately, the spectacle of a black man bound and gagged in a United States courtroom was too much even for Judge Hoffman, and a mistrial was declared for Bobby Seale. The Chicago Eight then became the Chicago Seven.

McGill suspected that Mumia would like nothing more than to ravage Judge Sabo's nerves and thus provoke him to similar madness. "My thought is that perhaps Mr. Jamal is, if not the most, then one of the most intelligent defendants by far that I have ever run across," McGill said to Judge Sabo, "and I'm quite sure that everything he's doing is strategic." McGill continued, "I think perhaps Mr. Jamal is attempting to not only divert their minds from guilt or innocence and to some sort of condition that he believes he is in unjustifiably, but that he may well wish to have himself ejected so that learned counsel would be in a position to try a case, and since he has a great deal of experience in it, and gain some sort of sympathy from the jury." To McGill, this display of protest and disruption was a fusion of Black Panther and MOVE tactics—derail the trial proceedings, inject chaos into the courtroom, and then seize the moment to convert the entire process into political theater. McGill would later use this display, which repeated itself endlessly through the whole trial, to powerful effect in arguing for the death penalty.

For the time being, McGill wanted to secure as much advantage as he could from Mumia's protestations. "You stay here and represent yourself and don't try to chicken out," McGill needled.

Mumia was too fired up to leave McGill's goading alone. "I'm not chickening out. That's unimportant for me. What I want is a representative of my choice, not of your choice, not of his [Jackson's] choice, but of my choice. It's my life on the line."

Jackson sat bemused, his emotions bordering on lassitude. The thought came to him, inexplicably, that maybe he could now make another pitch to be cut loose, even though Judge Sabo emphatically refused his earlier earnest requests to be relieved of the nightmare. "May I say something?" he interjected. "I most respectfully request to be removed from this case. I feel uncomfortable in this position being backup counsel."

McGill and the judge could be excused from suspecting that, perhaps, Jackson was conspiring with Mumia to prolong the arguing. Jackson's futile request did nothing to advance the possibility of his excusal, but it provided Mumia with a segue into another line of protestation. "I do not want him sitting there in defense of my life," Mumia declared.

Judge Sabo, at that point, realized Mumia was not going to let the proceedings continue. He warned him that this time, he would not be held in contempt or sanctioned in some other way but that he would be stripped of his right to represent himself.

Mumia's response was the same: "Judge, your warnings to me are absolutely meaningless. I'm here fighting for my life. Do you understand that? I'm not fighting to please the Court, or to please the DA. I'm fighting for my life."

There was nothing Judge Sabo could realistically say to that in response. A man facing execution has no genuine interest in being cooperative or congenial, Judge Sabo reasoned. Because there was no apparent way for the trial to proceed smoothly without allowing John Africa to displace Jackson as backup counsel, by day's end Judge Sabo had rescinded Mumia's status as his own attorney and put Jackson back into the lead role. It was a decision that ensured continued protests from Mumia, but at least it provided a way for the trial to continue—Judge Sabo's sole concern.

The jury, meanwhile, had already been shuttled back to the hotel, a wasted day in the halls of justice.

■ Jackson didn't expect he would be handling the trial as the lead law-yer. More than six weeks earlier, on April 29, he had requested appoint-ment of a second attorney because he felt he couldn't handle the case himself. He had told Judge Ribner at that time that he was overwhelmed by the sheer volume of work left to be done on the case. Yet, two weeks after confessing his unpreparedness and desperate situa-tion, he learned that he wouldn't have to do any trial preparation after all, because Mumia would be handling his own defense. Now, on the day of opening statements, he was thrust back into the lead counsel role, and thus into a more desperate situation than he had been in on April 29. He was too shell-shocked even to ask for a continuance.

Actually, Jackson had one last hope to avoid the unwanted duty of representing Mumia. Judge Sabo gave Jackson permission to take an emergency petition to the Pennsylvania Supreme Court to chal-lenge his decision to strip Mumia of his pro se status. Late in the day on June 17, Jackson, Mumia, and McGill appeared before Justice James T. McDermott, two flights above Judge Sabo's courtroom. Jus-tice McDermott, a onetime trial judge who enjoyed his reputation as a hanging judge and who himself had issued thirteen death sentences before gaining a seat on the Pennsylvania Supreme Court, was not expected to be sympathetic to Mumia's desire to have John Africa at his side, as he had denied requests of MOVE members to represent themselves in the MOVE Nine trial. He didn't take long, nor did he agonize over the matter, before issuing his decision: Jackson had to stay on, and John Africa had to stay out.

After McDermott issued his decision, he rose to leave the bench. "Where are you going, motherfucker?" Mumia wailed. The crudity of the epithet, uncharacteristic of the young journalist, shocked even McGill.

■ The day after the wild proceedings on June 17 would be no less significant for the trajectory of the trial. The one vestige of Mumia's activity as his own counsel was soon to be taken from him. Mumia arrived in court on June 18 from his holding cell unaware that the only juror he had selected, Jennie Dawley, the elderly black woman he had personally selected as his first choice on the jury, would no longer be sitting on his case.

Dawley had told a court officer, after the jury was excused early on June 17 that she had to make a quick trip home. She explained that her cat was sick and had to be taken to the veterinarian by 7:00 P.M. The court officer ordered her to stay. Dawley left anyway. It turned out that Mumia's instincts about Dawley were right; she had an independent streak about her, a feistiness that would serve him well in the case. The court officers on the night crew assigned to watch over the jury at the hotel noticed her missing when the jurors assembled for dinner. Her clothes were still in her room, which indicated that she intended to return, but she had broken Sabo's strict rules of sequestration. At about 9:00 P.M., Dawley returned to the hotel, only to meet up with angry court officers.

Judge Sabo, who had received a report of the events the night before, told McGill and Jackson about Dawley's violation of the sequestration order during a private conference in his chambers on the morning of June 18. Mumia was not present for the conference. Much of the discussion actually centered on how the three of them were going to deal with Mumia's strong-willed insistence on representing himself with John Africa's assistance. But, during the course of the conference, Judge Sabo made it clear that it was his intention to remove the insolent juror. Jackson expressed some reluctance to go along with the move, indicating that he wanted to get Mumia's input. It was a dubious practice to discuss such a sensitive matter without Mumia's presence in the first place. It was arguably illegal to arrive at a resolution of the issue without according Mumia the opportunity to express his own views on the matter, especially given that Dawley had been selected while he was acting as his own attorney.

McGill knew that Mumia would never allow the removal of Dawley without protracted argument and protestation. He began pressuring Jackson with claims that Dawley should never have been selected, as she obviously disliked Mumia. Judge Sabo, a wily jurist, echoed that observation, telling Jackson that "she'll hang him." The tag-team coercion worked: Jackson finally acquiesced to the decision to remove Dawley, without consulting Mumia. Getting Jackson to withhold any objection was important to Sabo and McGill because it is difficult to raise an issue on appeal where the defense attorney does not interpose an explicit objection to a particular action by the court or the prosecutor. Comfortable now that Jackson had eliminated any realistic chance of Mumia's challenging his actions on appeal, Judge Sabo told the court clerk to send Dawley home.

Edward Courchain, the elderly white man who said he couldn't be impartial due to the media coverage in the case, now became juror number one. The jury now consisted of ten whites and only two blacks. It couldn't have been scripted better for the prosecution.

■ The twelve jurors and three alternates took their seats in the jury box on June 18 expecting to hear the opening statements that should have been delivered the day before. When they heard the first words of the day, they were rightly dubious that they would be needed anytime soon.

"Who is representing me?" Mumia awaited an answer. Jackson sat frozen. "Why is he representing me?"

"He's representing you by order of the Supreme Court," Sabo finally replied.

Mumia again insisted that Jackson was not *his* lawyer. Getting nowhere, Judge Sabo ordered the jury removed once again. "Mr. Jamal, it is obvious to this Court that you have been intentionally—"

"Why is he representing me?" Mumia interrupted, speaking more loudly now.

"You have been intentionally disrupting the orderly proceedings in this courtroom," Judge Sabo remarked in a businesslike tone. It was clear where the judge was going. He was laying the groundwork to have Mumia removed from the courtroom so the trial could finally proceed. But before he could do that, without risking reversible error on appeal, he needed to be patient. Judge Sabo was an intemperate judge, quick to anger against lawyers, but he was no fool. He knew what it took to protect his record.

Protecting the record is a skill that trial judges gradually learn, some quicker than others. What exists on the record is the universe of facts that come into play after a case is over at the trial court level. An appeals court will not go outside that record. So if something is said, or if something happens, and it is not memorialized through words spoken while the court stenographer is there, then, for all practical purposes, those remarks just weren't said or those events just didn't happen. Regardless of whether Judge Sabo had any concerns over Mumia's rights as an accused person, he had to utter the proper set of words on the record to construct a particular universe of facts from which an appeals court would later review the fairness of the proceedings.

Playing the game of protecting the record, Judge Sabo issued endless warnings to Mumia about the possibility that he could forfeit his right to be present at his own trial. Judge Sabo wasn't going to take the tack of Judge Julius Hoffman, strapping Mumia to a chair and gagging him. That particular judicial tactic, widely reported in the news when it occurred to Bobby Seale, appalled the country. Judge Sabo would simply dispatch Mumia to his jail cell after justifying the move sufficiently on the record. Mumia was nowhere near as savvy about constructing a favorable record. He repeatedly castigated the judge for stripping him of his right to proceed on his own behalf and for summarily dismissing his request to have John Africa's assistance. Through it all, Judge Sabo methodically advised Mumia of the rights he would forgo if he continued to disrupt the proceedings, including his right to view the witnesses testifying against him and his right to confer with his attorney during the course of the trial proceedings.

Mumia was unmoved, convinced that every action by the judge was freighted with ill-will. "It's very curious that the court seems protective of certain rights and clearly doesn't give a damn about others.

The right of self-representation is an absolute right. But that right has been stolen by you several times during the voir dire, and it's been stolen before this actual trial began."

By 3:00 P.M., Judge Sabo reached the end of his patience. Arguing wasn't getting anywhere. He thought that maybe, just maybe, he could squeeze in the opening statements before adjourning for the day. The jury was brought back in, even while Mumia was still arguing for his right to represent himself. The jurors took their seats, and Mumia kept talking. It had to have been puzzling to those fifteen people, being shuffled in and out of the courtroom, with a criminal defendant seeming to hold the whole process hostage with his filibustering.

But McGill knew that his words, at the end of the trial, would put it all together for the jury. These events inside the courtroom—an oddity, at the least, for the jury—would all make sense in the end: McGill would see to that. McGill would use these events as further evidence that Mumia had killed Officer Faulkner, not out of a momentary flurry of anger but as an outgrowth of who Mumia had become.

Recognizing that Mumia would not stop talking, Judge Sabo motioned to have the jury escorted out of the courtroom again. He had that look that trial judges acquire when they're about to alter the course of events in a trial. His face broadened, became less rigid and less wrinkled. It was, one might even say, a look of serenity. He lost the appearance of someone whose composure was about to become unhelmed. Even before the last juror walked out the door to the jury room, Judge Sabo made his proclamation. "Mr. Jamal, you have interrupted these proceedings *for the last time*. The Court is ordering the sheriff to remove the defendant from the courtroom. We'll proceed in your absence."

Two spectators energetically leaped from their seats as Mumia was escorted out of the courtroom. "This is a fucking railroad!" one of them yelled above the chattering of the rest of the people sitting in the audience.

"What *is* this?" the other said defiantly.

The outcries seemed to stoke the anger of the Mumia supporters, as the chattering grew louder. MOVE members flourished defiant gestures at the court personnel. The clerk sensed that things were about to get out of control. About a dozen deputy sheriffs quickly descended on the two men who had yelled at the judge and forcibly dragged them out of the courtroom. Most of the spectators sat stunned at the pell-mell violence. A court of law is the last place one expects to *see* physical aggression; it is a place of harsh and sorrowful words, not physicality. Newspaper accounts referred to the incident as an "angry brawl" that nearly got out of control. "With arms swinging and people shouting," the *Philadelphia Inquirer* reported, "the fighting threatened to spread to the numerous police officers and supporters of Abu-Jamal in the courtroom."

"Does anybody know who those men were?" Judge Sabo asked, referring to the two contemptuous spectators.

"Yes," said McGill. McGill told Judge Sabo they were Billy and Wayne Cook, Mumia's two brothers.

Judge Sabo threw up his hands in scalding fury and ordered the clerk to tell the sheriff that the jury would have to be sent back to the hotel for the second day in a row. He then directed court officers to bring Mumia's brothers back into the courtroom. They were still struggling and shouting as they were forcibly brought in front of the judge. These men weren't facing execution, so a contempt citation and a jail term would have some meaning, which is why Judge Sabo held them in contempt and ordered them imprisoned for sixty days.

McGill gave reporters his own spin on the day's events: "Mr. Jamal's eviction from the courtroom may very well be his best shot. It's difficult to make decisions on someone you don't see."

■ On June 19 Mumia was back at the defense table when Judge Sabo ascended to the bench. He glanced at Mumia with a grave expression, wary of him. It was now the third day of the trial since the jury was empaneled, and opening statements had not yet been delivered. Sabo was tense, undoubtedly still unnerved by the "melee" the day before, as McGill characterized it. He was not about to bring the jury back in until he received an assurance from Mumia that there would be no more outbursts. "I want to first ascertain from Mr. Jamal whether or not he will behave himself in this courtroom so that he can stay for the proceedings." Judge Sabo then looked directly at Mumia, still seated at the table. "Mr. Jamal, are you going to behave yourself and not disrupt the orderly proceedings of this courtroom?"

Mumia didn't seem to take offense at the patronizing tone. In fact, he affected one himself: "I sure will, Judge."

Jackson diffidently requested that the jury be dismissed and a new one selected, arguing that the jurors had been privy, to some degree, to the acrimonious exchanges of the past two days. McGill, not unexpectedly, argued vigorously that, because any prejudice arising from those events was generated by Mumia's own deliberate actions, he'd have to live with it (actually, risk dying because of it). McGill applauded Judge Sabo's "extreme patience" in dealing with "yesterday's melee" and urged the denial of the defense motion. It was typical overkill on McGill's part, as Judge Sabo's decision was never in question. "The motion to dismiss the jury," Judge Sabo announced, "is denied."

Within minutes, the jurors were again seated in the jury box and McGill, finally, was giving his "bird's-eye view of what the evidence will be." The jurors stiffened in their seats as McGill, once again, strode up to the railing and peered at them. He never pandered to juries, preferring instead to be looked upon as an authority figure, a man to be respected, not necessarily liked. He recounted the "facts" concerning the events of December 9 as Cynthia White was expected to tell it. Although he planned on calling four eyewitnesses, it was White's account that would provide the seamless narrative upon which the prosecution's theory was to be built. He described how Officer Faulkner pulled over Billy Cook's Volkswagen, which led to a physical scuffle between the two. Mumia darted across the street toward Faulkner and his brother. The spark that set in motion a killer's rampage was clear: Mumia, harboring intense antipathy for cops, was intensely enraged by the fact that a cop was clubbing his own brother over the head with a flashlight.

McGill explained to the jury that Mumia was also shot at the scene. According to McGill's theory, again rooted in Cynthia White's anticipated testimony, Officer Faulkner spun toward Mumia after receiving a bullet wound to the back. "And you will hear the testimony that as he fell down, Officer Faulkner was grabbing *for something. . . .*" Grabbing for a gun, McGill implied, which young Danny Faulkner bravely used to fire off a round, striking the murderer in the chest as he, the officer, fell to the pavement.

Reaching the climax to this tragic narrative, McGill slowed his speech, the better to impress the jury at how despicable the crime was. Like a good storyteller, McGill began speaking in the present tense, to transport the jury to that time and place, helping them to reenact the events in their minds as a present occurrence. "Officer Faulkner now is on the ground," McGill said in a husky whisper; "and then you will hear the testimony of various witnesses that this defendant walks right over to Officer Faulkner"—his voice rising—"who at this point is on his back, and within twelve inches of his head, he points the gun that he had that was loaded, and unloads the gun. One makes contact, and that was the fatal shot, right between the eyes, literally blowing his brains out." McGill didn't just use words. He showed the jury the cruelty of the act. He stretched out his right arm and bent over, simulating the recoil of the revolver as three rounds were discharged.

McGill was experienced enough to understand the power of a good opening statement. He sensed that he had this jury on his side, even at that moment, before a single witness was called. But it is one thing to persuade a jury early on in a case that the defendant is guilty. It is quite another to get the jury to *hate* the defendant, to wish him dead.

Mumia was taken to a hospital, McGill explained. A sad irony, he noted as an aside, because this hospital was the same one to which Danny Faulkner was taken. In one emergency room lay an innocent victim, designated to protect us from violence and lawlessness; in another, the very embodiment of lawlessness. He promised the jury that it would hear evidence that "symbolizes the entire episode."

"This man, this defendant, you will hear and you will see throughout this trial as the evidence goes on, is a picture of extreme arrogance, defiance, even a strange boastfulness as to what he did in his deliberate killing of this police officer." McGill's cunning was slowly coming to light. A "picture of extreme arrogance" that "you will see throughout this trial": McGill was sure that Mumia would play right into his hands and continue to disrupt the proceedings with his rancorous barbs at the judge. McGill wanted the jury to watch for this, and think about it, and then reflect on what Mumia supposedly said at the hospital. Wasn't Mumia's utter contempt for the judge and for the sacredness of the trial proceedings nothing more than an extension of the vileness that led to his crude confession?

Mumia was lying on the emergency room floor, McGill stated, when Officer Faulkner's partner knelt down to look into the killer's eyes. "This defendant, you will hear, looks up at him when the officer is just dying, and said, 'I shot the MF'er and I hope he dies.' Arrogance, defiance, you will see it."

McGill ended his opening abruptly. He didn't need to rally his audience, not yet at least. He asked for their patience, signaling that the trial was both a formality and an emblem of our society's intrinsic goodness, a necessary road to travel on the way to executing justice.

■ If ever a defense attorney needed to say something, now was the time. An advocate cannot, must not, let the jury absorb the prosecutor's story like a dry sponge. The jury wants to know, *needs* to know, what the defendant's answer is to the prosecutor's blistering allegations. Those twelve human beings, at the very least, need to know that there is an answer, no matter how feeble it might eventually be taken to be. But not to render an answer, immediately and forcefully, is tantamount to admitting defeat.

Jackson went to his feet, his arms outstretched toward the table with his fingers holding up his forward-leaning torso. He didn't make a move toward the jury; he wouldn't move toward the jury, even though those men and women sat there with expectant stares, waiting to be told why the prosecution had it all wrong. He had no opening statement prepared, unsurprisingly, as he hadn't expected that one would be needed from him. "Your Honor, I reserve making opening remarks till a later time." Several jurors slumped deeper in their seats as Judge Sabo, with a tinge of glee, said simply, "Very well, then."

McGill could not have been more delighted.

They [the police] were getting on me telling me I was in
the area and I seen Mumia, you know, do it, you know, do
it, you know, intentionally. They were trying to get me to
say something that the other girl [Cynthia] said. . . . They
told us we can work the area if we tell them.

WITNESS VERONICA JONES, 1982

10. PRIMING FOR DEATH

A court of law enshrines cold logical reasoning; securing a
death verdict demands a conflagration of emotions. Vital to an
effective death penalty prosecution, therefore, is a villainous defendant
juxtaposed to a blameless, morally upright, and, preferably, physically
attractive victim.

To the elderly men and women on the jury, Danny Faulkner, a
handsome young white man they would have been proud to call a
son, sacrificed his life on the front lines in the war against lawlessness.
He was the quintessential capital punishment victim. Yet, within
Courtroom 253, as the trial got under way, the victim was an abstrac-
tion; only photographs and words permitted a glimpse into who he
was. If only there was some way to get the jury to feel the weight of
the loss, so that that weight could be felt against the counterweight
of the defendant's viciousness. This was McGill's dilemma. Maureen
Faulkner was his solution.

Maureen walked deliberately to the witness chair, her eyes angled
toward the floor, as if she had somewhere to go with no time even to

exchange a greeting. She went up the two steps and contorted her body slightly to position herself in front of the witness chair without hitting the microphone. She made a motion to sit down but then saw the Bible and realized that she had to take the oath. She raised her right hand to announce her willingness to tell the truth before God. She was subdued, sitting in the witness chair, expressionless, waiting for McGill to ask his first question—a virtual model of the grieving young widow. Just a year from her wedding when she had said that she would stay with Danny until death, Maureen Faulkner was now the prosecution's first witness in Mumia's trial. McGill allowed the jurors to absorb the moment.

They looked at her with soft expressions, momentarily (but only momentarily) helpless to ease her sorrow. They had before them not so much a witness with information, for she added little to the evidentiary mix, but something far more powerful, something that operated on their humanity at the deepest level. Maureen was also a victim—of loss, of heartache, of cruel and irrational violence. More than that, she was an attractive victim, easy to look at, and hence, easy to feel for. Even more than that, she was a delicate victim, young and deserving of the love of a husband and the promise of children. She was, most importantly of all, an undeserving victim, undeserving of the loss she suffered. Therefore, she deserved justice.

McGill picked his jury to give Maureen, and the city of Philadelphia, a measure of justice. The jury would be a party to an implied compact, wherein he would present proof of Mumia's guilt and they would deliver the gift of justice. But gifts are given from the heart, prompted by feelings *for* the recipient. McGill presented Maureen to the jurors so that they could *feel* for Maureen, feel Danny Faulkner's presence in the courtroom, and, paradoxically as it may seem, at the same time feel his absence from the human family. Maureen was there not only to display her loss but also to convey *our* loss. A death penalty trial, McGill understood, is as much (if not more) about feelings as it is about logic.

She told the jury of Danny's last day at home; how he stepped out into the cold in his uniform at 11:30 P.M. to begin his night shift, the most frightening for any cop's wife. She identified her husband's hat, which he dutifully placed on his head before he began his walk over to the driver's-side door of the Volkswagen—an insignificant evidentiary detail but a powerful theatrical display: a hat with no one to wear it—the ultimate symbol of absence. Further, that hat was the physical incarnation of Officer Faulkner's pride as a police officer, and its pristine condition at the trial symbolized the abrupt rupture of the thin blue line.

Maureen's testimony was strategically brief. She didn't need to tell the jury that she had a ritual with her husband—he was not allowed to leave for work, ever, without giving her a kiss.

The truth is, Maureen Faulkner would continue to "testify" throughout the rest of the trial without ever retaking the witness stand. She remained in the courtroom after the questioning was over, a conspicuous presence in the spectator section for the balance of the trial, surrounded by family and friends, and a consistent crew of police officers. The only time she wasn't there for the jury to see was when her husband's bloody shirt was taken out of the evidence bag and unfurled in open court. She broke into sobs at the sight of the shirt and hastily headed for the exit. Several jurors turned their eyes downward as the proceedings seemingly froze for an instant, a brief, grim armistice within the capacious courtroom.

Quiet and grieving, Maureen radiated a power of her own, energized subtly by the electricity of the proceedings. Maureen's power was in direct proportion to Mumia's rebellion, because the two were indissolubly linked in the courtroom drama. Her victimization and her sorrow seemed more acute in the heat of Mumia's embittered courtroom denunciations.

Maureen Faulkner was a vital ingredient in the life-death calculus that is played out in all capital cases: the defendant must be worthy of being killed by virtue of his acts; but the victim, too, must be worthy of the jury's act of vengeance. The death penalty is designed, its proponents argue, for the absolutely worst criminals, for people who have committed crimes so ghastly that society can no longer countenance their presence among the living. But that is so in the realm of logic. In reality, the death penalty, no matter how justified, speaks to the need for vengeance and cultural expiation. Consequently, an absolutely essential component to most successful death penalty prosecutions is the message that someone who is worthless killed someone who mattered, someone who lived by societal rules and had the promise to succeed by society's particular standards of success, leaving alone others who are undeserving of the loss.

McGill's opening statement and Maureen's testimony and presence sustained the emotional tone of the trial as a series of crime scene investigators testified to what was observed and found at the location where Officer Faulkner was shot. Photographs, diagrams, clothing stiffened by caked blood, and two .38 caliber pistols (one police issued, the other belonging to the accused) were introduced into evidence. These prosaic aspects of the evidentiary presentation had their own subtle power. It gave the prosecution a desirable ethos, an image that it was the district attorney's office that was devoted to truth and to seeking out justice. Jackson, in his rambling cross-examinations, only reinforced this prosecutorial ethos, painting himself as one seeking only to kick up dust.

But McGill counted on the circumstances of the arrest to propel the jury into accepting uncritically what the four eyewitnesses had to say. He sensed that the jury would have no trouble finding Mumia guilty in large measure because he was apprehended in under two minutes of the shooting just a few feet from Officer Faulkner's prone body. P.O. Robert Shoemaker was called to testify to develop this point. Shoemaker had heard Faulkner put out over the radio that he needed a "wagon," which, he explained to the jury, meant that he planned on making an arrest. What had caught Faulkner's attention to prompt the desire to take the driver of the Volkswagen into custody will never be known. Shoemaker and his partner were the first to arrive at the scene, and when they did, they found Mumia sitting on the curb with his bent legs protruding into the street and his right arm crossing his chest.

Shoemaker, with his gun already drawn, ordered Mumia to freeze. "We made eye contact probably about the same time," Shoemaker testified, "and the male did not freeze, his arm started to move to the left." At that moment, in the darkness, Shoemaker couldn't tell what Mumia was reaching for. He moved slowly to his left, with his eyes fixed on Mumia's outstretched left arm. Mumia was either gesturing toward, or reaching for, something. Shoemaker then noticed that a revolver lay on the pavement about eight inches from Mumia's outstretched hand.

Unsure of Mumia's intentions, but recognizing that something awful had just happened, Shoemaker kicked him in the face: "My heel contacted his throat area and the sole of my shoe hit him on the face."

Shoemaker was a Stakeout Unit cop, which meant that he had to have absorbed that unit's flaming anger over the shooting death of Officer Ramp, supposedly by a MOVE member, in 1978. Did he recognize Mumia as a MOVE sympathizer? Was the kick in the face a small form of retribution? One witness, Robert Chobert, would say a little later in the trial that Mumia, with his dreadlocks, had MOVE-type of hair. To the white population in Philadelphia, in 1981, dreadlocks on a black man was a virtual neon sign saying, "I am connected with MOVE." Shoemaker, and his partner, immediately felt that they had another MOVE killing on their hands.

"I'm shot, I'm shot," Mumia murmured after being kicked in the face.

Shoemaker called his partner over to keep an eye on their suspect—indeed, their enemy in the outrageous war against MOVE—as he walked the four feet to where Officer Faulkner lay dead, another casualty of that war, he must have thought. He looked down and saw the small hole between Faulkner's eyes, and it sickened him. Soon the entire block was teeming with movement, brightened by a confluence of flashing turret lights. Bundles of uniformed men, huddled together in clusters, formed at various spots around where Faulkner had been shot. When the police wagon arrived, Shoemaker and other officers lifted Faulkner immediately into the back of the wagon, refusing to admit to themselves the obvious, and he was then whisked away to Jefferson University Hospital.

The last thing left for McGill to do, before putting his eyewitnesses on the stand, was explain how Mumia was taken from the scene. This array of evidence was no incidental matter for the prosecution. McGill expected the defense to raise the claim that police officers brutalized Mumia at the crime scene. Police witnesses were called to give the "official" version. Mumia, they said, resisted arrest, flailing his arms and legs as officers tried to place him in a police wagon. Whereas Mumia had claimed in a police brutality complaint that cops rammed his head into a light pole like a human battering ram, police witnesses insisted that Mumia's head "made contact" with the pole as a result of his own physical aggression. That aggression also accounted for the injuries to Mumia's face, as officers claimed that they "accidentally" dropped him face first onto the pavement.

The official version was important for another reason. McGill would later bring in evidence of Mumia's supposed bellicose and insolent confession. That he had the strength and audacity to struggle against arresting officers, after having shot one of their brothers in blue, showed that he had the energy and proclivity to confess in the manner that he did. It was yet another manifestation of Mumia's utter hatred of "the system."

Before the end of that particular day, June 19, McGill would have cab driver Robert Chobert on and off the witness stand. Mumia had, in Judge Sabo's words, "behaved himself" the whole day, and the case was now proceeding quickly.

■ For the next few days the jury heard from the other eyewitnesses (Cynthia White, Michael Scanlan, and Albert Magilton), from witnesses who had information about Mumia's gun ownership, from a witness who explained that the rifling characteristics of the bullet found in the officer's brain were consistent with the rifling characteristics of the gun found eight inches from Mumia's outstretched hand at the crime scene, and from two witnesses who claimed to have heard the hospital confession. This array of evidence, discussed in Chapter Two, formed the core of the prosecution's case against Mumia, and it is that core that gave it an open-and-shut quality. Four eyewitnesses, a murder weapon, and a confession—that is what the jury had before it when the prosecution announced that it was resting its case.

But it wasn't smooth sailing getting there. Although Mumia sat as silent as a package throughout the first day of actual testimony, his quiescence was short-lived. By the third day of testimony, June 22, Mumia was again rebelling.

That morning, Jackson alerted the court clerk that he wanted to raise an issue before the jury was brought in. He went over to the railing to talk with a MOVE member who wanted to pass a message on to Mumia. The conversation was interrupted when the clerk announced that the judge would momentarily be coming into the courtroom. The MOVE members abruptly left their seats, as they always did when Judge Sabo was about to enter the courtroom, and stepped out into the corridor. Judge Sabo insisted that audience members stand when he took the bench. Anyone who refused to stand would be held in contempt and fined. Rather than give him the satisfaction of standing, the MOVE members, and others sympathetic to Mumia, left the courtroom until it was "safe" to come back in.

Jackson went over to the defense table and sat next to his client, who had been brought in a moment before the announcement. Judge Sabo then took his seat on the bench. "What's your problem, Mr. Jackson?" His tone registered that he was in no mood for posturing. Jackson was about to answer the judge, but Mumia abruptly cut in.

"*I* wanted to address you before the jury came in," Mumia declared, emphasizing that it was *his* idea, not Jackson's, to delay the proceedings. Judge Sabo had decided days earlier that he would not engage in any more repartees with Mumia; they were too exhausting and tended to bring the wheels of justice to a grinding halt. So he told Mumia that he'd have to make requests through his lawyer. That was the one thing Mumia did not want to hear.

"He's not representing me," Mumia again announced, pointing at Jackson. Judge Sabo turned away, a rude gesture that many judges resort to when they are displeased with an argument. "Judge, I want to talk to you." Mumia had chosen this moment, for no apparent reason, to reclaim control over his case—which is to say, his life.

Judge Sabo stood his ground, indicating that he too had come to an understanding within himself. "Mr. Jamal, I told you I will not talk to you. I want you to sit down." Mumia didn't budge. "I'm telling you, unless you sit down and behave yourself—"

Mumia interrupted him: "Judge, I am not being disruptive."

"You are. You are preventing me from proceeding with this trial."

Mumia continued to argue that he should be allowed to represent himself, seemingly trying to wear down the judge by sheer persistence. Never betraying a concern over being ejected, Mumia didn't so much as dare the judge to do so as exhibit a nonchalance, an immunity to Judge Sabo's exercise of judicial authority. He pressed on, at times raising his voice to the verge of breaking into shouts. He never did, however. Mumia could deliver with his mellifluous voice the most heartrending account of a sad story without maudlin displays of emotion. Listeners to his radio broadcasts and his newsroom colleagues had marveled at the gift. People in the courtroom quickly saw that this same gift allowed him to express firmness and outrage without unseemly exuberance. This frustrated the old jurist.

"I am not going to hear any more about it," Judge Sabo pleaded. "If you do not permit me to proceed with this trial right now, I'm going to have you removed from this courtroom."

"You can do what you wish to do," Mumia whispered with a heavy breath.

"That's exactly what I'm going to do."

Judge Sabo was again laying the groundwork to justify banishing Mumia from the proceedings. He knew instinctively, however, that this time the banishment would be weightier, because it would entail Mumia's absence while critical testimony was being rendered. The situation would call upon all of his experience in crafting a court record that would be looked upon favorably by the appellate judges who operated high above the hurly-burly of trial litigation. He was by no means a judicial scholar, but he knew enough to protect his record well at a moment like this.

McGill, however, was nervous. He had practiced criminal law long enough to recognize that there are very few, if any, rights that are more sacrosanct in a jury trial than the defendant's right to be present during the taking of testimony. The spirit of due process is infused with the notion that the criminal process isn't supposed to happen *to* the accused; it is supposed to happen *with* the accused. The accused is deemed a participant in the process while simultaneously its target. Due process in a criminal trial is, therefore, the melding of two goals: maintaining respect for the dignity of the accused (no matter how despicable the crime) and devising an effective method to extract vengeance. Overemphasizing the latter at the expense of the former can jeopardize a conviction.

True, the right to be present at one's own trial could be forfeited by disruptive behavior. But McGill didn't want the case of *Commonwealth v. Mumia Abu-Jamal* to be the test case on when behavior is sufficiently disruptive to justify banishing a capital defendant from his own trial. As much as he relished trying this case in Sabo's courtroom, he knew from experience and from his colleagues that he had to protect his case against the judge's tendency to go overboard with his anti-defendant gusto. He wasn't about to have this case reversed by an appellate court and sent back for retrial. Retrying a case, it is said, is akin to putting on a wet, sandy bathing suit.

McGill thus tried to broker a deal. He asked Judge Sabo to consider letting Mumia say what he had to say in the hopes that it would palliate his distemper. The judge had never had a defendant like this before. He had always been able to compel obedience by counting on the fact that he was the *judge*. It had, in a very real sense, become a contest of wills. And it would remain so for the remainder of the trial.

McGill gently prodded, and Judge Sabo, looking up at the clock and noticing that it was now well past 11:00 A.M., slowly began to back down. But Mumia would have to give in a little as well. There could be no break in the impasse unless the judge could save face. Judge Sabo agreed to consider a renewed motion for reinstatement of Mumia as pro se counsel, but it would have to be Jackson arguing it. "I will not allow him to address the court," he shouted at Jackson. "If you have a motion you want to make on his behalf, make it. You've got a motion, make it!"

Jackson desperately wanted out of the case, and he still harbored hopes that he would be liberated from the obligation, so he was arguing the motion as much for his own sake as for Mumia's. He first conveyed that Mumia's "aggressiveness" was rooted in his "sincere desire to represent himself." But more than that, Mumia had a certain outlook about what was happening around him, and *to* him, and Jackson wanted to communicate that point as well. "I believe that, under the circumstances, his aggressiveness with which he has spoken to this court with regard to his activities in this court is as a result of what he perceives to be a bias and prejudice within the system and, specifically, in Your Honor."

Judge Sabo stared blankly as Jackson continued, his arms crossed tightly across his chest, as if to immobilize himself. He tended to do that when a defense lawyer made an argument that he had no intention of taking seriously. It was unnerving to argue a point and see the judge sitting motionless like a lifeless statue; it made a lawyer feel silly. And a silly lawyer is not an effective lawyer.

Jackson asked, at Mumia's insistence, that the trial proceedings be stayed—suspended temporarily—to permit him to file a motion with a federal judge "so that he would have the issue of self-representation decided by what he considers to be an impartial and unbiased judiciary." Jackson also reminded Judge Sabo that "one black juror (Jennie Dawley) was removed for what one might consider to be mysterious reasons," and that Mumia regarded that judicial act as symptomatic of the abridgment of rights inflicted upon him. He didn't get to conduct his own voir dire, and the one juror he did select was removed literally behind his back. Those facts, Jackson argued, constituted an impairment of Mumia's right to a jury of his peers, which he should have had a hand in selecting, as well as an abridgment of his right to represent himself.

Judge Sabo, stone-faced, let Jackson speak without interruption. When Jackson sat down, Sabo's rigid features melted away and his eyes came alive, and he made a speech of his own. He complained that Mumia "does not take my rulings as a final ruling at this level." As he has said countless times to virtually every criminal defense lawyer who has ever tried a case before him, "If you don't like my ruling, you can appeal it." That was Judge Sabo's mantra, his signal that he's heard enough and wants to move on.

Hours were expended, largely against Judge Sabo's will, to cut through Mumia's insistence on having his rights respected. He acceded to McGill's entreaties to let the motion be argued extensively. He listened patiently. He had lived up to his end of the bargain. He had indulged in the charade long enough. Now he wanted the jury to come in so that the trial could continue.

"Judge, before the jury comes in I'd like to—" Mumia was again standing, his eyes fixed on Judge Sabo's.

Sabo interrupted him midsentence. "I don't want to hear from you," the angry judge fumed.

The interruption only caused Mumia to stand taller, with an almost military bearing. Courtroom observers have described him as majestic, standing erect at the defense table, straight and still, like a sturdy fence pole, with his full dreadlocks giving him a commanding presence that made him difficult to ignore. He spoke with a steady, deep baritone voice that dominated nervousness or fear. That too commanded attention, even among those who would rather not listen.

Just by the sound of the two men's voices, one could detect that Mumia had a power that Sabo could never have. Sabo was a weak-willed man; he couldn't command respect by the force of his own personality and character. Wearing judicial robes could not change that fact. But power of personhood was all Mumia could draw upon in this fight of his life. In addition, Sabo's concerns were petty in comparison to Mumia's concerns: the judge wanted to move the case along; the defendant wanted his rights acknowledged so he could present his case in a way that he saw fit.

Yet the undeniable trump card was the fact that Judge Sabo had authority—authority vested in him by the law. With that authority Judge Sabo quickly ordered Mumia to sit down.

"Judge, I have a point to make, and you can order me to sit down. You can order me thrown out of this courtroom. That's your prerogative." Like a fence post, Mumia still stood.

"Sheriff!" Judge Sabo cried out. "Sheriff, take him out!" Judge Sabo was exercising his authority but actually betraying his lack of power.

"I am *not* disrupting, Judge."

Shaking his head, Judge Sabo muttered, "I am not going to put up with it."

"I am *not* disrupting. You are disrupting *my* right to defend myself. I'm *not* disrupting." A court officer took Mumia by the elbow and he walked cooperatively to the exit. "You're playing hangman, Judge!" The turmoil was grinding everyone to pieces. The door slammed and, for a moment, one could hear birds outside chirping above the hum of midday traffic.

■ In all, Mumia was absent for about half of the trial proceedings. The *Philadelphia Inquirer* noted that "Abu-Jamal's actions in court have in many ways paralleled those of the nine MOVE defendants tried in 1979 for the death of a police officer during the shootout at MOVE's west Philadelphia headquarters. There, too, the defendants said that they did not want any lawyers to represent them, and there, too, the presiding judge ultimately ordered some lawyers to defend them anyway."

The colloquy typically sounded the same: Mumia vociferous in his insistence on representing himself; Judge Sabo ever more cantankerous in his rebukes—all contributing to an increasingly fierce straitjacketed tension. If anything, Mumia became more emboldened with each new day in the proceedings, as he soon began to hurl questions at the witnesses after Jackson completed his cross-examinations. He became more explicit in his disavowal of Jackson as his court-appointed attorney, repeatedly reminding Judge Sabo that Jackson was forced upon him against his will. A typical remark by Mumia:

Mr. Jackson is representing your *interest. He's not representing* mine. *He was employed by you, not by me. He's being paid by the court, not by me. I would like the assistance of counsel of my choice. I'm not being disruptive. I'm fighting for my life. This is my* trial. *[Judge orders Mumia removed, and the sheriff escorts him toward the door.] Your Honor, you're behaving in a way to get me killed, get me convicted, aren't you?*

The exchanges never advanced beyond Mumia's demand for recognition of rights to which he felt entitled and Judge Sabo's demand for order in the courtroom to which he felt equally entitled. It never took long before they were at loggerheads, and Judge Sabo's frustration inexorably led to Mumia's banishment from the courtroom, with the judicial order of removal increasingly sprinkled with sarcasm and less-than-dignified language from the judge ("Take a walk," was one of the judge's favorites). It was a quotidian pageantry of rebellion confronting authority. But it would later become, by the prosecution's telling, confirmatory "evidence" that the killing was no aberrational flash of anger.

■ The defense case began on June 28 with Jackson's opening statement delivered to a jury already growing weary and already won over nine days earlier by McGill's own compelling account; that McGill's opening statement was now backed up by evidence hardened the outlook of the men and women in the jury box. They were in no mood to hear a belated opening statement. Jackson had bypassed the opportune moment for that—a reflection not of considered strategy but of his unpreparedness. He spoke to the jury for only a few minutes, mostly in platitudes about the importance of keeping an open mind as the defense puts on its evidence. What that evidence would be, Jackson didn't say. In fact, he wasn't even sure. When Jackson thanked the jury for listening to his brief remarks, McGill felt secure that his good-versus-evil narrative was the only real show in town.

Jackson's shoot-from-the-hip response to the prosecution's evidence continued into the defense case. He had no firmly developed plan to counter the account given by Cynthia White, or to diminish the incriminating power of Robert Chobert's prompt on-the-scene

Mumia with his son Mazi—and a smile that reflected the promising journalism career ahead of him. 1981. COURTESY OF MUMIA ABU-JAMAL

More than a routine traffic stop—Billy Cook's Volkswagen parked in front of Officer Daniel Faulkner's patrol car at Thirteenth and Locust, on December 9, 1981. CRIME SCENE PHOTO

A puddle at the end of a stream—blood from a point-blank gunshot wound to Officer Faulkner's head. CRIME SCENE PHOTO

The parking lot through which Mumia ran to aid his brother. Was killing on his mind as he raced towards his brother, Billy Cook, who was in a scuffle with Officer Faulkner? CRIME SCENE PHOTO

Lost freedom and lost promise— Mumia being transported to court after his recovery from a gunshot wound from Officer Faulkner's gun. PHILADEL-PHIA DAILY NEWS

Fighting back—Officer Faulkner's wife, Maureen, leading a counter-demonstration against Mumia supporters. AP/WIDE WORLD PHOTOS

Thin blue line—Police Officer Daniel Faulkner, young and proud.
PHILADELPHIA DAILY NEWS

Court of public opinion—attorney Leonard Weinglass (standing)
debating prosecutor Joseph McGill (seated) at Villanova University.
PHILADELPHIA DAILY NEWS

Court of law—the author arguing in court. THE STAR LEDGER

The King of Death Row—Judge Albert F. Sabo. AP/WIDE WORLD PHOTOS

The Free Mumia movement on the move—Ossie Davis speaking at a Mumia rally in New York, 1999. AP/WIDE WORLD PHOTOS

Taking it to the streets—supporters at the April 24, 1999 "Millions for Mumia" demonstration. HARVEY FINKLE, IMPACT VISUALS

No justice, no peace—the trial and conviction of nine MOVE members for the 1978 killing of a police officer was a harbinger of tragic events, including Mumia's own entanglement in Philadelphia's judicial system and the 1985 bombing of the MOVE compound. COURTESY OF CLARK KISSINGER

Mobilizing a revamped progressive movement—Mumia's supporters listening to speakers rail against the death penalty and his conviction. HARVEY FINKLE, IMPACT VISUALS

Mumia's son Jamal in Philadelphia, August
1995. GABE KIRCHHEIMER, IMPACT VISUALS

Family members of Mumia speaking to a crowd protesting his pending
execution. August 1995. Judge Sabo later issued a stay of execution.
CHRISTOPHER SMITH, IMPACT VISUALS

A face and a cause—Mumia's case as the flashpoint for opposition to the death penalty and racism in the criminal justice system. HARVEY FINKLE, IMPACT VISUALS

The whole world is watching—protest banner in France, one of many countries with a large and active pro-Mumia support network. HARVEY FINKLE, IMPACT VISUALS

No "business as usual"—
clogging the streets,
people from around the
world descend on
Philadelphia.
AP/WIDE WORLD PHOTOS

Feelings run high—
protesters block the
entrance to ABC head-
quarters to protest the
lack of coverage of the
1995 court proceedings.
CHRISTOPHER SMITH,
IMPACT VISUALS

Thousands march for Mumia in downtown Philadelphia. GABE KIRCHHEIMER,
IMPACT VISUALS

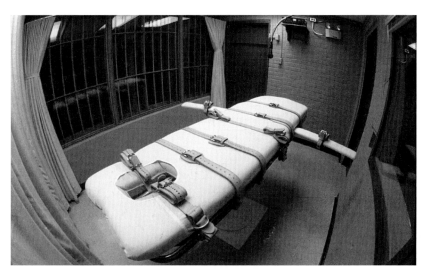

Bearing the cross—death chamber for carrying out lethal injections: the
method of choice for carrying out capital punishment in Philadelphia.
JACK KURTZ, IMPACT VISUALS

On the other side of the glass—Mumia Abu-Jamal answering questions in an interview for an HBO documentary. OTMOOR PRODUCTIONS

identification. He was so dispirited by the devastating impact of the "confession" evidence that he couldn't bring himself to think about ways to counter it. He had considered fashioning a defense that would portray Mumia as killing the officer in a momentary bout of rage—exacerbated by having been shot—but Mumia vetoed the plan. "They want me to buy into that, to say I'm crazy," Mumia complained to Jackson, referring to armchair litigators who offered advice as to how to defend the case. The best that Jackson could do, so he thought, was to hinge Mumia's defense on two witnesses—a young accounting student named Dessie Hightower, and a young prostitute named Veronica Jones—to establish the possibility that the shooter had fled the scene seconds before the arrival of police. He also hoped to demonstrate for the jury—for what purpose, Jackson never made clear—that Mumia was, in fact, intentionally abused by police when he was arrested.

Jackson's first witness was an emergency room physician, a young third-year surgical resident named Anthony Coletta. On December 9, 1981, Dr. Coletta was undergoing that rite of passage for young residency doctors: enduring long stretches of hospital duty, sometimes laboring without sleep for twenty-four to thirty-six hours. Dr. Coletta was trying to catch a few winks of sleep in the predawn hours of December 9 when his dreaded beeper went off. He had become adept at quickly shaking out the cobwebs in his head, and he knew that he had to fasten onto reality quickly now because he saw it was a trauma code. Dr. Coletta explained to the jury that a trauma code indicates that there are patients in the ER who face life-threatening injuries for which surgery may be needed. The trauma code was for Mumia.

Mumia was lying faceup, his clothes soaked in blood, when Dr. Coletta scanned his body for evidence of trauma. That is what emergency physicians are trained to do: scan the body, detect trauma, and quickly prioritize the order of treatment. Dr. Coletta, fully awake by now, immediately saw that his patient had sustained numerous traumatic blows to the body.

The most serious infliction of trauma that caught Dr. Coletta's eye was a gunshot wound to Mumia's chest, located just below the right nipple. He knew that Mumia was "on the verge of fainting," having lost a considerable amount of blood. He later determined that about a fifth of Mumia's blood had been lost.

There were other injuries of which the doctor took note. He noticed swelling over Mumia's left eye below a four-centimeter laceration on his forehead, a laceration on his left lower lip, and swelling on the right side of his neck and chin. To a lay person, it looked as if Mumia had been given a beating. To a doctor, Mumia was a victim of "blunt impact and penetrating trauma"—whether from a beating or from some fall, medical science couldn't determine definitively. In any event, it was the gunshot wound that concerned the young surgeon, and he took action to save Mumia's life. Through family intervention, he convinced his reluctant patient to submit to anesthesia. Had he not, Mumia would have died.

Jackson's questioning lingered on the issue of Mumia's facial injuries, which noticeably puzzled Dr. Coletta, who thought that the gunshot wound was the most relevant injury. Jackson wanted to prove that Mumia had been beaten at the scene by angry cops who immediately jumped to the conclusion that this dreadlocked young black man, perceived to be a member of the MOVE organization, had killed a brother officer in cold blood. While Jackson was trying to substantiate a rush-to-judgment theme in his defense, the jury didn't quite see it that way. He had not primed them for that message, leaving them alone to speculate that Jackson was doing the best he could to represent his client without any real ammunition to shoot down the prosecution's case. It was folly to expect that the jurors would, without guidance and ardent advocacy, independently arrive at a judgment that the police force, the embodiment of evil, were seeking to nail an innocent man on a capital charge.

He had lost all sense of proportion, a not atypical occurrence with a defense lawyer who hasn't mastered the art of advocacy. A trial advocate must always be guided by the jury, not by ego. A trial is no time to score points for the sake of scoring points. Something might seem extremely vital to the lawyer, but utterly trivial to the jury. *Is the jury with me on this?* a trial lawyer must ask herself constantly. *Or are these jurors letting this testimony slide by them?* Jackson never stopped to take a breath to gain a sense of perspective. Did all of this emphasis on Mumia's facial injuries, and the notion that the police beat him up, really matter to *this particular jury?*

Probably not. Had Jackson looked over at the jury, had he switched roles with them in his imagination, he would have realized that his approach conveyed the impression that the defense had nothing relevant to say about the key issue in the case: did Mumia fire those bullets into Officer Faulkner? Nor did Jackson's advocacy seek to focus attention on a genuine mystery in the case: how had Mumia been shot? The prosecution offered its theory on the matter, but it was ripe for attack, as none of the witnesses could actually account for it. Jackson failed to understand, again due to lack of preparation, that Mumia's gunshot wound could actually provide evidence to exonerate him.

Instead, Jackson's advocacy was never more vigorous than when he extracted testimony from witnesses about police handling of their prime suspect. The jury was probably right in their judgment of Jackson—he really had little to say in defense of his client. If this were a police brutality trial, Jackson might have been able to put a victory notch on his belt.

The truly important issue *was* the gunshot wound. In fact, it would become one of the most critical areas of the evidence in Mumia's struggle for a new trial. Dr. Coletta noted that the bullet had lodged in Mumia's lower back, at the twelfth thoracic vertebra. Because it had indisputably entered in Mumia's chest area, the bullet had traveled downward through Mumia's body. The bullet had passed through Mumia's right diaphragm, punctured the liver, and then come to rest on the lower spine. McGill quickly grasped the implications of this testimony, but what about Jackson? If he had, he didn't let the jury know it. McGill quickly tried to put out the fire.

The downward trajectory of the bullet through Mumia's body seemingly contradicted the prosecution's theory, derived from Cynthia White, that Faulkner fired a round as he was falling. That scenario suggested an upward trajectory, not a sharply downward one. McGill tried to guide Dr. Coletta into giving opinions that he was not equipped to render, but Jackson didn't raise any resistance. McGill first asked the doctor if he could determine "the position of the body of the defendant at the time that the gun was fired." Dr. Coletta admitted that he "would not be qualified to speculate about that." The prosecutor was satisfied with Dr. Coletta's conjecture that the bullet could have tumbled downward after ricocheting off bone. If the bullet did ricochet off bone, it would allow for the possibility that Faulkner had fired upward at Mumia as he was falling to the pavement. This "ricochet" theory should be sufficient, McGill thought, to leave Cynthia White's testimony fully intact. And McGill surely had no worries about other medical evidence presented by the defense contradicting this ricochet theory; the penny-pinching judiciary saw to that.

■ Dessie Hightower, a young accounting student at a local college, was the next defense witness. Hightower, and his friend Robert Pigford (who later became a Philadelphia police officer), were in the vicinity of Thirteenth and Locust Streets when they heard popping sounds. The two young men were in the area to pick up another associate at a local bar, but they had arrived too late. The bar had closed, so they were walking back to the car when they heard the pops. Hightower initially thought they were firecrackers, but by the third or fourth report, he realized they were gunshots.

Hightower and Pigford were across the street from the shooting. "I was able to clearly see across the street to where the incident happened," Hightower explained. He noticed a person running eastbound, toward Twelfth Street, just as he glanced in the direction of the shooting. He couldn't make out if it was a male or female. Within seconds, police units descended upon the scene. He watched the events unfold as eight or nine officers surrounded a figure sitting inert on the sidewalk. He described how the police hit and kicked this inert figure before grabbing him by the dreadlocks. They then stretched him out to transport him to a nearby police wagon, but not before ramming his head into a light pole.

A police officer summoned the two men to come closer, and

Hightower explained that he saw someone run eastward past a hotel in the middle of the block. Hightower was then escorted over to the van to look at Mumia. He saw him crouched in the van, blood thickly dripping from his forehead. He told the investigators that he couldn't say if Mumia was the shooter because he didn't see the actual shooting. Hightower and Pigford were then taken to the homicide precinct for questioning.

Jackson ended his examination on that point, mistakenly believing that he had exhausted this witness's value. Hightower had more to say, however. But Jackson didn't know that, because he had not talked to Hightower before calling him as a witness. Thirteen years would pass before Hightower would explain what else he experienced with law enforcement.

Nonetheless, Jackson secured the most important point that Hightower could offer as a witness: evidence of someone fleeing the scene immediately after shots were fired. He was confident he was going to have another witness corroborating Hightower's observation, but before he called this corroborating witness, he put the lead detective on the stand.

Detective William Thomas was, at the time of the trial, a relatively new detective. As he described it, his role in the investigation was to be the hub and the other investigators would be the spokes. It was his job to be familiar with the investigation as a whole. Jackson wanted to get more mileage out of Hightower's testimony, and he felt he could do it with Detective Thomas. He asked him a series of questions about the exploration of other leads or clues, insinuating that law enforcement officers simply assumed Mumia's guilt once they saw him at the scene, within feet of the slain officer, with an empty gun by his side. But once Jackson began inquiring into whether investigators tried to locate this fleeing person that Hightower described, McGill became nervous.

When trial lawyers get nervous, they object. Even if a bona fide legal justification for the objection is unavailable, they object anyway; the important thing is to buy some time by objecting. And that is what McGill did when Jackson asked Thomas if the fleeing person had ever been located. Even Judge Sabo, not known to be liberal in his allowance of defense attorneys to bring in marginal evidence, couldn't see the basis for McGill's objection. In fact, McGill really couldn't conjure up a coherent legal argument to bar Jackson's query. He just blurted out: "You open up one big can of worms if you permit this to continue." The evidence code has never had a can-of-worms provision to justify the exclusion of evidence. But that didn't matter to McGill. If McGill insisted, with sufficient vigor, that evidence shouldn't come in, then Judge Sabo would oblige him and rule the evidence inadmissible.

McGill was absolutely right. Over a decade and a half later, the whole issue of the fleeing person was a huge can of worms for the Commonwealth of Pennsylvania.

Jackson, of course, wasn't thinking about the long run. He had a case to try, and he knew that he had to keep pushing the point about flight from the crime scene. Detective Thomas was actually unimportant to him. It was his next witness who would enhance his theory of the case.

"The defense calls Veronica Jones to the stand." As with Hightower, Jackson hadn't talked to Jones before putting her in the witness chair. But he wasn't worried. He had a police interview report clutched between his thumb and index finger, the document dangling in the stillness of the courtroom air, when he announced her name. That police report was all he needed to feel good about Veronica Jones. After the court session the day before, Jackson confidently told reporters that he would be presenting a witness who would corroborate Hightower's account that someone had fled the scene immediately after the shooting.

Although it was summer in Philadelphia, Jones was sniffling as though it were February. Stuffy headed and lethargic from a cold, she didn't enjoy being in the courtroom. Plus she hadn't had a shower in days. Her hair was matted down, unlike the bloated Afro she wore out on the street. If she wasn't in the courtroom, she would have been nursing her cold inside her jail cell, incarcerated pending trial on a weapons and robbery charge. It was a considerable step up from her usual prostitution arrests.

She scanned the large courtroom in what appeared to be a gesture of disrespect, as if to say, "What are all of you looking at?" She immediately noticed that the spectators to her left, which was the prosecution side, were mostly white males with closely cropped hair and constipated expressions. There was nothing distinctive in their clothing, other than the fact that some were in police uniform. Jones couldn't get over how they all seemed to have dour expressions on their faces. On the right side of the spectator section, however, black men and women, with a smattering of light-skinned folks, sat with animated expressions and varied hairstyles. She knew instantly, despite her watery eyes and stuffy nose, that there were competing factions in this case: one side was for the dead cop; the other for the brother who faced execution.

And here she was, stuck in the middle.

"Good afternoon, Miss Jones." Jackson didn't give her a chance to acknowledge the greeting. "I want to direct your attention to December 9, 1981, about three-fifty A.M. Tell us where you were." Jackson dispensed with the usual introductory questions and jumped immediately to the heart of the matter.

McGill had been slow and deliberate in bringing out the important facts supporting his case. Jackson, by contrast, was peripatetic and anxious. His voice quivered and he spoke rapidly.

Jones, remarkably unself-conscious of her unkempt appearance, explained that she was working a corner on Twelfth and Locust, about three-quarters of a block from the shooting. She was a prostitute, like Cynthia White, lingering on the sidewalk to take advantage of the inebriated crowds emptying out of the closing nightclubs and bars.

"And what did you see?" Jackson casually asked, quickly glancing over at the jurors to assure himself that they were paying attention.

"All I seen was two men and a policeman."

Jackson took a step toward the witness box and looked at her with a quizzical glare. Jones sensed that this lawyer, whom she had never met, wanted her to keep talking. "I seen a policeman on the ground—what else can I say?"

Jackson wasn't sure what was happening. He peered down at the police report, now clutched tightly in his hand. What did she mean, "what else can I say?" It was all right there in this police report. All Jackson wanted from her now was to answer the question in the way he expected, which meant that she just had to tell the jury what she had told investigating detectives six days after the shooting.

On December 15, 1981, two detectives caught up with Jones at her mother's home in Camden, New Jersey, just across the Pennsylvania border. Cynthia White had told homicide investigators that Jones was in the vicinity of the shooting. Jones admitted to the two visiting detectives that she was at the corner of Twelfth and Locust Streets when she heard three shots. "I looked down Locust Street towards Johnny Dee's and I saw a policeman fall down. After I saw the policeman fall I saw two black guys walk across Locust Street and then they started sort of jogging. The next thing I saw was a wagon coming." Det. Daniel Bennett, the investigator who memorialized Jones's statement in the police report, was "positive" that Jones meant that the two men were running *away* from the scene of the shooting.

Jackson asked Jones about that day when the two detectives paid her a visit. She acknowledged that she was interviewed. That was a start, Jackson thought.

"What, if anything, did you see anyone do when you turned around and looked up Locust Street?" he probed, hoping that this woman would just spit out what was in the report.

"I didn't see anyone do nothing. *No one moved.*"

"No one moved at all?" Jackson pressed, trying to hold back the panic swelling up in his chest—the type a child feels when he senses he's lost. His head bobbed up and down, as he repeatedly looked at Jones and then at the report now held with two hands at chest level.

Jones replied, "Not that I seen, no."

Jackson asked for a sidebar, furious. The jurors weren't following the testimony anymore; they were now interested in something much more interesting, something that broke the boredom of hearing words piled upon words, hour after hour, each day followed by another. The drama now was Jackson himself. They could see from his hurried and repeated glimpses at the document in his hand and then at the witness that he was floundering and panicking. How would he swim to shore? Would he be able to?

Jackson called for a sidebar because he wanted to have the police report read to the jury, but he knew he'd have trouble from McGill and the judge. Jones was, after all, his witness, and there are strict rules against impeaching one's own witness. The only way to avoid those rules is to claim that the witness has become hostile or adverse to the party calling her to the stand. Jackson made that precise point at the sidebar conference.

"This is incredible," McGill declared.

"I am now going to plead surprise, because she is now claiming nobody moved," Jackson responded excitedly. "Mr. McGill knows from the statement what she said."

Judge Sabo was amused. "He pleads surprise," he said to McGill.

"I am going to cross-examine her!" Jackson blurted out, nearly shouting and whispering at the same time. The panicked feeling in Jackson's chest was now unleashed.

"Don't get excited," Judge Sabo cautioned. "Are you telling me you never talked to her?"

"I never talked to her, no."

Judge Sabo shook his head. Even he knew that it was virtual malpractice to put a witness on the stand without speaking to her first. Because McGill didn't seem to be objecting, Judge Sabo granted Jackson's request to impeach her with the interview statement, but he warned Jackson to keep it narrowed to that issue only. Jackson exhaled in relief.

He quickly showed Jones a copy of the police report and tried to walk her through it. But the darkened tunnel that he was in was a lot longer than he had thought. She disputed making the statements attributed to her in the report. She even denied placing her signature at the bottom of four of the five sheets comprising the report.

"How did your signature get on five sheets?" Jackson was angry, and he lost his concern over showing it.

"My mother is a witness," Jones declared, fighting back, "I signed one blank piece of paper." Jones not only disavowed seeing flight from the crime scene, she was irrationally claiming that the police fabricated a police report with an account that favored the accused. Jackson couldn't figure out what was going on.

Jackson pressed on, but to the jury and court observers, he was still floundering. Jones was supposed to be a short witness, nothing more than corroboration for Hightower. Instead, Jackson had her on the stand for what seemed like forever, hoping that he could undo the catastrophe that had befallen his plans. He gave up his efforts to get Jones to speak about flight from the crime scene when she angrily told the jury that she was a "nickel bag high" from marijuana when the detectives came to visit her.

And then, on a lark, he asked her, "Other than this one time when detectives came to your home in Jersey to interview you, had you talked to any other police at any other time?" Jackson was violating the rule—much overstated, but still worth remembering—that you don't ask a question to which you don't know the answer. But desperate times call for desperate measures, so he just threw the question out there for Jones to answer.

Veronica Jones unwittingly exposed the prosecution's underbelly. "I had got locked up, I think it was in January," she stammered. "I am not sure. Maybe February." Jones paused to think for a moment. "I think sometime after that incident. They were getting on me telling me I was in the area and I seen Mumia, you know, do it, you know, intentionally. They were trying to get me to say something that the other girl said. I couldn't do that." The revelation froze the entire courtroom; even the reporters sat motionless, trying to grasp what Jones had just said. Jackson had no idea this was coming, and he was unprepared to exploit it. Meanwhile, Jones continued to provide the defense with gifts: "It came about when we had brought up Cynthia's name and they told us we can work the area if we tell them."

McGill objected. "She is now going into facts and trying to say that the police are telling her she could work the area if they would tell us that the defendant shot the officer."

Indeed she was saying precisely that, but Jackson was so stunned he could only think to apologize. "I am not responsible for her answers," he lamely asserted. There was, of course, no reason to apologize for Jones's spontaneous revelation that law enforcement officers tried to get prostitutes to incriminate Mumia with the inducement that they would be permitted to work the streets with impunity. No one on the defense side of the case could be accused of generating this testimony, as Jackson's lackluster pretrial efforts never brought him to an encounter with any of the witnesses.

Judge Sabo recognized that Jones was now catapulting the case into a different direction, so he gave a sympathetic ear to McGill's protestations over the defense's incursion into "irrelevant" terrain. "Why are you putting her on the stand?" Judge Sabo asked. "You told me you were putting her on the stand for one purpose and that is to tell what she saw that night. Let's limit it to that."

Jackson argued that he was now entitled to use her for another purpose, in this case something far more significant for the defense. This witness, he pointed out, was now exposing the underbelly of the prosecution. The seamless narrative that White provided to the jury, which formed the bedrock to the prosecution's theory of the case, was being exposed as the product of law enforcement manipulation, and all Judge Sabo could do was rebuke Jackson for using her as a witness for evidence beyond that which he had anticipated.

Jackson's suspicions, which he had harbored since January when he first cross-examined Cynthia White, were now confirmed. He had heard that Philly cops manipulated prostitutes in criminal cases, but never had he been able to put such evidence before a jury. Now he had a witness on the stand talking about it. Jackson couldn't believe he'd even have to argue the matter. What judge in his right mind would block the defense from going down this path? Judge Sabo called a recess and ordered Jackson to "talk with" Jones.

Ten minutes later, Jackson gave a report to Judge Sabo, based upon his first and only conversation with Jones. "Just a summary of what she said," he began. "She was picked up and she believed it was in the first week of January. She was picked up by uniformed officers who took her, as well as some other people, aside and said, 'Look, we will let you work the street and we will do for you just like we have done for Lucky.'" McGill placed his palms on the table, signaling he was going to stand up. "Lucky is Cynthia White's name," Jackson explained. "The police then said to her, 'We want to ask you some questions about where you were, because we know Lucky said you were out there that night and you saw what happened,' and all of that. They told her that *if she would give a statement that backed up Cynthia White, they would let her work the street just like they were letting her work.*"

"I object to the whole area," McGill retorted, undoubtedly agitated.

"She is your witness," Judge Sabo admonished Jackson. "What she saw on Locust Street that night you can go into as thoroughly as you want to. All this other stuff is not relevant."

It was unbelievable. The judge was admonishing *Jackson* because the witness was revealing police manipulation of eyewitnesses. Jackson argued a point that he felt was beyond dispute; he was absolutely entitled to bring out this sort of evidence. But Judge Sabo insisted that he could not have a witness testify to matters that were not within the scope of what she was initially offered for.

"All this other stuff is not relevant"—how could that be!? He was stunned by the degree of Judge Sabo's obstinate bias for the prosecution. How could he rule that this evidence was not relevant!? He clenched his teeth, frustrated with having to deal with two prosecutors, one of whom wore a robe. He walked back to his chair, and just as he was about to sit down, looked up at Judge Sabo. He thought about saying something more—what, he didn't know. In the end, gravity got the better of him and he dropped down into the chair. What little fight he had inside fled the moment Judge Sabo blocked this line of inquiry. The jury would never get the full impact of "all this other stuff." The *Philadelphia Inquirer* said the events were a "blow to defense attorney Anthony Jackson and Abu-Jamal."

Jackson never could figure out the mystery of Veronica Jones. Why had she so firmly recanted what she had told detectives six days after the shooting? He would have gladly turned his back on that question if only he could have brought out the full story for the jury of police manipulation of Cynthia White. Little did he know those two facets of Jones's ill-fated moment in front of the jury were but two sides of the same evidentiary coin.

■ Jackson left court at the end of the day on June 29 wondering what he should do the next day. While about one hundred Mumia supporters marched in the rain from city hall to the site of the shooting to hold a rally, he took another look at the file and noticed a police report memorializing a statement by another witness, Debbie Kordansky. It reminded him that he had wanted to track her down weeks ago, but just couldn't find the time. It was another thing that fell through the cracks. He called McGill to tell him he wanted to call Kordansky as a witness the following morning, but that he didn't have any means to locate her, as the district attorney's office had a policy of withholding phone numbers and addresses of witnesses. McGill claimed not to have a current address but did have a phone number.

Jackson dialed the number McGill gave him and a woman answered. It was Debbie Kordansky. Jackson mumbled into the phone that he represented Mumia Abu-Jamal. Kordansky knew instantly why Jackson was calling, and she made it clear that she wanted no part of the trial. Jackson tried to be friendly, telling her that she was an important witness and that it was her obligation to tell the jury what she knew. Kordansky didn't even ponder what Jackson was saying to her. She immediately began telling him that she was in no shape to get to court.

"What do you mean?" Jackson asked.

"I was in a bike accident, my face got all scratched up. I can't do this, sir."

Jackson was dubious. He pressed her some more, his waning patience evident in the way he began snapping at her.

"Listen," Kordansky finally exclaimed, "I am afraid to tell you what I said because I really don't want to help you."

"Look, you just have to testify," Jackson insisted.

"I really don't want to help you, understand?" Kordansky wasn't kidding. "I really don't like black people. I was raped by a black man about five years ago and if I could avoid coming into court I will."

With that, Jackson laid the receiver down, gently, as if not to wake a baby. He cursed in disgust. He didn't want this damn case. Mumia didn't want him on the case. The people in the audience either thought he was a fool or a cop hater. And now he was having more witness trouble. He didn't have any money to hire an investigator to track Kordansky down. He sure wasn't going to play detective and do it himself.

The next morning, Jackson told the court clerk that he wanted a conference with the judge before the jury was brought in. McGill and Jackson went into chambers, as Judge Sabo played his usual round of solitaire before the start of the day's session.

"What can I do for you fellas?" Judge Sabo asked, laying down another card. He was quite good-natured when he was off the bench. Some lawyers who hated to appear before him even claimed that he could be downright charming. The old judge realized that the lawyers were waiting for him to put the cards down, so he put the deck atop the unfinished game and looked up at McGill. McGill leaned his head to the right, indicating that it was Jackson who wanted to speak to him. "What is it, Counselor?"

Jackson explained that he was having problems getting Kordansky to come into court. Judge Sabo wanted to know what "this girl" had to say. Jackson explained that she had described seeing someone run eastbound on the south side of Locust Street after she heard shots ring out. Kordansky was to be Jackson's third witness on that point, but he feared that he would ultimately have only Hightower testifying to it.

Judge Sabo tried to dissuade Jackson from calling her to the stand. Hearing that she didn't like black people, Judge Sabo took on a false avuncular affect and advised Jackson to dispense with her. "Maybe you are better off without a witness like that," he warned. Sabo was not giving genuinely helpful advice to a defense lawyer. In all likelihood, self-interest—in particular, ending the trial before the Fourth of July holiday—was his motivation.

Jackson disagreed. "I think I would be remiss if I did not make some further attempt to get her in court."

Judge Sabo's initial good-natured mood immediately disappeared. He wanted to move the case along. He sensed that it was winding its way toward a conclusion, and anything that bogged the process down irked him. His patience, always tenuous in the first place when it came to criminal defense attorneys, was paper thin now. He complained to Jackson that it was his fault for being in this predicament. He castigated the beleaguered lawyer for not making arrangements to bring Kordansky in weeks ago.

"I was forced into this situation," Jackson explained in defense of himself. "I can't afford and I can't pay for an investigator. I have to run around and do it. That is my problem, Judge. But I have to make an attempt to bring her in." Judge Sabo's frustration toward Jackson was irrational, akin to poking a man's eyes out and then blaming him for being blind.

It would be thirteen years before Kordansky took the witness stand in the case of *Commonwealth v. Jamal.* This jury would never hear from her. Jackson just didn't have the wherewithal—financial or emotional—to secure her attendance. The momentum of events was overcoming his will completely. An effective defense lawyer is able to stop that momentum. He is able to slow the pace of the trial down, if need be, to give his client and himself a chance to deliberate on what will come next. But Jackson wasn't acting as an effective defense lawyer at this point, or at any point in the trial. The machinery of justice was steamrolling over him.

Jackson's cynicism turned out to be correct: there would only be one witness to the fleeing person, even though he had expected that the jury would hear from four witnesses on that vital point. The jury, not irrationally, thought that one witness was the best the defense could do.

You and your attorney goofed.

JUDGE SABO

11. DECIDING ON
GUILT

Death penalty trials are unlike any other. The participants feel the difference the moment jury selection begins. The heaviness of death gives the jury selection process a lumbering quality, as people are asked to engage in quick archaeological excavations into their souls to determine whether they can be part of a process where human beings will decide whether another human being should live or die.

The process of determining guilt remains the same, except, perhaps, that the presentation of evidence is done with greater solemnity to express recognition of the gravity of the ultimate aim. In an odd way, the routinized procedures of a trial serve as a comfort to the jurors who long for some reassurance that they, mere mortals with ordinary lives, can carry out the job more appropriately assigned to Fate. The jurors are reminded, before they retreat to determine whether the prosecution has proven guilt beyond a reasonable doubt, that their verdict must be rendered without regard to punishment.

But unlike a conventional trial, a capital trial is broken into two phases. If guilt is established (in the guilt phase), then those same jurors must sit through another phase, one that is more wrenching, more ineffable, and often more contested than the former. This phase, known as the penalty or sentencing phase, is devoted to determining whether the defendant's moral worth as a human being has been so vitiated by his crime that he is no longer fit to remain among the living.

The guilt phase is often just a prelude to the penalty phase. The penalty phase is where the jury plays God.

Criminal defense lawyers are, deep down, an optimistic lot, once they are in the midst of a trial. No matter how bad it gets in a trial, they seem to cling to the idea that they can pull out an acquittal with a stellar summation, or with some Perry Mason moment. Jackson was no different. He had done little to undermine the prosecution's open-and-shut case. He had done nothing, as of yet, to attack the prosecution's "confession" evidence. He virtually conceded that the gun registered to Mumia was the murder weapon. Yet, with the trial winding down to its last two days, he had not given a moment's thought to the penalty phase.

This was a mistake. No lawyer entering into a death penalty case should look upon the penalty phase as a mere appendage to the guilt phase of the trial. It is not an afterthought. In most death penalty cases, where guilt is essentially conceded, the real fight begins in the penalty phase. But even where guilt is contested, even where hopes for an acquittal run high, even where reasonable expectations may justify such optimism, competent representation in a death penalty case mandates intense and thorough preparation for the penalty phase.

■ It was June 30, and Jackson had several witnesses lined up to testify; none, however, to attack the extremely damaging evidence of the emergency room confession. He had really put all of his evidentiary eggs in one basket—the "fleeing man" basket, if you will. That effort, in large measure, didn't pay off, with Robert Chobert and Veronica Jones both recanting their original claim to police of seeing someone run from the scene, and Debbie Kordansky unwilling to come into court. He was now scrambling with the logistical difficulties of lining up over a dozen character witnesses to testify.

In a close case, character witnesses can make a real difference. The theory behind allowing witnesses to testify as to a defendant's character is intuitive: a person with good character traits is less likely to commit a crime in defiance of those traits than one who is without them. Mumia had no criminal record. The Faulkner shooting was his only ensnarement within the web of the criminal justice system. Jackson, therefore, wasn't concerned about rebuttal testimony to the slew of character witnesses he was to call. What he didn't expect, however, was that he was doing McGill a terrific favor by marching down that road.

Jackson's first character witness was Sonya Sanchez, a poet and writer, known largely for her forays into issues of social justice in the United States. At the time she took the stand in Mumia's trial, she had been teaching at Temple University in Philadelphia for five years. Before that, she had taught at Amherst and University of Pennsylvania. Sanchez knew Mumia personally, but Jackson was compelled to stay within the narrow framework of the law and limit his questions to Sanchez's awareness of Mumia's reputation for nonviolence. She testified that Mumia "has always been viewed by the black community as a creative, articulate, peaceful, genial man." Her direct testimony lasted about three minutes.

McGill, without an obligatory greeting, went into his questioning as if a golden moment would slip through his fingers if he didn't move quickly. "Miss Sanchez, in reference to your writings, you wrote a foreword, did you not, for the book *Asata Speaks,* correct?"

Sanchez lifted her eyebrows in apparent recognition of where McGill was heading, but oblivious to the assiduity with which he would pursue his line of questioning. "That is correct," she answered simply. Asata Shakur, an ex-Black Panther who later joined the violent Black Liberation Army, had been convicted in New Jersey of killing a New Jersey State Trooper.

"Did that not deal with convicted police killer Joanne Chesimard's case?"

"Did you read it?" Sanchez replied, defensively.

"I am asking you." McGill wisely refrained from answering the witness's question.

"It has nothing to do with that at all. It has to do with her as a black woman in America."

"Were you not in sympathy with her position?"

"That is not correct. That is why I asked you, 'Did you read it?' " Sanchez answered defiantly.

"Is it a fact, Miss Sanchez, it does deal with Miss Joanne Chesimard, is that correct?"

"It deals with her as a black woman."

McGill then moved in for the clincher. "And was she not convicted of killing a policeman and is presently a fugitive from justice, is that correct?"

"I think so."

The damage was significant—even devastating: the only picture the jury had of Sanchez was of a person who seemingly supported cop killers. Is this the type of people Mumia associated with? the jurors must have asked themselves. Jackson decided to pose some additional questions to Sanchez in his redirect examination to dilute the damage done by McGill's questioning. He was hoping to give the jury a more well-rounded picture. Instead, he unwittingly brought the picture into sharper focus.

"Has there been a purpose in any of your writings to criticize the police department?" Jackson asked.

Sanchez was apparently oblivious to the dynamics of the courtroom—at least, of that particular courtroom, with that nearly all-white, predominantly male and elderly jury sitting just a few feet angled to her left. "I have written about many facets of America," Sanchez answered. "I have written about the oppression in a place called America."

"Oppression in a place called America"? McGill knew that *his* jury would not comprehend Sanchez's words, because they didn't occupy Sanchez's universe; they didn't share her outlook or embrace her political commitments. "Oppression in a place called America" to this jury was nothing more than sloganeering by people who wanted to do away with the blessings of American liberty. This "place called America" was their home, and it was, in their minds, the envy of the world. Attacking "this place called America" was tantamount to attacking the jurors' own identity.

Sanchez continued: "I teach also at Gratorford Prison. I teach young men in prison and have also talked to the guards there. You cannot talk about America without talking about oppression and the police department and the courts."

McGill wasn't going to belabor the point, but he stood up to cross-examine Sanchez again to reinforce the threatening message. "When you are talking about *oppression* in your answer to Mr. Jackson, the question is simply, are you including oppression by police on black people?" McGill didn't know what the answer would be, but the answer mattered little. Sanchez tersely replied, "By everyone."

And so it went for hours. A few minutes of direct examination in which, as if by rote, each of the fifteen character witnesses vouched for Mumia's nonviolent reputation, was followed by lengthy cross-examinations calculated to portray Mumia as a political radical who viewed law enforcement, and governmental authority generally, as the enemy of black people. At several points, McGill attempted to introduce that one item of evidence that he was unable to bring out earlier at the bail hearing: that mysterious newspaper article, which he felt would crystallize this theme and would make sense of this entire sordid affair—make sense of the killing, the confession, the courtroom outbursts, all of it. Though not a legal scholar, and never one to give the defense the benefit of the doubt on an evidentiary ruling, Judge Sabo instinctively recoiled at the attempt to bring in the newspaper article. He felt that McGill had enough to secure his conviction and death sentence, and he wasn't going to let McGill's thirst for more risk a reversal years down the road.

■ Jackson must have been astounded. There, buried in the file, was a police report that he had completely forgotten about. How could that have happened, given what the report contained? He could only blame it on the fact that he had just been too overwhelmed with the sheer volume of material in the case and his assumption, which he harbored right up to the start of the trial, that he would not be trying the case. He went into court on July 1 armed with the report and dedicated to making one more request of the judge, perhaps his most urgent request to date—a request even Judge Sabo surely would not deny.

McGill was thrilled when he walked into court. The guilt phase of the case was going to be over by the end of the day. Notes for his closing argument were tucked away in his briefcase. He could give the closing argument in his sleep. Those he had delivered to other juries, in less notorious murder cases, served as the template for this one. Guilt was a lock, he thought. Never had he had such an overwhelming case of guilt. McGill had his eyes set on the penalty phase.

Jackson nudged McGill at the prosecutor's table. "Joe, we gotta see the judge." McGill asked Jackson what for, but Jackson refused to say. "We gotta, that's all," he said.

"Your Honor, there is another matter I would like to bring to your attention," Jackson announced in the judge's chambers. He waited for the judge to say something, and discerning that the judge was waiting on him to say more, Jackson cleared his throat to explain. "We have now found there is another police officer that we would like to have testify."

Predictably, Judge Sabo wanted to know what this officer would say. He reacted to Jackson's statement not as a request but as a signal that the defense was seeking a delay in the trial. He was not inclined, to say the least, to allow for more delay, as he too had grown weary of the trial. Jackson explained that Officer Gary Wakshul was one of several officers who brought Mumia into the emergency room on December 9.

"So?" Judge Sabo impatiently interrupted. Jackson continued to explain that this officer had signed a police interview statement. "So?" the judge interjected again.

Jackson knew by the judge's impatient tone that he was going to have trouble. "The statement indicates, Your Honor, that . . . well, it says: 'During this time the Negro male made no comment.' " Jackson could barely get the words out. He felt a tightness in his chest, as it was clear to him that the judge was upset by this news. Wakshul was with Mumia when he supposedly twice blurted out the confession, Jackson explained, and yet he informed investigators that Mumia had said nothing. Sabo registered no reaction to indicate that he understood the import of what Jackson was saying. McGill, however, knew exactly what Jackson was driving at.

Jackson was about to enter a litigation twilight zone.

"He is not around," McGill informed the judge. "I am going to object to bringing this guy in. He is not around. I am not bringing him in at the last minute." Jackson was puzzled by McGill's hostility. He had been aggressive throughout the trial, but not hostile—not toward him, at least. But now there was a discernible edge to his voice.

Judge Sabo nodded in agreement. "You knew about this before. I am not going to hold up this trial."

Jackson protested, confessing that he had been unaware of Wakshul's statement. "I was forced to try and remember everything that everybody said and I couldn't do it," he admitted. It was a replay of Jackson's remarks on April 29. He had pleaded desperately with Judge Ribner then to give him some help by appointing a second attorney on the case. He had openly admitted that he was in over his head, with pretrial hearings and trial a little over a month away. And then, two weeks later, Mumia took the burden away from him by opting to represent himself. Judge Sabo himself told Jackson that he could now relax, because being backup counsel was really no big deal. When he was unexpectedly thrust back into the lead counsel role, the jury had already been selected and testimony was about to begin. It was enough just to keep his head above water, preparing for the next day's proceeding the night before, with six-day-a-week court sessions. He just didn't have the time or energy to digest all of the nearly two hundred police reports in the file. Couldn't Judge Sabo, in the interests of justice, just cut him a break?

Judge Sabo remained unmoved. "I am not going to delay the court," he reiterated. In any event, Judge Sabo averred, the statement was ambiguous. "I don't know what he means by this. 'During this time the Negro male made no comments.' That may be as far as he is concerned. Look, there were a lot of police officers in that room. There were other people that were there that may not have heard it."

Judge Sabo was missing the point. Frustrated, Jackson tried to explain that this wasn't a situation where a police report reflected an *omission* of a fact. "Judge, he didn't say, 'I didn't hear anything.' He said, 'He made no comments.' "

"It doesn't mean it wasn't said," Judge Sabo snapped back. That the jurors were the ones who properly should be evaluating Wakshul's statement was lost in the exchange. Judge Sabo had a penchant for tendentious reasoning to defeat an argument by a defense lawyer, and it was coming into play with full force now. "He didn't hear it as far as he is concerned. He can't speak for everybody else that is in that room. I am not going to delay the case any longer."

McGill gently offered reinforcement to Judge Sabo's anxiety to complete the trial, noting that the July Fourth holiday was fast approaching. It was a Thursday. The upcoming weekend was the holiday weekend, in the cradle of American liberty. "You could have had this man long ago," Judge Sabo stated with finality. "I am not going to delay the case anymore. There has been enough delay."

Earlier in the trial, the judge had suspended the trial proceedings for a half day to allow a white male juror to take a civil service exam. That delay didn't count, presumably because this juror, unlike Jennie Dawley, was deemed favorable to the prosecution.

Jackson refused to quit. He knew that he had to do something about that alleged confession, and he felt terrible in overlooking Wakshul's report. A man's life hung in the balance. He wasn't too exhausted to forget that. Trying to make the point that his request to bring Wakshul in to testify really didn't entail much of a delay at all, Jackson asked, "How long is it going to take to get a police officer here?"

"How do I know? He could be on vacation." Vacation? Why would Judge Sabo offer that conjecture? Was he privy to information that was unavailable to the defense?

Judge Sabo called a short recess, ostensibly to allow McGill to inquire about Wakshul's availability. McGill picked up the courtroom phone and chatted in a low voice. He placed the receiver down and Judge Sabo motioned for the court reporter to begin typing.

"Your Honor, I have made efforts to find out where Officer Wakshul is and I am informed that he is on vacation until July 8." Judge Sabo's conjecture—was it conjecture?—turned out to be correct.

Jackson continued to press. "Well, does that mean he is not in the city? Can we call him at home? Maybe he's still in the city."

Judge Sabo could only shake his head. He had never seen Jackson so insistent. He had, up until then, looked upon him as a team player in the judicial system: make an application, state your reasons, and then accept the ruling of the court. This sort of persistence could earn Jackson a bad reputation, which would jeopardize future court appointments on criminal cases.

"I am not going to go looking for anybody now," Sabo growled. "I have reached an end to my patience with this nonsense."

That was the end of it. Jackson knew that he wasn't going to get this witness on the stand. Like Kordansky, Wakshul never appeared in front of the jury. He finally did take the stand in the case of *Commonwealth v. Jamal* over a decade later. Jackson had no way of knowing it at the time, but Wakshul was a far more explosive witness than he could have ever imagined. And on top of that, he was in Philadelphia, just a phone call away.

Mumia wasn't privy to the events in chambers that morning. It was nearly noon on July 1 when the proceedings resumed in open court. The defense had no other witnesses. It now came time for the most difficult decision a defendant must make—whether to testify. Judge Sabo asked Mumia if he intended to take the stand. He and McGill expected that this highly intelligent defendant, a man who had made a name for himself in the communication business, the voice of the voiceless, would sit in the witness chair and explain how it is that he found himself slouched on the curb with a gunshot wound to the chest, just a few feet away from a dead police officer. Mumia stood up and glared at the judge.

"My answer is that I have been told throughout this trial, from the beginning of the trial, the inception of the trial, that I had a number of constitutional rights. Chief among them the right to represent myself. The right to select a jury of my peers. The right to face witnesses and examine them based on information they have given. Those rights were taken from me." Mumia paused and looked over his shoulder at the black faces in the audience, at the people who had become his brothers and sisters in MOVE. He continued but it was clear he was now speaking not to the judge but to everyone in the room. "It seems the only right that this judge and the members of the court want to confer is my right to take the stand, which is no right at all." Mumia's voice then began to rise. "I want *all* of my rights, not some of them. I don't want it piecemeal, I want my right to represent myself and I want my right to make a closing argument. I want my rights in this courtroom because my life is on the line."

Jackson stood as soon as Mumia took his seat. He announced, "The defense rests."

Mumia catapulted to his feet. "The defense does *not* rest!" Mumia exclaimed. He wanted to know why Officer Wakshul was not slated to appear. Mumia understood fully that a failure to rebut the confession evidence would destroy any hope of an acquittal. He also couldn't stomach the rank outrageousness of it. He refused to let the police frame him without a fight.

Judge Sabo said it was "impossible" for Wakshul to come in, because "the officer is on vacation."

Mumia scrambled through documents strewn on the table, and, locating what he was looking for, pointed to it. "On here it says no vacation," Mumia countered. A typewritten notation on Wakshul's police report of December 9, a notation that Jackson had overlooked, contained the reference "no vac" on the top of the first page. The judge waved that point off, pointing out that he had "the right to ask for him before and you didn't do it." Mumia thundered, "I had a right to represent myself, but you stopped that, didn't you?"

"Your attorney and you goofed," Sabo answered back, too embroiled in the exchange to notice the cruelty in the remark. Mumia had been fighting throughout the trial for his right to control his own defense, resulting in numerous expulsions from the courtroom, but instead he had foisted upon him an unprepared, overwhelmed, and unwilling advocate who simply dropped the ball in failing to subpoena Wakshul. Now Judge Sabo was telling him that he'd have to accept the consequences—the deadly consequences—of Jackson's dereliction. "You stole my right to represent myself," Mumia retorted.

Judge Sabo was completely sucked into the argument. "You did by your own actions."

"By fighting to defend myself, I stole my right? That is a lie, Judge."

The whole process was a lie in Mumia's eyes. He had always insisted on his innocence. The eyewitnesses saw him run across Locust Street—that much they got right. But in the darkness, illuminated only by a red flashing and twirling bulb on top of Officer Faulkner's patrol car, they had missed the fact that he was felled by a bullet when he came within a few feet of the officer, stepping toward the curb with the officer slightly elevated on the sidewalk. Cynthia White, the most damaging of the prosecution's eyewitnesses, was a liar; she was a prostitute who was induced to lie, and when a witness, Veronica Jones, was about to blow the lid off that dirty little secret, Judge Sabo kept the lie packaged up. And now, as Mumia saw it, the most brazen of all of the lies, the "confession" in the emergency room, was immune from attack because an officer with an opposing story was supposedly away on vacation.

"I am not going to allow this court to proceed to lynch me without speaking in defense of my life. Damn!" Members of the audience began shouting in support. Jackson held his head in his hands, shocked that even Sabo, the most notoriously unfair trial judge in the courthouse, which was not an easy distinction to earn within Philadelphia's criminal justice system, would descend this low in railroading Mumia. He wouldn't even allow a simple phone call to Wakshul's home when it was obvious that Mumia desperately needed this witness. "I know you want to kill me," Mumia continued. "It has been made abundantly clear."

◼ Closing arguments are the crown jewel of the trial lawyer's craft. Many trial lawyers like to think of closing argument as a time of oratory; a platform for eloquence and brilliance to penetrate the seemingly impenetrable logic erected by the opponent's stack of evidence; an opportunity to bring coherence to the myriad pieces of information extracted from witnesses, question by question, forged through evidentiary injunctions that act as minefields to the trial lawyer as he tries to reach his destination. But the truly great summation is something far more sublime. Yes, it must be disciplined by logic and constrained by reason. Yes, it must be uplifting, imbued with the passion of an ardent advocate who genuinely believes in his client and in his client's cause. Yet—and this is difficult for most trial lawyers to accept—he or she must become invisible.

Invisible? But it is my moment to shine, says the trial lawyer. It is my chance to persuade that jury of the justness of my client's cause. It may very well be my only chance to save my client from the gallows. How can I become invisible!? The trial lawyer must strive to have the jury forget that it is the skilled and silver-tongued lawyer speaking of injustice; the jury must *feel* the injustice itself, unmediated by oratory and eloquence. It is an art form, carried out through a cultivated skill, not unlike the skill of a virtuoso musician who becomes invisible as the audience is swept away by the music.

Anthony Jackson stood in front of the jury, not too close, lest he intrude on their space. He had not earned the right to approach those men and women with an air of intimacy. He wouldn't admit it; he couldn't admit it at that moment, but he knew deep down that his client faced an inevitable conviction. The jurors themselves likely knew that Jackson, deep down, knew this basic truth. Not on some conscious level, but deep inside their souls, they could sense the vibes of resignation coming through Jackson's words. *Jackson apologized to the jurors.* Some watched him with dour expressions; others with crossed arms and stiffened shoulders. He hadn't even allowed himself to say anything about the evidence, or about Mumia, or about the spectacles that they, the jury, had witnessed throughout the trial. He apologized for the slow pace of the trial, betraying his own sense of relief that his ordeal was about over. "This trial has now come to an end. I am sure most of you and many of you said, 'Thank God.' " Fifteen days had passed since those jurors assembled to hear the evidence.

If the trial was an ordeal, it was such because of Mumia. An apology for the plodding pace, and expressing relief that it is over, served only to isolate Mumia in that courtroom. His own lawyer, probably without awareness, had abandoned him within the first minute of the closing argument. And that abandonment, unwitting as it probably was, underscored Jackson's more conscious abandonment of the case on May 13 when he pleaded unsuccessfully with the judge to cut him loose from the case.

Mumia had spent much of his energy during the trial trying to expose the betrayal of American justice. It was not so much an ordeal from the defense perspective as it was a challenge to the ethical underpinnings of the system. Jackson would never reveal whether he ever allowed himself to understand that. He told the jurors, even before discussing the evidence, that they could be proud of this system of justice of which they were now a part as direct participants. "We in America, unlike many other countries, are fortunate in that we are here today as a result of the struggles of a number of people, people that we don't know and people perhaps that we have never even read about who have fought and died to make this system work." Whether the jury agreed with this politician-like verbal applause for American justice didn't matter. Jackson was not speaking *for* his client; he wasn't giving voice to his client's cause. His talk of the greatness of American justice did not spring forth from truths borne in the contest that took place in the courtroom, right before the jury's eyes.

Jackson continued with the point: "It may seem kind of strange to you when I say to you that Mr. Jamal, aside from the fact he was arrested, is indeed fortunate, fortunate in an ironic kind of way. When I say he is fortunate, he is being tried in America in a courtroom, in an American courtroom." Strange, indeed. The point, if anything, actually seemed to underscore the idea that his client's political harangues were irrational, and thus, by extension, that he was capable of irrational acts of violence. It was an odd point as well, given that an American courtroom is one of the few places in the Western world where a defendant is exposed to the death penalty.

The first half of Jackson's summation consisted of meaningless platitudes that did nothing to help Mumia. For example, against the mountain of evidence presented by the prosecution, Jackson pitted the presumption of innocence. He argued that the presumption of innocence is genuine evidence from which the jury could acquit. Literally true, but the words were empty, drained of spirit and blood. It was shallow, a manifestation of absolutely no preparation and commitment to the case, to insist that some lofty legal principle could eviscerate the evidence presented by the prosecution.

The final half of Jackson's summation urged the jurors to question Cynthia White's credibility, noting her vulnerability to police pressure, and highlighted discrepancies in the eyewitness testimony. "Looking at the inconsistencies in the evidence, you'll know that Mumia Abu-Jamal did not shoot Officer Faulkner," he asserted. He suggested that perhaps the police jumped to the conclusion that Mumia was the culprit based upon his reputation as a trenchant critic of the police. "Did they want Jamal because he is a well-known journalist, primarily in the black community?" he asked rhetorically. The jurors stared back blankly. Where was the evidence for that thesis? How does that explain the prompt on-the-scene identifications? These were questions McGill would later thrust upon the jurors. As for the confession, Jackson implied that Mumia, facing death on the emergency room floor, falsely implicated himself to protect his brother. "When he thinks he's dying, would love of your brother allow you to say that you were the one who did the shooting?" Jackson asked.

Some of Jackson's points respecting the troublesome nature of the eyewitness testimony were valid, if not astute, but they were delivered with a mind-numbing tone, almost as if he were reading a shopping list. He had no coherent story line about what happened on the night in question; he had no deep understanding about his client or the social backdrop to the investigation. He was presenting a grab-bag closing argument, offering a menu of choices to justify an acquittal, hoping that the jurors would be enticed to select just one. It had the trappings of a closing argument, but not the substance of persuasive rhetoric. As a criminal defendant facing the death penalty, Mumia was not constitutionally entitled to persuasiveness. He received the accoutrements of due process, and that was more than many of his brothers and sisters on death row had received.

Most importantly, as Jackson ended his closing argument it was plain that he had never taken away the momentum McGill acquired after he addressed the jury in his unopposed opening statement. There never was any question who stood for good and who embodied evil. The trial had worked out beautifully for McGill. His evidence had been contested by a criminal defense lawyer, giving it a veneer of legitimacy. A jury assumes, for it can hardly assume otherwise, that when evidence is challenged by the defense, it could not have been challenged more thoroughly. A jury does not know what it cannot know—that other evidence that could counter the prosecution's case exists outside of what they heard in the courtroom.

When McGill began his closing argument, he reinforced the point, telling the jury that the defense had had the prosecution's file at its disposal, a right accorded a defendant to permit the fair challenge of the prosecution's evidence. He was essentially echoing Jackson's American-justice-is-great theme. The prosecution's evidence had been challenged in the way the great American justice system says that it should be, and he wanted the jury to understand that. Jackson had given it his best shot and he could do no better—not for lack of skill or preparation but because his client was manifestly guilty and the evidence was too compelling to rebut. The jury was now privy to all of the relevant information bearing upon the guilt-innocence inquiry, as the defense had the wherewithal to present its own evidence of innocence, if such existed. McGill wanted the jury to appreciate that fact as well. Only then can the jury truly hold in appropriate esteem the value of that evidence, for the prosecution's case had withstood a robust challenge, thereby endowing it with a power from which there was no escape.

McGill had been shrewd throughout the trial, but at times that shrewdness led him to deliver low blows. He told the jury that it could acquit the defendant and there would be "nothing that anyone could do about it." Acquittal, McGill argued, was an "immense power" that the jury retained, and like all immense power, it must be used with restraint. McGill was undermining the scope of the presumption of innocence and the unique judicial calculus that is the hallmark of American justice: it is better that ten guilty go free than one innocent be convicted. The finality of an acquittal, McGill argued, must be weighed against the fact that "if you find the defendant guilty . . . there would be appeal after appeal after appeal." McGill was arguing that caution should be exercised in favor of conviction, not acquittal; that it was better to err on the side of the prosecution, because that sort of mistake might be remedied by some appellate court at some future date.

The low blows continued. Throughout the trial, McGill graciously advised Judge Sabo on ways to mitigate the prejudice associated with the acrimonious exchanges between Mumia and the judge. McGill and Judge Sabo shared a desire to "protect the record" against an appellate reversal. But McGill felt no constraints in making use of Mumia's difficulties with the judge as a fulcrum for generating sympathy for Officer Faulkner and outrage over Mumia's "arrogance and defiance." Mumia's dogged insistence on his right to represent himself, and his repeated reminder that he was on trial "for his life," became the focal point of McGill's advocacy.

"Let me tell you this, let me make this clear," McGill enunciated slowly, moving down the railing. "You have heard constantly, constantly you have heard about the facts that this defendant is on trial for his life. You have heard this all the time." The bitterness in McGill's tone revealed the depth of his disgust at Mumia's courtroom behavior. "Let me add this. Will you understand that this defendant is on trial for taking somebody's life, too. That is one thing we hadn't heard much about."

This was utter nonsense. The whole trial was about the accusation against Mumia for "taking somebody's life." But McGill didn't pause for the jury to consider the absurdity of this point. It was only a bridge to the emotional chord McGill wanted to strike: "It may be true and indeed it is true that Daniel Faulkner on December ninth, at three-fifty-eight as he looked up at the barrel of this gun, did not have an opportunity to ask for any type of counsel, or to make any type of abusive remarks in relation to anybody, the system, the laws, or anything. No one quickly ran down and said, 'Do you want an attorney? Do you want something? Do you want this? Do you want that?' He was just shot in cold blood with this weapon."

The two mutually reinforcing images were compelling: on one mental screen was a helpless police officer, looking up at a gun-wielding angry black man dedicated to destroying American values, and on the other, Mumia Abu Jamal at the center of numerous court-room spectacles where judicial authority and the legitimacy of the system were under verbal assault. Mumia's struggle for recognition of his rights, his quarrels with the judge, were now the organizing force to the evidence against him. McGill's strategy was coming into sharper focus, and it would later dominate the proceedings when McGill turned to advocating death. This was no spur-of-the-moment killing. To understand the evidence, McGill was saying, you must understand who Mumia is; and who this man is was displayed in the well of the courtroom throughout the trial proceedings.

Why else would Officer's Faulkner's brain be shattered with a high-velocity Plus-P bullet that explodes upon contact? That Mumia would have Plus-P bullets was consistent with his attitude toward authority—those bullets destroy, and that was the essence of Mumia's radical political sentiments: destruction of the white power structure, of the status quo. Why else would Mumia blurt out a profanity-laced confession that boasted of a cruel assassination? Only an arrogant and disciplined warrior could muster the bravado to do this in the company of scores of police officers while lying vulnerable on an emergency room floor with a potentially fatal gunshot wound to the chest. Mumia was no ordinary street thug. To McGill, the confession revealed that Officer Faulkner was a casualty of a certain kind of war, and that war would, three years later, lead to the highly publicized and much criticized bombing of the Osage Avenue MOVE residence. Whereas Jackson's closing argument had no resonating theme, Mc-Gill's closing packed a wallop derived from a tightly drawn portrait, the accuracy of which was seemingly irrelevant to this prosecutor, this judge, and this trial process. The important fact was that this portrait was tailor made for this nearly all-white blue-collar jury.

The actual eyewitness evidence was really an afterthought, a form of confirmation of what the jury already believed to be the case. That is why McGill reserved his discussion of the eyewitness evidence for later in the closing argument. McGill understood the rhetorical value of imprinting an image on the minds of the audience before launching into the more logical aspects of an argument. The mental image, the picture of a helpless cop looking up at an antiauthoritarian black radical poised to blow his brains out, fertilized the emotional soil from which "rational" justifications for conviction would grow.

"What you have, ladies and gentlemen, is an individual who was observed by the witnesses and who never left the scene." Four witnesses! None of those four, McGill emphasized, had any motive to implicate an innocent man in such a barbaric act. "What more compelling identification testimony would you need than that?" McGill airbrushed out of his rendition of the evidence the confusion that must have suffused the scene, with witnesses looking upon events through a flashing turret light atop a patrol car. McGill glossed over the discrepant physical descriptions of the shooter, and the evolving narrations about what was supposedly observed. These nuances were precisely that: nuances that had no significance in the face of *who* the defendant was. It was enough to fasten upon the fact that four witnesses observed Mumia dart toward Officer Faulkner, and that seconds later, a dark figure stood over the uniformed young man, bent over him and fired the Plus-P bullet into his brain. Mumia never left the scene, McGill repeated over and over. "That is the type of evidence that you may well find compelling."

The only thing left for McGill to do, as he wound his way to a conclusion, was to rally his audience. It is not enough to *convince*. The trial lawyer ultimately must *persuade*, must induce action in others, which is a far more difficult thing to do. Because the jury will eventually assemble in a small room with a mandate to take action, trial lawyers must find a way to rally the jury to *act*. "This is one vicious act," McGill said with controlled anger, crouching down on the floor and looking up to reenact the horror that Faulkner must have experienced, seeing a gun pointed at his face. "This is one uncompromising, vicious act. This is one act that the *people* of Philadelphia, *all of them*, all of you everywhere are outraged over." McGill wanted the men and women in that jury box to understand that they were being watched, that their actions would be judged by their fellow citizens. "This act demands action! Responsibility and courage!"

The jury was asked to do something for the "people of Philadelphia." How could they resist that plea?

■ The following day, Friday, July 2, 1982, didn't begin well for Jackson. He was awoken at 6:30 A.M. by fire engines parked in front of his house. Apparently, and it wasn't the first time during the trial, someone falsely reported a fire at his home. After resolving matters with disgruntled firefighters, Jackson readied himself for the day. He stopped by his office shortly before 9:00 A.M., fully expecting to make it into Courtroom 253 by 9:30. He then received a call from his fifteen-year-old son just as he was about to trudge over to the courthouse. His son had received a threatening phone call, apparently a threat of kidnapping. Jackson tried to keep calm as he instructed his son to get over to his grandmother's home. His son called back a couple of minutes later. He had received another call, from a different person but with a similar message. Jackson rushed over and took his son to his grandmother's.

It was remarkable that Jackson was able to keep enough focus to sit through the soporific verbiage that precedes jury deliberations. Before juries are allowed to evaluate the evidence—they are constantly reminded during the trial not to come to any conclusions until deliberations begin—they must receive instructions on the legal principles applicable to a case. Such instructions generally fall into two categories: first, the judge explains the general principles that operate in all criminal trials, such as the burden of proof and the presumption of innocence; second, the judge sets forth the particular elements of a crime, each of which the prosecution must prove beyond a reasonable doubt.

Shortly after 11:00 A.M., Judge Sabo began delivering the instructions on the law to a jury anxious to begin deliberating. At 11:48 A.M., the twelve men and women assembled in a room and began discussing what they had seen and heard in the courtroom. Meanwhile, Mumia sat alone in his cell, writing and waiting. Jackson and McGill also waited, passing the time nervously in their own ways. They waited for about six hours, with a startling intercession before the verdict was rendered. The jury had sent in a note, at 2:30 P.M., asking for further clarification on the law of manslaughter. The note signaled that the jury was beyond the whodunit question. Perhaps, the note implied, Mumia was guilty of manslaughter, and not murder, because he had killed the officer in a state of uncontrolled rage, induced by the maltreatment of his brother. It was a stretch. Whoever killed Officer Faulkner committed an act that appeared to be the quintessence of first-degree murder. Was the requested reinstruction on manslaughter simply a bump in the road on the way to a guilty verdict for murder in the first degree?

The jury foreman, George Ewalt, a telephone lineman and Vietnam veteran activist, stood up and looked to the court clerk for guidance. He had been chosen foreman by the others in the jury room because he seemed able to keep the discussions organized. The jurors never questioned in their deliberations that Mumia was the man who pulled the trigger to his .38 revolver which propelled the bullets that struck the young officer, once in the back and once between the eyes. They had spent some time debating whether the tricky element of premeditation—a key ingredient to a first-degree murder charge—had been established beyond a reasonable doubt. When Judge Sabo reinstructed the jury on the law of manslaughter and the varying degrees of murder, he accurately told the jury that premeditation can be formed in an instant. That clarification put the deliberations back on track, leading to the announcement of the verdict.*

With a slow cadence, the clerk asked the jury foreperson if the jury had reached a verdict on the weapons possession count. Whether the clerk inquired of the trivial weapons possession count for dramatic effect or simply out of convention is unclear. Everyone, of course, wanted to know about the first-degree murder count. Ewalt punctured the drama, so anxious was he to announce the verdict. "Guilty of murder in the first degree," he said. No one in the courtroom had trouble hearing the announcement. Propriety, of course, is the bedrock of solemnity, so the clerk again asked Ewalt to announce the verdict on the weapons possession count. With that guilty verdict announced, Ewalt was then given the green light to announce, once again, the jury's verdict adjudging Mumia Abu-Jamal a cop killer.

"The initial response to the verdict was one of uncharacteristic calm for a courtroom that has seen as much turmoil as Courtroom 253 has during the month-long Abu-Jamal trial," one reporter wrote. Maureen Faulkner wept quietly with her hands clasped tightly together. On the other side of the aisle, Lydia Wallace, Mumia's sister, put her hand on her mother's lap. Edith Cook was visibly ashen; her precious son—the one who always unabashedly showered her with love, the one who refrained from eating meat because it was too decadent and itself the product of violence against other living creatures, the one who cared little for conventional success because too many continued to suffer the sting of poverty and loneliness, the one who she looked to with distinct pride—the precious baby who she brought into the world and strived to protect against the psychic wounds of

*My understanding of what occurred during the deliberations derives from interviews of actual jurors.

poverty; this young man who had lived his life to get to this point had been adjudicated a convicted murderer.

Mumia was sitting deep in his chair, his legs crossed, torso curled and his face tightened, as the verdict was read. Was it anger, or just holding back the hurt, that caused him to sit motionless for the entire ten minutes that it took to record the verdict? When the deputy sheriffs moved in to escort him out of the courtroom, he rose gingerly from his chair and looked out toward the audience. He exclaimed: "Ona Move! Long live John Africa! This system is finished!" His defiance revealed nothing about how he was really feeling.

It was the end of the day on a Friday of a holiday weekend. Judge Sabo called the lawyers to the bench and gave them a choice: start the penalty phase immediately (meaning, that very night) or begin promptly the next morning. "What is your pleasure, gentlemen?" he asked, evidently pleased with the outcome. Jackson was too emotionally winded to respond. He'd had enough of Judge Sabo, McGill, *and* Mumia. He wanted the whole ordeal over. McGill, noticing Jackson's reticence, chimed in, "Judge, I think the first thing tomorrow morning would be in order." There would be no respite for Jackson to collect his thoughts on how to advocate for Mumia's life. He had done no preparation, absolutely none, for the penalty phase. He had no witnesses lined up. He had no strategy in mind. The jury would decide whether Mumia should live or die, but it would not receive meaningful assistance from Anthony Jackson. Thirteen years later, when asked how he passed the time that evening, Jackson confessed that he had no memory of it.

Jackson walked past the railing and into the spectator section on his way to the courtroom exit. Suddenly shouting jolted him like an unexpected slap in the face, causing him to stop midstride. "You're a traitor," MOVE member Jeanette Africa screamed. "You're going to pay for this!" Jackson had put up with a lot of berating for the past month, and he had kept his own feelings bottled up in order to forge ahead with his unwanted duty. But, with his emotional guard down, this particular verbal attack especially stunned him. Others joined in the screaming, angered by his failure, as some were saying, to "get off the case." Jackson tried to get to the exit door. Jeanette Africa quickly moved toward him and bumped into him. "Don't touch me!" Jackson warned, speaking for the first time in response to the screaming. The brief outburst uncorked his pent-up emotions. He collapsed onto a seat and began to cry. Jeanette Africa continued to shout obscenities at him.

Reporters observed the scene with dismay. They felt sympathy for Jackson, a man who, from their vantage point, had tried his best to help a totally ungrateful client. They saw from their spectator seats Mumia's open disdain for "this shyster," his repeated castigation and insults. He toiled in the barren fields of a criminal courtroom, doing a thankless job, and in the end, he was reduced to tears by a barrage of insults. And tomorrow he would have to convince this same jury, in this hostile milieu, to spare Mumia's life.

After the supporters and Mumia's family emptied out of the courtroom, the Faulkner family and police officers quietly celebrated, hugging each other and shaking hands. McGill, meanwhile, met the waiting news reporters outside: "I'm especially proud of the courage of the jury. To stand up to the shouting, the antics that have gone on in this courtroom, takes something special. I'm also very proud of the way the Faulkner family has stood up to this—they're a fantastic example to all people. They kept their cool at all times, even when they were being abused inside and outside the courtroom." McGill's comments appeared underneath banner headlines the following morning: "Abu-Jamal Found Guilty of Murder."

Political power grows out of the barrel of a gun.

MAO TSE-TUNG

This decision today proves neither my guilt nor my
innocence. It proves merely that the system is finished.

MUMIA ABU-JAMAL AFTER THE JURY'S VERDICT

12. DECIDING ON DEATH

How juries decide cases is shrouded in mystery, and, it seems
to me, it should be so. Researchers, however, have expended
considerable effort to penetrate the mystery of jury decision making
in capital cases precisely because the question to be resolved is so
profound. Their published studies, therefore, are important not simply
because they examine a highly unique process in the criminal justice
system but because they teach us something about ourselves. After all,
jurors in a capital case are plucked out of their daily routines to sit in
ultimate judgment of another human being, even though they are not
taught, either in school or in the crunch of daily living, how to judge
whether a human being should live or die.

In the guilt phase, the jury searches for facts from which a deter-
mination is made about an actual criminal episode. The jury understands, at bottom, that their decision is connected to a real-world event
from which the verdict can be adjudged true or false. At the penalty
phase, by contrast, there are no events that the deliberation process
seeks to capture within a verdict. The moral decision whether to vote

for death cannot be judged as true or false. The penalty phase decision making process propels human beings into that metaphysical wall separating life and death. How are human beings to decide whether to extinguish another human being? Are we even equipped to do that?

In 1990, a group of researchers, experts in widespread fields of law, sociology, political science, and criminology, from over a dozen universities in the United States, assembled to begin a research project known as the Capital Jury Project. Their aim was to study how human beings arrive at their decisions in a capital case. It is clear from the studies that the most important factor in the jury's life-or-death quandary is whether the defendant will pose a future danger to society. Killing, in short, is palatable only if done in the name of life itself.

This finding by the Capital Jury Project reveals how important it is for a jury to be aware of alternatives to the death sentence. When a jury is made aware that a life sentence without possibility of parole actually means *life without parole,* then the chances of a life verdict increase dramatically. According to the Capital Jury Project, "one of the primary influences on jury behavior in capital cases is the fear—often based on misunderstanding—that a defendant who does not receive a death sentence might return to society in a relatively short time and commit more crimes of violence." Some states, like Texas, refuse to implement a true life-without-parole system because their legislatures fear that juries will be less likely to impose death under those circumstances. While these politicians cynically castigate the parole system, they keep it on the books in order to keep the death machinery operating.

Another critical factor in the jury's life-death decision is the notion of juror responsibility. The researchers found that jurors understandably enter into penalty phase deliberations deeply troubled over what they are being asked to do. One juror in an interview conducted by a Capital Jury Project researcher reported: "The first thing we did was everybody just collapsed literally in each others' arms and cried, knowing that we had to do that. . . . Somebody just said, what right do we have to decide if somebody should live or die? And then, we had a large discussion about that, about whether we as people had that right." The emotional barrier expressed by this juror is the chief enemy of a death penalty prosecutor. A prosecutor who wants the jury to vote for death needs to tear down that barrier. He or she needs to diminish the sense of responsibility that most jurors feel when given the power to decide between life or death.

Here, too, the findings of the Capital Jury Project illuminate the process. One of the most common jury reactions to this emotional barrier is to look to "the law." If it is "the law" that is doing the killing, then the jury decision rests not on individual moral judgment but on an abdication of responsibility rooted in the comforting notion that the goodness of "the law" decrees the result. The fact is, "the law" does not tell the jury which sentence to choose—indeed, the Constitution forbids it. The Constitution requires that the jury be given the discretion to choose life, no matter how horrendous the crime. Yet the Capital Jury Project found that jurors are prone to misinterpret jury instructions—indeed, are emotionally driven to misinterpret them— in order to convince themselves that the law dictates a certain result.

In one North Carolina case, out of forty-nine jurors questioned, according to researchers, "only two were able to tell us properly what the legal requirements of mitigating testimony were. And in every instance, where the jurors were mistaken, their mistake made a death sentence more likely. The misunderstandings are very deep."[1]

Another dynamic the Capital Jury Project research reveals is that jurors will ignore the fact that they are engaged in a morally weighty decision whether to authorize the killing of another human being and will transform the penalty phase into a mechanical process of weighing facts to derive an outcome that the law decrees is the "right" one. Stated another way, jurors treat the penalty phase as no different from the guilt phase inasmuch as the penalty phase is looked upon as simply a process of factfinding. Jurors, then, take comfort in the notion that the law is doing the killing, not them.

The jury in Mumia's case was probably no different from most capital juries. The men and women who were being asked to decide whether Mumia should live or die were susceptible to the same emotional barriers, and thus the same need to avoid responsibility, that were discovered in the research by the Capital Jury Project. They had the same concerns over future dangerousness and the same impulse to justify killing with rationales rooted in the preservation and sanctification of life.

It would be up to the lawyers to channel this amalgamation of human complexity, either toward life or toward death.

■ Reasons to let live, reasons to kill. It is sometimes best to think of complex things in their starkest terms. The penalty phase is, when handled conscientiously by a dedicated capital defense lawyer, a complex, difficult process. But, stripped down, it is quite basic: reasons to let live, reasons to kill.

For the defense attorney, the penalty phase presents a unique challenge. A case reaches the penalty phase only after the jury has rejected the defense lawyer's closing argument in the guilt phase. In a noncapital case, that rejection stings, but at least the trial itself is over. In a capital trial, that rejection spills over to the next phase, because the rejected defense lawyer, credibility shaken, if not shattered, must urge the jury to accept what he now has to say. Conversely, the prosecutor enters the proceeding already triumphant in the battle of good over evil.

McGill's penalty phase evidence was already part of the record even before that phase began. The evidence that justified the guilty verdict would be the evidence that would justify death. A skilled death penalty prosecutor, McGill had litigated this case from the very beginning with an eye toward getting a death verdict. He sensed that the jury didn't need to hear more evidence. They only needed motivation to do that which most human beings are reluctant to do. McGill turned over the case to the defense, poised to shoot down whatever evidence Jackson could muster to save his client's life.

At 10:34 A.M., Mumia Abu-Jamal rose and announced that he "would like to read a statement." McGill knew that Mumia would issue a statement, because he had attempted to do so after the guilty verdict was announced. McGill spent part of the prior evening preparing his strategy to attack his target. Jackson, for his part, had no idea what Mumia was about to say; nor did he particularly care. Mumia had treated him badly throughout the trial, berating him openly as a courtroom hack whose true allegiance was to the assembly line justice system that carted away beaten-down human beings to metallic warehouses. Jackson had had enough.

Mumia had had enough of Jackson also. He did not consult with him about the wisdom of the statement he was about to give. In fact, the only meeting the two had in reference to the penalty phase was a brief exchange in the lockup area outside the courtroom earlier that morning. The jury looked upon the man they adjudged a cop killer as he began to speak without interruption.

"Today's decision comes as no surprise. In fact, many will remember that I said this would happen last week when John Africa predicted and prophesied this jury decision. I want everyone to know it came after a legal, trained lawyer was imposed upon me against my will. A legal, trained lawyer whose interests were clearly not my own. A legal, trained lawyer named Tony Jackson, a man who knew he was inadequate to the task, and chose to follow the direction of this black-robed conspirator, Albert Sabo, even if it meant ignoring my directions. . . .

"It was a legal, trained lawyer who followed Sabo's direction not to introduce the testimony of Policeman Gary Wakshul, a cop who, according to his statement of 12-9-82, arrested me, carried me to a wagon, accompanied me to Jefferson Hospital, guarded me, and returned to [the] Homicide [precinct] later that morning to make a statement. According to Wakshul, "We stayed with the male at Jefferson until we were relieved. During this time, the Negro male made no comments. . . ." According to Sabo, Wakshul is on vacation, so despite the fact his testimony is directly linked to a supposed confession, he would not be called in to testify. How convenient! It was a legal, trained lawyer who told the jury "You have heard all the evidence"—knowing that wasn't so. The jury heard merely what Sabo allowed—nothing more. Many jurors were told I would cross-examine witnesses, make opening and closing arguments, and explore evidence. What they also heard was I would act as my own attorney. What they saw was a man silenced, gagged by judicial decree.

"A man ordered not to fight for his life. Every so-called 'right' was deceitfully stolen from me by Sabo. My demand that the defense be assisted by John Africa was repeatedly denied. While, meanwhile, in a city hall courtroom just four floors directly above, a man charged with murder sits with his lawyer and his father, who just happens to be a Philadelphia policeman. The man, white, was charged with beating a black man to death. . . .

"But isn't justice blind, equal in its application? Does it matter whether a white man is charged with killing a black man or a black man is charged with killing a white man? As for justice, when the prosecutor represents the Commonwealth, the judge represents the Commonwealth, and the court-appointed lawyer is paid and supported by the Commonwealth, who follows the wishes of the defendant, the man charged with the crime? If the court-appointed lawyer ignores or goes against the wishes of the man he's charged with representing, whose wishes does he follow?

"I am innocent of these charges that I have been charged of and convicted of, and despite the connivance of Sabo, McGill, and Jackson to deny me my so-called rights to represent myself, to assistance of my choice, to personally select a jury who's totally of my peers, to cross-examine witnesses, and to make both the opening and closing arguments, I am still innocent of these charges.

"According to your so-called law, I do not have to prove my innocence. But, in fact, I did have to do so by disproving the Commonwealth's case. I am innocent despite what you twelve people think and the truth shall set me free.

"This jury is not composed of my peers, for those closest to my life experiences were intentionally and systematically excluded, peremptorily excused. Only those prosecution prone, some who began with a fixed opinion of guilt, some related to city police, mostly white, mostly male, remain. May they one day be so fairly judged.

"Long live John Africa!! For his assistance in this fight for my life! It is John Africa who has strengthened me, aided me, and guided me, and loved me! Could John Africa have done worse than this worthless sellout and shyster who promised much and delivered nothing? Could he have done worse than Tony Jackson?

"On December ninth, the police attempted to execute me in the street. This trial is a result of their failure to do so. Just as police tried to kill my brothers and sisters of the family Africa on August the eighth, 1978. They failed, and hence, a so-called trial was conducted to complete the execution. But long live John Africa for our continued survival.

"This decision today proves neither my guilt nor my innocence. It proves merely that the system is finished. Babylon is falling!! Long live MOVE!! Long live John Africa!"

The moment McGill hungered for had arrived. It would have been reasonable for him to expect Mumia to testify during the prior guilt phase, proclaiming his innocence then—but he had refused in protest over the unfairness of the trial. McGill's image of Mumia as an arrogant and highly intelligent man warranted the expectation that he would testify. The opportunity to cross-examine his prey was merely deferred, it turned out, as McGill asked, "May I proceed, Your Honor?" Judge Sabo swept the air with his right hand, as if he were welcoming someone into a room. "Go ahead," he said.

Jackson noticed in McGill's hands a collection of newspaper articles. He had seen McGill attempt on several occasions during the trial, and even at the bail hearing, to use old publications containing statements attributed to Mumia when he was a teenage member of the Black Panther Party. Jackson was astute enough to know that injecting black nationalist political discourse into the penalty phase would be disastrous. He immediately asked Judge Sabo for a sidebar conference.

He argued that McGill's use of the publications would "prejudice the minds and inflame the jury." McGill knew that Jackson was right, and that was the point of it. He wanted—he needed—the jury to be inflamed; anything less and the jury might not have the gumption to authorize the Commonwealth of Pennsylvania to kill the defendant. McGill wisely refrained from speaking with such bluntness. Instead, he employed one of the favorite arguments used by prosecutors—the opening-the-door argument. When a defendant introduces evidence to make a point, he "opens the door" to the prosecutor to deliver otherwise inadmissible evidence to rebut the defendant's point. Thus, McGill argued, Mumia brought it on himself by making a speech espousing his views of the trial and the criminal justice system. The prosecution, he argued, was now entitled to bring in evidence of his political views and affiliations.

McGill's opening-the-door argument was manifestly pretextual, as he had long wanted to confront Mumia with his past affiliation with the Black Panther Party. Mumia's political affiliations well over a decade earlier had nothing to do with his expression of outrage over the jury's verdict and his disgust with the way Judge Sabo handled the trial. To his credit, Judge Sabo kept McGill at bay throughout the trial when it came to injecting hard evidence of Mumia's radical political leanings into the trial. But now it was different. Mumia had spoken, and spoken harshly. It was only fair, Judge Sabo reasoned, to give the prosecutor some latitude.

Mumia signaled immediately that he would not be a cooperative witness. McGill first asked Mumia to repeat a quotation from John Africa contained in his statement. Seated at the defense table, Mumia refused, telling McGill to get it from the stenographer. McGill didn't push the point. He understood well the trial lawyer's delicate power over a witness, and how easily that power can be lost.

A good trial lawyer knows not to get entangled with a witness. It is, Gerry Spence once taught me, like fighting a gorilla in a cage. If you get inside the cage, you have relinquished the source of your power. It is best to stay outside the cage, thus keeping the gorilla neutralized, while you poke at him with a stick. A good trial lawyer pokes at the witness with pointed questions, and the witness is stuck inside the witness box constrained by the rules of court, which only allow the lawyer to ask questions. The more the lawyer pokes with his metaphorical stick, the angrier the witness gets; and soon, like the enraged gorilla, the witness begins to unravel, rattling the invisible cage. The jurors don't see the invisible stick and the invisible cage, only the unraveling witness, and conclude that the trial lawyer has done his job.

It was Mumia's job not to get flustered, to maintain the aplomb that characterized his other heated exchanges in the trial.

"Let me try something else, then. What is the reason you did not stand when Judge Sabo came into the courtroom?" McGill asked, poking through the cage.

Mumia reacted just as McGill had hoped. "Because Judge Sabo deserves no honor from me or anyone else in this courtroom." Mumia then slid his chair back and stood up, the better to underscore his point. "Because he is an executioner. Because he is a hangman. That's why."

"You are not an executioner?" McGill asked.

"No. Are you?" Mumia replied sharply, sitting back down.

McGill didn't take the bait. Hostile witnesses try to induce the trial lawyer to climb into the cage by lobbing their own questions at the lawyer. Answer the question and the trial lawyer risks getting inside. McGill wisely moved on to the next question.

In fact, McGill moved quickly into the heart of his examination. He was using a January 4, 1970, newspaper article in the *Philadelphia Inquirer* containing excerpts of an interview with a precocious teenager named Wesley Cook, Mumia's name given at birth. "Mr. Jamal, let me ask you if you can recall saying something some time ago and perhaps it might ring a bell as to whether or not you are an executioner or endorse such actions." McGill lifted the newspaper closer to eye level and he began to read. " 'Black brothers and sisters, and organizations, which wouldn't commit themselves before are relating to us black people that they are facing—we are facing the reality that the Black Panther Party has been facing, which is . . .' " McGill paused, took a step toward the jurors and brushed his eyes across the panel, and then enunciated very slowly. "Now, listen to this quote, you've often been quoted saying this: 'Political power grows out of the barrel of a gun.' Do you remember saying that, sir?"

McGill had been insinuating that Officer Faulkner was killed because of ideology from the moment the trial began. It was the core thesis in his good-versus-evil narrative, which he suggested in his opening statement, telling the jury that it would see firsthand that the killing was more than just the act of a no-good street predator. It was a revolutionary act, an assault upon "the system," by a black revolutionary who had lost his grounding in the real world when he embraced the system-hating MOVE organization. It was, in short, a political crime. Mumia's courtroom conduct suggested it; Mumia's teenage statement confirmed it.

Mumia explained that the quotation was from Mao Tse-tung, the Chinese communist leader. "It's very clear that political power grows out of the barrel of a gun," Mumia expounded, "or else America wouldn't be here today." He said nothing of the fact that it was a favorite slogan among Black Panther Party members in the '60s. Nor did he explain that, as a member of the Black Panther Party, he was required to absorb the essential teachings of Mao contained in the famous *Little Red Book*—a slim volume which was popular among college kids. In fact, the Panthers sold Mao's *Little Red Book* on college campuses nationwide to raise money for the organization. As a teenager, Mumia was only regurgitating a slogan that suited the times.

Many of Mumia's supporters were pleased that the trial had taken this turn; to them, this was terrific testimony simply because Mumia was espousing "political truths." To the journalists who had been sitting through the trial, mystified by much of Mumia's behavior, it was disastrous. These journalists, better suited to assess how middle America felt about radical political discourse, viewed the situation correctly; the jury was not impressed.

"It is America who has seized political power from the Indian race, not by God, not by Christianity, not by goodness, but by the barrel of a gun," Mumia continued, speaking confidently, somewhat like a debater in front of a university crowd. What was Mumia saying, that America was a fraud? Was he saying that killing is justified? This was a political perspective that the jurors didn't encounter on network television. It was an outlook, a self-referential critique, that was not part of the American landscape, and therefore could not at that moment take root in the jurors' consciousness. It only caused them to see red.

But Mumia was not speaking to persuade. If he was, he was playing the fool; and Mumia may be many things, but he's no fool. He was rebelling. He knew that the sentencing hearing was not about capturing the truth, about elucidating the arc of his own political awareness, about shining a light on *who* he really was. But in his rebellion he lost sight of how McGill was coaxing him into projecting a caricature onto a canvas that salt-of-the-earth Americans have no ability to critique themselves.

"Do you believe that your actions as well as your philosophy are consistent with the quote, 'Political power grows out of the barrel of a gun'?" McGill continued.

"I believe that America has proven that quote to be true."

"Do you recall saying that: 'The Panther Party is an uncompromising party, it faces reality'?"

"Yes. Why don't you let me look at the article so I can look at it in its full context, as long as you're quoting," Mumia countered.

McGill quickly agreed—he could hardly contain his delight, in fact. The article talked of the Black Panther Party's antipathy toward police who, the Panthers believed, engaged in murders as a "calculated design of genocide and a national plot to destroy the Party leadership," as evidenced by "a bloody two-year history of police raids and shootouts." It also noted that Mumia was committed to "helping Black Americans gain a sense of dignity" and that the Philadelphia chapter was "more socially activist than militant." But Mumia's teenage commitment to social justice for Philadelphia's impoverished blacks was obscured by the article's frequent references to guns. "All Panthers must learn to operate service weapons correctly," the article stated. This surely jolted the jurors, perhaps caused them to jettison everything else.

When Mumia finished reading the article, McGill again began poking the stick inside the cage, asking a series of questions about his courtroom behavior. The juxtaposition was not accidental, of course. McGill wanted to demonstrate that Mumia's courtroom behavior was nothing short of a display of what the article described: an angry black nationalist who sees political change coming only through armed insurrection. Mumia resisted the questioning, trying to wrest back control by throwing out questions of his own.

"Are you going to just keep on asking questions like you did to Judge Sabo, and constantly playing with words?" McGill asked. "Did you not continually question Judge Sabo and disagree with his rulings continually after he ordered you again and again and again and again?" McGill kept the questions coming, bringing up as well Mumia's outbursts at Judge Ribner and Justice McDermott.

Satisfied that the jury now had before it the true measure of the man, McGill announced that the prosecution rested.

■ McGill's use of the article was entirely unfair. The reference to the saying, "Political power grows out of the barrel of a gun," occurred in a paragraph within the news article that reads:

> "Since the murders," says Wesley Cook, Chapter Communications Secretary, "Black brothers and sisters and organizations which wouldn't commit themselves before are relating to us. Black people are facing the reality that the Black Panther Party has been facing: Political power grows out of the barrel of a gun."

The jury never heard the phrase "since the murders," which preceded the quotation that McGill found so inflammatory. What was Mumia referring to?

On December 4, 1969, shortly after 4:00 A.M., fourteen Chicago police officers, under orders from Cook County state's attorney Edward V. Hanrahan, burst into the home of Fred Hampton, the leader of the Chicago chapter of the Black Panther Party. Gunfire erupted. When it was all over, Hampton lay dead in his bed; Panther member Mark Clark was also killed. Other Panther members survived their gunshot wounds. The newspaper article McGill used in the 1982 trial reported on an interview with Wesley Cook that took place a month after this Chicago shooting (January 4, 1970). The phrase "since the murders" was a reference to the Hampton and Clark killings. Mumia's observation that "political power grows out of the barrel of a gun" was not a reflection of his attitude toward guns and violence, but an observation about the *government's* manifest willingness to use violence against the Panthers. The Hampton and Clark killings revealed the truth of Mao's maxim, a blatant illustration of the government's use of guns to exert political power. Twelve years later, McGill plucked out the Mao quotation, stripped it from its context, and unfairly attributed it to Mumia as a reflection of his personal penchant for violence. Unfortunately, Mumia did nothing in his repartée with McGill to project a more appealing image to the nearly all-white jury.

■ Although Jackson had called several prominent citizens as witnesses six months earlier at a bail hearing, he had no one lined up to testify now. When the debacle was over and Mumia took his seat, Jackson could think of nothing else to do but formally put an end to the penalty phase proceedings. He said softly, "The defense would rest, Your Honor." All that was left were the closing arguments for and against imposing death.

Jackson spoke first, and this time, instead of platitudes, he offered a mechanical analysis of the death penalty statute. Under Pennsylvania law the jury is required to impose death if certain specified aggravating factors outweigh whatever mitigating factors the defense can point to. One of the aggravating factors that a jury may find to justify a death verdict under the Pennsylvania statute is the fact that the victim was a peace officer. With no genuine mitigation evidence introduced into the penalty phase, Jackson seized upon the language of the statute. It said "peace officer" not *police* officer, he argued. Had the state legislature wanted to include "police officers" within the ambit of the death provision, it would have used that title in the statute. "I'll bring that to your attention," Jackson lamely declared, "as a matter I think you need to consider." Jackson's plea for a life verdict descended to the level of arguing that Officer Faulkner was not a "peace" officer within the literal terms of the statute. The jury could only react with one emotion: disgust.

In another blunder, Jackson unwittingly suggested to the jury that a life sentence for Mumia might not in actuality be a full life term behind bars. "Some cases" exist, Jackson pointed out, where a person is given a life sentence and he is "out in a few years." This outrageous remark by a lawyer who was supposed to be giving jurors reasons to *spare* Mumia's life actually triggered the life-preservation impulse that would justify killing him—after all, would the jury fear that Mumia might someday gain his freedom and kill again?

Jackson also argued that the death penalty has had a tortured history in the United States, and in Pennsylvania. He tried to convince the jurors that imposing death is wrong. He should have known that this was a Sisyphian task, as these jurors had been death-qualified through their acknowledgment that they did not have conscientious scruples against imposing the death penalty. Jackson succeeded only in revealing that he had nothing meaningful to say on Mumia's behalf. He never attempted to close the political and cultural distance between the jury and his client, perhaps because bridging the divide was simply impossible. It was true that the race-conscious jury selection, coupled with the *Witherspoon*ing process, created a huge chasm between the two.

It was a sorry display, but it wasn't yet over.

McGill asked for a five-minute break before he began his closing.

He quickly scribbled notes on a legal pad, obviously jotting down points arising from the morning's events.

McGill began by telling the jurors that they had "the opportunity to actually hear this defendant . . . you had the opportunity to see the person, the type of person he is, and how he is." He asked the jury to think about that when "reflecting back upon the incident, the events at the time." McGill sensed that he now had permission from the jury to elevate the venom in his delivery, saying, "What we're dealing with now and who we're dealing with now is a convicted murderer." McGill pointed to Mumia: "This man over here is a killer." He let a beat of silence reinforce his anger while giving him an opportunity to connect more forcefully through eye contact with each of the jurors. He then told the jury, in the starkest terms, what their guilty verdict meant. "You're looking at and have heard a killer. That's who we're dealing with."

McGill retreated from the railing a few steps—itself a form of communication. He put out both arms, like a human scale, and explained that they, the jurors, had to weigh the aggravating factors against the mitigating factors. "If the aggravating outweighs the mitigating, then the law requires the death penalty." This balancing of the aggravating factors (the factors that merited imposition of death) against mitigating factors (factors supporting a life imprisonment sentence) was the essential task for the jury. The argument was crucial to McGill. He couldn't bank on the jury imposing the death penalty merely out of outrage or fear. The human capacity of empathy for another human being is too resilient to be fully extinguished by negative emotions. McGill wanted the jury to see its role in a banal way. His strategy was to emphasize the mechanical nature of the sentencing decision, and thus eviscerate its subtle, individualized, and morally weighty aspects. The effect of this mode of argumentation was to blunt the jury's sensitivity to what the United States Supreme Court characterized as its "truly awesome responsibility." McGill invoked the notion of legal duty, not to emphasize the importance of legal duty in its own right but as a reassuring escape from the anxiety of moral choice. In effect, he was telling the jurors that they were technicians in a larger legal apparatus from which Mumia would receive "appeal after appeal after appeal"; that the painfully difficult choice about life or death is, in reality, no choice at all, for the law makes the choice for them.

McGill understood instinctively what the Capital Jury Project uncovered years later through research: jurors seek out ways to put the decision-making onus on the law.

"Law and order. Ladies and gentlemen, this is what this trial is all about, more than any other trial I have ever seen; and certainly more than any other I have been involved in." McGill was moving closer to the central motivation behind the need to execute Mumia. "Because you yourself have seen, you have heard things that are going on, and you have heard testimony of things that are going on as to what is lawful and what is not lawful, and actions, arrogance, reactions against the law. Law and order. So, ladies and gentlemen, at least ask yourselves the question, are we going to live in a society with law and order, and are we going to enforce the laws consistent with the intention of law and order, or are we going to decide our own rules and then act accordingly? That's really what we are talking about. . . . Because once we have the opportunity presented that anybody can kill a cop and it doesn't matter, you may as well forget about law and order, just throw it right out."

Effective trial lawyers are distrustful of abstractions. Powerful, readily understandable images are far more effective. McGill gave the jury a short vignette to underscore his law-and-order message. "This morning, before I left—actually, my mother actually called me up and we were talking about the case a little bit and before I went down here, she said this to me. She simply said, you know, and I won't go into some of the other things that she said about this case, but she specifically said this, 'Joe, if you can come up'—and this is a lady who is in her seventies—she said, 'Joe, if you can come up and kill a police officer, who is going to protect me?' "

"Who is going to protect me?" McGill's vignette revealed that his argument about law and order was really a device to tap into fear—

the fear, cultivated by media obsession with violent crime, that law-abiding folks are in constant danger. Fear is the wellspring of law and order; and McGill needed to talk about fear, because anger, the emotion that paves the way for a death verdict, is a secondary emotion. Anger sustains itself within the human heart against the competing impulses to preserve life, to sanctify life, by the more primary emotion—fear. McGill needed to use fear to nourish the anger that would ultimately compel the jury to demand death.

"That's what she said," McGill continued. "But that, ladies and gentlemen, is really what it is all about. Because that is what our system and the kind of constant battleground that we have during the course of every day in this city. The only symbol of people that are attempting to enforce the law, to control and protect people, are police officers. And if you can at will kill police, ladies and gentlemen, you then make that extra step towards the area which is without law enforcement, which is an outright jungle. We are one step from the jungle without the opportunity of individuals to enforce the law."

Mumia repudiated social order, McGill argued. "Order, ladies and gentlemen, that you may not have seen; order that this defendant has decided is not good enough for him." McGill could now explicitly state what he had long insinuated: "This is not something that happened overnight." The capacity to execute a police officer had brewed within Mumia since he was in his early teens. That, McGill argued, was the true significance of Mumia's endorsement of the Mao quote.

The rhetorical noose was now securely fastened around Mumia's neck. "The horror, the horror," Kurtz says at the end of Joseph Conrad's *Heart of Darkness.* Western colonialists conquered the jungles of Africa and Asia, and in so doing, propagated a cultural image of the jungle as a place of chaos, darkness, and horror. McGill's closing argument reached its apex with the imagery of an "outright jungle," and thereby tapped into something deep in the collective psyche of the largely white, blue-collar jury. Mumia was to be feared, and thus hated, for his murderous act, which was the fruition of his revolutionary politics, which, in turn, threatened the encroachment of the jungle. To stave off chaos, darkness, and horror, McGill was telling his jury—and it was never more his jury than at that moment—they must eradicate the jungle by executing this man. But by voting for his execution, McGill reminded the jurors, "you are not asked to kill anybody. . . . You are asked to follow the law. The same law that I keep on throwing at you, saying those words, law and order." The jury was to be the expression of law and order no less than Mumia was the expression of the jungle. McGill had succeeded in pitting the jury against Mumia, placing the two in irreconcilable conflict. The jury could no longer be the detached dispenser of justice. The jury would be the preserver of law and order. There could be no doubt what the jury would do.

■ The jury left the courtroom to begin its life-or-death deliberations at 12:27 P.M. after receiving the legal instructions regarding the weighing of aggravators and mitigators. Less than four hours later, at 4:20 P.M., the jury announced its verdict. The jury had deliberated for less time on the issue of whether Mumia should live or die than it did on the issue of his guilt.

One juror had griped that they should hurry up with the decision because he still hoped to attend a barbecue event. No one was happy sacrificing even a portion of their Fourth of July weekend on such a grim task.*

Before the jury was brought into the courtroom to announce its decision, the clerk telephoned for more sheriff's deputies. The courtroom was soon ringed by twenty of them. Mumia glowered at the jurors as they shuffled toward their designated and familiar places in the jury box. The court clerk ceremoniously posed the query to the jury foreman: "Having found the defendant, Mumia Abu-Jamal, guilty of murder in the first degree, what is your verdict as to penalty?" The jurors sat motionless and without expression. The jury foreman's answer was short: "Death."

---

*A juror who had apparently relocated to Ohio disclosed this fact to a local ABC reporter.

■ *Philadelphia Inquirer* reporter Marc Kaufman wondered aloud whether Mumia had a death wish. In an article entitled, "Did Abu-Jamal Want the Jury to Find Him Guilty?" Kaufman wrote that "Abu-Jamal conducted his unsuccessful defense with what appeared to be an intense and perplexing will to offend and even the desire to fail." Kaufman recounted Mumia's frequent verbal jousting with Judge Sabo; but more dismaying was Mumia's attack upon the jury itself and the justice system overall. Why, Kaufman asks, did Mumia adopt this "strategy of John Africa"? It puzzled many of Mumia's friends and admirers. But one thing seemed clear to Kaufman: "The strategy [of John Africa] helped convict him and, incidentally, communicated a largely negative and one-dimensional picture of a man believed by many to be an exceptional individual."

Kaufman reported that "some friends and observers" believed that Mumia was "committing 'an indirect suicide.'" Others speculated that "the pressures and disappointments of his life had grown so great that he literally lost touch with reality." And then there was McGill's theory, which would revive itself over a decade later when a new legal challenge was brought against the conviction and death sentence. Mc-Gill told reporters that Mumia's attack upon the judge, the jury, and the justice system as a whole was a ploy to derail the proceedings in order that a successful appeal could someday be launched. As Kaufman put it: "Injecting the kind of chaos that MOVE can bring to a court, this reasoning goes, helps create an environment in which judicial error is more likely, and so the verdict would be overturned on appeal."

To McGill and others in the district attorney's office, there was a method to all of Mumia's courtroom madness.

TWO

RECONFIGURING GOOD
VERSUS EVIL

This court is not going to be intimidated by mob pressure. Understand that. If the day ever comes that the mob can control the courts, then, indeed, we are in dire circumstances. I will not tolerate it. No threats, nothing is going to intimidate this court. No mob pressure is going to intimidate this court.

JUDGE SABO, JULY 18, 1995, TO COURTROOM SPECTATORS

I've never seen a Jim Crow court until today. The whole atmosphere of this court is Mississippi 1955, and that's what's sad about it.

CORNEL WEST, COMMENTING ON JUDGE SABO'S COURT

13. A NEW TEAM, A NEW PORTRAIT, AND AN OLD JUDGE

"I'm shook up," a juror told a local reporter. "When you have to condemn a man to death, it's rough." Mumia's adamantine behavior, however, apparently made a rough job a bit easier. Another juror pointed to Mumia's in-court behavior to mitigate the severity of his judgment: "His behavior made it easier to believe he could be a killer."[1] And yet another juror was even more blunt: "The man is intelligent, but he was acting stupid."[2]

The death verdict against Mumia was the twentieth in Philadelphia alone since Pennsylvania reinstated the death penalty in 1978.* Mumia happened to be the third Philadelphian hit with a death verdict within a ten-day period. It was McGill's sixth successful death penalty trial, the

---

*In the first five years of New York's death penalty, by contrast, only one individual from New York City was sentenced to death.

largest number in Pennsylvania. Even at this early stage in Pennsylvania's implementation of the death penalty, legal observers perceived a thirst for death in the Philadelphia district attorney's office.

Today, the reputation of the Philadelphia district attorney's office is unmatched among capital punishment jurisdictions. District Attorney Lynne Abraham was dubbed in a 1995 *New York Times Magazine* article as "the deadliest DA"[3] because her office seeks the death penalty in 85 percent of all homicide cases—a staggering percentage. Philadelphia death verdicts account for more than half of the state's death row population, now at 223, even though it makes up only 14 percent of the state's total population. The death penalty is meted out eleven times more frequently in Philadelphia than in Pittsburgh, even though the populations of the two urban locales are roughly the same and the disparity in their murder rates comes nowhere close to explaining the death verdict disparity. Nationwide, the *city* of Philadelphia has sent more people to death row than twenty-eight out of the thirty-eight *states* with the death penalty.

■ McGill, like Jackson, was emotionally depleted after the death verdict was announced. He was also enormously satisfied, dispensing brawny handshakes to the cops and FOP representatives who attended much of the trial. Heartfelt hugs were reserved for Maureen and the Faulkner family members, many of whom harbored concerns that the jury would not have the courage to mete out a death sentence for a man who, they grudgingly had to admit, was both intelligent and charismatic. All of the spectators on the prosecution side of the courtroom had deepened their antipathy toward MOVE over the past several weeks, disgusted by their vociferous condemnation of "the system" that was trying to "railroad a brother." To them, the death verdict—a token of justice for a young police officer and his widow—meant that they prevailed over the forces of destruction.

Exhausted, McGill spoke briefly with reporters, his fatigue giving way to the enmity that bubbled beneath the surface: "The citizens in

Philadelphia have just had enough," he declared. "They've had it with hearing about reasons and excuses for people who have committed serious, vicious, malicious acts." A profile of McGill appearing in *Philadelphia Magazine* applauded his stewardship of the trial, noting that it had been a sideshow for the hated MOVE organization:

> *Countless times during the Abu-Jamal trial, MOVE members who were present to lend moral support to the accused attempted to take over the courtroom. Soon, Abu-Jamal and Faulkner were practically relegated to the status of sideshow, as MOVE transformed the tense scene into a guerilla theater confrontation, pitting their cult against the community. That summer, McGill felt more like a ringmaster than a prosecutor. Eventually, his name, too, was added to MOVE's Manson-like death list.*

Danny Faulkner's partner, Officer Garry Bell, left the courtroom more subdued than his colleagues and friends. He was dubious that the death sentence would ever be carried out. "Danny was shot like a dog," Bell told the *Philadelphia Inquirer*. "There was no justice at all for him. This man will have appeals and appeals, and I really don't think he'll ever be electrocuted."*

■ On March 6, 1989, the Pennsylvania Supreme Court issued its decision in the appeal of *Commonwealth v. Mumia Abu-Jamal.* Mumia's trial had been fair, the Court ruled, and his death sentence was an appropriate sanction for the cruelty and hideousness of his crime. Whatever irregularities marred the trial process was not the fault of the trial judge, but rather, was the by-product of an obstreperous defendant who refused to sit quietly. The description of the trial contained in the Court's judicial opinion bore scant resemblance to what

---

*In 1982, the mode of execution was by electric chair. It is now by lethal injection, the method of choice in the vast majority of death states.

really happened, which is hardly surprising. Rarely does an appellate court decision bring a trial proceeding to life.

The Pennsylvania Supreme Court, which is the oldest supreme court in the United States (predating even the United States Supreme Court), consists of seven justices. It is a court with a proud history of judicial leadership and scholarly jurists. It is also one of only eleven state supreme courts that still chooses its justices in partisan elections. The elected terms are only ten years, which means the justices are perennially burdened with raising money and avoiding overly controversial decisions. One retired justice from that court remarked that "this is the very worst possible method of selecting judges—it doesn't have a single redeeming grace."

During the 1980s, this proud institution came close to dissolving amidst torrid accusations of racism, fraud, and Machiavellian maneuvering. At the center of the controversy was the chief justice on the court, Robert N. C. Nix, Jr. The son of an esteemed Pennsylvania congressman, Nix was the first black justice ever to sit on the Pennsylvania Supreme Court. A fellow jurist, Justice Rolf Larsen, apparently coveting Nix's position as chief justice, tried to coax Nix into running for the U.S. Senate, thereby vacating the slot. When Nix refused, Larsen threatened to expose to the public that Nix is black, which, Larsen believed, would undermine Nix's chances for reelection in 1981. Here is Nix's recounting of the conversation, rendered during hearings on the scandal:

> *After a short discussion of the wisdom of that decision [to run for Senate], Justice Larsen indicated: "Well, you know that you have to run for retention next year." I said: "Yes, I was certainly aware of that fact. He then indicated . . . to me, "You must be aware of the fact that when you ran for election in 1971 many of the residents of the Commonwealth were not aware of your race, and that fact could make a difference in a retention election." That was the end of the conversation.*

A parade of witnesses was called during the hearings, which corroborated Nix's accusation that Larsen attempted to coerce Nix's retirement from the bench through race baiting. For example, the Democratic chairman of Allegheny County, Cyril Wecht, testified that Larsen had "talked about his plans to expose the fact that Justice Nix is a 'nigger,' as he put it."

Larsen was caught using the *N* word on other occasions. One witness, a law clerk on the Pennsylvania Supreme Court, testified at the hearing that Larsen made the following remark about the MOVE Nine trial: "They should put those niggers in a cage and hang them from the ceiling."

Larsen's behavior grew even more bizarre. A story leaked that Larsen had used an aide to secure prescription drugs illegally. Incensed, Larsen lashed out at two of his colleagues on the court, claiming that they had tried to run him over in a car. On November 1, 1993, Larsen was indicted by a grand jury that heard from over two hundred witnesses, including all seven members of the Pennsylvania Supreme Court, regarding the illegal drug purchases. Larsen ultimately left the court in disgrace. The scandals prompted the Pennsylvania Senate to consider disbanding the court and reinstituting a new one.

Mumia's case hit the Pennsylvania Supreme Court docket during this turbulent period. And things didn't seem quite right with the court when Mumia's case was decided. Two justices (one being Larsen) inexplicably didn't participate in the oral argument or in the decision of the court. During the oral argument, Nix asked pointed questions of the appellate lawyer with the district attorney's office concerning McGill's reference in his closing argument that Mumia would have "appeal, after appeal, after appeal." The court had earlier reversed a death sentence handled by McGill for invoking precisely that argument, noting that it impermissibly waters down the weightiness of the jury's task in deciding between life and death. It was apparent to many observers of the oral argument that Chief Justice Nix was going to push for the overturning of Mumia's death sentence. Without explanation, when the decision was issued fifteen months later, Nix joined the other two absent colleagues and recused himself without explanation. An editor for the *Philadelphia Inquirer* thought it odd that Nix would raise probing questions about McGill's conduct and then not participate in the court's decision.

Nix refuses to explain why he did not participate in the appellate decision on Mumia's case. Facing reelection in 1991 (the decision was issued in 1989), Nix was apparently caught in a dilemma. He couldn't, from a political point of view, side with Mumia on the appeal, even though, by the looks of it, he agreed that Mumia's trial had been unfair; but, equally true, he couldn't bring himself to join the other members of the court in whitewashing the trial with an opinion endorsing Judge Sabo's and McGill's conduct. He apparently reached for the escape hatch and recused himself. Justice Nix abdicated his role as a jurist a second time when, almost a decade later, another appeal to the Pennsylvania Supreme Court was filed on Mumia's behalf. Because he abruptly opted for early retirement, he did not sit for that appeal. On top of that, the district attorney at the time of Mumia's original appeal, Ronald Castille, became a member of the Pennsylvania Supreme Court. He refused to recuse himself from Mumia's second appeal to that court, even though his name appeared on the prosecution briefs submitted in opposition to Mumia's original appeal.

Interestingly, the 1993 grand jury that indicted Justice Larsen issued the recommendation that, from here on out, "the reason for recusals should be documented in court records."

Defeated in the Pennsylvania Supreme Court in 1989, Mumia then asked the United States Supreme Court to review his case. The U.S. Supreme Court refused. Its refusal to consider one issue in particular remains especially troubling: McGill's politicization of the penalty phase hearing through his use of the twelve-year-old newspaper article containing the Mao quote. Mumia's appellate lawyer argued, as did Jackson, that this injection of political affiliation into a criminal trial violated Mumia's First Amendment rights. No one, the argument went, should be punished, certainly not risk death in a criminal proceeding, in whole or in part, because of one's political beliefs or organizational affiliations. Actions, not thoughts, are the relevant criteria.

The Pennsylvania Supreme Court noted that Mumia's former teenage membership in the Black Panther Party, "an unpopular political organization" with a "perceived violent philosophy," demonstrated his "longstanding disdain for the system." This was, in the sterile terms suitable for appellate judges, precisely what McGill had argued. The court held that McGill properly used this alleged aspect of Mumia's character to argue for imposition of the death penalty. With that ruling, *Commonwealth v. Jamal* entered the constellation of legal precedent.

■ David Dawson could never have predicted, and would probably have been appalled at the thought, that his life would in any way intersect with Mumia's. He certainly had nothing in common with Mumia in terms of social outlook or political philosophy. Dawson liked to call himself Abaddon, meaning "one of Satan's disciples." He landed on death row after being convicted in Delaware for brutally murdering a woman during a burglary spree. During the penalty phase of Dawson's trial, the prosecutor proceeded in much the way McGill had. He endeavored to link Dawson's criminal rampage to his political beliefs. The prosecutor sought to introduce evidence that Dawson was a member of the Aryan Brotherhood, a white racist group, and had multiple tatoos reflecting his racist and satanic views (including tatoos and paintings of swastikas). Although Dawson's lawyer objected to this evidence, the trial judge permitted the prosecution to proceed with its politicized attack, but excluded all of the swastika-related evidence. Dawson received a death sentence.

Dawson appealed to the Delaware Supreme Court, arguing that the use of his Aryan Brotherhood affiliation in the penalty phase violated his First Amendment rights. The Delaware Supreme Court, either because it was impressed by the Pennsylvania Supreme Court's analysis or simply too lazy to engage in an analysis of its own, adopted verbatim the reasoning contained in the published decision of *Commonwealth v. Jamal*. Right-winger David Dawson and left-winger Mumia Abu-Jamal were joined at the hip in the world of legal precedent.

The two cases weren't linked for long. David Dawson's lawyers petitioned the United States Supreme Court to take a look at the issue. The Court agreed to do so. Mumia's earlier certiorari request, raising the same issue, had been rejected by the Court. In 1992, the United States Supreme Court ruled that the Delaware high court was wrong to allow the penalty phase to become politicized in that way. "Whatever label is given to the evidence presented," the Court explained, "Dawson's First Amendment rights were violated by the admission of the Aryan Brotherhood evidence . . . because the evidence proved nothing more than Dawson's abstract beliefs." *Dawson v. Delaware* is now a significant precedent in Supreme Court death penalty jurisprudence.

Mumia had every right to expect equal treatment from the United States Supreme Court. The Delaware Supreme Court, after all, had relied exclusively on his case, and the United States Supreme Court ruled that that court was wrong for doing so. Mumia had a compelling basis for Supreme Court action, and he asked again that the Court take his case. The response, however, was terse: "Petitioner's application for writ of certiorari is denied."

Barely into the new decade, the road was paved for Mumia's execution—unless his case could be deconstructed to undermine the reliability of the jury's guilt and penalty phase verdicts.

■ Leonard Weinglass took on Mumia's case in 1992. Several lawyers were considered for the job, but none had the credentials matching Len's as a lawyer for leftist causes—an essential criterion for selection. Len came into prominence as a direct result of a friendship he forged with Tom Hayden in 1967 in Newark, New Jersey. A leading figure in the student movement of the '60s through his work with Students for a Democratic Society (SDS), Hayden was engaged in community organizing in Newark at the time. After a stint in the air force, Len returned home (he grew up in nearby Kearney) and set up his small-town law practice there, a somewhat unusual career choice for a Yale Law graduate. It was that friendship that led to his later involvement in the famous Chicago Seven trial in which Hayden was one of the defendants. The Chicago Seven trial was Len's launching pad to countless other left-wing political cases, big and small.

I first met Len in November 1987, while working as a well-paid young associate at a large San Francisco law firm specializing in labor and securities litigation. Coming from an uneducated family (I was the first to graduate high school), I was perhaps entitled to feel deserving of my success and the road that success put me on. But the money and all that it promises in the material world didn't seem to fill a vacuum inside me; the corporate world was not so much a gilded cage as it was a platform for slow death, an opulent milieu that withered the spirit, which thrives on genuine human connectedness. I was living a dual life back then, slaving away for corporate America but secretly squeezing in activities for various left-wing causes and reading existentialist and postmodern philosophy (I read virtually all of Nietzsche's books on company time). I hungered for human connectedness.

One day, a young activist named Katya Komisaruk, who I knew slightly, threw out the idea that I represent her in a federal criminal trial. An MBA graduate out of U.C. Berkeley (I had gone there as an undergraduate and met her once during that period of my life), Kayta was an impassioned antinuclear activist under federal indictment for sabotage and destruction of government property. She explained to me that she had entered onto Vandenberg Air Force Base, located north of Santa Barbara, California, and taken a hammer to a sophisticated computer system that was an integral part of a system called Navstar. Navstar was part of Reagan's first-strike nuclear defense policy, premised on the lunatic theory that a missile defense system could be designed, with the aid of computers, to intercept incoming enemy nuclear warheads. Protected by this computer-driven umbrella of missiles attacking enemy missiles, our military and political leaders salivated over the prospect of being able to launch a nuclear attack against the "evil empire" with virtual impunity.

The madness of it all was too much for Katya. She decided to take matters into her own hands and destroy the computer system herself, which she did in the early morning hours of June 2, 1987, with nothing more than a hammer and a can of spray paint (the paint was used to write in bold lettering "International Law," "U.N. Charter," and other words to capture the legal justification for her actions, which she hoped would be considered by a jury). She then held a press conference in San Francisco, telling the world what she had done, to the deep embarrassment of the United States government. Her action was part of a nonviolent tradition in the antinuclear movement made famous by Catholic theologians Daniel and Philip Berrigan—a tradition known as the plowshares action, inspired by Isaiah 2:4: "And they shall beat their swords into plowshares, and their spears into pruning hooks; nation shall not lift up swords against nation, neither shall they learn war any more."

I told Katya that I was not equipped to handle a criminal trial but expressed my amazement at her gumption. I had never even seen a real-life trial before, let alone participated in one as a lawyer. I was a well-paid, sit-behind-the-desk lawyer, which suited my Ivy League legal training. I didn't have the foggiest notion how to be a "real" lawyer, which is what she needed. Law schools, especially the most esteemed ones, don't teach their students how to be courtroom warriors. Katya wisely reached out for a "real" lawyer—Len Weinglass. I didn't read many books about law as a kid, but I remembered reading a book about the Chicago Seven trial. Even as a kid I more readily identified with Len than with the more voluble William Kunstler, the other lawyer in the trial. When I learned Len Weinglass agreed to handle Katya's case, I immediately sought permission from the powers that be at the firm (begged is probably more accurate) to let me assist him in the trial.

I was the "law person" at the defense table, which meant that I was responsible for preparing legal motions and researching legal issues. Mostly, however, I watched Len do his work as a courtroom advocate, mesmerized and enchanted. Here was a lawyer who actually spoke words that evoked feelings and painted mental pictures; a lawyer who, unlike the stuffed shirts at my law firm, gave of himself in a spirit of generosity within the austere environment of a courtroom. Watching Len, I realized that he used the trial process to *share* information and to *share* important truths about the human condition—sharing, not proselytizing or lecturing pedantically.

Well, that was the beginning of the end of my days as a corporate litigator. When I first met Len I was still grieving over the loss of my mother, who had died three weeks earlier of cancer. In hindsight, it's clear to me now that I was open for any escape from my sorrow, and working with Len provided it. Watching him do his magic, I decided to abandon my plans of eventually entering the slow-paced bucolic world of academia, and vowed to become a trial lawyer like him. Nine months later, I moved from San Francisco to New York with nothing more than a backpack and a guitar. It was as if my mother's death was her gift to me—the impetus for me to break free and take Robert Frost's road less traveled.

For seven months, I slept on the living room floor of Len's modest-sized Manhattan loft, earning a pittance of what I had as a corporate lawyer, but thrilled nonetheless. Len and I worked together for several years, as I soaked in how to be a trial lawyer. They were among the best years of my life. One evening, tucked away in sleeping bags under the stars at Len's Catskills hideaway, Len recounted an experience he had as a young lawyer that crystallizes his approach to advocacy before a jury.

After finishing one of his first jury trials, Len went back to the trial judge's chambers, having been summoned there.

"Mr. Weinglass, where did you go to law school?" the judge inquired.

"Yale, Your Honor."

"Where are you parents from?"

"Rumania," Len answered, befuddled by the judge's curiosity.

"Well, next time, young man, a little less Yale and a little more Rumania."

It was only natural that Len would recruit me to work with him on Mumia's case. Two other lawyers officially came onto the team in 1994 as active participants: Jonathan Piper, a closet leftist working as an associate in a big corporate firm in Chicago, and Rachel Wolkenstein, a never-in-the-closet leftist with the Partisan Defense Committee, an organization founded upon the Marxist ideology of Leon Trotsky. Another lawyer, Steve Hawkins, experienced in capital litigation through his work at the NAACP Legal Defense Fund, Inc., helped out sporadically as a consultant.

Nineteen ninety-four was a crucial year, because that is when I began drafting the petition for a new trial pursuant to Pennsylvania's Post-Conviction Relief Act (PCRA), the statute authorizing inmates to challenge their convictions even after their original appeals have been exhausted. Jon helped considerably in beefing up the nearly two dozen separate constitutional claims we were intending to raise. Meanwhile, Len and Rachel stoked up the political movement, which blossomed at around this time. Rallies for Mumia were regular events throughout the United States (many on college campuses), and in France, Germany, Denmark, Holland, and Italy. For example, in 1993, two thousand protesters took to the street in front of the U.S. Cultural Institute in Berlin. T-shirts, bumper stickers, mouse pads, buttons, posters—all bearing Mumia's internationally recognized face appeared everywhere. I couldn't go on vacation without seeing "Free Mumia" slogans. Fund-raisers were commonplace as well, and they went beyond those sponsored or endorsed by celebrities such as Ed Asner, Ossie Davis, Mike Farrell, Danny Glover, Alice Walker, and others. Nine San Francisco high schools in the spring of 1994, for instance, held a ten-kilometer race to raise money for us. There existed at least twenty national and international groups devoted to supporting our efforts to secure a new trial.

I was virtually oblivious to it all at the time. I hovered over the trial transcripts and perused the massive quantity of legal precedent like a scientist in a laboratory. I felt that all of my legal training and my experiences as a lawyer were in preparation for this case. Freeing Mumia was not a political cause to me; it was a personal mission.

Len, who admired Clarence Darrow, felt likewise. Darrow had ended his illustrious career with a magnificent plea against the death penalty in the famous 1924 case of Leopold and Loeb (in which two intellectually gifted teenagers, in seeking to commit the "perfect crime," kidnapped for ransom and then murdered the fourteen-year-old son of a prominent Chicago businessman). I sensed that Len regarded Mumia's case to be his Leopold and Loeb moment—a fitting capstone to his own devotion to the legal profession. In many ways, my devotion to this case is also my gift to Len.

After years of investigation and careful analysis of the trial transcripts and the voluminous police reports, we finished putting together
our PCRA petition in late spring of 1995. When we filed it on June
5, it felt to me as though we were launching a rocket into space,
nervously wondering whether it would take a nose-dive into the ocean.

■ At the time we had decided upon the June 5 filing date, in late
May, Governor Thomas Ridge had not yet signed a death warrant. In
fact, even though Mumia's original appeal to the Pennsylvania Supreme Court had been decided in 1989, no death warrant had ever
been issued against him, and we were confident that it would stay
that way while we litigated the PCRA petition. Len wrote to Governor
Ridge in April informing him of our intention to file the PCRA. The
correspondence was not a courtesy communiqué—in death penalty
litigation, like any serious litigation, nothing is done without some
tactical judgment undergirding the decision. We wanted to put the
governor on notice that Mumia fully intended to take advantage of
the rights afforded him under the PCRA. We felt that this notification
would foreclose the governor from issuing a death warrant before the
PCRA petition was litigated, lest he appear to be overly bloodthirsty.
Len's letter didn't tell the governor *when* we were filing the PCRA
petition, because we had not yet decided on a date.

The situation on June 5 was not, however, as we had expected it
to be. On June 1, four days before our intended filing date, the governor signed a warrant for Mumia's execution, scheduling it for August
17, 1995. At the time, we didn't know how the governor timed the
signing of the death warrant so perfectly. All that we knew at that
point was that we would have to litigate this case under added pressure, which is exactly what the governor probably wanted.

Unbeknownst to us, the governor was aware of much of the legal
team's thinking on the case. We learned four months later, after the
PCRA proceedings concluded, that government officials had been in-
tercepting, reading, and photocopying Mumia's mail, including privileged correspondence to and from his attorneys, beginning in August

of 1994. Needless to say, the attorney-client correspondence contained sensitive information about our tactical and strategic assessments of Mumia's case, as well as our plans to file the PCRA petition. The revelation came about as a result of a civil rights lawsuit Mumia filed against prison officials in the United States District Court for the Western District of Pennsylvania, alleging that his mail was being illegally tampered with.

Mumia's civil rights suit went to trial before a federal magistrate in September 1995. Prison officials argued that they justifiably inspected Mumia's mail to prevent the conducting of a business from within the prison—the business being the sale of his writings, notably his first book, *Live from Death Row*, a collection of essays containing Mumia's harsh critique of the prison system. The magistrate didn't quarrel with the rationale; the problem was that the assistant general counsel for the Department of Corrections, David Horowitz, read Mumia's privileged legal mail, photocopied the correspondence, and then, in the words of the magistrate, "forwarded" them to the Office of General Counsel, "in their entirety and with no redactions."

The magistrate was rightly disturbed by this activity, because, as he noted, "the Office of General Counsel is an Executive Office and a source of advice to the Governor of Pennsylvania for, among other things, questions concerning the signing of death warrants." The magistrate condemned Horowitz's actions; as a lawyer, he knew better than to pass on attorney-client communications to the governor's office. The magistrate ruled: "Here, however, Horowitz, operating entirely outside of the procedure set forth in [the Department of Corrections regulations], obtained information relating directly to [Mumia's] state court collateral appeal, containing his attorney's work product and advice concerning possible claims, and he did nothing to prevent that information from being disclosed. In fact, finding himself in possession of material which had nothing to do with the suspected violation of Department of Corrections policy, and having much to do with [Mumia's] state court appeal, he sent that material on to Brian Gottlieb [deputy counsel at the Office of General Counsel]."

A federal judge adopted the findings of the magistrate on the issue of impermissible interception of legal mail, ruling that it "interfered entirely with counsel's ability to represent [Mumia Abu-Jamal] during his collateral appeal."[4] Among other things, the interception of the legal mail allowed the governor to issue a preemptive strike against us, forcing us to litigate our PCRA petition under the heat of a death warrant.

■ We soon received notification to appear before Judge Sabo on July 24. With that notification, and with the execution date set for August 17, Rachel and Jon panicked and urged that we should request from the court an earlier date. Steve Hawkins and I, the most experienced in the area of appellate and postconviction death penalty litigation, disagreed, arguing that we needed the time to prepare for the hearing and that we would secure a stay of execution from *a* court—not necessarily from Judge Sabo, but from a court somewhere. Rachel and Jon naively believed that we could march into a Philadelphia court, pick and choose the legal issues we wanted to present for resolution, and then demand an adjournment to begin the hearings at some later date. Steve and I weren't so sanguine.

"But we can't sit and do nothing; there's an execution date," Jon solemnly reminded us during a meeting in a conference room at my Greenwich Village office where the defense team usually met.

"It's bullshit," I said. "There won't be an execution on August seventeenth." The law was crystal clear: a death row inmate is constitutionally entitled to one habeas corpus challenge of his conviction and sentence. An execution before resolution of the habeas corpus petition is, for obvious reasons, a denial of that constitutional right. "We can start the hearings at the end of the month without putting Mumia at risk," I pressed. "We should file a stay application, and if it gets denied, we'll get one from a federal judge."

Len, rarely one to openly offer an opinion on a legal issue, stayed silent while we debated the issue. He ultimately sided with Rachel and Jon, figuring that moving up the date to secure a stay of execution would not have a downside and would satisfy the clamor among some supporters for us to do something.

The difficult task of putting thought onto paper and the crafting of legal strategy, back in the mid-'90s, was something that Jon Piper and I handled, which, speaking for myself, caused me to be more legalistic in my assessment of how we should proceed. Len played virtually no role in writing legal briefs, and little in developing the legal arguments. He reexamined the case with the trained eye of a seasoned trial lawyer but had little to offer in packaging an appeal. Because we weren't preparing for a trial but instead pursuing an appeal, Len spent much of his time as the ambassador for the case, the public spokesperson. While he traipsed around the world giving speeches at "Mumia" rallies, providing the "face" to the defense team, Jon and I wrote the legal briefs that served as the blueprint for the upcoming courtroom litigation. Rachel, not an actual practicing lawyer and with little litigation experience, supervised our investigators, maintained close contact with Mumia and the political support network, and kept the files in order. The media often characterized us as a "large, high-powered defense team," which both unnerved me and made me chuckle. Len relished the description because it enhanced his stature as the field marshal to a huge bevy of troops in this holy war to free Mumia. In reality, Jon and I were the intellectual forces behind the case up to that point, and Jon had to squeeze in time from his busy corporate law practice to provide his contribution—which was uniformly excellent in quality. Working with Jon in putting together the all-important legal briefs for the case, I certainly didn't feel as though I were part of a "large, high-powered" defense team. Often I felt the anxiety of working alone on a mammoth task.

I say all this because it seemed to me that Len's "ambassador" role caused him to be much more sensitive to "the movement" than I was, and somewhat cavalier in his attention toward the legal issues with which we had to grapple. In fact, at times I felt he was too sensitive to how our actions would be judged by the diverse contingent of pro-Mumia activists, and too willing to be influenced by Rachel's ideologically driven assessment of how we should proceed. Rachel's view of me, of course, was just the flip side: I was too analytical and too legalistic. In this instance, Len was understandably concerned that the Mumia supporters (including MOVE), who took the August 17 date quite seriously, would not understand the legalistic rationale for acquiescing to a court appearance on July 24. Len didn't want to tell throngs of sign-carrying activists that Mumia would not be executed on August 17 lest it dampen their ardor. We sent a letter requesting that the court date be advanced. The administrative judge for the Court of Common Pleas granted our request and moved the date to July 12.

■ We appeared in Courtroom 253 on the morning of July 12 having to fight through the crowded corridor. Hundreds of Mumia supporters jammed onto the second floor, making it almost impossible to get to the courtroom. A huge crowd—some shouting "Free Mumia" and carrying banners with the same message, others distributing leftist literature, and still others looking on with wide-eyed detachment—were outside in the city hall courtyard, fully exposed to the blistering morning heat.

When Mumia strode into the packed courtroom, dreadlocks still flowing but considerably heavier than he was the last time he had been there, it was as if a rock star had come onto the stage. Mumia beamed a smile out to the audience and flourished an enthusiastic clench-fisted salute. This is how *Time* magazine reported it:

> *Like rival clans thrust together at gunpoint, the two halves of a Philadelphia courtroom audience watched each other warily last week, begrudging good behavior. Then a convict with cascading dreadlocks entered, and the people to the right of the aisle erupted. "Free Mumia!" they screamed. "Mumia, we love you!" Women blew kisses. Men punched the air with salutes. To the left of the aisle, the other half watched, silently enraged that the defendant might get another chance.*

The scene would replay itself at every court appearance when Mumia walked into the courtroom with his bouncy steps: throngs of cheering fans sitting behind the defense table, disgruntled spectators, including Maureen and Faulkner family members, sitting silently on the prosecution side. I frequently tried to sneak glances at the Faulkner family and at Maureen, who had relocated to southern California shortly after the killing and had not remarried. They always sat impassively when the supporters cheered, but I know—because they had said as much—that, while we were energized by the support, a part of them died a little inside at the sight of the adulation. "It's wearing me down," Maureen tersely admitted later in the proceedings. I understood what she meant, the erosion inside from feeling embittered and powerless. Others seated on the prosecution side were more voluble. "Have you ever seen anything more disgusting?" one young cop angrily complained to reporters. "Cheering a cop killer!" "He should fry!" the anti-Mumia forces in the courtroom were fond of saying in response to the "Free Mumia" chants. "If Mumia dies, there'll be fire in the skies," the pro-Mumia folks would yell back.

Several close relatives of the slain officer, including his older brother, Tom Faulkner, attended the proceedings. Tom always had a pained expression on his face. He told reporters that he had trouble sleeping at night, especially because he would catch glimpses of Mumia's face on posters and placards at various places. I learned one day during the hearings that things had not gone well for the Faulkner family in the years following the killing. Danny's other brother, Joseph, died prematurely in 1985, as did his sister in 1987 and his mother in 1989. "Danny's mother died of a broken heart," Maureen said. Tom insisted that the heartbreak from Danny's early violent death contributed to the deaths of his brother, sister, and mother. I was struck by the profound sadness in that notion.

Judge Sabo, white-haired, small but not frail, and admirably agile at seventy-four years of age, energetically mounted the bench and wasted no time in letting everyone know that this was *his* domain and that he was not going to tolerate "improper decorum" in *his* courtroom. "Before we proceed," Sabo announced, "I just want to remind everyone that this is a court of law. We are not out on the street. This court will not tolerate any outbursts. If that should occur, the sheriffs are instructed to remove that person immediately and they will not be allowed back into the courtroom. Everything must be proper and decorum must be maintained." At that moment, a spectator let out an incoherent shout. The first ejection from the courtroom thus occurred within seconds of Sabo's warning. There would be many, many more.

Calm temporarily restored, Len stood to make an argument that had no realistic chance of succeeding—namely, that Judge Sabo had to recuse himself because of his bias. The reason for Sabo's presence in the first place, after all these years, had more to do with efficiency and custom than anything else. Postconviction appeals (which is what we were engaged in, sometimes called collateral appeals) are handled in the first instance by the original trial judge. The theory is that the original trial judge would have the most familiarity with the case, thereby putting him in the best position to evaluate legal challenges to the original trial proceedings. The problem, of course, is that the original trial judge is not inclined to conclude that he permitted a defendant to be convicted in an unfair trial.

The heart of our argument for recusal was the undeniable fact that Mumia and Judge Sabo despised each other, and the judge had made his antipathy known during the course of the 1982 trial. We claimed that Judge Sabo could not set his strong feelings aside and fairly adjudicate the issues we intended to present, most of which dealt with his conduct and decision making during the trial. On top of that, we brought forward material indicating Judge Sabo's bias against criminal defendants generally, including an affidavit from one lawyer, and statements from six others, that characterized the judge essentially as a defendant's nightmare. We even presented evidence demonstrating that Judge Sabo had been reversed on appeal more often than any other judge in the United States.

In his long argument, Len emphasized the judge's longstanding connections to law enforcement. "Your Honor has served prior to becoming a judge for sixteen years as an undersheriff in Philadelphia.

And while you were in that capacity you were a member of the Fraternal Order of the Police, as I understand it, and you were a member of the Sheriffs' Association. And we don't know what this court's relationship is to those organizations, but we do know that one of the organizations that this court has had a long-standing relationship with is the Fraternal Order of the Police, and that association is now currently, today, actively involved in a campaign to see to it that Mr. Jamal is executed." Len was right: the FOP had taken out newspaper ads, erected a Web site, and sponsored protests and rallies advocating that "Mumia should fry."

Len concluded with a gratuitous observation, but resourceful nonetheless: "I just want to say, I don't think Your Honor is aware of it, but we have two attorneys here from Japan, and two attorneys here from Germany, who were sent by lawyers' associations in their home countries because of their concern over this case. I myself have had a call from the consul general of Italy who said the foreign office in Rome wants a report on these proceedings." Because Len's skills as a lawyer are more jury-oriented, he has a knack for injecting information into a proceeding that adds texture to a legal argument. Many appellate specialists who spend most of their time in law libraries and in front of computer screens fail to humanize their arguments, preferring the world of abstractions. That certain notables were in the audience had nothing to do with the legal issues, of course, and would not have been mentioned by a pure appellate lawyer; but they had everything to do with advocating for Mumia in the larger court of public opinion. It was a resourceful bit of name-dropping.

I, for one, was unaware of whether any notables were in the audience until Len made the announcement. I turned and noticed for the first time that Cornel West, the Harvard philosophy professor, was intensely observing the proceedings. I was pleased, as I believed that we needed witnesses of Cornel West's stature to document what we would experience in Sabo's courtroom.

The prosecution's swift response reflected what we were to experience throughout the litigation: hard-hitting, aggressive, and highly personal attacks. The prosecution came in with a team of four lawyers, each with unique skills and each committed to defusing the political notoriety this case had achieved. (McGill had left the district attorney's office in 1986 to enter private practice.) Prosecutor Hugh Burns, a bald, portly, and humorless man who is an appellate specialist in the district attorney's office, was the first to speak for the prosecution team. Burns was the prosecution team's most relentless advocate. What he lacked in charisma and oratorical flair, he made up with a certain doggedness in his advocacy. I had the impression that Burns had taken a few beatings in elementary school from playground bullies and being a lawyer was his revenge. Len had a darker view of Burns, joking that watching him in action gave new insight into how things were done in a Nazi Germany courtroom.

Pumped up by the excitement of the proceedings, Burns told Judge Sabo in an uninterrupted and rapidly delivered speech that our mission was only to disturb the peace in Philadelphia. "The bottom line in regard to all of the statements that have been made that are contradicted by the record, refuted by the record, refuted by appellate decisions, that the defense attempts to rely on is this: It demonstrates that the defense in this case does not care about the truth, does not care about the law, does not care about the record. What it cares about is making inflammatory statements which are intended to in-flame and feed an atmosphere of public pressure which is directed at you, which is intended to pressure you." Burns urged the judge to resist this "campaign of public pressure."

Burns then held up a piece of paper. "I have seen, in addition to all else I have seen, fliers distributed by I do not know who, in which they include your fax number, and they say put pressure on this judge, send him a fax." Burns then directed a question at the judge: "I won-der if we could ask you for the record, Your Honor, if you have received any faxes?:

Judge Sabo happily obliged, stretching his arms wide the way my little daughter, Hannah, does when I ask her how much she loves me. All the while the judge flashed a smile that gave him a certain childlike charm.

Burns smiled back and swung his head from side to side to signal his disapproval. "I suspect you have received quite a few. I suggest that that is all part and parcel of the strategy that's been adopted by the defense in this case."

It didn't take Judge Sabo long to deny the recusal motion. No one abides being called biased, prejudiced, and unfair. Judges, it's important to remember, are no different. And to be called these things by an out-of-town New York City lawyer with a history of representing political radicals—well, this was no way to get invited to the Sabos' for dinner. As soon as the arguments were concluded, he announced that he had "given serious thought to this, and I see no reason why this court should recuse itself." He claimed that he had been "fair to the defendant during his trial and could be fair to him at this time." The pro-Mumia side of the pews erupted in laughter and snickers, as sheriff's officers took several steps toward the audience, poised to follow the commands of the judge. "I will not tolerate these outbursts," he warned. He then declared, in self-congratulatory fashion, that "mob pressure" and "threats" would not influence him as a jurist.

With the recusal motion summarily disposed of, we pushed to have the stay of execution issued. It was obvious, given the scope of the challenge we were mounting against the prosecution's case, that we would never complete the hearing before the designated execution date. Additionally, Mumia was absolutely entitled to have recourse to an appeal to the Pennsylvania Supreme Court, and then to the federal courts thereafter. The process would take several years. Issuing a stay was pro forma. But we quickly learned firsthand what Mumia has known for years—that with Judge Sabo, nothing can be taken for granted.

In response to the motion for a stay of execution, Judge Sabo wanted to know when we could put on our first witness.

Len began to answer, "We can start that process—"

"Tomorrow? Today? Tomorrow?" Judge Sabo interjected.

"Your Honor, I really do not believe in a death penalty case, we ought to be proceeding under this kind of pressure," Len protested.

"Well, you have to proceed as promptly as possible. As I said before, justice delayed is justice denied." Judge Sabo concerned about justice? The sarcasm in his voice was palpable.

Another prosecutor, Joey Grant, a rough-talking assistant district attorney who had spent several years as a defense attorney with the federal public defender office in Philadelphia, took the judge's cue and pushed to have the proceedings begin in haste. "I think the only recourse for Your Honor," Grant volunteered, "is to say 'Counselor, with all due respect, come on, I don't want to hear it, you made some allegations, now is the time to put up or shut up'—and that's what I suggest we do here." We likened Grant, a talented prosecutor who I grew to like, to Christopher Darden, the black prosecutor on the O. J. Simpson prosecution team, which was fresh in the news at the time of these proceedings. We suspected, perhaps unfairly, that Grant, an African-American, was brought in to defuse the incendiary imagery of a legion of white prosecutors seeking to execute a black man. More disturbing was Grant's reputation as an overzealous, "cross-the-line" litigator. In 1992, a Pennsylvania court reversed a murder conviction against a man named Nicodemo Scarfo on grounds of prosecutorial misconduct. The court stated: "We are especially concerned that prosecutorial misconduct seems to arise in Philadelphia County more so than in any other county in this Commonwealth." The court went on to advise prosecutors to take a "more thoughtful approach to the prosecutor's role in our society." One of the two prosecutors whose conduct was under scrutiny in the *Scarfo* case was Joey Grant.

Burns attacked us from a different angle, saying that because we had time on our hands to stoke up the protesters at rallies, we surely could be ready to present real evidence. "Yesterday," Burns said, "Mr. Weinglass was outside trying to incite the crowd."

Len has always had to battle the legacy of his experience in the Chicago Seven trial. Some people in the legal community still think of him as "that wild man Weinglass," an opprobrium from Judge Hoffman that stuck. Anyone who knows Len—a gentle human being, if there ever was one—realizes how absurd the characterization is. Len shot back at Burns: "This is the kind of thing I'm talking about, Your

Honor. I come to Philadelphia, I expect lawyerly-like conduct." With that, the trappings of dignity in the proceedings melted away in the heat of the dialogue.

The fix was in. We now understood the real function of the August 17 execution date. There would be no execution on August 17, 1995—of that I was certain. The governor established the August 17 date so that Judge Sabo could use it as an artificial deadline by which the PCRA proceedings were to be completed; it thus provided a justification for him to create a climate of haste, which heightens the likelihood of mistakes and omissions. Mistakes and omissions would then be exploited by the prosecution in any future proceedings in federal court, where the real fight would take place. Judge Sabo refused to grant the stay, the better to keep the pressure on.

But he also did something that was rather cunning. He didn't deny our request for a stay either. He ruled that he would "take it under advisement." By doing so, we couldn't take the issue to the Pennsylvania Supreme Court on an emergency appeal, because a litigant can only appeal an actual denial of a request. Judge Sabo made it clear that he wasn't denying our stay application. He just wasn't granting it as of yet. He blindsided us, and he clearly enjoyed the feeling of having the upper hand.

The governor's decision to issue a death warrant—something the legal team knew was a symbolic gesture—galvanized the Mumia supporters, not only those who packed the courtroom but supporters worldwide. To them, August 17 was a *real* deadline, a date that could mark the end of the line for Mumia. To them, the fight for a stay of execution was highly significant, and we opted to pursue our legal strategy with that premise in mind. To the lawyers and to Judge Sabo, the fight over the stay was really about power. Judge Sabo couldn't abide the notion of giving us anything; and to the prosecution, the quibbling over the stay suited their desire to pressure us into putting on a case without the psychological comfort of being fully prepared.

Of the July 12 proceedings Cornel West said: "I've never seen a Jim Crow court until today. The whole atmosphere of this court is

Mississippi 1955, and that's what's sad about it." Throughout the proceedings, we could hear the chants outside: "Justice, Now!" "Free Mumia!" and "Sabo Must Go!"

◼ We never were able to secure the stay of execution before the start of the hearings. Judge Sabo wouldn't even grant our request to have the hearings begin on August 1, only three weeks away. We reluctantly put forth that proposal as a compromise to the prosecution's insistence that we begin immediately. The judge wasn't interested in compromises; if the prosecution thought it best to begin immediately, then the PCRA proceedings would begin immediately.

Faced with a rushed schedule that threatened our ability to present our evidence, we filed an emergency application with the Pennsylvania Supreme Court seeking more time to prepare for the hearing. Jon Piper and another prosecutor on their team debated the issue before Justice Frank J. Montemuro, Jr., of the Pennsylvania Supreme Court, as Len and I prepared ourselves for the courtroom battles to come. Len and I were the designated courtroom litigators; Rachel handled certain motions and logistical matters; and Jon, to the extent that he could squeeze in the time (no small feat given that he was an associate in a corporate law firm), would help me with legal research and drafting of legal memoranda. At the end of the day on July 17, we received word from Jon that Montemuro pushed the start of the hearings back to July 26—a surprising result, given that we were the ones who advocated having the case advanced in the first place. In any event, it still wasn't much time, but at least it gave us a chance to catch our breath. One newspaper article reported in its headline, "Raucous Appeal Hearing Aborted in Abu-Jamal Case." Raucous it was, but aborted it was not.

The next day, July 18, Judge Sabo let it be known that the protesters who appeared outside his home over the weekend—eleven people of the hundred-plus who showed up with placards and healthy lungs were arrested—would not influence his actions. He figured that we lawyers orchestrated, or at least encouraged, the incursion into his private sanctuary, but we had actually had no involvement whatsoever. Although rightfully upset by the protests at his home, he didn't let on that he was miffed by the Pennsylvania Supreme Court's intervention, but he must have been, at the least, a bit annoyed. He quipped to Len, "It reminded me of the old Biblical story of Solomon." Len said that "we felt like that child" who Solomon proposed splitting in half. "So do I," Sabo responded good-naturedly, "because I wanted to start today and you wanted to start August first. And the Supreme Court broke the bone, gave you a piece, gave me a piece, and said now you lawyers chew on it." Sabo seemed to enjoy the back-and-forth. To Sabo, temporarily taken out of retirement to handle this case, the events in his courtroom were a game. It probably broke the monotony of sitting at home playing solitaire.

■ The courtroom dramatics were a boon for the reporters. The media chastised Judge Sabo for his rank partiality. The *Philadelphia Inquirer* remarked after the first few court appearances: "The behavior of the judge was disturbing the first time around—and in hearings last week he did not give the impression to those in the courtroom of fair-mindedness. Instead, he gave the impression, damaging in the extreme, of undue haste and hostility toward the defense's case." A front-page headline in the *Philadelphia Daily News* on July 19, 1995, put it bluntly: "Sabo Must Go." One *Philadelphia Inquirer* columnist, calling Sabo "Mr. Magoo with an attitude," warned that his "behavior" does not "inspire confidence in the court's impartiality." I thought that the reference to Mr. Magoo was interesting; Abbie Hoffman had observed that Judge Julius Hoffman in the Chicago Seven trial looked like Mr. Magoo.

Even Senator Arlen Specter, an unexpected ally, told the Republican National Committee that this case was being mishandled by Judge Sabo. In a speech at the Wyndham Franklin Plaza Hotel, Specter, a former Philadelphia district attorney, stated that, although he did not know the merits of the case, "once the judge says he is entitled to a hearing, it has to be a realistic hearing and a meaningful hearing and a hearing that has adequate time for preparation."

The media impression of Judge Sabo didn't improve over time. In an August 13 editorial, the *Philadelphia Inquirer* had this to say: "Over the last several days in a handsome City Hall courtroom, the search for justice in the case of the death-row inmate Mumia Abu-Jamal might have been a serious, sober, rational affair—a proceeding that enhanced respect for the law. That, unfortunately, has not been the case. And it has been, in large part, because of the injudicious conduct of presiding Commonwealth Court Judge Albert F. Sabo." *The New York Times,* noting that Judge Sabo "has sent more people to death row than any judge in the state," cited actual courtroom occurrences at the hearing to illustrate that Judge Sabo "has been openly contemptuous of the defense." The article further observed that "Judge Sabo has sustained virtually every prosecution objection while shooting down almost every defense objection."

Legal commentator Stuart Taylor, writing for the conservative publication *American Lawyer,* was shocked by the way Judge Sabo conducted the hearings, observing that he "flaunted his bias, oozing partiality toward the prosecution." Taylor faulted Judge Sabo for barring Mumia from presenting witnesses and for "sharply restrict[ing] Jamal's lawyers in their questioning of witnesses, and block[ing] them from making offers of proof on the record to show the import of the precluded testimony."

Throughout the nation, people, many with high-profile names, voiced their concerns over the fairness of Mumia's trial and the 1995 proceedings. A full-page ad in the *New York Times* summarizing our legal claims appeared in early August with an eye-popping list of names. Professor Charles Ogletree, the Harvard Law professor, and three of his colleagues wrote to Governor Ridge on August 4, 1995, urging clemency. So did Jesse Jackson. The National African American Leadership Summit issued a statement on June 10, 1995, expressing its "deep alarm" over Mumia's case. A petition signed by two dozen members of Congress was sent to Attorney General Janet Reno, stating with reference to the impending execution date that a "grave injustice is about to be committed."

The events in Judge Sabo's courtroom reverberated in distant lands. A few thousand supporters marched through downtown Berlin a day after we began the hearings. Protests in France, Denmark, London, Rome, Brasilia, Mexico City, and other cities followed. Early in July, South Africa's largest black newspaper, *The Sowetan,* issued an editorial stating: "When a country's criminal justice system is riddled with racism, it is only the international community that can uphold the rights of its victims. One such victim is award-winning journalist and former Black Panther Mumia Abu-Jamal, a Pennsylvania death-row prisoner who is fighting from his cell the racism of America's justice system." The African National Congress and Nelson Mandela wrote to Governor Ridge. The European Parliament voted a resolution calling upon Judge Sabo to issue a stay of execution and urging a fair review of Mumia's case. Human Rights Watch "joined with many other human rights organizations in raising serious doubts about the fairness of his trial. . . ." French president Jacques Chirac directed his ambassador in Washington to urge the federal government to intervene and spare Mumia's life. Danielle Mitterrand even visited Mumia. The German foreign minister also urged the federal government to intervene. Italian parliamentary deputies, in tandem with a writer's group headed by Salman Rushdie, urged that Mumia's death sentence be lifted. Belgium dispatched a communiqué to the State Department asking for the same thing. The foreign reaction even crossed into violence. In Greece, for example, two bombs went off in American-owned banks, with a radical group taking responsibility for the blasts, saying they were in protest of Mumia's death sentence.

■ The court session on July 26 began, not surprisingly, with Judge Sabo picking a fight with us. We had just taken our seats when the court crier issued the solemn pronouncement, "God save this Honorable Court."

"Take a seat back there!" Judge Sabo shouted to some people in the audience within a fraction of a second after taking the bench. He then directed his anger at one of Rachel's assistants, MOVE member Jeanette Africa. He ordered her away from our table, demanding that she sit in the audience. Len tried to explain that she was assisting the team, but Sabo scoffed at the argument.

"She is not a lawyer," he said sharply. "I am asking her to take a seat back there in the audience."

Len didn't want to back down, but he didn't want to start the proceedings with unnecessary bickering either. "I think it should be noted that she has sat there [at the defense table behind Mumia] without disruption of any kind for the last court session."

"I am not talking about disruption. I am saying that is not the proper place for her to sit. She had too much to say in the last trial and that's why we had a lot of trouble." Age and the passage of over a decade had not dimmed the judge's memory. He remembered that Mumia had consulted with Jeanette throughout the 1982 trial. This recollection of the 1982 trial prompted some shouts from the audience. Judge Sabo shouted back: "Any outbursts and you will be evicted from the courtroom. You are not out on the street. What you do on the street I don't care, but in this courtroom you will show proper respect for the proceedings that are going on here now."

Len waited for the judge to finish his warning. "Your Honor, the court's last comment about the first trial is reflective of an attitude—"

"It is not reflective of anything," Judge Sabo interrupted. "I am just telling you plain ordinary facts that occurred, Counselor." Judge Sabo was fond of using that appellation, "counselor." He said it with an edge, using the word as a verbal jab at a lawyer. He didn't give Len a chance to respond, opting to change the subject. "I understand you subpoenaed the governor and his staff."

Indeed we did. We wanted the governor and four of his aides to testify as to the timing of the issuance of the death warrant. We didn't yet know about the forwarding of intercepted legal mail to the governor, but we knew that the timing of the death warrant was not coincidental. The governor, of course, was moving to quash the subpoena and an argument date had been set for Monday, July 31.

Len tried to shift the focus back to Judge Sabo's attitude. He renewed our recusal motion, pointing out that numerous news outlets had been critical of the judge's handling of the proceedings thus far. Len was waving photocopies of newspaper articles, arguing that "community sentiment" is a relevant criterion for determining whether a judge should continue to sit on a case.

"Community sentiment does not control, Counselor. This court does not buckle under community pressure. Let's go! The recusal request is denied. For the tenth time, the twentieth, the thirtieth time, it is denied! Let's proceed with the case, Counselor."

Prosecutor Grant chimed in, "May the Commonwealth call its first witness, if he declines to do so?"

"One way or another we are proceeding," Judge Sabo said, speaking directly toward the prosecution side of the room.

"The Supreme Court has ordered this court to stop hurrying us," Len pointed out.

Judge Sabo glared momentarily at Len, undoubtedly fuming over Len's willingness to use our minor victory with the Pennsylvania Supreme Court to embarrass him before a packed courtroom. He spoke again of King Solomon, as if the telling of the story would convince everyone that the higher court had not personally repudiated him when it ordered that we be given additional time to prepare. "They have taken a bone and broken it and given you a piece and given me a piece," Judge Sabo said bitterly. "And as I told you before, I ate my piece. And that's spelled A-T-E, for the news media. Now let's proceed." He didn't want the media to misunderstand what he had said and erroneously report that he "hated" what the Supreme Court had done. There was no doubt that he was sensitive to how the media was reporting the courtroom events. Truth be told, everyone was.

■ I knew that we had to eviscerate the good-versus-evil story that McGill had deployed so successfully at the 1982 trial, and I thought the best way to do that would be to develop a good-versus-evil story of our own. A useful first step, in my view, would be to undermine a critical premise of McGill's narrative: namely, that Mumia was a dangerous, violence-prone radical who was nothing more than a time bomb. That's how I proposed to begin.

We arranged to have in court on July 26 six mitigation witnesses: State Representative David P. Richardson, journalists E. Steven Collins and Joe Davidson, Mumia's high school teacher Ken Hamilton, a longtime family friend Ruth Ballard, and Mumia's sister, Lydia Wallace. These witnesses, who I prepared and would question, were exemplars of the type of evidence that could have been presented to the jury back in 1982 as a basis for advocating for a life sentence. Since I would be the first to question witnesses in the PCRA proceedings, I would have to play it by ear as to how much latitude Judge Sabo was going to give us in the questioning.

■ My image of a good penalty phase defense is Richard Wright's *Native Son.* The hero in that book, Bigger Thomas, committed a ghastly crime—killed a girl, hacked up her body, and burnt it in an incinerator. A prosecutor's presentation to a jury would focus only on those few minutes of Bigger's life. If a juror/reader focused solely on those few minutes, she would likely be quite inflamed and perhaps amenable to imposing a death sentence. But I dare say that few readers of *Native Son* come away from the experience anxious to send Bigger Thomas into the death chamber. The reason is because Richard Wright does a masterful job of bringing us into Bigger's world, allowing us to understand him, to see him as a complex human being with intrinsic dignity and worth, without sugarcoating the hideousness of his crime. A dedicated trial lawyer gets inside the emotional universe of his client, and in so doing, is able to remove his client from the presumptive category of evil he finds himself in at the start of a capital trial. Richard Wright, like so many other great-souled artists, shows us how it is done.

It is often said that a great trial lawyer, like a great novelist, preacher, or prophet, is a great storyteller. An effective death penalty trial lawyer must be the ultimate storyteller.

Anthony Jackson never thought about how to advocate for Mumia's life in the event of a conviction. He never assembled evidence about Mumia's life; he never consulted with people who had known him at various stages of his life; he never even talked with Mumia about the subject. It was, therefore, inevitable that the penalty phase would be, at the least, a perfunctory affair, and at worst, a disaster.

McGill had focused almost exclusively on Mumia's early association with the Black Panther Party, knowing that the jury probably held an image of that organization as destructive, ruthless, and threatening to all that white middle-class America holds dear. The Panthers were indeed fond of Mao's remark that "all political power grows out of the barrel of a gun." Mumia's early political awareness could not have sidestepped such sloganeering. But it was too much for McGill's jury, nurtured on network news and sitcoms, to understand that the Panthers in general, and Mumia in particular, embraced Mao's remark as an observation, a pithy distillation, of European and American history. Mumia tried to explain that point to the jury, but the transmittal of that message, occurring in Judge Sabo's pressure-cooker courtroom with the fog of death hovering over the proceedings, was lost upon an audience that had already adjudicated Mumia a cold-blooded cop killer.

Mumia did indeed embrace radical politics. He still does. What the jury did not hear was that Mumia's commitment to radical politics was not, as McGill suggested, the scaffolding upon which Mumia built his desire to kill police officers. Rather, like many others, Mumia came to radical politics, the Black Panther Party, and advocacy journalism because he felt that social justice requires attacking the roots of our society's ills—notably racism and poverty, which flourish in an unjust economic system. Violence was not the trajectory of his radical politics; community service was.

There was no excuse for Jackson's failure to bring in mitigation witnesses to counteract McGill's distorted caricature of Mumia. He had the good sense to bring in respected Philadelphians like Representative Richardson and Senator Street at the bail hearing six months earlier. Newspaper accounts of the crime were often filled with commentary by people who knew Mumia, expressing shock that he would be involved in such a violent incident. A December 10, 1981, report in the *Philadelphia Daily News*, for example, noted that "Jamal's arrest for murder seems another contradiction in the life of a man remembered by friends as calm and peace-loving." The article further reported that those who knew Mumia described him as "talented, brilliant, compassionate." It went on to say: "He was an award-winning journalist of immense talent . . . whose work showed deep compassion and understanding of the city's minority community." The *Philadelphia Inquirer* came out with a profile of Mumia on the same day. It noted that, according to those who knew him, "Violence was something alien to Jamal—despite his association with militant groups." The *Inquirer* piece added: "Jamal's friends described him as a gentle man, a good reporter with an excellent radio voice and a social activist who never preached violence."

Acel Moore, an associate editor at the *Philadelphia Inquirer*, was in shock when news came out of Mumia's arrest. "Mumia, whom I have known professionally for several years, was a gentle man who I would not consider capable of a violent act," Moore stated to other reporters. The news director at public radio station WUHY, Nick Peters, underscored the point: "I never detected anything in him that would suggest violence."

My strategy for the hearing was to explore four areas of Mumia's life to illuminate his personal qualities: his commitment to community service and empowerment, his commitment to family, his commitment to peace and nonviolence, and his commitment to the craft of journalism. Three individuals with reputations beyond challenge were slated to be our core witnesses: Representative Richardson, Philadelphia radio journalist E. Steven Collins, and *Wall Street Journal* reporter Joe Davidson. Mumia's sister, his high school teacher, and his mother's close friend would be complementary witnesses, adding more color to the portrait that the core witnesses would paint.

State Representative David Richardson was the first of our witnesses. He testified that he came to know Mumia through their shared commitment to the community: "We were very actively involved in the community through a number of organizations, groups, to try to help promote and motivate the community around cultural and positive aspects of the African-American community here in the city of Philadelphia." He added: "It was Mumia's compassion for people and compassion for those issues that impacted directly on vital issues, such as housing, such as health care, such as feeding the homeless, that drew me closer to Mumia."

Richardson's testimony showed how Mumia's talents and activism flowed from his deep devotion to the voiceless. He looked upon Mumia as a fusion of slain black leaders: "[I]t was the compassion and heart and feeling of Dr. Martin Luther King but the tenacity of a Malcolm X, and also the conviction of a man like Medgar Evers. And I think if you tied them together and you look at what we have here today you would have that in a total, comprehensive sense in Mr. Jamal, who has been actively involved in our city and struggle for a long time."

Richardson's invocation of martyred black leaders was echoed by E. Steven Collins. Collins testified that Jamal "had a way of translating human emotion through radio so that no matter where you were you understood the circumstances. I think of him as I think of Dr. King. Because Dr. King did that." Collins's and Richardson's assessment of Mumia was not at all surprising. Mary Mason of radio station WHAT, a prominent radio broadcaster with a popular morning radio show, described Mumia to a reporter from the *Philadelphia Daily News* the day after the shooting "as a Malcolm X, Dr. Martin Luther King, and the Rev. Jesse Jackson rolled into one."

Richardson also led the way with strongly worded answers about Mumia's peaceful disposition and commitment to nonviolence. Richardson described him as a "strong advocate" for peace, a "peacemaker" who "abhorred violence." Collins said he could not "remember one time where there was ever a discussion, any hostility, verbal or otherwise, towards any law enforcement, or even a philosophical view that would suggest that." In trying to articulate his view of Mumia's attitude toward peace and violence, Collins stated that he "search[ed his] mind" but could not find any indication of a proclivity toward violence. "In my mind I thought a million times about this whole preoccupation with his supposed philosophical bent on hurting law enforcement or whatever," Collins explained. "And I don't remember ever, ever, ever hearing that or having a discussion with Mumia or other people where that came up or that was principal or centerpiece as he has been treated in many news stories since this occurred."

I knew that much of Mumia's self-image was wrapped up in his activities as a journalist. I wanted the witnesses to explain that Mumia never separated craft from politics: what he did as a journalist was entwined with his commitment to social change. Journalism was, I intuited, an outlet for his acute sensitivity to the voiceless in society. At the time of his arrest, he was serving as president of the Philadelphia Association of Black Journalists. His mastery of the craft was well-known and admired. Every profile of Mumia published in the immediate wake of the shooting, of which there were several, focused primarily on his immense talents as a journalist. The *Philadelphia Inquirer* reported on December 10, 1981, that "one of [Mumia's] former news directors said yesterday, it was his searing and skillful interviews and radio reports on 'the system' as it affected the swirling forces and subtleties of inner-city life that made him a well-known figure in local broadcast journalism." Nick Peters, the public radio station news director, remarked, "If you ever heard his reports it was incredible. People would hear his reports and always wanted to know more about the subject. He had an incredible presence."

Radio personality Mary Mason felt Mumia was "one of the best in the business." Mason, who had her run-ins professionally with Mumia, still viewed him as "an extraordinary news person. Jamal could have been a network anchor." A colleague at WUHY where Mumia once worked, America Rodriguez, explained that Mumia had "a dramatic flair." "He didn't make his stories dramatic. He could draw out the drama of an event."

Collins testified that he would have told the jury that Mumia was "the greatest voice and greatest journalist I had met," someone his peers expected would rise to the level of broadcasters like Charles Osgood and Ed Bradley. According to Collins, Mumia's commitment to the community was "seemingly his trademark" because his journalism spoke for "people who needed a voice. People who were out of work . . . [I]f you are standing in an employment line or in a welfare line and you get short treatment, as the people do on that level, Mumia would articulate and illuminate their condition in an incredible way." Joe Davidson, the *Wall Street Journal* reporter, testified that Mumia was "the best radio journalist in the city."

I prompted Representative Richardson to remember the time when Mumia aired an appeal to the community to help locate a missing child. He explained that this particular broadcast "sticks out more so than a lot of other cases . . . because it was the compassion that was shown directly as it related to human life." As a Temple student, Collins recalled hearing a commentary by Mumia on the pointless shooting death of a young black man. "[I]n three minutes it felt like I had a keen insight into what happened and Mumia's conclusion was compelling and it encouraged people to think about the value of life."

Mumia's older sister, Lydia Wallace, explained in her testimony that her brother had a passion for justice even as a child growing up in the housing projects. "He cared about people. He wanted everyone to have a fair shake. . . . He was sensitive to the people's plight, hardship, oppression."

A longtime neighbor and family friend, Ruth Ballard, recalled Mumia as a young boy giving Bible lessons to others: "There is one particular incident where in the summertime mainly they would have Bible classes. And a teacher would come around and teach them at the community hall different things about the Bible and the Lord. And Mumia would go as well as other children, but Mumia would do something different after the class was over. He would go home and he would gather up the little children and he would read to them from the literature that he had received in Bible class. As though he was the preacher or the teacher."

Mumia's generosity was underscored by his high school teacher, Kenneth Hamilton, who said that "Mumia was just very eager to share with other classmates." Hamilton also remembered Mumia for his intellect and his voracious reading. "I was impressed by his intelligence, his sincerity," Hamilton explained. "He was very well read for a young man of his age and he stood out far from the rest of the class." Hamilton's testimony was reminiscent of a comment made by Mumia's principal at Benjamin Franklin High School, Leon Bass, in the wake of his arrest. Bass told a reporter that he remembered Mumia as one who helped lead an unsuccessful student effort to change the school's name to Malcolm X High School. He described Mumia as having "great potential."

With all the emphasis on Mumia's work as a journalist, I did my best to explore his private life, which I had come to learn displayed the same compassion he expressed publicly. The problem was that Mumia is an intensely private person, one who is highly reticent when it comes to exposing private feelings and personal information about his childhood. Mumia's sister testified that their family life during Mumia's childhood was structured, spiritually based, and loving. Mumia fostered a loving relationship with his siblings. Lydia explained that her brother was especially close to his mother, visiting her frequently even after he went out on his own. He also was a father at the time of his trial, and his devotion to his children was visible to those who knew him. In fact, Representative Richardson carried with him the following image of Mumia: "You could picture Mumia with his son on his shoulders and his microphone in his hand interviewing people in the community as he was actually out in the community doing his work."

The struggle to reconfigure the good-versus-evil narrative that would redefine the case had a positive start. Faced with the vivid and compelling portrait these witnesses provided, prosecutor Grant recognized, in his words, the "immense talents of Mr. Jamal," his "obviously talented journalistic voice, and his activism." He then admitted, to our amazement, that the killing of Officer Faulkner could not be squared with Mumia's true character: "From all the descriptions of everybody that has come here—and they all are good people from what I can see, I believe—I don't think the shooting of Officer Faulkner is characteristic of this defendant." Quite a change from McGill's blistering assessment.

■ The court session ended on July 26 the way it began, with angry shouts. After I finished up the questioning for the day, the judge wanted to know who we would be presenting the next day. After some discussion on the matter, Judge Sabo quickly left the bench. Rachel had walked up to the podium to address certain problems over visitation with Mumia. Judge Sabo had obviously ignored her. The slight aroused the pro-Mumia spectators and they began chanting "Sabo must go!" Someone went back to chambers and moments later Judge Sabo returned to the bench.

"There is too much noise in this courtroom," he angrily exclaimed. "If you don't shut up I will put you all outside."

Someone yelled out, "This is bullshit!"

"Take him out!" Judge Sabo ordered.

The spectator, an elderly and frail black man, raised his hands to indicate that he would leave voluntarily. As he gingerly made his way toward the aisle from his seat, he shouted out to Sabo in a strained voice, "You are a judge! You are a judge!" It was a powerful moment, the perfect thing to say. Judge Sabo needed to be reminded that, as a judge, it was his duty to rise above the agitation engendered by strong feelings stemming from the case.

It seemed to me Sabo was ruffled and embarrassed, but he tried to mask it with bravado. "Put him out!" he demanded again. Court officers moved in to take the elderly black man by the arm when he abruptly swung at one of them, protesting, "I can walk! I can walk!" I suppose it was because of his age and evident frailty that the court officers didn't get overly physical with him. On several occasions during the hearing, court officers literally threw spectators out of the courtroom.

Sabo pounded both fists on the bench. "It is getting to be a circus here, Mr. Weinglass. Stop this nonsense." Another outburst of laughter instigated the court crier to demand silence. "Boy, I will tell you, this is getting to be a circus. It *is* a shame. It's a disgrace." With that, the judge trudged toward the door to his chambers.

I just shook my head. It was only the beginning.

I did the best I could with the resources that
I had.

ANTHONY JACKSON

14. REVISITING
THE PAST

It was only a matter of time before Judge Sabo would start
threatening us with contempt, for which he was famous among
the local criminal defense practitioners. It happened for the first time
on the second day of the proceedings, July 27. Judge Sabo wanted me
to call the next witness. While we had intended that our next witness
would be Anthony Jackson, we weren't sure if he was fully prepared
to handle the stress of answering uncomfortable questions about his
performance in a very difficult case. Len and I were huddled in a
conference with Mumia, as the judge peered impatiently at us. We
were discussing the other possible witnesses to call before putting Jackson on the stand.

"It is past nine-thirty now, Counselor, call your next witness." We
were still deep in conversation, oblivious to the judge. "Mr. Williams.
Mr. Williams! Mr. Williams!" I looked up, startled. "The court has
directed you to call the next witness. I don't want to have to hold
you in contempt."

There it was: the contempt threat. We entered the PCRA proceedings having heard much about Sabo's penchant for threatening lawyers with contempt. It was a relief of sorts to have him use the word early in the litigation, almost like taking an early punch in a boxing match to remove the frightening aura of the contest. The threat would be issued numerous times during the course of the hearings, and actual citations issued twice, against Len and Rachel. In fact, the threats became so routine we eventually didn't even take notice.

After some squabbling with the judge over scheduling, we called Jackson to the stand. Len had been working with him for days, and he would be doing the questioning. I liked Jackson, because he struck me as compassionate and genuine. I remember him, Len, and me having dinner one evening several months before the hearings, and I marveled at how unguarded he was. He knew what we were hoping to do: paint him as an incompetent. It says a lot about Jackson that he was willing to spend hours going back over a time in his life that he probably wanted desperately to forget when he knew what our mission was. As horrible as the experience in 1982 was for him, he still retained a generous spirit.

During the times when I observed Len preparing Jackson as we approached the day he would take the stand, I could see his eyes gradually deaden and his stamina wither. There came a point when he just wanted the whole thing to be over with—finally and definitively, over. I felt pained at what we would necessarily subject him to in the PCRA hearing. It is never easy for a lawyer to take the witness stand, especially for a trial lawyer whose psychological makeup is geared to having control in the courtroom. It is especially stressful for a criminal defense lawyer to relinquish control by being questioned in the context of a claim that he didn't provide constitutionally adequate representation. The stress is magnified when the case is receiving worldwide attention. On the one hand, Jackson didn't want to see Mumia executed; no defense lawyer wants that for a client. On the other hand, no lawyer, and Jackson was no exception, enjoys having his performance put under a microscope and critiqued with the benefit of hindsight for any semblance of performance deficiency. As lawyers for Mumia, we would be unforgiving in our critique; but as a fellow trial lawyer, I was more tempered, because I know that it is impossible to go through a trial without making mistakes.

■ Jackson took hesitant steps as he approached the witness chair. Beads of perspiration had already formed on his brow and his tie seemed to be tightened unnaturally around his neck. Len first lobbed simple questions to Jackson about his personal background, a standard way of warming up a witness. Len then gently moved into the area of his experience with capital punishment litigation. Jackson claimed that he had handled upward of twenty capital cases before getting involved with Mumia's case. This was plainly wrong, and I jotted a quick note to Len to indicate why I thought so. Jackson had spent three years with a public interest agency doing civil litigation; at the time of Mumia's arrest, the revived death penalty in Pennsylvania had only been on the books for those same three years. There was no conceivable way Jackson could have handled a single capital case, let alone twenty. Len wisely didn't launch into an attack of our own witness at this early stage of the questioning, notwithstanding my initial exuberant backseat-driver instinct to attack. It is usually better to get what you need from a witness with friendly questioning, then attack later, if necessary.

I was pleased that Len took my suggestion to get the "good stuff" concerning the penalty phase before entering into the thornier area of Jackson's guilt-phase representation. Our prep sessions with Jackson revealed that his inadequate performance in the penalty phase was straightforward and undeniable. He quickly admitted on the stand that he had talked with no one about testifying in the penalty phase, had subpoenaed no witnesses, and had not developed a plan for re-buffing McGill's vigorous advocacy for death. "We were working six days a week for a couple of weeks," Jackson explained, oddly using the word "we" when in fact he had worked alone on the case. "I assumed that we would have had at least an extra day to prepare for the sentencing." That's what you get for assuming anything in Sabo's courtroom, I thought to myself.

Len then nailed the point: "So that we are clear, Mr. Jackson, prior to the verdict of guilt on Friday afternoon, July second, you hadn't done anything to prepare for the penalty phase hearing, is that right?" Jackson nodded and acknowledged that this was true.

Jackson's admission that he did nothing to present a case for life on Mumia's behalf was, in my judgment, very important. For many supporters, and for Jon and Rachel, it meant little because the sentiment was that nothing would be acceptable short of Mumia's release from prison. As important as that goal was (and remains), the reality that any death penalty litigator understands is that saving the client's life is paramount because it presents the most immediate problem to be solved. The foundation upon which the death penalty can be overturned having been laid, the lawyer can then work for his client's exoneration, if that is feasible under the circumstances. If too much emphasis is placed on complete exoneration at the expense of developing a powerful case against the death verdict, one risks losing the entire case—and the client dies. It is like doing emergency medicine: save the patient's life, and then deal with restoring him to full health, if that is possible. It was always my orientation, and that of Steve Hawkins—which made us (the two death penalty litigators) the lone voices on the defense team—to place at least as much emphasis on the penalty phase as on the guilt phase in litigating Mumia's case.

After questioning Jackson about his mishandling of the penalty phase, Len moved into the far more delicate area of Jackson's guilt-phase performance—delicate because Jackson felt that it was wrong to fault him for the jury's verdict. He felt he had performed adequately, and he still had some understandable remnants of bitterness toward the MOVE members who castigated and threatened him during and after the trial. But, to his credit, he kept those feelings hidden from view as he testified before the packed courtroom. Len identified each of the witnesses called by the defense and asked Jackson if he had talked with any of them before testifying. Jackson admitted that he put all of them on the stand cold.

Len then brought up the subject of Debbie Kordansky. Jackson explained that he was too swamped to arrange for her attendance in advance of the trial. "In this case, unlike any other homicide case that I had tried before," he explained, "the district attorney was pretty much in control of all of the witnesses. They had redacted the addresses and phone numbers of the witnesses and cut them out literally. There was no way for the defense to contact these witnesses without going through the district attorney's office. Miss Kordansky was one person I wanted to speak to. Why? Among other things, she said she saw a man running from the scene. Obviously I wanted to see her."

Jackson paused to see if Len wanted to ask a question. Len just looked at him, which prompted Jackson to continue. "I remember bringing this up to the judge and Mr. McGill. As I recall, Mr. McGill said words to the effect that she didn't want to talk to me, she had nothing to say, she'd hurt me or something of that sort. This was the kind of thing Mr. McGill always kept telling me, that these witnesses don't want to testify for the defense or won't be good for the defense."

Len questioned Jackson about other mishaps in the trial, seeking to get Jackson to take responsibility for them. He admitted to certain lapses, including his failure to attack cab driver Robert Chobert with evidence of his probationary status arising from a conviction for throwing a Molotov cocktail into a public school. He also admitted that he should have arranged for Officer Wakshul's attendance to undermine the reliability of the confession evidence. Another lapse was Jackson's failure to notice that the medical examiner who performed the autopsy made a hand-written notation on the first page of the autopsy report that the bullet penetrating the slain officer's skull was a .44 caliber.

At first blush, it appeared that there had been a finding that the fatal bullet was a .44 caliber, which would have ruled out Mumia's .38 caliber pistol, and therefore would have exonerated him. Jackson totally missed this avenue of attack upon the prosecution's case. The wrinkle, however, is that our own ballistics expert concluded that the fatal bullet was, indeed, a .38 caliber. That fact has not deterred many to proclaim, erroneously, that Officer Faulkner was killed by a .44 caliber bullet. When we realized that we could not, in fact, make out a case that the fatal bullet was a .44 caliber, we pursued a more limited point. Jackson's failure to notice the ".44 cal." reference on the first page of the autopsy report spoke volumes about his shoddy trial preparation. It would be one thing for him to decide, as a practical matter, that he would not use this reference in the report to undermine the reliability of the medical examiner's testimony; it's an entirely different matter to bypass its use completely because it simply wasn't noticed. It is difficult to fathom how any modestly prepared lawyer could have overlooked the ".44 cal." notation on the first page of the medical examiner's report. Jackson's failure to notice it illustrated just how ill prepared and overwhelmed he was.

Jackson seemed relieved when that line of questioning was over. He insisted that he had not "given Mumia second-rate service." He said that he had given him "the best that I could with the resources that were made available to me." Jackson much preferred answering questions about "the resources that were made available" to him. He had no problem blasting the Philadelphia court system, in part because the attention was deflected away from his own conduct and performance; but most importantly, he seemed invigorated by the opportunity to expose the stinginess of the system, because, to him, that was the true source of the evil.

Jackson explained that the court system allocated $150 for a pathologist. "I telephoned five, six, seven pathologists in this area of Pennsylvania, New Jersey, Maryland, Delaware. The best I could get was a pathologist in Pittsburgh who said if I would mail it to him he would read [the autopsy report] and tell me something over the telephone. For a hundred and fifty dollars he says he doesn't walk out of his neighborhood. And he was the cheapest. I had no success in finding a pathologist who would even consider reviewing [the report], talk to me or anything, for a hundred and fifty dollars."

As for a ballistics expert, Jackson said it was "almost an identical situation." He had contacted a ballistician he knew from his days as an evidence technician with the police department, George Fassnacht. Jackson was able to muster about $350 from Judge Ribner, but as Jackson explained, "I did not have enough funds for him to perform any tests, any examinations, nor for his appearance in court."

Jackson testified that he received "a grand total" of about $800 to secure expert assistance in the trial, including the services of an investigator. To exacerbate the difficulty, Jackson added, "Assuming even the amount given by the court was acceptable, you then had to ask that they wait approximately a year before they receive the money."

Len finished his questioning by the lunch break. When we returned for the afternoon session, I noticed a shouting match outside the courtroom entrance between Mumia's family members and supporters and court officers. I couldn't make out what the problem was because the shouting garbled the arguments; all I could see was that folks were angry and Maureen Faulkner was reduced to tears.

I tried to ask Rachel what had happened in the hallway as the afternoon court session was called to order, but was interrupted when two spectators were forcibly removed for standing with clenched fists in the air after court officers had ordered them to sit down and a third spectator was ejected for raising his hand in a Hitler salute. By the time that flare-up was under control, Rachel was already at the podium complaining that the off-duty police and Faulkner family members were permitted to enter the courtroom without going through the metal detectors. This apparently agitated the Mumia supporters. Rachel complained that this sort of favoritism was unfair. I heard Maureen whisper loudly, "That's not true!" Yelling then erupted behind us; more spectators were ejected for hurling insults at the judge.

Grant disputed Rachel's assertion, stating: "I don't know where she gets her information but I wish she would start researching some of the statements she makes prior to opening her mouth."

"She does that all the time," Judge Sabo added.

The personal attack on Rachel was not unusual. The prosecutors and the judge had a particular dislike of her, either because she was the most strident one in the courtroom or because they had investigated us and learned that she was not a genuinely practicing lawyer and was the most ardent leftist on the defense team. Len, of course, received grudging respect as an old warrior. As for me, Grant and some of the detectives pulled me aside in the hallway during one of the breaks in the proceedings and chided me that I was still young enough to salvage my otherwise promising career as a trial lawyer if only I would cross over that great divide and fight on the side of the angels. I simply laughed at the mock invitation and joked that I was having too much fun representing bad guys. "You'll be sorry," one of the detectives warned with a wry smile.

Grant made the suggestion that the pro-Mumia supporters enter through one set of metal detectors and those sympathetic to the Faulkner family enter through another set. He explained that this solution suited the hair-trigger atmosphere that pervaded the court proceedings. "Since July the twelfth when we started these proceedings, there has been a constant tumult, incessant horns blaring, crowds shouting, right underneath the window where the proceedings are taking place," Grant recounted. "We've had three outbursts, four outbursts in the last three days. People shouting and directing comments to Your Honor. People have been escorted out today. There's been a sum total of about sixteen people ejected from the courtroom. Now, I am not suggesting that the defense team is orchestrating any of this, but certainly emotions are very volatile and spirits are very high. I would suggest for counsels' own protection and everybody else that there be two separate entrances and they have metal detectors at both entrances."

As it turned out, the judge didn't quite understand what Grant was proposing. He ordered the court officers to set up a separate entrance for use by the Faulkner family *and* Mumia's family, while everyone else had to use the general public entrance. We were pleased with that arrangement. We weren't so pleased with Sabo's offhand remark that he approved of off-duty officers attending the proceedings carrying concealed guns. When we protested, he waved our concerns away, stating that they did so for his "protection."

The afternoon session was devoted to Joey Grant's cross-examination of Jackson. Grant was a tireless questioner, though at times overly enamored with big words and long complex sentences. His convoluted locutions frustrated Jackson. Wording aside, however, the message was clear: any deficiencies in Jackson's performance had nothing to do with his preparation or commitment to the case; rather, it had everything to do with Mumia's "control" over it.

"I don't envy the position you were in," Grant said as a preface to a question, "but tell me if this is a fair statement. Basically, Mr. Jamal was telling you what to do and dictating both the strategy and the witnesses to be called."

"No, sir," Jackson fired back. "Mr. Jamal was not dictating anything to me."

Grant then proceeded to confront Jackson with various snippets from the trial transcript. There were several occasions during the trial when Mumia had consulted with various MOVE members during court recesses. Grant brought out those occasions to suggest that Mumia was taking orders from MOVE. Grant also quoted several passages where Jackson told Judge Sabo that Mumia wished to follow the "strategy of John Africa" and did not want "a legally trained lawyer" representing him.

"Were you running the show?" Grant didn't even give Jackson a chance to answer. "You weren't running the show, you were part of the show, Mr. Jackson, weren't you?"

Jackson fought back, answering, "I don't know what you mean about 'the show,' Mr. Grant." Jackson was feisty, but Grant's badgering was beginning to wear him down. It was getting close to 4:00 P.M., and he needed a break. "He did not dictate to me . . . he did not dictate strategy to me," Jackson griped. "If he did, I would have walked out of the courtroom then."

The cross-examination continued, with long incoherent statements by Grant couched as questions. Then, without any real catalyst, Jackson inexplicably broke into tears. He simply stopped talking and tears began rolling down his cheeks. He tried to compose himself but couldn't stop his stammering speech. He had to be helped off the witness stand, manifestly overwrought. Grant told me years later that he thought Jackson had stopped breathing, which frightened him momentarily. It was a bizarre moment because he wasn't talking about an emotional subject when he began to cry; he was fielding questions about the possibility that Mumia's supporters raised money for him during the pretrial phase of the case. No one could figure out what had prompted the display of emotion at that moment. I watched Jackson slowly step down from the witness stand and thought to myself that the glare of attention had taken its toll. Upon reflection, it occurred to me that Jackson had reason to be very sensitive over suggestions of financial impropriety—which is what Grant was insinuating.* Jackson was suspended from the practice of law several years after Mumia's trial due to the mishandling of client funds—a fact that Grant didn't expose because, deep down, he regarded Jackson as a friend and as a noble man.

I had my run-ins with Grant during the proceedings, but I respected his forbearance in that instance. He could have drilled in the knife and really bloodied Jackson. But he didn't, out of simple human decency. Too often, in the heat of battle, we forget to be decent.

■ It wouldn't be a day in Judge Sabo's courtroom without an acrimonious exchange between the judge and the defense team. When Jackson left the courtroom out of a side exit, Len moved to the podium to address the judge. Sabo was on his way off the bench. "Your Honor, one last thing," Len cried out.

"What is it Mr. Weinglass? Why don't we wait until tomorrow morning?" Fatigued, Sabo was in no mood for more verbal sparring.

"Tomorrow might be too late," Len said, gripping the podium with both hands. "I just want to make one simple request of the district attorney." Len explained that he needed the prosecution to provide a document to us that was part of the court record.

Fatigue had gotten to Grant also, as he reacted testily. "I am sick of giving them everything!" he shouted.

Judge Sabo, anxious to get home, simply didn't want to get into the middle of a shouting match. "Well, I don't have it."

*Jackson was appointed by the court, which meant that he was not allowed to accept money from sources other than the court.

"I am sure the district attorney has it," Len said, maintaining his calm.

"Try to find it tonight," Judge Sabo responded.

"I don't have it, Your Honor."

"Well, I don't have it, either."

The calmness in Len's voice was slowly giving way to the high-pitched sounds of stress and frustration. "I am not asking the court for it; I am asking the court to ask the district attorney to provide it for us."

"Well, ask them for it," Judge Sabo responded, apparently forgetting Grant's earlier outburst.

"I have, and they refuse," Len explained.

"Go and ask the Supreme Court for it," the judge advised. "I don't have it. What do you want me to do, dig something up for you? I don't have it."

Judge Sabo, either through maliciousness or idiocy, refused to acknowledge the nature of Len's request. "I want you to perform as a judge interested in the rights of my client," Len said, now fully rebuking the judge.

Judge Sabo rose from his chair. "Don't leave the bench," Len commanded. *Uh-oh,* I thought.

"I am leaving the bench now because I am tired of this, Counselor. Let's deal with this tomorrow!"

"Same old game . . . Tomorrow . . . You will tell me then that it's too late."

Grant, who had been packing his files, quickly moved to the railing. "Oh, shit," I muttered to myself. I had never seen Len become unhinged like that in a courtroom.

"You know what, Judge," Grant advised, "I think counsel needs to be reprimanded. I don't think he understands the rules of decorum and the profession in a courtroom."

Judge Sabo glared at Len. "Do you understand, *Counselor,* that you are here by permission of this court?" The threat was real. We had no right to appear as lawyers in a jurisdiction for which we had no license. Judge Sabo had the power to strip us of the privilege of handling this case in his courtroom.

"I understand that," Len answered—he too sensing that we needed to be careful.

"You could be removed. So please. Don't go too far." With that last remark, Judge Sabo strode toward the door to his chambers.

■ Judges like to pretend that they are oblivious to news coverage of their cases. The events inside Courtroom 253 were front-page news in the papers and the lead story on the local news broadcasts during the 1995 PCRA proceedings, just as the trial proceedings were in 1982. When Judge Sabo entered the courtroom on Friday morning, July 28, he had something to say to the news media that left no doubt that he read the papers. "To you people of the news media. I do wish that you would report the proceedings in here correctly," he complained. "You said that we had evicted three people yesterday because they refused to sit. We actually evicted four. Three of them were evicted because when they stood up they turned their back to the court. The fourth one was evicted—he was a rather stocky white male who had stood up and gave the court a Nazi salute." Sabo moved his microphone closer and he put his mouth up against it. "Well, nobody in this courtroom will address this court with a Nazi salute. He not only was evicted but he was told that he could not come back any further in these proceedings. I will not tolerate any Nazi salute in this courtroom." I suppose the judge had a point. Refusing to stand or raising a defiant fist in the air are, in my view, acceptable signs of disapproval even inside a courtroom (so long as a jury is not present to witness it); a gesture that equates this case with the horrors of Nazism, however, is not something that any judge will tolerate.

Judge Sabo had one more point to make. He was taking a real hit in the press and on the local news broadcasts. His unguarded remarks and his undisguised favoritism to the prosecution prompted numerous commentaries about his unfitness to preside over the case.

Some lamented that he was doing the prosecution and the Faulkner family a disservice, which I thought was absolutely true. For the life of me, I do not know why the powers that be in the Philadelphia criminal justice system allowed Sabo to preside over the PCRA proceedings. Allowing a respected jurist to handle the matter would have given the proceedings a semblance of legitimacy. In any event, the media suggestion that he was actually a detriment to the prosecution side of the case had to have wounded him.

"I also read in the news media that there is constant bickering between defense counsel and the judge," he said. "Well, that's going to stop. When I make a ruling, that's final. I will not tolerate any arguing about it. The matter, as you all know, is on automatic appeal to the [Pennsylvania] Supreme Court. I will not tolerate any bickering; there is not going to be any more bickering." He then brought up the occurrence at the end of the previous day with Len. "Yesterday, I had adjourned. I wanted to leave. It was a long day. I don't want any motions or arguments at that time. There will not be any more of that. And if you continue to do that, I will have no alternative but to hold you in contempt and fine you."

■ Jackson resumed the stand, haggard and testy. Jackson stomped bitterly toward the witness stand, his shoulders drooped and a scowl on his face. I noticed at that moment that Sabo had handed Grant a document. I couldn't tell if the judge was trying to be sly about it. After the obligatory greeting, Grant showed the mystery document to Jackson. It was his fee petition—the invoice he submitted after his obligations on the case were over. It was apparent that Judge Sabo had done some digging of his own; digging to help the prosecution, of course. The fee petition showed that Jackson was wrong in his estimate that the court system allotted about $800 for expert and investigative services; in fact, the figure was around $1,400—a figure that was still woefully insufficient for a capital case, but damage was nonetheless done to Jackson's reliability as a witness. It wasn't so much the discrepancy in the figures that hurt us; it was the impression it left. It suggested that Jackson was willing to shade his testimony in our favor because he wanted to see us prevail. When Len objected to Sabo's apparent willingness to act as a second prosecutor, he offered a disingenuous explanation. "I just wanted to correct the record," he claimed. "I only gave it to Mr. Jackson because I saw he was having difficulty remembering what the fees were. So I gave it to him to assist him." Someone behind us yelled out "Bullshit!"

When Grant finished his questioning about the fee petition—questioning that seemed to go on forever, with endless editorializing—he began focusing on Jackson's claim that he did little trial preparation for the five-month period before Mumia announced his decision to represent himself in May 1982. Here, too, Grant scored some points. He stroked Jackson's ego, telling him, "I have seen you work, Mr. Jackson, and I know you are very thorough." Grant and Jackson had been adversaries in several cases. It's difficult for an ego-driven trial lawyer (and there is no such thing as a non-ego-driven trial lawyer) to resist the flattery, even when it is a transparent tactical ploy.

"You must have read through those reports ten times, at least," Grant asserted.

"At least," Jackson agreed. *Ouch,* I thought. As the one who would be writing the briefs later on in the case, I listened to answers and envisioned how they would be deployed on paper. Jackson's answer was the type that gets paraded in legal briefs to show that Mumia received excellent and diligent lawyering. I'd have to find a way to deal with it in our legal briefs.

Grant then sought to discredit Jackson's sworn statement in his affidavit where he claimed to have done little preparation. "You state in your affidavit," Grant began, "and I am paraphrasing—"

Len immediately rose from his seat. "Beg your pardon," he said.

"I'm paraphrasing because I don't really care about the exact wording," Grant explained.

"You have to give him the precise wording, otherwise it is not proper impeachment," Len argued. He was absolutely right. The rules of impeachment don't permit paraphrasing. A witness who is the subject of the impeachment must be confronted with the exact words he supposedly uttered or attested to on a prior occasion. Grant was obviously unfamiliar with the rule.

"Could counsel cite some law for that proposition," Grant demanded.

Len restated the proposition: "You can't paraphrase and say you are impeaching at the same time."

"This is Mr. Weinglass on evidence, Judge. I never heard of this rule." The audience behind the prosecution table—the anti-Mumia spectators—burst into guffaws at Grant's sarcasm.

"Let the record reflect that there was loud laughter from the right side of the courtroom and no admonishments from this court." There was a moment of silence as Len remained standing, awaiting a response from the judge. Judge Sabo apparently thought that Len would be satisfied just saying something on the record; it was evident that Len expected the judge to admonish the anti-Mumia spectators.

Judge Sabo capitulated. "All right. I am admonishing *everybody*. No laughing, no speaking out, no nothing." It was a weak warning, couched in terms of putting everybody on notice. For good measure, to disabuse anyone of the notion that he had given in to Len, Judge Sabo childishly added, "And that goes for you too, Mr. Weinglass."

Grant eventually returned to his favorite theme: Mumia's purported control over the defense case, rendering Jackson a victim of Mumia's ill-fated reliance on MOVE members as his legal advisors. Grant pointed out that Mumia had control over which character witnesses to call. Jackson explained that when it came to character witnesses, it is expected that the client would dictate who would be eligible as witnesses. "I didn't know Mr. Jamal all my life; I couldn't tell him who to call as a character witness."

Grant then pointed out that Mumia had withheld the names of the character witnesses from Jackson until the moment that they were to be called. "It's because you weren't in control, Mr. Jackson," Grant propounded.

"You are still on this control thing," Jackson said, frustrated.

"Yes, and I am going to stay on it," Grant replied.

"Well, let me just tell you this, Mr. Grant, and I am going to try to tell you for the last time. I have been practicing law for a long time. At no time, at no time that I know of have I not been in control when I was the lawyer. When I was backup counsel—that's when I wasn't in control." Jackson took a sip of water, and then leaned toward the microphone to continue, hoping his answer would put a stop to the unceasing inquiry about who was in control. "For some reason, you seem to think Mr. Jamal was in control. Mr. Jamal was in control when he got the Commonwealth to respond to some political thing. When I was the lawyer, I was the lawyer and I was doing what I wanted to do. When Mr. Jamal wanted me to do something, I said, 'Your Honor, Mr. Jamal wants me to do this.' If I didn't preface my remark that way, then I was in control." It turned out that Jackson had prefaced his remark with the caveat that Mumia was ordering him to take a particular course of action only once during the trial (and it was an incidental episode where Mumia wanted Jackson to move for a dismissal of the murder charge—a futile act, but one that Jackson agreed to perform to mollify his client).

Jackson's little speech didn't deter Grant from asking still more questions about Mumia's supposed control over the case. It was tiresome to watch, because Grant had it all wrong. True, Mumia repeatedly rebuked Jackson openly; true, he repeatedly ordered him to stop acting as his lawyer; true, he attempted on several occasions to question witnesses himself; true, he refused to cooperate with Jackson. But all of these things didn't add up to what Grant suggested was the reality. The reality was, Mumia never had control over his own case, which is precisely why he rebuked Jackson, protested his presence and his actions in court, and refused to cooperate. Mumia's conduct didn't reflect that he was *in control*; it proved that he was *stripped of control*. Grant refused to see the distinction.

In fact, Grant seemed to fuel the distinction with his questioning: "He shouted in your face a number of times, didn't he?" "You have never been so humiliated in any case that you can remember, true?" "He shouted at you during the course of a trial in a public forum, right?" The questions only established Mumia's frustration and rup-tured relationship with Jackson. To Grant, it supposedly bolstered the prosecution's claim that Mumia controlled the case.

Grant craftily ended his questioning with an effort to undermine an article of faith within the pro-Mumia movement—that Mumia is an innocent man. "Now, the truth is, that no matter how much in-vestigation you did, over how much time, and notwithstanding all the resources and groups available to Mr. Jamal and to you, and notwith-standing all the organizations offering monetary and other support, you just did not find any evidence that showed him to be innocent; isn't that the simple truth in this case?"

There were ways of answering that question without really an-swering it. Jackson could have attacked the premises to the question; after all, he had not been given adequate resources, and had not per-formed any investigation, and had not received money or support from any organizations. Whether from fatigue or just a lack of will, Jackson answered as if he no longer wanted to engage in a duel with Grant. "The simple truth is," Jackson said slowly, "I didn't find it. That's right. If I had more resources I may have. I don't know."

Grant had more staying power than Jackson, and for that I ad-mired him. Nontrial lawyers don't realize how tough it is to question a witness for days, which is what Grant had done, never seeming to let up. He followed up on Jackson's answer with a final question: "And you may have found out that there was no such evidence that you could unearth no matter how much money or how much time you could have had?"

"You are absolutely right," Jackson said.

No matter how careful courts are, the possibility of perjured testimony, mistaken honest testimony, and human error remain all too real. We have no way of judging how many innocent persons have been executed, but we can be certain that there were some.

JUSTICE THURGOOD MARSHALL, *FURMAN V. GEORGIA*

15. ATTACKING THE OPEN-AND-SHUT CASE

Except for those who believe the death penalty is morally wrong as a matter of principle no matter to whom it is applied, the most potent argument for its abolition is the possibility that factually innocent people may be executed. The fact that the death penalty is racially discriminatory rarely alters people's position on the subject. Some may be sufficiently moved by the statistics of discrimination to call for an overhaul of the system, but their support for capital punishment as a form of criminal sanction remains unaltered. To many death penalty supporters, discriminatory application of the death penalty only means that *more white* defendants should be executed. But even the staunchest supporters of capital punishment shudder at the thought of an innocent person executed *pursuant* to the law. Not surprisingly, therefore, the stridency in the public discourse over Mumia's case converges principally on his guilt or innocence.

The most puzzling aspect to Mumia's entire case, which is also its greatest irony, is that all of the second-guessing over Mumia's guilt or innocence could theoretically have been avoided with rudimentary crime scene investigative techniques, which, if Mumia was indeed the shooter, could have conclusively linked his .38 caliber Charter Arms revolver with the death of Faulkner. McGill did his best to create the impression with the jury that this linkage could be made. In reality, however, all that the prosecution could show was that the bullet removed from the slain officer's brain was "consistent with" the rifling characteristics of bullets that would be expelled from the recovered revolver, which Mumia had begun to carry with him shortly after he was robbed while moonlighting as a cab driver.

What puzzled us was the absence of evidence indicating that Mumia's gun had recently been fired, and that he had recently fired it. Because officers arrived at the crime scene in less than two minutes after the shooting, it would have been extremely easy to make those determinations. We didn't believe for a moment that investigators forgot to perform the requisite crime scene tests—not in a police killing investigation. We suspected that law enforcement had deep-sixed the results.

In 1994, we retained a ballistician named George Fassnacht, whom Jackson had unsuccessfully attempted to retain in 1982, to review the police ballistics reports and the trial testimony of the prosecution experts. We called him to the stand on August 2. Fassnacht testified that he refused to accept an appointment on Mumia's case in 1982 because of "a shortage of funds." Asked if he made a decision as to the acceptance of court appointments generally, Fassnacht replied: "It was soon after [I rejected the appointment in the *Jamal* case] that I stopped taking court-appointment cases in Philadelphia for a period of close to ten years." Why, Fassnacht was asked. "Because Philadelphia either wouldn't pay sufficiently, would arbitrarily slash the bill in half, or make you wait one, two years for payment."

Fassnacht found, to his astonishment, that there were no reports indicating whether Mumia had lead residue on his hands or face—a telltale sign of recent firing of a revolver. Crime scene investigators had conducted other more cumbersome tests on various items of evidence, including lead residue tests on the slain officer's tie and on a nearby wall. Yet investigators incredibly claimed they did no lead residue tests on Mumia's hands or face—obviously the most relevant area for lead residue testing. When a gun is discharged, it not only expels the bullet from the muzzle, it releases microscopic particles of lead residue back toward the shooter. Much of that blowback residue—how much depends on such factors as the type of gun and weather—lands on the hands and face of the shooter. A revolver, by virtue of its construction, releases far more residue than a rifle, and somewhat more residue than an automatic pistol. The greatest concentration of residue would be found on the web area of the hand holding the firearm at time of discharge. It is on the web area of the hand that crime scene investigators, at the very least, conduct the lead residue test.

A lead residue test is routine in crime scene investigations where a suspect is apprehended shortly after an incident involving alleged gunfire. Crime scene investigators are fully aware of the fact that the highest concentration of microscopic particles flying out from a discharged revolver on the hands of the shooter exists shortly after the shooting. Fassnacht testified that a lead residue test "could have been accomplished without too much difficulty to determine if, in fact, he had fired a firearm." Fassnacht pointed out that a simple hand-wipe analysis could have been performed on Mumia's hands. A hand-wipe analysis involves brushing the skin of a suspect with a cotton swab, which is moistened with a certain chemical. Obviously, the most promising area to swab would be the hands; but crime scene investigators often swab the suspect's face and forearms, as some firearms (especially revolvers like Mumia's) blow out considerable amounts of microscopic lead particles. The swabbing procedure, when done only on the hands, takes a minute or two. The residue lodged in the pores of the skin are transferred onto the swab, which is then submitted for laboratory analysis. No crime scene unit in any major city in 1981 operated without this inexpensive firearms residue kit. Fassnacht testified that he "would have expected them (the crime scene investigators) to have performed that test."

Equally astonishing was the claim that no one bothered to notice whether Mumia's gun was still warm or smelled of gunpowder. It is possible to detect the smell of gunpowder for four to six hours after a gun is fired. Recently fired guns, especially pistols, also emit heat. Police officers are trained to sniff a recovered gun for the smell of gunpowder, and to feel for warmth on the muzzle, to determine if it had been fired recently. Jamal's gun was picked up at the scene within minutes of the incident and then delivered to the Firearms Identification Unit by 5:55 A.M. on the morning of December 9, 1981, about two hours after the alleged shooting. Yet homicide investigators insisted that no one bothered to smell or feel the muzzle.

Because these sorts of tests were easy to perform and customary for crime scene investigators, it simply made no sense that law enforcement accidentally bypassed them when positive results could have definitively proved Mumia's direct involvement in the killing. The suspicious nature of the claim was heightened by the fact that this was a crime scene investigation involving the killing *of a police officer*—a crime that undoubtedly provokes enhanced efforts to produce inculpatory evidence. Although we never ferreted out direct proof that test results were withheld from the defense, we felt that the inference was compelling that that was precisely what happened.

■ After Fassnacht, we called a witness who actually saw the shooting but never testified at the trial. This was remarkable, because out of all of the eyewitnesses, this one provided to crime scene investigators the most complete account of what happened. Why did McGill, as thorough a prosecutor as he was, keep this eyewitness from the jury?

Robert Harkins, a rotund and bellicose fifty-six-year-old man, wanted no part of the drama taking place in Judge Sabo's courtroom. We had, on several occasions, visited his home and workplace in an effort to talk with him. He refused us each time, once telling our investigator that "detectives downtown" told him he didn't have to talk to us. On one occasion, at about 9:00 P.M., I knocked on his door while Len and Steve waited down the block. I've had good success in the past schmoozing hostile witnesses, and I boasted to Len that I could accomplish what the investigators could not. "Give it a try," he said. A young girl answered the door, probably around twelve years old. The blood drained from my head and I choked up as I asked to speak to Robert Harkins. As soon as I saw the young girl, thoughts of Harkins's criminal record intruded into my thoughts—a record containing information that he had been convicted of sexual offenses, including corrupting a minor. To see a young girl living in that home, fair or unfair to Harkins, made me queasy. When he came to the door, I stumbled through my introduction, telling him that I was very sorry to disturb him at that hour of the night but it was a life-or-death matter. I guess my insincerity was evident because as soon as Harkins caught on that I was working on behalf of "that cop killer," as he put it, he cursed and slammed the door.

We stated in our PCRA petition that we wanted to call Harkins as a witness in order to establish that he had viewed a photo array—an assemblage of photos (usually six) lined up for a witness to determine if he is able to select the suspect. We had no independent proof that a photo array was shown, only a gut instinct based on the fact that McGill never put Harkins on the witness stand. Why did McGill forgo another eyewitness who was no more than thirty feet from the shooting? One explanation that suggested itself from our investigation was Harkins's legal problems. It was possible that McGill didn't want to expose Harkins to cross-examination, in view of his distasteful criminal record. This, however, was doubtful; McGill was too aggressive a prosecutor to dispense with an eyewitness because of solicitude for the witness's feelings and privacy. Indeed, White and Chobert were no angels. It seemed to us, however, that another plausible explanation, which we were obliged to explore, was that investigators attempted, unsuccessfully, to secure a positive identification from Harkins shortly after the crime. A failed identification would not only further support our claim that Mumia was wrongly accused, it would add yet another layer to our evidence of prosecutorial misconduct. A prosecutor is constitutionally compelled to disclose to the defense all evidence of failed identifications. The prosecution had never indicated in any of its disclosures that Harkins failed in making an identification. If we could prove that the prosecution suppressed a failed photo array identification, we would have good grounds for a reversal of Mumia's conviction.

The problem, however, was that we had no solid evidence to back up our speculation that Harkins had viewed a photo array. Harkins was my witness, and I was dubious that he would testify that he had been shown a photographic array containing Mumia's picture. Prosecutors are certainly not above doing nefarious things, but suppressing a photo array is too easily discoverable for a prosecutor to risk. But, on the other hand, Harkins hadn't denied viewing a photo array to our investigator, who had succeeded in exchanging a few words with him. In any event, I had a more ambitious goal. I pressed for the calling of Harkins as a witness because I strongly suspected that McGill had not used him as a trial witness for a more basic reason: his observations severely undercut the prosecution's theory of the case. In fact, I believed that Harkins, a witness who probably had the best vantage point to the shooting of all the prosecution witnesses, could go far in bolstering our claim of Mumia's innocence.

Len and I went back and forth over Harkins. I relished those moments with Len because I felt privileged to witness firsthand the thought process of a veteran courtroom warrior. Unlike most other trial lawyers with whom I've worked, Len is unafraid to express doubts and fears about litigation tactics. He thinks aloud, willingly exposing himself to rejection and judgment (and oh, how willing lawyers are to pass judgment), because he cares little of appearing powerful and mighty. Ironically, his power in the courtroom comes from his manifest lack of hubris and, as I mentioned earlier, his approach to jury persuasion as a process of sharing.

We both agreed that Harkins was a witness to be feared, not only because of his overt hostility but because he was a loose cannon. We didn't know what he would say about his observations of the crime. We had police reports containing his interview statements, which, we believed, blew a gaping hole in the prosecution's theory of what happened at Thirteenth and Locust; but, as Jackson had painfully learned with Veronica Jones and Robert Chobert, that was no guarantee that his in-court testimony would be consistent with them. Moreover, the detectives assisting the 1995 prosecutors had their hooks in Harkins. After our failed attempts to get Harkins to cooperate with us, we could only gain access to him through arrangements with certain detectives. When we tried to interview him at a police precinct, where he was being "protected" from us, he simply refused to talk. Ultimately, primarily through my urging, we decided to put him on the stand, knowing that we would need some latitude from Judge Sabo to deal with Harkins's expected hostility. In retrospect, I wonder what gave me the notion that Sabo would cut us any sort of slack in questioning a witness—a naive belief in justice, perhaps.

"Petitioner calls Robert Harkins," I announced.

A rather pathetic, overweight, and rumpled man waddled precariously to the witness box and stopped, nervously fidgeting with his fingers. Harkins stood there a moment, apparently thinking that he needed permission to ascend the two steps to the witness chair. The clerk motioned for him to take a seat, and he stumbled while trying to place his large frame in front of the microphone. He sat with a straightened back on the edge of the seat, his lips pursed and tightened to reveal his tension.

"Now, on December ninth, 1981, at about six A.M., do you remember being interviewed by a detective?" I asked Harkins as he glowered at me from the witness chair.

Harkins acknowledged that he had been interviewed and had signed a police interview report. The report indicated that Harkins saw a scuffle between the shooter and the officer, which resulted in the officer falling to the ground on all fours. Cynthia White, the prosecution's key witness, never said anything about a scuffle between the officer and the shooter; indeed, she never claimed that the shooter touched the officer at all (or vice versa). White had said that Mumia shot the officer in the back as he was running to the scene, and as a result of that gunshot, the officer stumbled and fell. According to Harkins's statement, the officer was hit in the back with a bullet *when he was on the pavement on his hands and knees struggling to regain his balance.* The officer then "rolled over" onto his back—again, an observation in stark contrast to that offered by White. At that point, the shooter fired two more shots. When asked if he could identify the shooter, Harkins answered, "Maybe."

A week later, Harkins was interviewed again. Undoubtedly, investigators were perplexed with the starkly different scenario that Harkins provided from that of White. In fact, the whole case, from an investigative standpoint, came down to a choice between Harkins and White. Chobert, Scanlan, and Magilton could not provide the kind of detail in their testimony that would allow for a complete accounting of what happened. None of those witnesses claimed to have seen the entire incident from beginning to end; White and Harkins, however, gave as complete an accounting of the events as could reasonably be expected. The other three witnesses could complement either Harkins or White. For this reason, McGill could not put White *and* Harkins on the stand at the trial; it would have to be one or the other. The interesting question, then, is why did McGill choose White over Harkins?

When Harkins was brought back in for a second interview, the decision as to which of the two would be the bedrock of the prosecution's case was still very much up in the air. Harkins spoke again of a physical scuffle between the officer and the shooter, this time with more detail. He told the investigator that the shooter "grabbed the officer with his hand and spun him"—no gunfire, not even the brandishing of a gun, just the physical act of grabbing the officer with the hand and spinning him. The interviewing detective asked Harkins again if the shooter actually grabbed Faulkner—to which Harkins again explained that he had. He reiterated that Officer Faulkner then lost his balance as a result, fell to all fours as the shooter hovered over him, and was then hit in the back with a bullet. At that point, the officer rolled over and was then struck by the fatal bullet.

Significantly, Harkins never saw Faulkner discharge his gun at the shooter. In fact, he saw the shooter "shrug" his shoulders after firing into the officer, as if, in his words to the police, "somebody was watching him." Nowhere in any of the interview statements did Harkins mention that the shooter went over to the curb and sat down. Harkins actually left the scene immediately, because, as he put it, "if there was any more shooting, I didn't want to be the one shot."

The shooter, under Harkins's account, who he described as bigger and heavier than Faulkner, was never wounded, was seemingly non-chalant about having just killed a cop, had been in a physical scuffle immediately before discharging his gun, and fired at the officer in the back when he was on the ground. No wonder McGill didn't call Harkins as a witness. His account thoroughly contradicted that of Cynthia White, a far more malleable witness—hence, more desirable for law enforcement. It didn't have the primary virtue of White's account—an explanation as to when and how Mumia was shot through testimony that the officer had "grabbed for something" as he was falling toward the pavement. Whereas White resolved that mystery, Harkins deepened it.

The prosecutors at the 1995 hearing undoubtedly knew that Harkins posed a major problem for them. It was in their interest to keep the prosecution story line of the killing clean and straightforward. Harkins would only muck things up with an account that could never be reconciled with the account that was presented to and accepted by the jury in 1982. So they had a strategy: object, *and object often*, and count on Judge Sabo to be Judge Sabo—a fellow prosecutor in black robes. It was, of course, an excellent strategy in Judge Sabo's courtroom. There is not supposed to be a home-court advantage in litigation, but reality departs from theory quite often in the rough-and-tumble world of court-room combat. Every single objection interposed by the prosecution during the 1995 hearings—and this is no exaggeration, as the transcripts themselves attest—was sustained by the king of death row.

"Do you remember telling the detective that the first thing you saw was Police Officer Faulkner grabbing a guy?" I asked.

"Objection, Your Honor!" Grant bellowed.

"We are not here to rehash that," Judge Sabo replied on cue, playing his role as second prosecutor to the hilt.

"Do you remember what you told Detective Sutton on December ninth, 1981, about the shooting?" I pressed on.

"I was coming down Locust Street—"

Grant immediately interrupted Harkins. "Objection."

"Objection is sustained."

I kept going, asking the same sorts of questions in varying ways, hoping, naively, that Grant would get fed up with objecting. I was never naive enough to believe that Judge Sabo would tire of sustaining Grant's objection. But Grant catapulted out of his chair after each of my questions, no doubt enjoying the home-court advantage.

There was a time in my life as a trial lawyer when the repeated sustaining of objections to my questions would discombobulate me. I'd become flushed with shame and long for a place to hide in that austere pit in the middle of the courtroom. I learned to hide the fear and shame from the jury, but those feelings would cause me to lose my power as a courtroom warrior. Over time, with each new jury trial, I learned not so much to hide my fear and shame but to put it out in the open for the jury to see it. I came to realize that it is not unwise to show the jury that you are human, that you, like them, are afraid at times. I struggled to reach that point in my personal development to understand that in a jury trial, it is okay to be vulnerable, because vulnerability allows for human connection, which in turn allows for authentic communication. And if there is one thing a trial lawyer must understand about advocacy, it is this: When you're not communicating, you're not advocating.

I didn't concern myself with fighting with Grant or the judge. I wanted to expose information, and if I had to stumble through an examination to do that, then so be it. I began protesting, but Judge Sabo simply agreed with Grant's position, without even the pretense of pondering the issue, that we could only ask Harkins about whether he viewed a photo array. Questions about what he saw on the night in question were off-limits.

"Let me ask you this, Mr. Harkins. There were discussions, were there not, on December ninth, 1981, about what happened, right?"

"Yes."

"And you told the police that you were very near where the shooting happened, right?"

"Yes."

"And that you saw the shooter, is that right?"

"Yes."

"You didn't see the shooter get shot, did you?"

"No, I did not."

"Did you see a man running across the street?"

"No, I did not."

Grant stepped in again. "I object." I had been wondering what had taken him so long.

Judge Sabo, growing impatient, rebuked me. "Would you get right to the issue here, *Counselor?*"

I decided to go into the photo array issue before going back to Harkins's observations of the shooting, just to get Grant off my back. During the course of that questioning, Harkins blurted out, which stunned everyone, apparently even the prosecutors, that the shooter "walked, then sat down on the curb." He had *never* even hinted at seeing such a thing before. As I said earlier, he had actually told the investigator that he immediately fled the scene for fear of being caught in gunfire. This inculpatory remark, which was akin to Chobert's surprise claim at the trial to the same effect, came out of the blue. Grant, of course, didn't object to that piece of testimony about the night in question. I was ready to launch into my attack, and I believed that even Sabo would allow it now. After all, Harkins had just "opened the door" to a full exploration of what he saw by virtue of his volunteering that he saw the shooter lumber over to the curb.

"When you talked to the police on December seventeenth, 1981, did they ask you about the description of the shooter?"

"I object."

"Why don't you get right to it, Counselor?" Judge Sabo demanded, again referring to his expectation that we only question Harkins on the photo array issue.

I ignored the judge. "Now, you mentioned something about the shooter sitting down. Do you remember that?"

"Yes."

"Did you tell that to any of the detectives?" I looked over at Grant and extended both my arms out toward him, indicating, sarcastically, that it was his turn to say something.

"Objection," Grant said as he gave me a wink. Grant enjoyed the theatrics of courtroom battles, just as I do, and we related on that level. I didn't begrudge him the wink, just as he didn't take umbrage at my sarcastic gesture. The proceedings, deathly serious, had devolved into a game where each side did its best to create a court record that would enhance the chances of success later on in federal court.

I then challenged Grant to allow me to question Harkins about what he saw. It was a last-ditch effort, hoping that I could goad his macho competitive nature. "Let me be clear to Mr. Grant. If he wants to throw the gauntlet down, if I were allowed the latitude to question Mr. Harkins, I could demonstrate to the court that in fact his scenario, his own testimony, exonerates Mr. Jamal." A strong claim, packaged within a bold challenge—would Grant take the bait?

Judge Sabo didn't let Grant respond. He immediately interjected, harping on the fact that we never submitted an affidavit from Harkins encompassing the issue of his eyewitness observations. That Harkins was not amenable to talking with us, to say the least, never entered into the equation for the judge. I should have remembered how Judge Sabo shut Jackson down when Jackson tried to question Veronica Jones about police manipulation. There, too, this same judge refused to allow questioning to go beyond the parameters that were set out before the witness took the stand.

I continued to ignore the judge and threw out the challenge again, this time injecting the suggestion that the prosecution was afraid. "I appreciate the Commonwealth's fear in my questioning this witness, but what I'm saying to the court is that I could demonstrate actual innocence through this witness."

"Counselor, you show me—"

"The court is barring me from doing that," I thundered, the frustration probably evident in my audacity to interrupt the judge. My interruption could have earned me a contempt citation, but Sabo was too caught up in the quarreling. "How does Your Honor's ruling advance the cause of justice?" I asked.

"What do you mean by justice?" the old jurist asked.

"To ensure that an innocent person is not executed," I answered. "If I could demonstrate through this witness actual innocence—"

Judge Sabo fired back before I could finish, "His guilt has already been demonstrated by a prior jury." I shook my head, which prompted Judge Sabo to express his own view of justice: "Counselor, justice is an emotional feeling. That's all it is."

The spectators let out a gasp. Judge Sabo, seemingly oblivious to the shallowness of his remark, addressed the crowd: "All right, quiet in the room or you will be asked to leave. You are going to go out."

Could he really mean that we were not fighting for something substantial, something beyond the triviality of emotions? "Justice is an emotional feeling," he said again. "When I win my case, it's justice. When I lose my case, I didn't get justice, you know. So take it from there." To Sabo, justice was "an emotional feeling" wrapped up in a contest, a game—which, when played in his courtroom, is a rigged event. In this instance, and in so many others in his courtroom over the past twenty years, the courtroom battles were a life-or-death game.

"I think there is a concept that we call truth, which you're missing," I responded.

"You didn't say you were going to call him to show that there was actual innocence. You said you were calling him to show that the district attorney's office did something wrong."

I saw that the judge was being highly formalistic because Grant had fought hard to silence Harkins through saturation objections. I informed the judge that we wanted to amend our Petition so that Harkins could be presented to show actual innocence.

"I object," Grant announced, unsurprisingly.

"Of course they object," I declared. "Of course they don't want the actual innocence evidence to come out."

And it never did through the live testimony of Robert Harkins. We could never find the wedge to get him back onto the stand so long as Judge Sabo was presiding over the proceedings.

■ The day ended on August 2 with the usual acrimony, the usual feuding, but no ejections from the courtroom and no boisterous shouting. It's odd to characterize a court session as calm because there had been no fireworks during the proceedings. Yet, in a case where bitter exchanges with the judge and the prosecution were par for the course, we felt that stretches of time where no one was being ejected, or no one was shouting epithets, were moments of calm.

Although the proceedings on August 2 had those stretches of time that were calm by comparison to other occasions, it began as if it were going to be a brutal day. Before Fassnacht took the stand, Judge Sabo announced that he would be tightening his grip on the defense because we had been plastering the city with subpoenas. "I think it is time for the court to take back reins on the defendant here," he announced as soon as he took the bench. "Because I have been a little, I guess a little bit lax. I don't know if it's lax, but it's like leaving a bull unattended in a china shop that just goes through and knocks everything down."

It never took much for Rachel to tangle with the judge, and these remarks not unexpectedly rankled her. "Your Honor," she declared, "before we get to that, you indicated that you wanted us to proceed per our petition. And I would inform the court that claim number nine deals with the geographical and racial disparity question." Rachel was referring to our allegation that the jury pool was rigged to undercount the number of minorities eligible for jury service.

Judge Sabo didn't pay attention to Rachel's point, which was a good one. We were certainly entitled to present evidence to substantiate, if we could, this particular claim. Rachel kept arguing.

"Counselor, Counselor!" Judge Sabo yelled. Rachel kept on arguing, as if the judge were actually interested in hearing what she had to say. "Counselor! No more! I have ruled on that issue, you have an exception." Rachel kept going, and I sat there amazed. I wondered if she had taken lessons in oratory from MOVE members, who also had an unbelievable ability to engage in rapidfire speech and intense focus even when facing a hostile crowd. "If you keep talking," the judge warned, "you are going to find yourself up in the cell room. I am telling you I have ruled on that. You have an exception to my ruling."

The threat of jail didn't deter Rachel; I'm not sure she even heard the threat. "Your Honor—" She couldn't finish the thought.

"All right! Sheriff! Take her out of here, *please!*" Judge Sabo wasn't kidding. Several armed officers took Rachel by the arms, pinned them behind her and handcuffed her. She stood at the podium the entire time that she was being handcuffed, glaring at the judge. One officer took her by the arm and guided her down the center aisle. Len and I sat there paralyzed. In fact, the courtroom had never been that quiet during the entire three-week proceedings. Everyone just watched the arrest process unfold. As cantankerous and abusive as he was, Sabo had always been quite predictable in how he handled courtroom events. He'd chastise, ridicule, threaten with contempt—a range of responses that were never too dynamic. What immobilized Len and me, and what stunned the entire crowd in the courtroom, was the fact that Sabo's arrest order was like a bolt out of the blue. Rachel's conduct was hardly the most brazen act to be perpetrated in the courtroom. Len's earlier command to the judge not to leave the bench, and my audacious interruption of him during Harkins's testimony, seemed to involve more effrontery than Rachel's insistence on completing her statement. It all came down to timing and personality: Sabo was getting fed up with us (as we were with him), and he simply disliked Rachel far more than he did Len and me.

Rachel was taken to a holding cell upstairs, where she stayed for a few hours.

"I am telling you, I will not tolerate this," Judge Sabo muttered, as the audience shuffled and stirred. "When I make an order, that's it." He called a recess to collect himself.

We immediately visited Rachel in the holding cell, and she was buoyant. She didn't want to talk about her situation, only how we planned to proceed that day. Len kept reassuring her that things would be okay, that we would get her out, while she repeatedly tried to reassure us that she was unafraid. I'm convinced that, in fact, she *was* unafraid. I certainly had my differences with Rachel, but I never doubted her commitment to her politics and to Mumia's case. Her poise that morning, both in the courtroom and in the lockup, conveyed a strength that Len and I fed off. I doubt that I would have been so collected if it were me handcuffed and dragged from the courtroom.

Rachel later begrudgingly apologized to the judge, after we insisted that she do so, because Judge Sabo was making noises about removing her from the case. His actions were extreme, even for him. The daily chants out in the courtyard were apparently getting under his skin. Muffled sounds of "Freedom Now!" "Free Mumia!" "Sabo Must Go!" from the city hall courtyard below provided background music to the proceedings. On the day that Rachel was arrested, Judge Sabo, for the first time, angrily ordered the arrests of the protestors outside. Fortunately for the protestors, word reached them about Judge Sabo's order before sheriff's officers could apprehend them.

■ If Jackson had a defense strategy, it was developing the theory that the actual shooter fled the scene moments before the police arrived. Dessie Hightower, the young accounting student, carried the weight of that strategy through his testimony of seeing someone run eastbound after he heard the pops of gunfire. Robert Chobert and Veronica Jones were supposed to share the load, but they recanted their initial claims of flight from the crime scene. Debbie Kordansky, a fourth witness to flight whom Jackson forgot about until the night before he needed her, simply refused to appear in court.

We believed Jackson was on the right track, and thus pursued the flight theory, dedicating ourselves to presenting explanations as to why Jackson's efforts to develop that defense met with failure. Len liked to tell the press that the fact that four eyewitnesses spontaneously told investigators about flight proved definitively that there was another person at the scene of the shooting, aside from Cook, Faulkner, and Mumia. "Were these witnesses hallucinating?" he would ask rhetorically. I was struck by the consistency in the reported observations. All four claimed to see someone flee eastbound in the direction of a nearby alleyway. I've visited that alleyway numerous times and was impressed by its potential as an escape route. Jones and Chobert both asserted that two people "ran away," with the added wrinkle from Chobert that one of the fleeing persons was Billy Cook, who returned to the crime scene when the flashing turret lights of oncoming police cars made running useless. What was important to me was that the consistency in the description of flight refutes any suggestion that what these people saw was nothing more than a scattering of people away from the eruption of gunfire. Moreover, their observations were provided to investigators, not to give them a sense of the ambience of the crime scene in the wake of gunfire but to assist them in apprehending the actual perpetrator.

On August 3, we began putting on evidence to substantiate this proposition that a third person, probably a passenger in the Volkswagen, killed Officer Faulkner.

■ It would seem unnecessary to disrupt Dessie Hightower's life again by having him testify during these proceedings in view of the fact that he had provided testimony of flight at the 1982 trial. Hightower was never one who relished his involvement in this case. McGill had noted back in April 1982 that Hightower did not want to be involved. But if the police and prosecution had manipulated other witnesses, we reasoned, they probably tried to do the same to Hightower. We put him on the stand as our first witness on Thursday, August 3, to substantiate our suspicions, but not before detectives almost arrested him two weeks earlier.

On July 17, at about 8:00 P.M., detectives appeared at Hightower's home and banged on his door. Hightower was home with the flu. When he answered the door and noticed the badges held up against his face, he tried to reclaim as much focus as he could. The detectives, according to the prosecutors, were only there to subpoena the young man; Hightower, however, explained to us that they were there to arrest him because he had not appeared in Sabo's courtroom to testify pursuant to the defense subpoena—an account that was consistent with the fact that Judge Sabo had indeed issued a warrant for his arrest. Fortunately, they accepted Hightower's assurance that he would come into court as soon as he could overcome his illness. When we learned of these events, we complained bitterly. Why would detectives, the prosecution, and even Judge Sabo be concerned about the appearance of a witness who *we* subpoenaed? The prosecutors knew that Hightower was *our* witness, and his attendance was, therefore, *our* concern. It was quite apparent to us that the practice of witness intimidation, backed by the force of a judge, was alive and well in Philadelphia.

In any event, Hightower testified at the PCRA hearing that he had been interviewed by police on two occasions: shortly after the police took control over the crime scene, and then six days later. On both occasions he told police that he had seen someone flee eastbound on Locust Street before police arrived on the scene. The first police interview went by without incident and was conducted quickly. The interviewing detective wrote down Hightower's statement on a police form and had him sign it.

But on December 15, Hightower was summoned back to the precinct. He arrived at about 4:00 P.M., expecting to be there only for a few minutes, probably to clarify some minor point. He was kept there for over five and a half hours. A detective launched into questions about what Hightower had seen, and the young accounting student explained again, patiently, that he had seen someone run eastbound on Locust Street, past a hotel that was on the block. The detective seemed skeptical, bordering on annoyed. He pressed Hightower, asking if he had seen Mumia fire a gun. Hightower got the feeling that the detective didn't believe him.

Hightower was hooked up to a polygraph machine about three hours into the interview and was grilled about his denial of seeing Mumia brandish a gun. He was never asked a single question about his observation of seeing someone flee the scene, which was the most significant detail he provided to law enforcement. It was obvious that the polygraph examination was not administered for a legitimate investigatory goal. Of all the crime scene witnesses, only Hightower, a materially favorable defense witness, was subjected a polygraph test. This was unusual and suspicious, as the police never asked Cynthia White, Robert Chobert, Albert Magilton, Michael Scanlan, or any other prosecution witness to take a polygraph test. The prosecution could provide no explanation as to why a young college student with an unblemished record was subjected to a polygraph, and the other pro-prosecution witnesses—some of whom had criminal records— were not. But in view of the other evidence of law enforcement manipulation of witnesses, a fair inference arises that an effort to intimidate Hightower was afoot as well.

Hightower left the precinct that night unsure what had just happened. He comforted himself with the thought that he was not the only one to be polygraphed and that this was just normal police procedure. At the 1995 proceedings, the prosecution put on the polygrapher who testified that Hightower had failed the polygraph. We brought in a polygrapher of our own from the West Coast, at considerable expense, but Judge Sabo, prompted by an objection from the prosecution, would not permit our expert to examine the polygraph data.

Debbie Kordansky, the woman who refused Jackson's entreaties over the phone to testify, took the stand at the PCRA hearing in the afternoon of August 3. Her testimony was not as straightforward as her initial police interview statement, which on its face indicated that she had observed someone fleeing the scene. According to Kordansky's statement, on December 9, 1981, she lived in a hotel at Thirteenth and Walnut, overlooking the parking lot across the street from the scene of the shooting. It was that parking lot from which Mumia emerged before he began his run across Locust Street. That morning at about 3:45 to 4:00 A.M. she heard gunfire, which prompted her to look out the window onto the street. She then saw a man running east on the south side of Locust Street.

At the 1995 hearing, she claimed not to have a complete memory of the events. We weren't surprised by that claim, however, because that is what she had told an Internal Affairs investigator in April 1982.

She told that investigator that she had "certain prejudices that affect my memory against and for police, and black people." Consistent with what she had told Jackson when he virtually begged for her to co-operate, Kordansky explained that she had been raped by a black man. She then said that, based upon "logic" and not memory, she heard gunshots, heard sirens, and then went to the window. Only at that point did she see someone run.

The prosecutors seized on this so-called logic-based answer. Grant hammered the suggestion that her observation of flight was trivial because she made the observation after the police arrived. This speculation that she might have seen someone flee after the arrival of the police simply made no sense, which led me to believe that Grant was wasting his time with his questioning. What this speculative hypothesis overlooked is the obvious fact that she reported her observations of someone fleeing the scene to the police because she thought it would be helpful to them in their effort to apprehend the shooter— something she acknowledged as true when she testified. There would be no reason for Kordansky, a highly reluctant witness in the first place, to come down from her hotel room, introduce herself to investigators, and then subject herself to an interview that would ensure that she would be called later to provide testimony at a trial *if* what she saw was as meaningless as seeing someone run *after* the arrival of police. On top of that, the police are not in the business of recording irrelevant information that has no bearing on an investigation. Logic and common sense indicated that Kordansky felt compelled to report seeing someone run from the scene because that event was, in her mind, significant; and it would only have significance if the observed flight occurred before police arrived.

What about the other two eyewitnesses, Michael Scanlan and Albert Magilton? These two witnesses appeared to be untainted by law enforcement manipulation. We certainly didn't have any specific information indicating that they had been coerced or induced to testify. First of all, neither had the vulnerabilities that White, Chobert, and Jones presented—namely, previous encounters with the law. But more importantly, these two witnesses did not offer eyewitness accounts that, upon reflection, seriously advanced the prosecution's case. In fact, in crucial respects, Scanlan proves to be a very favorable witness for Mumia.

Scanlan had told detectives in 1982 that Mumia must have been the driver of the Volkswagen. How did he get that impression? we wondered. The answer is in the hair—Mumia's hair. Scanlan couldn't help but notice that Mumia had long, flowing dreadlocks. He couldn't have been the shooter, according to Scanlan, because he was "certain"—a word attributed to him in a police interview report—that the shooter had an "an Afro hairstyle." Jackson had not developed this point at the trial, and there appears to be a reason for that, which amounts to another annoying reminder that nothing in life is ever simple. Jackson probably didn't want to emphasize Scanlan's description of the shooter because he had pinned his hopes on the fact that Robert Chobert, Veronica Jones, and Dessie Hightower would all testify that the person they saw run from the scene had long dreadlocks. He probably had no interest in Scanlan's observation that the shooter had an Afro hairstyle because it contradicted his three "flight" witnesses.

While it is easy to play Monday morning quarterback, I felt angered by Jackson's apparent tactical judgment. It bespoke his cramped perspective as to how to mount a defense in this case. Scanlan was an excellent witness for the prosecution, primarily because he was well dressed, articulate, engaging, and untainted by even the hint of police pressure. He also gave the jury the impression that he had an excellent viewing of the shooting, especially in his description of how Faulkner's body "jerked" when the shooter fired into his head. An acknowledgment from a powerful prosecution witness that the shooter had a hairstyle that had absolutely no resemblance to that of the defendant on trial is simply too good to pass up. It is the type of evidence that a trial lawyer revolves an entire cross-examination around. Jackson let the point slide by, and then ultimately got burned by Chobert's and Jones's recantations of seeing flight from the crime scene.

The painful irony is that Mumia's dreadlocks symbolized at the trial his allegiance with MOVE, which was an explanatory point for why the killing occurred; and yet, those same dreadlocks, through a skillful cross-examination of Scanlan, could have been a powerful testament to the fact that he was *not* the shooter.

■ We had expended a considerable amount of resources searching for Cynthia White, without success. Without the ability to put White on the stand, we had to settle on other ways of undermining her credibility as a witness. I had naively counted on destroying Cynthia White as a witness through the testimony of Robert Harkins. The prosecution team, of which Judge Sabo was a de facto member, sabotaged that effort. But all was not lost, by any means.

White had thirty-eight prior arrests for prostitution in Philadelphia and three open cases awaiting trial when she took the stand. Significantly, those thirty-eight arrests were accumulated over a twenty-month period, from May 1980 to December 1981; from mid-December 1981 to the start of Mumia's trial, White went arrest free, even though she admitted to continuing to ply her trade during that six-month period. That paper trail strongly suggested she was receiving favorable treatment by the police.

She also had an extensive history of providing false information to law enforcement, and frequently revised her account over time to conform to the prosecution's theory. For example, she initially described the shooter as shorter than five feet eight—Mumia stands six feet one. She later tried to minimize the significance of this observation with the claim that she was poor at judging height. She implausibly insisted that it is possible to view Mumia, who is unquestionably a tall man, as being "short." She also initially claimed at the preliminary hearing back in January 1982 that Mumia brandished a gun in his left hand as he ran toward the officer. She later retracted that point, evidently because it didn't make sense in view of the fact that Mumia is right-handed and had a holster on his left side (which would call for retrieving a gun with the right hand). She oscillated between saying that the shooter wore a hat and that he had dreadlocks. Finally, she initially told police with respect to Billy Cook and Officer

Faulkner, "there was no struggle" between the two; she then gradually developed a graphic account of Cook punching Faulkner in the face. Each of her revised accounts came about in the wake of an arrest (the first on December 12, and the last taking place on December 17, after which she went arrest-free for six months), a fact that White admitted at trial was not coincidental. Indeed, a poster was displayed in Philadelphia precincts advising that any arrests of Cynthia White were to be routed to the Homicide Division. She understood that law enforcement regarded her as a valuable witness, and she was savvy enough to know how to parlay that importance to secure benefits for herself.

Veronica Jones, the other prostitute witness who ambushed Jackson with her recantation when she testified at the 1982 trial, had the potential to undermine White. She had begun to say, before Judge Sabo blocked further elaboration on the subject, that she and other prostitutes were offered the same deal that White was offered: they could work the streets with impunity if they would inculpate Mumia. It was difficult to corroborate Jones's truncated but momentous allusion to police manipulation without Cynthia White, whom we had feverishly tried to locate. But we were able to acquire evidence that certainly bolstered Jones's spontaneous remarks at trial. On August 1, Robert Greer, an investigator who briefly helped Jackson with Mumia's case until money ran out, testified.

Greer was a classic private investigator—gruff and wizened by over twenty years of law enforcement experience. He testified that when he attempted to interview White before the 1982 trial he was unable to do so because two men, who he surmised from his own law enforcement experience were plainclothes police officers, were always nearby in a small red car. In Greer's judgment, and he reported this to Jackson, White was being shadowed and protected by undercover officers—an observation bolstered by the documentary record indicating that White was never arrested by the Philadelphia authorities for the six-month period leading up to Mumia's trial. This explains why Jackson had expressed to Judge Ribner that he suspected White was being manipulated by law enforcement. Jackson understandably was reluctant to elaborate on that point in open court back in 1982 because he didn't want to tip off McGill that he had an investigator who was trailing a key prosecution witness.

Furthermore, it turns out that White had been arrested on five occasions between May 1980 and July 1981 by two police officers, Richard Herron and Joseph Gioffre, who were later convicted in connection with the federal probe into Philadelphia police corruption. In each of those instances, the charges against White were dropped. During this period, Herron and Gioffre were shaking down prostitutes and pimps for protection money, and one way they accomplished that extortion was to make arrests and then, for the right financial arrangement, see to it that the arrest was not ultimately processed for prosecution. Jackson's suspicions about White's connection to this police corruption, it turns, out, was worth exploring.

Another clue to the suspicion that White had some sort of arrangement with Philadelphia law enforcement rests with an event in 1987. In June of that year, White found herself again incarcerated, this time on armed robbery charges. She appeared in court for bail, and the judge noted that he was reluctant to release her because of her record of "seventeen failures to appear" and "page after page" of arrests. In a jam, White called Detective Richard Culbreth for help. Detective Culbreth acted as White's "police escort" at Mumia's trial. He appeared alongside White at a bail hearing and convinced the reluctant judge to free her without posting bail. Detective Culbreth had accomplished this amazing outcome after he informed the judge in a bench conference of White's involvement in Mumia's trial.

Finally, the most important proof that White's seamless narrative was a concoction centers on medical evidence. Science is the best way to refute testimony, because science, so long as it is valid science, rises above the vagaries of human motivation and behavior. With no money to retain a pathologist, Jackson was unable to make a point that would be crucial to attacking White's testimony. The prosecution's trial theory, based upon White's testimony, was that Jamal was shot by Faulkner as he (Faulkner) was falling to the ground. A defense pathologist could have shown that the prosecution's theory, rooted in White's testimony, was physically impossible.

■ We retained John Hayes, M.D., an associate city medical examiner from New York City, to look over the medical records of Mumia's gunshot injury. He testified at the hearing on August 4. I had previously encountered Dr. Hayes as a prosecution witness in a New York City murder case I had tried. I cross-examined him in that case. Len, appropriately, handled the examination of him now.

According to Dr. Hayes, Mumia had suffered a gunshot wound in the right chest just below the right nipple, and the bullet traveled in a straight line, backward and *downward* through his right lung, his diaphragm muscle, the right side of the liver, striking the twelfth rib, and ending up between the twelfth vertebrae of the spine and the first lumbar vertebrae, on the back, left-hand side. In Dr. Hayes's opinion, which the prosecution never even attempted to contest, the gunshot causing Mumia's wound had to have been angled downward toward his torso (assuming, as the prosecution does, that Mumia was standing upright when shot).

This downward angling of the gunshot was inconsistent with the prosecution theory at trial that a standing Mumia was shot by a falling Officer Faulkner. The prosecution had two avenues of explanation to undercut the value of Dr. Hayes's testimony: (1) that Faulkner could have angled the gun in a downward direction with his arm as he was falling; or (2) reviving the "ricochet and tumble" theory relied upon by McGill (the bullet ricochet off bone within Mumia's torso and then tumbled in a downward direction.) Neither passed the laugh test. The first explanation suggests that Faulkner fired his gun with his arm configured in an odd position, which is doubtful because that would probably have been noticed by the prosecution eyewitnesses. The "ricochet and tumble" theory was simply wrong, as the X rays conclusively established that the bullet traveled through Mumia's torso without any deflection. Dr. Hayes testified, without rebuttal, that a ricochet would have left some physical indication that could be detected in an X ray.

There was, in short, no realistic way that Faulkner could have shot Mumia as he was falling—the prosecution's theory of how the shooting took place was, plain and simple, wrong. McGill had made a choice to take White over Harkins. With White's account conflicting with rock-solid scientific evidence, that left Harkins. And his account could not in any way be reconciled with the theory that Faulkner had fired his gun *after* he had been hit in the back with a bullet. Under Harkins's account, Mumia had to have been shot sometime *before* the shooter grabbed Faulkner, spun him around, and then fired into his back as he struggled to regain his balance. I became convinced over time that Harkins was a disfavored witness to McGill because he only deepened the mystery over *when, and under what circumstances,* Mumia was shot.

■ At the end of the day on August 4, a Friday, Len addressed Judge Sabo on what, in a normal court proceeding, would be just a housekeeping matter. We were still trying to assemble exhibits from the original trial and were having some logistical difficulties. Len was asking that the proceedings resume on Tuesday, thus giving us Monday to take care of the logistical problems. Judge Sabo refused the request, noting that "maybe the DA will call some of their witnesses on Monday."

Len ruffled what little hair he had on the top of his head, a mannerism of his that I have come to notice reflected tension. "I know the court is concerned about the prosecutors, but there are two parties here," he said bitterly.

Judge Sabo's rancor matched Len's bitterness. "I am concerned with getting witnesses on that witness stand and testifying under oath in this courtroom as to what they know about this case. That's what I'm interested in. I'm not interested in a lot of hot air. I've had enough of that. It's hot enough outside."

The judge was right about the weather; it was a grotesquely hot summer in Philadelphia. After court we usually went straight from the air conditioning of the courtroom to the air conditioning of our hotel, with brief obligatory stops at daily rallies and media microphones outside city hall. The stifling heat wasn't conducive to exercising, which only exacerbated the stress.

"I wish the court wouldn't characterize advocacy as hot air," Len protested. He then proceeded to rebuke Judge Sabo for acting contrary to the Canon of Judicial Ethics. "You should conduct yourself as the canons require," he concluded. I gave a slight smile at that, because Len had told me years earlier that I should carry the canons with me when appearing in court to remind judges not to come down too hard on young lawyers.

"Don't tell me how to conduct myself," Judge Sabo retorted angrily. "You are a New York attorney. When you come to Pennsylvania, you show the proper respect to this court. And I am telling you one more time I am not only going to evict you but I am going to fine you a thousand. That's not a threat, that's a promise."

Len, Rachel, and I remained concerned about the judge removing us from the case. We knew that he had the authority to do it, and we didn't trust the Pennsylvania judicial system to stand in his way. That is why Rachel bit her lip and apologized after she spent a few hours in lock-up. Len wisely backed down and allowed the proceedings to dissolve into the much-anticipated weekend.

■ Jesse Jackson showed up at the city hall courthouse on Monday, August 7. He came not only to observe the proceedings but to provide spiritual comfort to Mumia. The two talked privately. The meeting prompted discussions in the defense team over the possibility that Mumia would dispatch a conciliatory message to Maureen Faulkner. I was 100 percent in favor of the overture. Rachel was understandably wary. She felt that it could backfire on us, in part at least because it could be misconstrued as a tacit admission of guilt. I argued that the message could be drafted to disabuse anyone of that notion, but I was sympathetic with Rachel's cynical outlook toward the media. Moreover, it was unclear how Maureen would react to any direct communication from Mumia. Mumia wanted to reach out to her, but he suspected that she would never accept an overture on his part that contained any suggestion that he did not kill her husband. In the end, we opted not to reduce anything to writing, and Mumia passed along a conciliatory oral message to Maureen through Reverend Jackson.

August 7 was a special day for us. With Reverend Jackson in the audience (coincidence or not, I don't know), Judge Sabo announced that he was now prepared to act on the stay of execution application. "We still have the question of the stay of execution here," he unexpectedly began. "And today is August seventh. The execution date is August seventeenth. It's getting rather close." Mumia tended to slouch a little in his chair, which I enjoyed witnessing because it reflected his confidence in how we were handling the courtroom presentation. He certainly never slouched in the 1982 trial. I noticed, however, he quickly came out of his slouch when he realized what Sabo was about to do. "And at the rate we're going, I don't see when, I don't even know when we're going to finish," the judge continued. "And then from here it is an automatic appeal to the Pennsylvania Supreme Court. I am sure they are not going to be able to resolve that issue before August the seventeenth. And from there you are going into federal court. And I'm sure no one along that line is going to be able to make all of these decisions before August the seventeenth of 1995." It was slow in coming, and it was obviously difficult for the cantankerous judge to capitulate. "Based on that reason alone, because this is the first PCRA petition, as I understand it, he is legally permitted to argue that one all the way up to the highest court in the land, including the United States Supreme Court. And I can't see that happening before August the seventeenth of 1995, and for that reason and that reason alone, I will grant your stay of execution."

The courtroom erupted into applause. Nobody noticed that implicit in the judge's announcement was an admission on his part that he had no intention of granting our PCRA petition, even though the evidence was not all in. After all, he was emphasizing *Mumia's* right to appeal. "Calm down," Judge Sabo said, not as a rebuke but as the beginning of a refutation. "Don't be too happy because that's only for this one." If anything exposed Judge Sabo's utter bias, his behavior at that moment did. He didn't want to grant that stay, but it is my guess he was forced into it by superiors within the Philadelphia justice system. The international pressure for a stay had become intense, with letters, faxes, and phone calls swamping the clerk's office from all over the world. My favorite communiqués were from Nelson Mandela and Archbishop Desmond Tutu. It was gratifying to feel a link to those two freedom-loving individuals. Judge Sabo couldn't abide the cheering, not because it disrupted the proceedings but because it signified that he had succumbed. He told the crowd "Don't be too happy," childishly insisting upon having the last word, if only to underscore that he was not going soft.

The police officers attending the hearings were visibly upset. One of them told a coterie of reporters, "It makes you wonder, maybe we should have executed him at Thirteenth and Locust where he executed Danny Faulkner."

Mumia's public reaction was tepid and impersonal. He told an interviewer shortly after the announcement, "I am not under an active death warrant, although I remain under an active death sentence; thus, I still sojourn in hell." He offered no spontaneous reaction, either through words or gesture, upon hearing Sabo's announcement. This man who hadn't let an hour pass without verbally jousting with the judge during the trial; this man who had spoken eloquently and often in a vain effort to recapture control over his own case; this man, throughout the PCRA proceedings thirteen years later, sat completely silent, infrequently whispering commentary to one of us lawyers. Now this lover of words and people, this incarcerated soul who hungered for meaningful human contact, seldom engaged in banter during the breaks in the proceedings. Long stretches of time alone in a cell clearly had affected him. His writings had become analytical and distant. He now tends to absorb events and then transmute them in his mind into intellectual abstractions. He feels comfortable in the realm of ideas—a realm that the state of Pennsylvania could not trespass upon until such time, if it should come to pass, that the liquid in the needle of death is drained into his veins. So his detached reaction to the stay of execution, and to all else that occurred in the courtroom, seemingly flowed from what he had been forced to become as a human being.

Many times I had wanted to grab his shoulders and ask him to speak of how he was really *feeling*. "What are you feeling, Mumia? What do you long for, and what do you regret? Are you still able to love?" Maybe someday.

■ We were back in court on Wednesday, August 9, and Judge Sabo was peeved about the media coverage of his decision to grant the stay. His first remarks from the bench were directed at our table, accusing us of misrepresenting the reason why he had granted the stay. Len, Rachel, and I had, indeed, gloated to the media and the throngs of supporters that we won that particular showdown with Judge Sabo. We needed to gloat as an outlet for our frustrations at having to deal with aggressive prosecutors who had an embittered judge in their hip pocket. Len in particular cited the "tens of thousands of people around the world who supported Mumia" as the reason for the stay. It was important, from an organizational standpoint, to infuse the support network with a sense that their vigilance was paying off.

In any event, we felt that it was, in fact, true that Judge Sabo was forced to capitulate. It may have been the result of the powers that be in the court system that twisted his arm; but someone within the system felt the heat from the protests. But Judge Sabo didn't want that suggestion to go unrebutted. "I did not issue the stay because Jesse Jackson had anything to do with it," he announced to the audience and the reporters in particular. "Nor did I issue the stay because of any national or international pressure. I did it because the law required it to be done."

This was pure nonsense, as we had argued vociferously back on July 12, and almost daily during the proceedings, that a stay was legally required, and yet Judge Sabo had repeatedly refused to issue the stay. "I told you at the very beginning that this little old judge in this little old courtroom will not buckle under any kind of pressure, whether it be national or international."

■ "I know who shot the cop, and I ain't never gonna forget it." With those words spoken thirteen years before, Chobert played his part in the prosecution's mission of securing a conviction against their prized defendant. But Chobert was an ambiguous witness, notwithstanding his unambiguous identification at trial of Mumia as the killer.

He never had the opportunity to observe Mumia in an upright position before identifying him to the police. Mumia was crouched in a police van, bleeding from the head and chest, when Chobert peered inside. Had Mumia been able to stand for an on-the-scene identification, Chobert might not have been so quick to identify him as the shooter. He admitted that Mumia didn't fit the physical description he gave of the shooter. He described the shooter as heavyset, weighing about 225 pounds—some 55 pounds heavier than Mumia. This shooter, who Chobert said "ran away," was wearing a light tan shirt and jeans—colors far more subdued than the bright red and blue ski jacket worn by Mumia on that fateful night.

Chobert delivered a devastating blow to the defense apart from his identification testimony. When Jackson asked about his statement to homicide investigators that the shooter "ran away," Chobert stunningly renounced the claim. "It was a mistake, just a mistake," he insisted. Jackson tried to shake Chobert, but that only fortified him. Jackson went after Chobert from another angle, confronting him with his criminal record. McGill, however, objected. At a sidebar conference, Chobert told the judge, "I threw a bomb into a school, a Molotov [cocktail] . . . I got paid for doing it." Chobert was still on probation for his conviction on this offense and Jackson wanted the jury to consider it so that they would have the full measure of the man who they were asked to believe. Judge Sabo sided with McGill and barred Jackson from doing so.

Jackson completely missed a more fruitful attack. Chobert didn't only say that the shooter fled, he also gave an account of what he personally did in the wake of the shooting. *He stepped out of his cab and walked toward the scene of the shooting to see if he could help the fallen officer.* Now, that's odd, I thought. Why would he do that? If, as he claimed at trial, the shooter remained at the scene, still armed, wouldn't he be jeopardizing his own life? I thought of Harkins: he drove off immediately because he feared being shot. Chobert would never have walked into the line of fire where a cop killer remained fully armed and capable of killing him. That he walked toward the sidewalk where the officer lay dead—a fact confirmed by police reports indicating that arriving cops told him to go back to his cab—powerfully confirmed that, in fact, he saw the shooter run away, just as he claimed to homicide investigators at the scene. Jackson never caught the absurdity of Chobert's revisionist account at trial.

The new prosecutors attempted to push these facts aside, arguing that Chobert had no fear of the shooter because he had been shot. Chobert, however, testified that he was unaware that Mumia had been shot. Nor could the prosecution say that Chobert felt there was safety in numbers, as he saw no one else at the crime scene other than Billy Cook.

We knew that there had to be more to this story. Why would he walk toward the crime scene when the armed killer was sitting on the curb? How could he have mistakenly told police that he saw someone "run away" a distance of some thirty steps eastbound on Locust Street, which happens to be the approximate distance of an alleyway that would have been a convenient escape route for the killer? Was it just a coincidence that Chobert's observation of flight from the crime scene matched that of other witnesses? There had to be more. We put Chobert on the stand during the latter part of the 1995 proceedings to find out if we could bring the full story to light.

We didn't expect Chobert to be a friendly witness. He really had no reason to be. During the trial in 1982, he had been led to believe that his life was in danger by testifying. He was put up in a hotel and provided police protection (two cops who stayed in the room next door) for a few weeks before his testimony—all for his own safety, he was told. He had no doubt in his own mind that Mumia was the killer, notwithstanding what he had reported to the police just minutes after the shooting.

We knew from the trial transcripts that Chobert was driving a cab and that he was on probation. We also surmised he had a drinking problem, because he had two prior DWI convictions. How was it that he was driving a cab? Wouldn't he have difficulties getting a chauffeur's license?

Len asked Chobert, "Do you recall if back in 1981 or 1982 whether or not you had a conversation with the district attorney who was prosecuting this case—Joe McGill—about your driver's license?"

"Yes, I did," Chobert answered.

A conversation between a witness and the prosecutor about how the witness earns his living? That is certainly worth pursuing. So that is what Len did.

"Do you recall what he said to you at that time?"

"Well, he said he'll look into it," Chobert explained.

The law is very strict on a prosecutor's obligation to turn over all information concerning any agreements, formal or informal, between a witness and the prosecuting authorities. A defense lawyer is entitled to that information for use in cross-examination, because a jury is entitled to consider whether such agreements might affect a witness's testimony. Chobert wasn't giving expansive answers—a reticence that was in keeping with the way he answered questions at the 1982 trial—and he surely wasn't giving us evidence of a detailed, formal agreement. But he was giving us more than we had expected going into these proceedings. We thought we would hit a brick wall with Chobert.

I slipped Len a note. I figured if McGill said that he'd look into Chobert's driver's license situation, it must have been Chobert who initiated the conversation. It only stood to reason, by my calculation, that this would be true, given that prosecutors are reluctant to extend favors or benefits to a witness unless absolutely necessary. McGill surely knew that to do so would require disclosure to the defense, which would create an avenue of cross-examination. A prosecutor much prefers a clean witness unburdened by any such favoritism. I suggested in the note that Len ask Chobert whether he initiated the discussion.

"And when he said he'll look into it, that was in response to something that you had mentioned, was it not?"

Chobert admitted that he had initiated the discussion. "I asked him if he could help me find out how I could get my license back," he replied in his typical laconic style. Chobert went on to explain that his chauffer's license had been suspended, which meant that he had been violating his probation by driving illegally. While McGill offered a carrot—to try to get the license back—it also carried a stick—the threat to Chobert's probation because of his continuing driving violation. Thus, Chobert was reaching out to McGill out of economic *and* penal necessity: he wanted to continue to earn a living and he didn't want to go back to jail for violating the terms of his probation. When McGill stated that he would look into the situation, Chobert expected that he would be receiving his assistance and his benevolence.

This was the best answer we could get, under the circumstances. The whole point to this line of questioning was not only that McGill and Chobert had a secret agreement, but that Chobert's state of mind was affected by it. Because Chobert raised the subject, it was obviously something that was important to him. McGill's willingness to help him could only have created an alliance between the witness and the prosecution, and the defense should have been told about it.

Because Jackson was kept in the dark about McGill's conversation with Chobert, so was the jury. Was this the reason Chobert testified that he was "mistaken" in telling investigators that the shooter "ran away"? Chobert wasn't about to admit in 1995 that he perjured himself at the 1982 trial. Instead, he clung to his claim that his trial testimony was the truth and that his statements in the police reports were a mistake. But Chobert's revelation at the 1995 hearing put things in their proper context. It provided a reason—a compelling reason, a jury might well conclude—for Chobert to slant his testimony in the prosecution's favor. It reinforced the highly suspicious nature of Chobert's trial testimony, particularly in regards to his conduct at the scene immediately after the shooting stopped. The only reasonable inference that could be drawn from *all* of the evidence is that Chobert *did* see the shooter run, and that shooter was considerably huskier than Mumia. With the shooter gone from the crime scene, Chobert felt it was safe enough to approach the wounded officer. He must have assumed that the arriving officers apprehended the fleeing shooter and placed him inside the police van. He identified Mumia, in all likelihood, based upon the assumption that he was the apprehended fleeing shooter, without having the opportunity to view Mumia's stature and weight. Nor was he able to see Mumia's brightly-colored ski jacket, as it had been removed when he was thrown into the van. Had Chobert been able to see Mumia in a standing position wearing his ski jacket, he probably would not have identified Mumia as the shooter.

McGill proved himself to be a shrewd prosecutor throughout the 1982 trial. The Chobert revelation exposed him to be ruthless. McGill, knowing that evidence undercutting Chobert's credibility existed, misled the jury by asking rhetorically: "What motivation would Robert Chobert have to make up a story within thirty-five to forty-five minutes later?" He brazenly suggested to the jury that Chobert had come in to testify without any taint of prosecutorial influence, knowing full well that he had had a questionable conversation with Chobert and that Jackson had no way of challenging his argument to the jury.

■ The "fleeing man" theory that Jackson had tried to develop at trial rested on a crucial premise—namely, that a third civilian, aside from Mumia and his brother, was at the scene with Officer Faulkner. The prosecution's theory of the crime rested on the equally essential premise that only two people were at the scene with the officer at the time of the shooting. Mumia's fight to prove his innocence, in large measure, hinged on our ability to undermine the prosecution's jealously guarded two-person theory. At the very least, evidence that raised the possibility that a third person was at the scene would puncture the image of a reliable open-and-shut case while simultaneously bolstering the observations of various witnesses that someone fled toward a nearby alleyway. We learned during the 1995 proceedings that the prosecution suppressed physical evidence that would have allowed the defense to do precisely that: undermine the prosecution's two-person theory.

Homicide investigators actually initiated an investigation in 1982—without following through—into the possibility that a third person was at the crime scene and that this third person fled. On the night in question, police picked up at least three black males—Cynthia White's pimp (known on the street as Sweet Sam), Billy Cook's business associate (a man named Kenneth Freeman), and one Arnold Howard—for questioning as possible suspects to the shooting. We put Arnold Howard on the stand on August 9.

Howard, a lanky, wiry, and talkative black man, had known Mumia since he was a child. "We grew up together in the same neighborhood," he explained in his testimony. He was extremely thin, a consequence of having his stomach surgically reconstructed as a result of five gunshot wounds he received in 1989. In the predawn hours of December 9, 1981, more than five law enforcement officers picked up Howard at his home in connection with the Faulkner shooting investigation. He was taken to the homicide precinct, known as the Roundhouse, for interrogation and for placement in a lineup. Additionally, Howard described how the police "put some kind of powder on my hands."

"Did the officers tell you why they were checking your hands?" Len asked.

"Yes, they said by my license being found at the scene of a homicide, that I was somewhat involved in it," Howard explained.

"Now, besides this test of your hands or whatever was done with your hands, were you asked to participate in any other kind of process?

"Yes, they put me and a Kenneth Freeman into a lineup."

Freeman worked with Billy Cook in a makeshift business, selling jewelry, hats, scarves, rolling papers, and other knickknacks from a self-constructed mobile shack. The two frequently rode together in Cook's Volkswagen. Howard explained that he had given his driver's license to Freeman a few days earlier.

Howard kept referring to his driver's license, but what he actually was referring to was a driver's license application form, which also served as a temporary driver's permit. There was no dispute that this document was found in the front pants pocket of Officer Faulkner—a fact that the prosecution disclosed for the first time at the 1995 hearing. The problem, of course, was that Jackson was never told about it back in 1982 when the information could have been put to use for Mumia's benefit. What was Faulkner doing with Howard's driver's license? Interestingly, prosecution witness Michael Scanlan testified that he saw Faulkner examining a document in his hand early in the encounter between him and Cook. Jackson had let that testimony slide by as an insignificant detail, understandably, as he had no reason to know or suspect that this document belonged to a *third person*— thanks to the prosecution's suppression of that fact.

Howard explained to homicide detectives that he lent the document to Freeman; they were justifiably dubious. If Howard was in fact at the scene and somehow involved in the shooting, he wouldn't be inclined to admit it. The fact of his license being in Faulkner's possession strongly suggested that he was there.

"Incidentally, Mr. Howard, were you there?" Len was referring to the crime scene.

"No, sir," Howard said firmly.

"Did you produce proof to the detectives as to your whereabouts at the time of the occurrence?"

"Yes, I did. A sales receipt from Pathmark on Aramingo Avenue"—a location some distance away from Thirteenth and Locust St. The sales receipt indicated a time of 4:00 A.M. Howard had an alibi, and, remarkably, it was good enough to satisfy the homicide investigators.

If it wasn't Howard in the Volkswagen with his own driver's license, then who was? Ken Freeman was the logical answer, not only by virtue of Howard's claim that he lent the document to him but also because Freeman was Cook's business partner. Len probed Howard's knowledge about Freeman, but the prosecutor, a woman named Arlene Fisk, who had inexplicably taken over the lead role (Joey Grant, without explanation, left the prosecution team), blocked the inquiry with persistent objections. Fisk struck me as extremely bright, and much more pleasant to deal with than Grant or Burns, both of whom enjoyed affecting a macho veneer. Her lack of a hard edge, however, didn't dampen her aggressive advocacy.

Freeman had died on the night that the MOVE house on Osage Avenue was firebombed. Len asked Howard if he knew anything about the circumstances of his death. "My understanding is he was hand-cuffed and shot up and dumped up on Grink's lot on Roosevelt Boulevard, buck naked," Howard said. In fact, Freeman died under highly mysterious circumstances. He had been brought to a hospital in a police vehicle, gagged, bound, and naked. The death certificate indicated he had died of a heart attack. He was thirty-one with no history of heart problems.

"He was handcuffed?" Len followed up.

"Yes."

"And shot?"

"No, shot up with drugs."

"And to your knowledge, did Ken Freeman have your license on the night in question?"

Howard nodded. "Yes, he did."

We were pleased with the information Howard provided. By itself, the undisputed fact that the deceased officer had within his clothing a driver's license belonging to a third person is more than just an interesting fact having a slight bearing on the question of Mumia's guilt or innocence, as it raises a question about the reliability of the prosecution's two-person theory. But in view of the remarkable fact that numerous independent witnesses saw flight from the scene of the crime (a fact never considered by the earlier jury), this uncontested item of physical evidence was tremendously significant. The eyewitness accounts *and* the driver's license mutually reinforce the indispensable message that the jury would have received in a genuinely fair trial proceeding—namely, that the prosecution's theory that only two people were at the scene who were in a position to shoot the officer is too unreliable to justify a conclusion of guilt beyond a reasonable doubt.

Most intriguing, Howard's testimony also increased the importance of Scanlan's observation of the shooter wearing an Afro, since Freeman sported one.

Ideologies . . . have no heart of their own.
They're the whores and angels of our own
striving selves.

JOHN LE CARRÉ, *THE SECRET PILGRIM*

16. FIGHTING IDEOLOGY

We returned to our hotel, a small no-frills Holiday Inn that was a few short blocks away from the crime scene (I could see it from my window), feeling good about Howard's testimony. If we hadn't contacted Arnold Howard, we never would have discovered that the prosecution had suppressed evidence that Faulkner was in possession of a driver's license form belonging to a third person. Howard's testimony compelled the prosecution to concede that this was so. Additionally, through Howard's testimony, the fleeing man began to take on an identity—Kenneth Freeman.

As with everything else in the case, the "Freeman" theory had its problems. Billy Cook didn't report to the police that his business partner was with him in the Volkswagen, let alone that he was the one who shot the officer. Instead, Cook blurted out to the police who arrived at the crime scene, "I ain't got nothing to do with it." Cook's instinctive reaction to protect his own interest was, to say the least, problematic. The prosecutors in the 1995 hearing never shied away from throwing this particular fact in our faces. It was clear that, to them, Cook's statement at the crime scene, more than the evidence that the jury considered at the 1982 trial, pointed to Mumia's guilt. They goaded us constantly to call Cook as a witness, as did Judge Sabo. We might very well have obliged, if we could have located him. We had investigators pounding the pavement looking for him, and at times they came close to finding him, but always ended up empty-handed.

There was another problem with the "Freeman" theory. Freeman was outspoken in his accusation that Philadelphia cops were responsible for burning down the vending stand that Cook and Freeman operated—a business that the two of them established through much diligence—four days after the Faulkner shooting. A person who had just killed a cop would have quite an incentive to keep his mouth shut. The circumstances strongly suggested that angry Philadelphia police officers were indeed responsible for the fire that destroyed Freeman's and Cook's treasured business. One officer in the sixth precinct (Faulkner's home precinct) told a news reporter that the precinct was abuzz over the fire. "It's entirely possible that certain sick members of this department were responsible for this fire," this officer said. "The place was filled with Cheshire grins." Why would Freeman be so brazen in his accusations against Philly cops if he was a hair's breadth away from being charged with a capital offense? Rationality would dictate silence; but then again, why assume Freeman was thinking rationally?

In any event, we didn't—because we couldn't—dwell on the implications of Howard's testimony for long. We had a major decision to make before the next day's proceedings began. Part of our investigatory strategy was to locate every single person who was at the scene of the crime when the shooting occurred. Our primary source of information on that score, of course, were the police reports. That's how we knew to reach out for Arnold Howard. Many lawyers, particularly those without the financial and human resources to do it, would have bypassed someone like Howard, because the cryptic police report pertaining to him created the impression that he was unimportant to the

case. We had the benefit of money, raised through diligent fund raising efforts, and a core of dedicated volunteers and paid investigators,
which allowed us to dig up witnesses over a decade after the incident that bound them together. We also had an extreme skepticism
about the good-faith investigative efforts of the Philadelphia police
department.

I was sensitive to the possibility that Mumia's sympathies with
MOVE might have prompted law enforcement to jump to a conclusion about Mumia's guilt. I even believed that law enforcement was
willing to fabricate evidence to help in the effort to convict a man
they *believed to be guilty*. Rachel and Jon held more extreme views;
they were convinced—actually, to them, it was sacrilegious to believe
otherwise—that law enforcement knew Mumia was innocent, knew
that the shooter fled the scene, and relished that a conviction and
death sentence would be a terrific coup in the city's war against
MOVE. Their view was an article of faith that grew out of their
ideological zeal. Len, probably motivated by a desire to keep the defense team intact, kept his views, for the most part, private, which
could be maddening when decisions had to be made and emotions
ran high.

Len and I nevertheless approached the case from a pragmatic
standpoint. Although we all adhered to the view that Mumia was
innocent, Len and I understood that we couldn't expect a judge to
share that view, or even to be sympathetic with it, at the outset of
litigation. We would have to develop a credible case to undermine the
reliability of the jury's verdict—that was the best we could realistically
shoot for. So even if Len and I agreed with Rachel and Jon, I felt that
we couldn't make the "knowing frame-up of an innocent man" theory
the centerpiece to our litigation strategy. It would be asking too much
from a judge.

Our differing views about the core of Mumia's case, as well as the
differences in the role ideology played in our personal and professional
lives, led us to stake out different strategic approaches to litigating the
case. On many occasions, I wondered whether there was enough room
on the defense team for all four of us.

■ Rachel had unique access to Mumia, and he understandably put his faith in her. An indefatigable and unrelenting advocate for the "Free Mumia" cause, she was a key player in bringing Mumia to the attention of the broader left-wing movements in this country and throughout Europe. It was Rachel's standing in the political arena that gave her stature within the defense team.

Mumia had always placed his faith in radical politics. At his trial, he stridently advocated the merits of conducting the trial according to the strategy of John Africa. After his conviction, Mumia put his future in the hands of MOVE. When municipal authorities, upon orders from Mayor Wilson Goode, dropped a firebomb on the MOVE compound at Osage Avenue on May 13, 1985, Mumia's important papers (including documents from his trial) went up in flames as well. Mumia's allegiance with MOVE was sincere and heartfelt; but it also paved the way for word to spread among left-wing organizations that an innocent man, an ex-Black Panther, was on death row. The first leftist group to carry the banner was an organization with which Rachel and Jon were affiliated—the Partisan Defense Committee.

The PDC, in the splintered world of left-wing backbiting, is a Trotskyist organization. The PDC had taken up advocacy for the MOVE Nine, imprisoned for what amounted to life terms, in connection with the Ramp shooting. Ramona Africa, the sole adult survivor of the 1985 bombing of the MOVE compound on Osage Avenue, urged the PDC to look into the case of Mumia Abu-Jamal, stating in a letter that he is "a journalist and activist who is on death row for his political beliefs."

At small leftist gatherings, and at larger rallies for progressive causes, the PDC hung banners and distributed leaflets with the bold, if not unique, slogan, "Free Mumia Now! Abolish the Racist Death Penalty!" This ardent advocacy for Mumia reminded me of the communists in the United States who trumpeted the Scottsboro Boys case in the 1930s, which ultimately led to the landmark Supreme Court ruling mandating adequate legal representation in capital cases. Mumia the symbol, and the most charismatic of political prisoners, latched onto the consciousness of progressive people hungering for a focal point around which to rally. Cold war dynamics, the nuclear arms race, and apartheid dissipated in the '90s as anchors for left-wing advocacy. Progressives began to look within and found that there was much to be angry about in this country, particularly the spectacular rise of the prison–industrial complex. The problem, however, is that few prisoners can rivet the attention of activists and progressive-minded people to spark or revive a movement. Mumia, however, fit the bill; he had a striking appearance, a poetic sensibility, a vocal gift, and an impeccable record as a revolutionary stretching back to the heady days of the Black Panther Party. The PDC was tapping into something big.

The next organization that embraced the cause with a fervent belief that Mumia was framed was the Quixote Center, a group of liberation theology Catholics. The Quixote Center, through its subsidiary, Equal Justice U.S.A., brought Mumia's cause into sharper focus, and lent it an enhanced credibility that the PDC could never provide. The case slowly transmogrified from one involving a political prisoner on death row to a referendum on the fairness of the criminal justice system itself. Mumia certainly helped in this development, using his writing skills to disseminate trenchant attacks on American capitalism and the rise of the prison–industrial complex. He provocatively averred that he was living in the most rapidly growing public housing project in the country—a prison. He described the people who lived there with him, and the people who kept watch over him. He provided vignettes of life on the "inside" to a public on the "outside" that has no idea what human beings are capable of doing to other human beings in the name of law and order. He wrote essays criticizing the Gulf War, ridiculing the O. J. Simpson trial, supporting the United Nations's condemnation of our embargo on Cuba, lamenting the rash of police violence and prison construction, and on and on. Mumia the cause, almost inevitably, seeped into the rarefied atmosphere of the literary elites and Hollywood celebrity circles.

Probably the defining moment in the pro-Mumia movement came when National Public Radio expressed interest in airing on its *All*

Things Considered program a series of extremely powerful radio commentaries by Mumia describing, among other things, life on death row. On the eve of the first broadcast, with the commentaries recorded on audiotape and after promoting the provocative idea, NPR capitulated to intense right-wing political pressure and withdrew its commitment to air the recordings. Then-senator Bob Dole and the National Fraternal Order of Police threatened NPR where it counts: in the pocketbook. Dole was quite explicit about it, stating on the Senate floor that "this episode raises sobering questions, not only for NPR but for the taxpayer-funded Corporation for Public Broadcasting, which has oversight authority over NPR and provides much of its funding." To this day, the *All Things Considered* recordings are under lock and key with NPR. NPR's abrupt cancellation of these radio commentaries, coupled with the manifest power of Mumia's vocal delivery and sharp insights, caught the attention of many intellectuals and celebrities.

Throughout the development of the "Mumia" phenomenon, the PDC remained rigid in its outlook. It was deemed counterrevolutionary, and thus contemptible, to advocate for a new trial for Mumia. To even suggest that securing a new trial was a worthy goal, in the minds of the PDC adherents, was to acquiesce in the bourgeois notion that the legal system was capable of fairness. It was for this reason that it was always an uphill battle to get the defense team to focus on the penalty phase issues. The only justifiable political call was for Mumia's release: no new trial, no calls for a moratorium on the death penalty, no advocacy that he was not a genuine candidate for execution. Mumia must be released, now!—and those holding the reins of power have to capitulate to this demand of the proletariat. With this sort of anachronistic rhetoric, had the PDC retained total control over the blossoming pro-Mumia movement, it would have forever remained a marginal cause. Fortunately, the extreme rigidity of the PDC is an anomaly in the progressive community—as I have experienced it. Not everyone was willing to accept on pure faith that Mumia was innocent; many, however, were willing to give a sympathetic ear to the claim that the criminal justice system had not produced a result in his case that was sufficiently reliable to justify our trust. Other political groups, recognizing the need to broaden the base of support, welcomed such persons into the pro-Mumia fold and lamented the rigidity of the PDC.

But all of that doesn't diminish the indefatigable efforts of Rachel Wolkenstein and the PDC; for that, Mumia would always be grateful. The question was how much would gratitude eclipse judgment.

■ Leaving aside the differences between me and the PDC contingent on the defense team, the important fact, in the short run, was that everyone on the team agreed that, at the least, the city's particular history with MOVE was an important backdrop to this particular case, and that law enforcement's intense antipathy toward this organization probably created a bias in the investigation, as criminal defense lawyers would put it. That core belief that united the defense team prompted us to ferret out every person identified in the police reports and learn for ourselves what they had to say. It paid off with Howard, as we would otherwise never have learned that the prosecution concealed evidence that Officer Faulkner had a license in his pocket belonging to a third person. Would it pay off with other witnesses?

William Singletary, a Philadelphia resident, was in the vicinity of the shooting at the time Faulkner was killed. A police report in the case file identified him by name, but expressly stated that he saw nothing. A less-than-thorough reexamination into the case would have bypassed Singletary as nothing more than an irrelevant bystander. Singletary was located and interviewed in 1990—two years before Len and I became involved in the case. Rachel and her assistants at the PDC received word that Singletary had information about the shooting. They tracked him down and on August 31, 1990, brought him into the office of Mumia's court-appointed appellate lawyer, Marilyn Gelb, the lawyer who encouraged Anthony Jackson to go to law school.

In a move that will forever perplex me, Gelb and Rachel submitted Singletary to questioning under oath before a stenographer. It was, in my view, a blunder if only because the defense is obligated to turn such material over to the prosecution in future litigation, thereby relinquishing one major advantage a defendant enjoys—the element of surprise. Gelb may have accepted without exercising independent judgment Rachel's representation that Singletary held the key to Mumia's exoneration and opted for the stenographic recording to account for the possibility that Singletary might later, through change of heart or even death, become unavailable. I say that Gelb may not have exercised independent judgment because Singletary told a fantastic tale. Even if his account was true, it was so beyond the pale, no judge would believe it, thereby rendering his testimony inconsequential at best; at worst, an embrace of the story would brand us lawyers as nothing more than a band of kooks.

At the time of the 1982 trial, Singletary was a thirty-one-year-old Vietnam veteran who managed a family-owned gas station in Philadelphia. He had no psychiatric history and no criminal record. He was married with children, living in a modest residence, far from the world Mumia inhabited as a journalist and political radical. By the looks of it, he appeared to be a perfectly normal, rational human being.

When I first met Singletary at his home in 1995, I whispered to Len that he was built like a football player, with muscular shoulders melding into an equally muscular neck. Len whispered back that he had heard that his cousin was Mike Singletary, the onetime all-pro linebacker for the Chicago Bears.

Len and I sat on a couch and Singletary took a seat in what appeared to be his favorite chair. He sank deep into it and relaxed. He then smiled broadly to indicate that he was ready to answer any question we cared to ask. The room was dimly lit and somewhat musty, but I thought it best to keep quiet about it, even though it made note-taking difficult. Because Len and I knew that Rachel had interviewed him several times over the past several weeks, we were sensitive to the possibility that he was growing weary of this intrusion into his life. We asked him to go over his story again, rarely interrupting him with questions. His demeanor never betrayed impatience or annoyance at having to repeat his story yet again. His account mirrored what he had said in the 1990 statement.

In that 1990 statement, Singletary explained that he had unsuccessfully tried to get into a nightclub on Thirteenth and Locust. He then began to walk toward the southeast side of Locust and Thirteenth, which is the corner of the intersection nearest where the shooting was to take place. When the shooting erupted, he claimed to have been a mere twelve to fifteen feet away, adjacent to a subway entrance. He saw the traffic stop and the encounter between Cook and Officer Faulkner. Singletary claimed to see "a very tall fellow" sitting in the passenger seat of the Volkswagen; he said that he noticed this passenger because "it looked funny for a tall guy . . . to be sitting in a small car." This much was helpful, but perplexing, as Kenneth Freeman was definitely not a "tall fellow," and the initial description of the shooter given by Cynthia White was that he was shorter than five feet eight.

The incident he was about to describe, however, made my eyes widen. The officer, Singletary said, "made the driver get up against the wall, spread-eagle. . . ." No one had ever suggested that any part of the traffic-stop encounter took place away from the parked vehicles. The two had a verbal confrontation, with the officer filling the night air with obscenities. Then, Singletary said, the following occurred: "After about maybe two minutes, the tall guy emerged from the Volkswagen and said, 'Billy, we don't have to take this. . . . We are tired of these fucking racists and so forth and so on. . . . They burned a newstand last night and we just finished fixing it and we turned it back over. . . . We don't have to take this.' So the police officer said: 'Get back in the car.' "

The "tall guy," who wore his hair in dreadlocks and had "raggedy, unruly hair under his chin," didn't go back to the car. Instead, he "reached in his right pocket and pulled out a small handgun and shot the cop in the eye." The shooter then threw the murder weapon against the right rear tire of the Volkswagen, and ran east on Locust Street, with the driver (Cook) running behind. As a result of the gunshot wound to the face, the officer "went right up against the building and slid down," sitting upright propped up against the wall.

It was at this moment that another man appeared on the scene, yelling "This is my brother's car, where is my brother?" Singletary didn't know Mumia by appearance, but knew of him as a prominent radio journalist. Mumia noticed Singletary and asked him what happened, to which he said that "the tall guy shot the cop." According to Singletary, Mumia then moved toward the bleeding officer with outstretched arms, offering to help. The officer had, moments earlier, mumbled to Singletary, "Get Maureen" or "Get the children." As Mumia approached, the officer, with his gun resting on his upper thigh and the barrel pointing upward at a forty-five-degree angle, pulled the trigger, then slouched back and "dazed off." Mumia, hit by a bullet discharged from the officer's gun, stumbled over to the curb.

The balance of his 1990 statement was devoted to a description of how detectives forced him to renounce this account and sign a false statement indicating that he had not seen the shooting. He also described how they had driven him and his family out of Philadelphia.

Should we call William Singletary? In the hyperrational world of the law, the answer was self-evident. In the commonsense world that most people inhabit, the answer was self-evident. In the world of PDC politics, it was a real question.

No other decision would plague the legal team more than that question. Len and I struggled over the issue, consulting numerous other lawyers, discussing it endlessly in late-night conversations over the phone, visiting with Singletary several times. We agonized not so much because we suffered delusions that Singletary's account of the shooting, as opposed to the police misconduct, was plausible—we knew that it wasn't; we agonized because in a death penalty case, you discard an exculpatory witness only after thorough exploration of the pros and cons. Plus, Rachel and Jon *insisted* that we use him. The consensus among those whom we consulted was that we shouldn't use him, for the obvious reason that his eyewitness account was too susceptible to attack. I hoped that this would persuade Rachel and Jon to abandon Singletary. My argument was simple: I felt it was a mistake to commit ourselves to such a preposterous version of events. Why, I asked, should we allow ourselves to be attacked by the prosecution? It is far better to go on the attack and maintain the smallest possible target for the opponent. Rachel and Jon were nonetheless adamant. As far as they were concerned, Singletary's story exonerates Mumia—that was enough to merit calling him. As far as I was concerned, using Singletary was akin to putting up a billboard with a bull's-eye drawn on it.

In every other case on which I have worked involving a team of lawyers—and I had worked on several, stretching back to my law school days with my first mentor, Professor Alan Dershowitz—major strategic and tactical decisions were not made democratically; nor were strategic and tactical judgments about which witnesses should be called delegated to the client. The one or two lawyers who have the most experience and most knowledge about the matter should have ultimate say. That, unfortunately, was not how our team operated back in 1995. Len clearly had the most experience in terms of years, but he had no particular expertise in the complex world of capital punishment jurisprudence. He relied on me and other specialists to educate him about the difficulties that would lie ahead in our appeals to the federal courts. That is one of Len's best attributes—his willingness to listen and his utter lack of hubris. I felt that Rachel and Jon's views on the Singletary issue should receive the least weight because they had no real criminal defense or capital punishment experience (indeed, no actual trial experience). As an aside, I was rather shocked by Jon's advocacy, because he made his living in the rigidly logical and no-nonsense world of corporate litigation.

But, as I alluded to earlier, there was one area that Rachel in particular had the upperhand on me and others. She was much more connected with the left-wing political movement to "free Mumia" than I was. I have never been a joiner. I was intellectually always attracted to progressive thought, and I had engaged in activist causes. But I disdained rigid ideologies. Rachel's deep involvement in "the movement"—whatever that might mean—meant that she had a tighter connection to Mumia, who understandably felt that his fight for freedom could never be disconnected from the political movements propelling his cause. I certainly agreed with Mumia that the mass left-wing support was important; but I also believed that *he* was important to the left-wing, and that he did not need to be concerned about losing support. At bottom, I parted company with the notion that ideology should, in any way, dictate the litigation strategy or tactics in a death penalty case.

My impression was that Rachel lobbied hard with Mumia in the hopes of forcing us into calling Singletary. I deeply resented Rachel's encroachment into an area in which she had no experience, especially because she used her stature within the PDC to wield influence over Len. Len sometimes gave the impression that he would allow concerns over how decisions within the defense team would influence the support network to affect his legal judgment. On that score, he trusted both Rachel and Mumia, and that trust trumped my legal analysis.

But, at the core, Len is an astute trial lawyer. He knew that Singletary's story about the night in question, if presented to a jury, would be disastrous to the case. He knew that no federal judge down the road would credit his story about what he had supposedly seen. He also ultimately agreed with my preeminent concern—namely, that our *credibility* as lawyers would suffer if we embraced Singletary, and that loss of credibility could be the most damaging consequence of all. But Len couldn't escape the apparent fact—about which I could be wrong—that Rachel had convinced Mumia to demand that Singletary take the stand. Len would never veto Mumia. Instead, he came up with a compromise.

■ "Okay, now are there any other witnesses you want to call?" Judge Sabo asked.

"If I may," Len said, "there is one additional witness who is referred to in the petition which counsel has had now for two months. And this is a witness who is a person whose recollection of what happened on the night in question we believe to be not entirely accurate." Len was speaking slowly, enunciating his words as if each carried the weight of the entire case. "We believe his recollection today is not entirely accurate," he reiterated. "We believe his recollection, which was given in a sworn statement in 1990, was not entirely accurate." Len said it three times. The repetition reflected his anxiety over the Singletary issue. Once Len told me that he was definitely going to call Singletary, at about 1:00 A.M. the night before, we crafted this approach—distance ourselves from Singletary's purported observations at the crime scene, in the hopes of preserving our credibility, while drawing on his testimony that he had been victimized by the police so as to scare away an exculpatory witness.

Because Singletary had not yet arrived in court, the prosecution team put on a witness of its own, an Officer Joseph Brown. We had not expected him to be called as a witness, and I was clueless as to what he would be testifying about—a trial lawyer's nightmare. "Len, you take him," I whispered, indicating I preferred that he cross-examine him. "I've gotta do Singletary, I can't," he replied. Len is a good friend, but sometimes he's like a father. If he tells me I have to cross-examine Officer Brown, then that's what I'll do.

I *hate* cross-examining any witness without pondering how I would go about it. I put an enormous amount of time and thought into a cross-examination. To me, cross-examination is an art form, an activity unlike any other, which deserves reverence for its powerful truth-seeking function. One early twentieth-century legal scholar said that cross-examination is the greatest device for ferreting out truth ever devised by humankind. That is true, if it's done skillfully. It is not an activity one should voluntarily engage in without appropriate preparation—to do so, in my view, is sacrilegious. But there are times when a trial lawyer is forced to cross-examine without the benefit of preparation. In those situations it is best to reduce the task to its most basic level: what is the story I want to tell with this particular witness?

It turned out that Officer Brown was called for a limited but important purpose: to impeach Arnold Howard. Howard had said the day before that he was brought in for questioning and a lineup in the predawn hours of December 9, 1981, and was detained for several days. Officer Brown testified that, according to the Roundhouse precinct logbook, Howard was brought in much later in the day, at around 12:30 P.M., and he had left about two hours later.

"May I have the logbook, exhibit C-eighteen," I said as I walked over to the podium to begin the cross-examination. The logbook contained Howard's signature, signing in and out as Officer Brown had said. It did contradict Howard's testimony that he was brought into the precinct early in the morning and was kept under arrest for several days. If the logbook entry was not undermined in some way, Howard's testimony would probably be disregarded by future courts reviewing this case.

My story line was simple: Officer Brown had no personal knowledge of who Arnold Howard was and his involvement in the case, and had no knowledge about what happened at the precinct on December 9. Everything he testified about was based solely upon the two entries in the logbook—Howard's signature signing in, and his signature signing out two hours later. If, in the process of telling that story through the cross-examination, I could secure something more helpful, then that would just be icing on the proverbial cake.

"Do you know, of your own *personal knowledge*, an individual by the name of Arnold Howard?"

"No, sir, I do not."

"As you sit here today, of your own *personal knowledge*, you don't know when Mr. Howard was brought into the Roundhouse," I declared, awaiting for his assent.

The officer at first equivocated. "I don't know whether it was—" I waved my finger at him so that he could see that I was asking about personal knowledge. "Oh, you're right, of my own personal knowledge, right," he corrected himself. Cross-examination lesson: never let the witness tell *his* story; only tell yours.

I then methodically went through the logbook and pointed out that virtually all of the civilian witnesses brought in for questioning in the early morning hours of December 9 had not signed the logbook. Officer Brown explained that when witnesses are brought in en masse to be questioned, they don't necessarily enter through the front entrance doors. The logbook is a sign-in book only for the front entrance doors, he clarified. That was the opening I was looking for.

"So if people were brought in earlier in the morning on December ninth, say between the times of four A.M. and six A.M., and they're not reflected in this logbook, how would they enter the building?"

Officer Brown explained that they would "walk through the police Detention Unit, walk through two metal doors after they are opened by the officer, go to an elevator and take the elevator or the stairs to whichever floor the unit that they were going to was on." No signing-in of the logbook when a person is brought into the building in this manner, I emphasized in the questioning.

I returned to the "no personal knowledge" story line, unabashedly sticking to a simple story. Simple stories are the best kinds to tell in litigation. "Can you testify today that sometime earlier on December ninth, 1981, perhaps between the hours of four A.M. and six A.M., whether Mr. Howard was brought in in the manner that you just described, can you tell us that?"

"Not if his name's in this logbook," Officer Brown answered.

I knew he was playing a word game with me—a game police witnesses are fond of. His logic was that Howard couldn't have entered through another entrance if he was brought in through the front entrance door. It was a flawed logic, because the fact that he was brought around the front entrance at about 12:30 P.M. on December 9 didn't rule out that he had been brought to the precinct earlier that morning. After all, he could have been escorted out to grab a bite to eat. Brown played the word game for several minutes as I kept pressing the same story line.

Finally, Brown broke down in the duel over words. "In other words," he asked, "what you are trying to say is that Mr. Howard may have been brought in with all these other individuals [that had been brought in through the Detention Unit entrance]?"

"Yes, that's what I am asking you," I replied.

"I cannot give you that of my own *personal knowledge*, I was not there." It is a good feeling when a witness parrots your language; it shows that you have won the psychological battle, because the witness is now operating on your terrain.

"That is precisely what I am asking," I asserted, confident that I had reached my goal. "So you can't tell us if Mr. Howard was there earlier, taken out of the building, and then brought in through the front entrance at twelve-thirty, can you?"

"No sir, I cannot."

"Precisely," I said, perhaps with a little smugness.

■ We returned from lunch and there was still no sign of Singletary. Rachel knew I was still very much against calling him as a witness, so she refused to talk about his whereabouts in my presence. I suppose she didn't want me to gloat over the possibility that he wouldn't show.

The prosecution team very much wanted Singletary to appear. In fact, Arlene Fisk announced immediately in the afternoon session that the prosecution would do whatever it took to bring him in for our benefit. Of course, the prosecution wasn't seeking to benefit us at all; they knew, as I knew, and probably Len as well, that Singletary would probably in the end help the prosecution more than he would help the defense. "We offer to the defense immediately, at this moment," Fisk told Sabo, "police officers, detectives, cars, persons who could go to whatever address defense counsel would like, any member of the defense team can accompany those officers, so that Mr. Singletary can be brought into the courtroom, placed on the witness stand, and offer whatever testimony the defense chooses to have that witness offer to-day." She then looked over at our table, pausing for a moment, baiting us. "I make that offer to the court so that there can be no question about the ability of defense counsel to produce the witness in this courtroom."

Judge Sabo solicited a response from Len. "Mr. Weinglass?"

"No response is necessary to that," Len replied.

I figured this was an opening for me, a last opportunity to end what I regarded as a self-destructive maneuver. "Len, what does *that* tell you?" I said. I urged him to change his mind, stating the obvious, that the prosecution's anxiousness—indeed, their undisguised enthusiasm for Singletary—clearly showed that calling him was a mistake. Rachel glared over at me as she engaged in a whispered conversation with Mumia. "This is madness," I grumbled to myself, frustrated and frightened.

Singletary eventually arrived, and he did take the stand that afternoon. But before that, we put on another witness, a medical doctor named Ian Hood, who testified about inconsequential matters concerning the autopsy. During Dr. Hood's testimony, Judge Sabo and Len became embroiled in another verbal spar. Len was using some autopsy slides in his questioning when Judge Sabo asked to see some of them.

"These aren't the photos Dr. Hood saw," Len said.

"How do you know what he saw? Give me back the photos," Sabo demanded.

"These are not the photos he saw."

"Give me back the photos. Will *you please*!" Judge Sabo growled.

"I am asking for the photos he bases his testimony on," Len answered. It was a silly quarrel, but the venomous tone reflected how the August heat, the constant verbal wrangling, and the intense interest that the case had generated began wearing everyone down.

"Give me back the photos! They are not your photos!" Sabo shouted.

"Let the record show that the court is raising his voice."

"And let the record show that counsel is not doing what I tell him to do. Counselor!"

How this silly dispute started and developed, I don't know. I was still stewing over the Singletary decision as this flare-up was taking place. And then . . .

"You are in contempt of court!" It was bound to happen, and perhaps it was fitting to happen on this particular day. "I am fining you a thousand dollars because you wouldn't do what I wanted you to do."

Len and the judge continued the verbal warfare. "Let the record show that the court was shouting and pointing its finger in a threat-ening manner to defense counsel."

"Not a threatening manner, a promising manner," Judge Sabo countered. "Promising. One thousand dollars, Counselor."

It was Len's first contempt citation since the Chicago Seven trial, where he was hit with a bountiful number of contempt citations, leading Judge Hoffman to sentence him to a jail term of one year, seven months, and twenty-eight days. Bill Kunstler, the other lawyer involved, was sentenced to an even longer term, four years and thirteen days. Those contempt citations, and the resulting jail sentences, how-ever, were overturned on appeal. Len later appealed Sabo's contempt citation to the Pennsylvania Supreme Court. He lost, and paid the fine. But in a final twist, fund-raising efforts to cover the fine netted more than $3,000. "I must give credit where credit is due," Len sar-castically told a reporter. "Judge Sabo has become one of our principal fund-raisers."

■ "Good afternoon, Mr. Singletary."

"Good afternoon."

It was after 3:00 P.M., and Singletary, the man of the day, was finally put on the witness stand. He was dressed casually but smartly. He didn't seem fazed by the crowds outside carrying huge "Free Mu-mia" banners; nor did he pay any mind to the fact that not a seat in the courtroom was unoccupied. He looked straight at Len, waiting for the questioning to begin, a flat expression on his beefy face.

Len proceeded slowly, bringing out background details and infor-mation about when he and Len had first met. Judge Sabo didn't like the sluggish pace of the examination. "Let's get to the heart of the matter, please."

Len didn't quicken the pace, still lingering on background mate-rial. "Judge, I object," Fisk interjected. "We are here in the pursuit of justice. Could we please get right to the matter."

Judge Sabo joined in. "Let's get right to the heart of the question, please, Counselor. I can't be here settling all the social problems of the world. Let's get to the issue, come on." It was eerie, as if the prosecution and judge knew we on the defense team were deeply divided over this witness.

Len still lingered, this time asking Singletary about his physical appearance back in 1981. Fisk again objected. Judge Sabo again pushed: "Let's get to it!"

Judge Sabo then said something that Len latched onto. "If you are going to go into other areas besides the manner in which the police took statements, you should have told the DA." We would have been delighted to limit Singletary to that issue. The one thing Len and I did not want was exploration into Singletary's purported observations of events on Thirteenth and Locust, despite Rachel's desires.

"That is the only area we will broach, and I am glad the court is limiting the area," Len immediately noted. "Consistent with the court's ruling, I will ask questions in the limited area of whether or not Singletary was with the police." And so he did.

Singletary testified to the police misconduct along the lines that he described in his 1990 statement. He explained that he was taken to the Roundhouse shortly after 4:00 A.M. on December 9. This much we knew from a police report that indicated that he was interviewed by investigators. He claimed that he was interviewed by a black detective named Green. An Irish detective was also in the room. According to Singletary, Detective Green took Singletary's hand-written statement and "ripped it up and threw it in the trash."

"Did you then have occasion to write a second time?" Len probed.

Singletary said that the same thing happened when he wrote out a second statement. Len was gingerly avoiding inviting any response from Singletary concerning what he claimed to have seen at the crime scene. Singletary explained that the detectives wanted him "to write what they wanted me to write."

"Did Detective Green threaten you in any way?"

Singletary said that he had. "He told me I wouldn't leave, that they would take me to the elevator and beat me up and that my business would be destroyed."

Singletary ultimately signed a police report purporting to reflect that he had not seen anything of consequence. He testified that he felt "badly" after the police "escorted" him out of the precinct, after he had signed a false police report. A couple of days later, "four guys came and said it was a burglary detail and told us to get on the floor." Singletary was referring to his place of business, a gas station that he managed. These "four guys," law enforcement officers, told Singletary, "This will give you something to remember." This sort of harassment continued, Singletary said, for several months, leading to his relocation in North Carolina in August 1982.

Then came the cross-examination.

Arlene Fisk wasted no time in getting to the issue of what Singletary claimed he saw on Thirteenth and Locust. Len objected, arguing that the questioning was going outside the scope of the direct examination. Fisk argued that she should be allowed to delve into it: "Your Honor, the witness and counsel, both on several occasions during the direct examination made reference to the fact that this witness was not telling the police what they wanted to hear. It is clearly permissible to find out what it is that the police heard and why they didn't want it." The judge gave her the green light. Our hopes of limiting the inquiry to what Singletary experienced at the police station were dashed.

"Tell us what you wrote," Fisk prompted him.

"Word for word?" Singletary asked.

"Word for word, tell us what you wrote."

"Well," Singletary began, "I brought my car, parked my car at the southwest corner of Thirteenth and Locust. I got out to go over to the club Whispers. The doors were locked. I came back across the street. There was a Volkswagen that was going south on Thirteenth Street. He made a left turn on Locust. Pulled to curb immediately. There was a police car behind it. The police car pulled behind the Volkswagen. The driver of the Volkswagen got out. The police officer got out and immediately started to walk to the wall. And immediately at that point, the police officer was frisking the driver of the Volkswagen. There was an occupant in the Volkswagen on the passenger side who started yelling and screaming, saying a lot of things. He had a long army, umm, overcoat on. He came from the car, stuck his hand in his right pocket, pulled a gun. I immediately moved over to the high-speed line [that is, the subway], the barrier there, and I ducked. I heard a pop. I ducked, I looked. And the, uhh, when I looked over I saw the guy again point the gun in the direction of the police officer, firing into his face. I didn't see the first shot. I only saw the second shot. And as I saw the second shot, the police officer fell backwards. This tall guy with dreadlocks looked to his right, looked to his left, placed the gun in the Volkswagen, started running. The guy who was driving the Volkswagen then started yelling a name or something and started chasing this guy.

"I peeped over to see, I peeped over to see if there was anything I could do for the officer. And I started backing up. There was a, the guy there said he was a cab driver and asked me what was that sound he heard. And I said the police officer was just shot, we need to get him help right away. And as I was talking to him he went towards the police car to make a call. Just to tell them the police officer was down and we would need help right away. And I started back to see the officer, then another gentleman came across the street. He wasn't as tall as the first guy. He had dreadlocks and he had said, 'This is my brother's car, where is my brother?' I said I don't know. I said there was two guys that took off running. I said the tall guy shot the police officer, he took off running.

"And he said, 'Oh, my God, we don't need this,' and he went over to the cop, 'Is there anything I could do, anything I could do to help you?' And he was laying forward, bending forward. And the police officer's gun, which was in his lap, discharged, striking him [Mumia] in the chest or someplace. And he screamed, 'I'm shot, I'm shot.' He staggered against the back of the Volkswagen. And then there was sirens and everything was becoming chaotic then. It was just like, you know. That's what I wrote down in the report."

Singletary later added that he saw a helicopter orbit overhead beaming a searchlight onto the area shortly after the police arrived at the scene.

Fisk allowed Singletary to tell his story without interruption, because she knew Singletary would now be an easy target. For his account to be believed, one would have to say that all four prosecution eyewitnesses were not simply mistaken, or slanted the details of their testimony to favor the prosecution, but rather, that their on-the-scene accounts were nothing more than wholesale concoctions, even on the seemingly trivial detail of where Officer Faulkner frisked Billy Cook. Slanting details to favor the prosecution, or even revising bits and pieces of a story later on as the case moves toward trial, is not only plausible, it happens all the time. But this notion that White, Chobert, Scanlan, and Magilton had all conspired to concoct a story at the crime scene, of course, is a difficult sell. "You can't sell what you yourself won't buy," I warned Rachel and Jon repeatedly.

Fisk went on to expose inconsistencies in Singletary's account on the witness stand from that given in 1990, as well as expose other provable errors in that early account. First, Singletary said that he left Philadelphia in February 1982, not August, when he gave his sworn statement in 1990. Second, Singletary, in 1990, said that the passenger in the Volkswagen uttered some remarks about being "tired of these FBI racists" and made certain allusions to the burning of a newstand. In fact, the arson of Cook and Freeman's vending shack occurred four days *after* the Faulkner shooting. Third, Singletary had said in the 1990 statement that the officer, at the moment that Mumia offered to help him, spoke directly to him (Singletary), saying, "Get Maureen or get the children or something like that." When confronted with this last point, Singletary reaffirmed that the officer spoke in this fashion, but this time insisted that the officer was directing the remarks to Mumia.

When Singletary claimed that the dying officer spoke those words, Maureen Faulkner, sitting three rows back, put her hand to her mouth, stunned. This aspect of Singletary's testimony, more than any other, exposed Singletary to be untruthful; our own expert, Dr. Hayes, confirmed that Faulkner died instantaneously from the gunshot wound to the head. It was medically impossible for him to have spoken a single word, let alone to have clung to consciousness for as long as he allegedly did. Finally, the 1990 statement makes it clear that the shooter Singletary described placed the gun on the curb near the Volkswagen, approximately where Mumia's gun was found.

It was the latter point that upset me the most. I had long argued that Singletary's story equates the murder weapon with Mumia's gun, because it just so happens that the discarded weapon Singletary described was found where the police recovered Mumia's gun. Rachel dismissed my concerns with the tendentious reply: "The police could have switched the guns." Anything is possible, but lawyers operate in a rigidly logical world that puts a premium on proof, not in the world of ideological fantasizing. Singletary, by my way of thinking, was as disastrous as I had feared.

Fortunately, the events of that day in the courtroom didn't faze the supporters; they remained galvanized by the overarching unfairness of the 1982 trial and the current proceedings. About six thousand protesters descended on Philadelphia and rallied for Mumia on August 12; nineteen buses came in from New York City alone; other buses came into town from Baltimore, Chicago, Milwaukee, Providence, Washington, D.C., Boston, Detroit, Pittsburgh, and Jersey City. Rachel told the crowd—the largest pro-Mumia rally up to that point—that Sabo was trying to intimidate the defense team and that we were being thwarted in our effort to prove that the Philadelphia police and the FBI worked hand in hand to frame Mumia. She promised the supporters that we would continue to attempt to prove a frame-up. The crowd, of course, cheered wildly.

Maureen, by contrast, expressed to reporters how hurt she was from Singletary's testimony—not because she regarded it as garbage but because he lied about her husband's supposed last words. "I knew Danny couldn't have spoken," she said. "He was dead instantly. What that man said was a lie, and it was cruel and it hurt."

■ There was one curious aspect to the "Singletary affair" that infuses it with ambiguity. The prosecution called to the stand the following day an officer named Vernon Jones. A highway patrolman who knew Singletary in 1981, Jones testified that Singletary was, indeed, a manager of a gas station, that there was "nothing unusual" about him that would indicate a proclivity to fabricate, and that he was not someone who disliked police. The prosecution called Officer Jones for one reason: to present a December 17, 1981, police report prepared by the officer. According to the statement, Singletary approached Officer Jones at the crime scene to ask, "What happened?" When Jones asked Singletary if he saw the shooting, Singletary allegedly told him that he had not. This police report, therefore, purported to refute Singletary's testimony. The oddity, however, is that the report concerns only Singletary and was apparently written to discredit in advance the suggestion that he had witnessed anything of consequence. Why would there be an entire police report, chock-full of details, devoted to an irrelevant bystander who had no information to provide law enforcement? Under cross-examination, Officer Jones could not explain why he was asked to give a statement that focused on a supposedly irrelevant bystander. Moreover, Officer Jones could not explain why this supposedly irrelevant bystander was taken to the Roundhouse to give a statement, which was a documented fact. Nor was there an explanation why this supposed irrelevant bystander who had nothing material to provide law enforcement remained for questioning at the Roundhouse for nearly five hours, another documented fact. Law enforcement's efforts to memorialize in such detail the conduct of Singletary just didn't jibe. In fact, the Vernon Jones police report, dedicated to the conduct of a supposedly irrelevant bystander, smacked of a defensive maneuver by law enforcement against the eventuality that Singletary would someday testify. Had he really provided an exculpatory account to the police, which was discarded, just as he claimed? He certainly didn't have a motivation to inject himself into this case, subject himself to grueling questioning, and even ridicule. If only Singletary's account of what he observed made sense.

■ Singletary remains, to this day, an enigma. He is a solidly middle-class man with a family. He speaks with a steady voice, coupled with direct and appropriate eye contact. He is well groomed, intelligent, and genuinely likable. He certainly had no ties to any left-wing causes or to Mumia; if anything, he appeared to me to be, at the least, indifferent to radical politics. Even the prosecution acknowledged that Singletary had no discernible reason to step forward and testify falsely. Most importantly, he was not someone who suddenly appeared over a decade later claiming he had information; it is indisputable that he was *at the scene of the crime* when the shooting occurred. Yet if what he said in court was a bold-faced lie, then he is a pathological liar of the first order.

Singletary was not, by any means, the only person to step forward with an exculpatory claim that he saw someone other than Mumia shoot Officer Faulkner. Jackson had told Judge Ribner back in 1982 that he was receiving numerous phone calls from people claiming they had such information. As is typical in high-profile cases, most communiqués of that sort are from crackpots who want their fifteen minutes of fame. Without adequate resources, Jackson couldn't winnow out the gems. We faced similar difficulties. Information from people who we knew were at the scene, by virtue of police documentation, received immediate and intense scrutiny. The quandary often concerned information we received from people who simply came out of the woodwork over a decade after the fact. The criminal justice system is rightly skeptical of such witnesses, and I felt that we should be too.

On August 10, a man named Michael Jones appeared at the Philadelphia district attorney's office and reported that he saw Billy Cook shoot Officer Faulkner. Prosecutor Fisk immediately informed us of Jones, as she was obligated to do under the law. We spoke to Jones in the hotel restaurant. Once I heard his story, I left the table to take a nap, leaving him with Rachel and others.

"What's up with this shit? Not another one," I said in frustration later that evening in a team meeting in Len's room. Salty language increased the deeper we moved into the hearings.

"Calm down, Dan," Rachel replied. "We're not going to use him."

"Well, that's a fucking relief." I didn't ask why Rachel came to her conclusion; I was simply relieved by the news. Rachel explained herself anyway, stating that she had sent him packing because she had no interest in pursuing a theory involving a scenario with Billy Cook as the shooter.

Billy Cook, unfortunately, remained in hiding. The word we received was that he was afraid that he would be killed by the police if he surfaced to help his brother. As far as I know, we never tried to convince him otherwise. I understood why the judge and the prosecutors kept baiting us to call Billy to the stand. Their mission was to undercut as thoroughly as they could any basis for claiming that an innocent man was convicted in 1982, and they desperately wanted our case for innocence to turn on Billy Cook's testimony. Prosecutors and defense attorneys appreciate that using a family member as a referendum on a client's innocence is a dangerous proposition. If Billy testified to exonerate Mumia, the prosecution would legitimately argue, and any jury would be entitled to agree, that the testimony is suspect because of their sibling relationship. It is for this reason that testimony from family members is a weak form of evidence. Calling Billy to the stand was, therefore, a no-win proposition for us. No matter how well he performed as a witness, his testimony would be discounted. But if he performed badly, then it would tarnish the entire case. The prosecution and Sabo comprehended this reality very well. A no-win situation for us is a no-lose situation for them. Even if Billy Cook had been available to testify, calling him in Sabo's courtroom would probably have been a mistake.

■ The following day, August 11, the court proceedings were consumed by the presentation of yet another man who claimed to have seen the shooting. William Harmon, a fifty-two-year-old career criminal, emerged from the proverbial woodwork to tell a story that outdid Singletary's.

Harmon, serving time on a drug-selling offense, wrote a letter to his attorney claiming that he had witnessed the shooting of Officer Faulkner. Harmon's attorney forwarded a copy of that letter to us and the district attorney's office. Because Len and I were busy presenting the evidence in the PCRA proceeding, Rachel took a trip alone to the Mercer County Prison to visit with Harmon. She spent about four hours with him on August 3. Rachel, Len, and I discussed Harmon's story over dinner at a nearby I-Hop restaurant. The arguments within the defense team over Harmon roughly mapped the arguments we had over Singletary. I advocated simply ignoring the man; Rachel said that we couldn't afford to do that, although she was less adamant about it than she was with respect to Singletary. Len agreed with Rachel that we should keep our options open with Harmon. With that two-to-one vote, we added Harmon's name to our list of witnesses.

On August 11, Harmon was brought into the courthouse from Mercer County Prison. Judge Sabo demanded that we put him on the stand. "No way," I said to Len, in a virtual panic. The thought of another twilight-zone story—which would make for two in a single case—horrified me to no end. Len didn't want him on the stand either, but his "never say never" approach led him to plead with Judge Sabo for more time. Judge Sabo wasn't buying it. He wanted Harmon on the stand that day, and he didn't want to give us any more opportunities to talk with him. Len argued that Harmon's recollection was stale and that we had to show him some photographs to revive his memory. Judge Sabo countered that we could show him photographs while he was on the witness stand. Len insisted that we were entitled to more time to investigate his story—what was there to investigate, I thought to myself. Judge Sabo wasn't budging.

I handed Len a note that said, "Strike him from the list, NOW!" Len was risk averse to a fault; he simply was unwilling to dispense with a witness unless absolutely necessary. I was risk averse to a fault as well, but in a converse way: whereas Len never wanted to risk *not* calling someone, I never wanted to risk putting someone on the witness stand unless I felt confident that the witness would not harm Mumia's case. We were about to learn one irony in life—that risk aversions carry their own risks. Len glanced at the note and nodded to me in agreement. He then signaled to the judge that we weren't inclined to call Harmon "under these conditions."

It was too late.

"I will call him," Judge Sabo retorted. "The court will call him for you. Anybody could ask him any questions they want. I will call the witness for you, okay?"

Everyone knew that Judge Sabo's only interest was to embarrass us. "But it is our record and it is our choice," Len protested, now desperate to strike Harmon from the witness list.

Judge Sabo seized the moment to take the high road, and it was disgusting. "I'm here seeking justice. The truth. And I will put him on." The more Len protested, the more gleefully Sabo trumpeted his solicitude for truth and justice.

William Harmon, dark-skinned and gaunt, took the stand as Judge Sabo's witness, for the sake of "justice" and "truth." He told the packed courtroom that thirteen years ago Thirteenth and Locust was "his" corner, the place where he pimped his high-heeled street-walkers under the nickname Bippy. In the predawn hours of December 9, Harmon was having "an early breakfast" with a girlfriend, whom he identified as Tina, at a diner on Thirteenth Street. He noticed Mumia outside, and, enthused at seeing a local celebrity, went out to tell him how much Tina and his mother, and "all the women that I know," loved his radio voice. The encounter was interrupted by a loud argument coming from Locust Street, a half block southeast of the diner. It was Faulkner and Cook.

According to Harmon, Mumia abruptly moved toward the scene, with Harmon following "a few steps behind." Mumia didn't even make it to the street when a single shot rang out. Harmon saw the officer fall back against a wall, much in the manner that Singletary had described, while a dreadlocked man ran eastbound. Mumia moved toward the officer. "I heard another shot and I saw Mumia fall," Harmon testified.

"Did you see Jamal shoot the officer?" Len asked.

"No."

"Did you see Jamal get shot?"

"Yes, I did." Harmon's description of how Mumia received his gunshot wound corresponded with Singletary's—Mumia was hit in the chest as he approached the wounded officer leaning with his back against the wall. Harmon's testimony simply reinforced the urgency of the question that arose from Singletary's testimony: if Mumia was indeed shot by Faulkner as the wounded officer was in a sitting position with his back against the wall, why had none of the other witnesses seen this? To Rachel and Jon, this evidentiary gap proved Mumia was framed. But, as alluded to earlier, for this frame-up conspiracy theory to hold, all of the eyewitnesses would have to have been brought on board within minutes of the shooting, because none of the initial police reports suggested that any of them had seen anything remotely akin to what Harmon and Singletary had described.

Harmon's story didn't end there. Seconds after the dreadlocked shooter fled eastbound, a red two-door Malibu with two men inside pulled up alongside patrol car 612. A passenger emerged, with "Johnny Mathis–style hair" and a black leather jacket. This passenger from the Malibu shot Officer Faulkner in the face from about ten feet away, then jumped back into the Malibu and sped away.

Prosecutor Fisk didn't need to ask questions, as it was clear that Harmon wouldn't provide the evidentiary basis for any judge to grant Mumia a new trial. But I suppose she couldn't resist having a little bit of courtroom fun. She asked Harmon a series of questions about why he kept such "vital information" to himself for so long. Harmon didn't appear to notice, and he certainly didn't take umbrage at, Fisk's over-the-top sarcasm. Harmon explained that he had promised his mother not to get involved, but now that his mother was dead, he had to do what his conscience called upon him to do. "I can sleep better at night, knowing I came forward," he said proudly. For good measure, Fisk went through Harmon's rap sheet, which contained about a dozen convictions stretching back to 1964, ten of which involved allegations of fraud, forgery, and burglary.

"It was another wild day at the appeals hearing for Mumia Abu-Jamal," the next day's *Philadelphia Inquirer* reported. Fortunately for us, it was patently clear, even to the journalists, that we didn't want Harmon on the witness stand.

Columnists, however, weren't so discriminating. In one column printed in the *Philadelphia Daily News*, we were dubbed the Scheme Team, a band of lawyers who "learned a few tricks from O. J. Simpson's Dream Team." The columnist castigated us for presenting "two radically different versions of the crime," and then asked: "So who's more believable—someone who works as a whore or someone who leeches off a whore?" Other columns were equally vicious.

■ Although damaged by Singletary and Harmon, at least we had distanced ourselves from them in a somewhat feeble effort to have our cake and eat it too. Pamela Jenkins was another story. She was a prostitute in the early '80s who also now claimed, *for the first time*, to have information about the Faulkner shooting investigation. We embraced her as an explosive new witness. We took notice of Jenkins even though she was one of those coming-out-of-the-woodwork-type witnesses, because she had been used by the Justice Department as a confidential informant in a federal probe into corruption within the Philadelphia police department. This meant that Jenkins had been screened by veteran federal prosecutors and was trusted enough by the FBI to wear a concealed wire; if she was good enough for the feds, we reasoned, she was good enough for us. Her story, in skeletal form, was straightforward.

In December of 1981, Jenkins was a troubled fifteen-year-old high school student. She claimed that she had had a sexual relationship with a police officer, Tom Ryan—a relationship to which Ryan admitted, though he disputed the time frame. During the course of that relationship, Jenkins provided information to Ryan. On the Saturday following the shooting, according to Jenkins, Ryan brought her into police headquarters.

"And did the name Mumia come up?" Len asked.

"Yes," Jenkins whispered in a husky voice.

"And what did the officers say in connection with Mumia?"

"They just told me—well, in other words, they were saying that it was a shooting and that Mumia had did it. And they was making slurs across me, trying to make, you know, trying to pressure me into saying I was somewhere that I wasn't." Jenkins then elaborated that the officers were trying to compel her to finger Mumia.

Jenkins testified that she withstood the pressure to implicate Mumia. But that was not our main purpose in calling her. Jenkins also was a prostitute, and she had befriended Cynthia White. She testified that White occasionally provided confidential information to police, and that shortly after the shooting White had confided in her that she was "scared, in fear for her life from the police." Soon thereafter, White disappeared.

Then the question that would lead to Jenkins's undoing: "When did you last see Cynthia White?"

"Umm, around the beginning of this year [1997]," she said, suddenly hesitant.

"And do you recall where you saw her?"

"Umm, on Thirteenth Street, at Yates house." Yates house was a local crack-smoking den. Jenkins said that she didn't exchange words with White on that occasion, because White scurried out "like she seen a ghost and, umm, she ran out the door and got into Ryan's truck."

Fisk was itching to cross-examine Jenkins. Throughout the entire direct examination, she was tapping her pen on a legal pad, a twinge of a smile on her face. When Fisk finished her examination, I knew we were set up for a devastating rebuttal. Fisk never attacked Jenkins; instead, she had her underscore the two main points of her direct examination—namely, that she was in the midst of a relationship with *police officer* Tom Ryan in December of 1981 and that she had seen White just a *few months ago*. Fisk especially emphasized the latter point.

"And there is no doubt in your mind that that was Cynthia who you saw earlier this year, the same Cynthia White that you spoke to in December 1981?"

"No. There is no doubt," Jenkins assured Fisk.

Fisk called her first rebuttal witness, Det. Raleigh Witcher. After doing enough trials, a trial lawyer's intuition becomes developed to the point where he knows when disaster is about to hit. There's something in the way the adversary calls out the name of the next witness; the sound of the voice becomes richer, and the enunciation more emphatic. The adversary grabs the moment and seemingly soaks it in, like a hiker reaching the top of the mountain looking over the expanse. Fisk let Jenkins retreat from the witness stand before announcing, with a limber and emphatic voice, that "the Commonwealth has a witness, Your Honor." Witcher walked up to the witness stand as Len and I puzzled over who this man was. Neither of us recalled seeing or hearing his name in connection with Mumia's case.

Fisk presented Witcher with a computer printout, which he promptly explained was an FBI printout for a person known as Cynthia White. It contained various identifying numbers which, when cross-referenced, indicated that it was *our* Cynthia White. The printout indicated that White was deceased. It didn't establish, however, when she died.

Fisk presented another courtroom exhibit.

"All right, Detective Witcher, can you tell us what is Commonwealth Exhibit number four?"

Witcher examined the document through his half-rimmed glasses, looked up and in a single stroke destroyed Jenkins as a witness. "It is a certificate of death issued in the state of New Jersey, State Department of Health. And attached is a report of death, Camden County Office of the Medical Examiner." The identifying numbers on the death certificate, including the social security number, left no doubt that Cynthia White had died on September 2, 1992. It wasn't White who saw a ghost; it was Jenkins who did.

Officer Ryan, who testified later in the hearing, offered further rebuttal, but it was anticlimactic. He admitted under my questioning that he did have a sexual relationship with Jenkins, but stated that it began after he first arrested her on a truancy charge in June of 1982— seven months after the shooting. He also admitted that he used Jenkins as a police informant. He testified, however, that he couldn't have had a relationship with Jenkins back in December of 1981, and he certainly couldn't have been involved in any police activity involving Jenkins at the time of the Faulkner shooting. Why? Because he wasn't even a police officer then—a fact that the prosecution confirmed with more official documentation. Moreover, school records proved that Jenkins wasn't even attending the school where she claimed that she had met Officer Ryan back in December 1981.

■ The Jenkins debacle really shook Len and me up. Like all other self-respecting lawyers, we were highly sensitive to the question of our credibility. A lawyer who loses credibility is a lawyer who loses effectiveness. I felt that the defense team took a major hit in the credibility department with Pamela Jenkins. The only salutary effect from it, I hoped, would be greater cautiousness in who we would embrace as a witness in the future. Perhaps, I thought, the embarrassment from it would actually heal the rift between me and the PDC contingent on the team inasmuch as we all would now be on the same page when it came to evaluating strategy.

My hope proved to be naive. In the spring of 1999, over seventeen years after the killing and nearly four years after the lengthy hearings before Sabo, Rachel and Jon announced that they had discovered yet another "explosive new witness." According to them, this new witness would testify that he and another unidentified individual received money from the mob to kill Officer Faulkner. The killing, however, was not to be a mob hit; rather, the mob was merely some sort of conduit for a killing which was sought out by high-level officials within the Philadelphia police department. Although the details were never fleshed out completely, this new account portrayed Officer Faulkner as an inside informant for federal authorities investigating corruption within the department. Exposed as such, Faulkner became the target of corrupt police officials who feared that he would be their ultimate undoing. According to this new witness, Faulkner was killed at the behest of corrupt Philadelphia officers to silence him.

When I heard the story at a defense team meeting at Len's loft, I bit my lip to avoid another unpleasant argument with Rachel. Actually, I was enraged, convinced that bona fide lunacy had set in.

When the meeting ended, I stayed behind to speak further with Len, fearful that we were close to ruining years of work and threatening to extinguish Mumia's hopes for justice.

"Are you *seriously* considering this?" I asked. Len was visibly distressed. He had been aware for a few months that Rachel was working on bringing this witness around to helping the defense. He agreed that the story was insane, but Rachel had already lobbied Mumia, as she had when Singletary was the issue. Concerned that Mumia would insist upon our presenting this evidence, Len sought out ways to push this witness onto the trash heap without further rupturing the defense team. We even had the witness undergo several lie detector tests (with mixed results, which further complicated the situation). Most frightening, the story somehow leaked out and was mentioned in a major attack piece on the pro-Mumia movement published in *Vanity Fair* in August 1999.

But what if Mumia wanted the witness? On the one hand, I felt that he was absolutely entitled to present him, because it was his life on the line. On the other hand, a lawyer must protect his client against his own tendency to destroy himself, especially in a capital case where desperation might cause a client to opt for an irrational course of action. But even if Mumia's wishes prevailed, that didn't mean he was entitled to have a *particular* lawyer do it for him. I made it clear to Len that I would not participate in what I regarded as an assisted suicide. I have to admit, I also wasn't about to embarrass myself by running with such a patently outrageous story on the most visible death penalty case in the world. I don't know Len's analysis of the situation, but he ended up with the same conclusion: if Mumia wanted the witness, he'd have to get another lawyer to present him.

Rachel and Jon took the same position, but on the flip side: If we convinced Mumia *not* to use this witness, then they would leave the defense team. Jon presented his position exactly as I presented mine: he too would not stand by and watch a client make a decision that might result in his death. He accused Len, Steve, and me of becoming the first death penalty lawyers in history who turned their back on an exculpatory witness. It was a shallow analysis inasmuch as it totally ignored the implausibility, if not the absurdity, of the story that we were rejecting.

Rachel and Jon are no longer on the case. They ceased their involvement in August of 1999, after Mumia decided that he would not demand that we use this witness. In retrospect, I feel somewhat ashamed for even thinking that Mumia would opt to pin his hopes for a new trial on such an absurd account. An innocent man on death row might grab at anything to get justice; but I should have had faith that Mumia would never get *that* desperate.

Remarkably, as I reflect on this particular episode, it actually deepened my commitment to this case and heightened my already enormous respect for my client. It became apparent to me that Mumia is far too honorable to propagate a lie upon which to build a case for his freedom.

I didn't realize it [the confession] had any importance
until today.

GARY WAKSHUL, 1995, EXPLAINING WHY
HE FAILED TO MENTION HEARING A
CONFESSION FOR TWO MONTHS

This is not going to change my testimony!

VERONICA JONES, 1996, IN RESPONSE TO
HER ARREST FROM THE WITNESS STAND

17. CONFESSING TO LIES

Confessing to a crime and proclaiming innocence mark the boundaries of a criminal defendant's response to an accusation. People are rightly dubious of a suspect's claim of innocence: the 'I-ain't-got-nothing-to-do-with-it' response to an accusation is perceived as instinctive, a subset of the larger instinct for survival. Conversely, people tend to be awed by a confession, precisely because it is perceived as cutting against the grain of that same survival instinct. No item of evidence is more dispiriting to a criminal defense lawyer than a confession.

A confession usually signifies defeat. The confessing suspect is telling the interrogators that he will no longer be the prey, that the tightness inside his soul has become too intolerable to bear. Confessing often springs from resignation, and it feels good to confess—in the same way that taking off a tight pair of shoes feels good.

Mumia's alleged confession was different. It signified victory, not defeat. Security guard Priscilla Durham testified that it sounded as if the wounded man on the emergency room floor was boasting, seemingly proud of the fact that he plugged a police officer with a bullet between the eyes. Prosecutor McGill took it one step further: it went beyond boasting; it was an acknowledgment that his was an inevitable act by a revolutionary warrior who viewed the man in the blue uniform as nothing more than a guardian of a deeply hated system that defiles the earth and oppresses the poor.

Mumia's alleged confession, therefore, established that the shooting had nothing to do with whether Officer Faulkner "deserved" to die, as that had nothing to do with it. Nor was the murder a by-product of self-interest, or even of uncontrollable rage. The confession, in short, was no mere boast but a revelation: the killing was an act of political will, akin to a soldier's act in wartime.

Jackson never grasped the psychological force this one item of evidence would have on the larger issues in the trial. McGill, by contrast, grasped well that the confession was more than a powerful piece of inculpatory evidence. He saw that it served a deep human need to imbue a murder with meaning. In most homicide prosecutions, the reason for a killing that sufficiently satisfies us is self-evident: a store owner is shot because the killer seeks money; a spouse or girlfriend is killed because possessive jealousy overpowers self-control; a gang member bleeds to death on a sidewalk because a murderous rival gang member knows no other way but violence to resolve disputes. In Mumia's case, the killing itself provoked confusion and disbelief. Intelligent, compassionate, and overtly life affirming, Mumia didn't seem capable of such an act—at least, that is how many family and friends reacted to the news of Mumia's arrest. But, in McGill's mind, the confession dispelled the confusion and revealed the killing to be a manifestation of the belief that "political power grows out of the barrel of a gun." It was proof positive that law enforcement was right to crack down on the Black Panther Party, MOVE, and other black nationalist groups—all of which were tangible threats to the social order, forces of sociopolitical entropy pulling at a tenuous social fabric stitched together by a potentially disintegrating thread called Law and Order. Mumia had given voice, not for the voiceless but for that jungle about which McGill adumbrated in his closing argument.

■ Jackson didn't plan his trial strategy around the evidence of the confession, something that a well-prepared trial lawyer would do. It was as if he ceded the issue to the prosecution, and therefore pushed it out of his consciousness. There seems to be no other explanation for why he did not, as priority number one, subpoena the police witness, Gary Wakshul, who could have damaged considerably the prosecution's case. Even the most inexperienced of trial lawyers would have known enough to ensure that Wakshul would appear as a witness. He would be, under virtually any circumstances, the highlight of the defense case. Yet, as Judge Sabo aptly, if not cruelly, put it, Jackson "goofed" in failing to subpoena Wakshul, and Mumia would have to pay the price for that mistake.

We didn't make the same mistake; a high priority in the hearings was to put Wakshul on the witness stand. Although he tried to skirt the service of a subpoena (calling in sick when he received word that a process server was looking for him), we slapped one on him in late July. The task of extracting as much benefit from Wakshul as possible fell on my shoulders.

The night before Wakshul was to be called to the stand at the PCRA hearing, I battled my nocturnal nemesis, insomnia. I lay in the dark of my hotel room with my eyes open, the hum of the air conditioner sealing out the sounds of traffic from the street below. I thought to myself that it would be no secret to anyone—particularly Wakshul himself—that the centerpiece to my questioning would be Wakshul's December 9, 1981, signed statement that recorded his report to an investigating detective that he "remained with the suspect the entire time" and that "the Negro male made no comments." I thought of Anthony Jackson begging that miserable judge for the opportunity—just a few minutes, for Christ's sake—to call Wakshul at his home. Spending my days in Courtroom 253 in the Philadelphia heat, I began to appreciate deep in my bones the ordeal Jackson had endured. And the more I thought of what a comfort it was to be litigating Mumia's case with Len, and having volunteers helping us and supporters cheering us on, the more I felt for Jackson's loneliness, fighting an impossible war in a rigged contest, alone and without a friend. How awful he must have felt when he realized that the "prosecutor" sitting up on the bench wearing his black judicial robes would not allow him to bring Wakshul in to testify. Jackson still felt the sting of that injustice, over a decade later. I drifted to sleep some time around 3:00 A.M., convincing myself that my goal the next morning would be a modest one: I would simply have Wakshul reaffirm that he reported to investigators that which was recorded in his December 9 statement.

I woke up four hours later wanting more. I wanted more, because, like McGill, I understood that the true meaning of the case turned on the confession.

■ I put the December 9 statement on the defense table when I walked to the center of the courtroom. I wasn't planning on using it for a while. I had other things to question Wakshul about. I hadn't noticed Wakshul walking up to the witness stand. He just appeared, waiting for the questioning to begin. I eyeballed him for a few seconds, letting the silence of the courtroom rest fully on his shoulders like a crushing weight. I stood in front of him with nothing in my hands, because I wanted him to know that I wouldn't be questioning him about the December 9 report until later. I figured that his anxiety over *when* I would club him with it would drain him of energy as the day wore on.

I asked a series of throwaway questions to establish that he sided with the prosecution, and he obliged with short answers and wary glances. It is axiomatic with trial lawyers that points you score with a hostile witness are far more valuable than points scored with a favorable witness. It is implicit in questioning a witness who already favors your side that the answers are a product of preparation between the witness and the lawyer. That doesn't make the answers untrue; it only makes them suspect, and therefore less potent. There is, in short, a direct correlation: the more hostile the witness, the more difficult it is to secure favorable information, and thus, the more valuable that information. I wanted it clear that whatever positive evidence we could extract from Wakshul, it should be given lots of weight.

Aside from extracting a psychological edge, there was another reason that I set the December 9 statement aside. It is a mistake to rush into using a document in an examination. It is best to credit a favorable document with maximum reliability beforehand. The document itself, aside from the particulars contained within it, must be portrayed as a treasured scroll. With that in mind, I went into Wakshul's familiarity with taking suspects into custody. Wakshul admitted to receiving training in handling suspects and training in recording facts in police reports that might be significant in a subsequent prosecution. Wakshul readily agreed that confessions from a suspect rank high among those things that a police officer should note in a police report. Wakshul further agreed that thorough, accurate, and complete police reports are essential ingredients to professional police work. He even volunteered that the "administration of justice" depends on it.

I gradually moved the subject closer to the matter at hand. "All of the things that we have been talking about apply even more forcefully when you have a cop killing, isn't that true?"

Wakshul sensed what I was doing. For the first time in the examination, he began to hedge. "I suppose," he said.

Suppose? This was Wakshul's first and only involvement in a cop-killing case. It had racked the city of Philadelphia. Media accounts of the killing, and of the celebrated suspect, permeated the city. If Mumia had confessed with such disdain for the life of a young police officer, then all of the hand-wringing in the media over whether Mumia had committed this crime would have been a farce. Wakshul obviously understood—how could he not?—that such a confession was exceedingly significant. There was no "supposing" about it.

I could have launched into an attack at that moment, but it's not my style to fight with a witness. Gerry Spence, a mentor of mine, is fond of saying that a good cross-examination is like a well-done bull-fight. No fighting with the bull by the matador, only an elegant dance that ultimately leads to an artistic kill, one stab at a time—that is the essence of a great cross-examination. I led Wakshul back in time, to the predawn hours of December 9, without displaying any aggressiveness toward him.

"When you got to Jefferson Hospital, what was your assignment?" The question was important to establish that he was in a position to hear a confession.

Wakshul was clear. "My assignment was to stay with him until released. And that's about what I did."

"And you had to guard Mr. Jamal because he was a suspect in a very, very serious matter." Wakshul stared at me blankly. "Isn't that so?"

"Yes, of course."

At that point in the examination, I opted for a detour, but it turned out to be a shortcut. I wanted to know whether Wakshul knew Officer Bell, Faulkner's partner, who insisted that Mumia had confessed. He stated that he did, and that he knew him well. "If Officer Bell had appeared in front of you, you would have recognized him as Officer Bell, isn't that true?" I asked.

"I would have recognized him, yes."

Had Wakshul seen Bell that night? He claimed that he could not remember seeing him. That was an interesting point that I had not expected. It didn't fit the scene as I had envisioned it from Bell's account at the trial. Bell claimed that Mumia blurted out the confession when he knelt down to look into the eyes of the person who he and other officers believed killed his partner. Bell allegedly responded to Mumia's confession with a threat of his own: "If he dies, you die." That was Bell's story, and yet, Wakshul couldn't say that Bell was present. It struck me that if Mumia had shouted a confession at that moment, Wakshul would have seen Bell kneeling down, staring into the face of that despicable, unrepentant killer.

Here is where the detour became a shortcut. When Wakshul said he didn't recall whether Bell was present in the emergency room, I followed up by asking if he was "mentally alert" that morning. I was trying to extract as much juice from the lemon as I could: if he was mentally alert, then the fact that he couldn't recall seeing Bell would add force to the argument that Bell, in fact, wasn't there to hear the alleged confession. I calculated that my question was a safe one. I didn't think that Wakshul would admit to being other than mentally alert while on duty performing a vitally important job. Wakshul used my question as an opportunity to stick it to the defense, to make us sorry for calling him as a witness. He launched into an answer that he was itching to give. "I was mentally alert when I assisted in getting Mr. Jamal into the hospital and placing him on the floor. At that point there was some discussions, some talk going all around, but I heard Mr. Jamal say, 'I shot him and I hope the motherfucker dies.' " I almost interrupted Wakshul at that point, but I could see he wasn't finished. "I was stunned at that point. I stumbled back into a little alcove and started to cry. Covered myself by going outside, closing up the wagon and getting myself together. I then went back into the hospital at some period after that. And I have—"

Wakshul paused, as his eyes rolled up toward the ceiling. "I have very little recollection of anything that happened after that point," he continued, "except for some snapshots in my mind of seeing Danny Faulkner's dead feet lying on a gurney." I nodded encouragement to Wakshul, goading him to continue. "I remember after that being in the precinct but I have no recollection of anything further that night until early in the morning, the following morning, when I was leaving work in my car, running into a cement pole with my car. And at that point I had more control over myself."

Wakshul was supposed to have been a witness who would establish that Mumia never confessed; yet he was now saying that he did. Ironically, I couldn't have been more pleased.

Wakshul's testimony was a replay of Officer Bell's. Bell had testified that he, too, became distressed after hearing the confession, which accounted for his failure to report it immediately. In fact, although Bell made a log report that night and volunteered a statement to homicide detectives the following week, he did not report to anyone for two months that this man who he confronted on the emergency room floor confessed so brazenly directly in his face. He said nothing to other officers, to friends, to his family, even to his wife. This highly significant piece of evidence—evidence that truly eliminates reasonable doubt of guilt—lodged itself deep in the back of Bell's mind. That is what Bell said under oath at the trial: "I kept it in the back of my mind." And his explanation was exactly the same as Wakshul's. Bell claimed he was too traumatized to report it.

Wakshul was, no doubt, attempting a preemptive strike against my examination, because he knew that I was going to confront him with his December 9 report. He became impatient, because he probably thought when he took the stand that I was going to make use of that report early in the examination. Unnerved, he undoubtedly felt the ax poised above him. Wakshul didn't understand, however, that his December 9 report was not the ax that would sever his head. It was just evidentiary leverage for a broader attack on the case. I was very pleased that he became impatient, because now it meant I was in control, and thus in a prime position to expose the absurdity of what he was saying, which would bolster Mumia's claim that the confession was an utter fabrication.

I finally showed Wakshul his December 9 report and I marched him through it. Shortly after being relieved of his duties that morning, he was interviewed by a detective named Kaminsky. Wakshul admitted that he wanted to be truthful and thorough in his answers to the detective and was motivated to help make sure the person responsible for the killing was punished. He admitted that he had no reason to withhold important information. He admitted that he signed the December 9 statement at 5:50 A.M. (hence, considerably less than two hours after the supposed confession). The signed report indicates that he told Detective Kaminsky that "We [he and his partner] stayed with the male at Jefferson Hospital until we were released. During this time the Negro male made no comments."

I let Wakshul reiterate that he was too distraught to tell Detective Kaminsky about the confession, which he characterized as "shocking," "disgusting," "unforgettable," "weighty." I asked one of our assistants to take a colored pen and begin writing down his answers on a large drafting pad propped up on an easel. I often do this for a jury because information that is seen as well as heard is far more persuasive. Although there was no jury here, I have found that writing down a witness's answer is also a great way to exert control. It is like tightening a noose on a wild animal; it's a form of imposing dominance upon a witness. And that is what I was aiming to do now: bring Wakshul down.

I asked Wakshul if he told Detective Kaminsky what time the incident occurred. Wakshul indicated that it occurred at about 3:54 A.M. I signaled my assistant to write that down. What about the color of the automobile driven by the person who had informed Wakshul and his partner that an officer had been shot? Wakshul told the detective it was a "dark-colored auto, possibly a Ford, with New York license plates." Add that to the list, I signaled.

"Not only were you able to describe the complexion of the car, the possible make of the car, the fact that it bore New York license plates, and the time that you received a radio call, you were also able to give some sort of description of the person who informed you that an officer had been shot. Isn't that true?"

Wakshul looked down at his report: "Yeah, according to this report, a white male approximately forty-two and well dressed."

For a man who was emotionally wiped out, too overwrought to report a confession, he had considerable ability to transmit details of far less importance. But, I thought, perhaps he would try to explain himself by saying that he was able to remember and report these trivial details precisely because they triggered no emotional response. I figured it would be valuable to include on my list the things he remembered about Faulkner himself, lying dead on the pavement.

"Now, Mr. Wakshul, were you able to help the investigator by telling the investigator the important detail about the positioning of Officer Faulkner?" That was surely an upsetting sight.

"I informed the investigator that we saw him lying on the south side of the street on the pavement."

What about Mumia—did Wakshul report where he was? "The only thing I stated in this report," Wakshul explained, "is that he was on the sidewalk at the curb near a dark-colored, or dark-blue-colored Volkswagen."

There was one more item for the list. Wakshul had the presence of mind and emotional control to report to Detective Kaminsky that Mumia had a press card in his wallet. The sight of Officer Faulkner, shot through the face, didn't prevent him from remembering that little tidbit of information.

I suspect that everyone in the courtroom understood the point I was making. But we on the defense team never expected a fair shot from Judge Sabo, so I was sensitive to how things would appear in the transcripts. Because it would be my job to write the briefs when the courtroom battles were long over, I had a self-interest in ensuring that the transcripts reflected clearly what was happening in the courtroom. With that in mind, I pushed Wakshul some more. "Now, for your benefit and for my benefit, I had my colleague write down some of these important details that you were able to communicate to investigator Kaminsky." I walked over to the list and pointed to it. "When you provided these important details that are listed up here, these seven categories, you were trying to be helpful, weren't you?" It was a throwaway question. The answer meant nothing to me. I just wanted the transcripts to reflect what was going on in the courtroom and hammer the point that Wakshul was in a position, emotionally and cognitively, to provide minute and numerous details to an investigator.

But the clincher was getting Wakshul to admit the obvious fact that a confession would eclipse in importance each of these items on the list; and indeed, it would override in importance all of the items taken together. He admitted this was so. Yet, I reminded him, the very last item in his report, just above his signature, was his statement that the "Negro male made no comments." There was the urge to ask him at that moment: How is it that you can now say that you were too emotionally distraught to report hearing a confession when you were fully capable of reporting all of these details? I resisted the urge, because there was even more dirt to dig up with which to bury Wakshul.

It turned out that Wakshul was interviewed again, a week later on December 16, this time by Detective Thomas, the lead investigator in the case. During the interview, Wakshul provided Detective Thomas such details as the color of Jamal's pants and shirt, and information about a camera Officer Faulkner had in the patrol car. It had been a week since the alleged confession and the unsettling events at the scene of the crime. But that passage of time didn't awaken in Wakshul the need to report hearing a confession. Instead, when Detective Thomas asked "Is there anything you wish to add to this interview?" Officer Wakshul responded "Nothing I can think of now."

At that point in the questioning, Wakshul knew he had to do something. I knew that he couldn't continue with his claim that he was too distraught to report a confession when it was now evident that he had reported abundant details to homicide investigators. I slowed the pace of the questioning, because I wanted to give him time to reach out for another explanation. I wanted to show, as graphically as I could, that Wakshul was now willing to perjure himself in claiming that he heard that confession. I wanted to show that this cop, when caught in one absurd lie, was willing to search out another absurd lie, all in the service of the "big lie"—the lie that Mumia confessed.

In order to do that, I took another detour in the questioning. I asked a series of questions about the fact that Mumia had filed a police brutality complaint. Wakshul acknowledged that there was an Internal Affairs Bureau investigation devoted to investigating that allegation. Wakshul and other officers were interviewed by IAB investigators. It stood to reason that, from the perspective of cops who truly believed Mumia was a cold-blooded cop killer, the filing of a police brutality complaint was the height of audacity. I put myself in their shoes, tried to look at the situation from the cops' perspective. They must have been outraged, I thought. They had to have wanted to put Mumia in his place, retaliate in some way.

Of course, Wakshul wasn't stupid enough to admit to all of that. But my assessment of what probably motivated the fabrication of the confession led me to explore the IAB investigation. After all, the whole

notion that Jamal confessed—which was undoubtedly a highly relevant investigative fact—never surfaced until *after* the IAB investigation
began. But more remarkably, a bevy of homicide investigators dedicated to assembling compelling evidence against Mumia for the district
attorney's office, failed to glean even a hint that Mumia had confessed
to the killing in a crowded emergency room, filled with over a dozen
to two dozen cops within earshot of it (as Priscilla Durham claimed).
Indeed, the homicide investigators produced precisely the opposite
conclusion: that Mumia had said nothing in the emergency room.
Instead, this highly relevant evidence of guilt suspiciously surfaced
within law enforcement through an Internal Affairs investigation that
had nothing to do with whether Mumia was the shooter.

If Mumia did indeed confess, then the homicide investigators were
unbelievable incompetents. Picture it. These senior investigators gather
evidence flatly contradicting the claim that Mumia confessed. They
were unable to secure a single statement from *anyone* indicating that
Mumia confessed. They claim never to have tested Mumia's gun for
evidence of recent firing. They claim never to have checked the muzzle
to see if it was still warm or smelled of gunpowder. These investigators,
in short, supposedly had the means to collect physical evidence of
guilt *and* a damning confession, and they didn't. Was that just in-
competence?

The beauty of it all was that Wakshul, the man who affirmatively
stated that Mumia said nothing in the emergency room, couldn't resist
the urge to stick it to him when he was interviewed by an Internal
Affairs investigator on February 11, 1982. It was then that Wakshul,
for the very first time, reported that Mumia had confessed. His account harmonized with that of his fellow officer, Garry Bell, who also
reported the confession for the first time in mid-February, over two
months after the fact, to IAB investigators. The security officer, Priscilla Durham (whose application to become a police officer, we learned
in our own investigation, had been rejected in the late '70s) went on
record with her claim about the confession a month after that, in
March, also to IAB investigators. Wakshul's partner, Officer Stephen

Trombetta, never mentioned anything about a confession, even when asked directly if he heard Mumia say anything.

Why, I finally asked, did he not report the confession until that moment on February 11, 1982? He couldn't stick to the story about being too emotionally overwrought—the list on the easel pad graphically precluded that answer. He took a moment to answer and I smiled at him. The bull was going to collapse with the final thrust of the sword.

"I didn't realize it had any importance until that day," he replied.

■ Caught in the lie that he omitted mention of the confession because he was too overwrought, Wakshul did precisely, it seems to me, what all liars do: pursue another lie. The jury should have heard this inane response, I kept thinking to myself. Early in the examination he admitted that confessions are extremely important, and they are recorded in police reports, which must be thorough and accurate "for the administration of justice," as he aptly put it. Yet, under the stress of the questioning, he nonetheless reached out for the ridiculous explanation that he didn't realize that Mumia's confession was important until February 11, 1982—a date at which he happened to be interviewed by IAB investigators.

I wondered how a jury would react to Wakshul's testimony. Could any juror seriously believe that Wakshul had really heard a confession but didn't know it was important for two months until he was interviewed by Internal Affairs investigators looking into charges of police brutality? If that was a lie, then Wakshul's initial report that Mumia "made no comments" was the truth. And if Wakshul's report that Mumia "made no comments" was the truth (after all, he was with Mumia "the entire time," according to that same report), then Bell and Durham had to have been lying. And if Bell and Durham lied, then what were the other officers capable of doing to enhance the investigation? Were they capable of entering into a secret pact with Cynthia White, giving her carte blanche to earn her living on the street in exchange for a seamless narrative of an event that the other witnesses could only provide in bits and pieces? Were they capable of deep-sixing crime scene test results indicating that Mumia's gun had not been recently fired and that no lead residue could be found on Mumia's hands, face, or clothing? Were they capable of surreptitiously forcing Veronica Jones to recant her initial claim of seeing two people flee the scene?

These were questions the jurors never had to ask themselves. They certainly didn't have to grapple with the fundamental question to this drama: who was good and who was evil? Wakshul's testimony, at the very least, made that question far more ambiguous than the 1982 trial proceedings would suggest.

■ Wakshul's absence from the original trial—he was in Philadelphia and could have been called, my questioning later revealed—was the greatest outrage. Veronica Jones's surprise recantation at the trial, leaving Jackson stunned, ran a close second.

Veronica Jones had always been a mystery. Unlike Cynthia White, Jones didn't step forward at the crime scene to tell police what she saw. When police arrived at the scene, Jones retreated from the activity, preferring never to get involved. She feared Philly cops, and, unlike the more street-savvy Cynthia White, had no use for them. If it wasn't for White, Jones might never have been involved in the case. White dribbled out information the way a zoo keeper doles out sardines to a hungry sea lion. One of those sardines was the fact that Jones was standing on Locust Street when the shooting erupted. Clued in to the possibility of another eyewitness to the shooting, two detectives visited Jones at her mother's home on December 15, 1981.

Jones's first foray into the case had been a mixed blessing for the defense. She recanted her original statement to detectives that she saw two persons run in the wake of gunfire. Yet she spontaneously blurted out that cops had tried to get her to bolster White's purported eyewitness account. Both aspects of her testimony stunned Jackson.

Jones's second time on the witness stand, over a decade later, was no less dramatic.

Our investigation, which continued even after Judge Sabo had rejected the evidence we presented in 1995, turned up Veronica Jones in the early spring of 1996. Armed with the results of that investigation, we sought, and then obtained, over the vehement protest by the district attorney's office, permission from the Pennsylvania Supreme Court to send the case back to Judge Sabo in order to take her testimony.

We appeared again in Sabo's courtroom on September 18, 1996, over a year after the first round of hearings on Mumia's petition for a new trial. He was not happy to see us again; we felt the same. We had gone through three weeks of testimony in July and August the year before, and we had thought we'd seen the last of each other. As maddening as the old judge could be, I marveled at his feistiness. He probably clung to life solely to see the jury's verdict against Mumia carried out. I can't say that he saw us lawyers on the defense team as evil people. Rather, it is more likely that Sabo saw in us the entirety of what was wrong with the death penalty in America. Our attitude, our relentlessness, our insistence on reexamining everything—these things rendered the justice system a mockery, in his view. What good is a death penalty when a band of lawyers, supported by misguided radicals and do-gooders in Hollywood, can thwart the will of the people and the considered judgment of a jury? To Sabo, the state of Pennsylvania was entitled to execute justice, and we had no right to thwart the process. That Len, Rachel, and I were New York lawyers, supported by people from around the world, rankled him all the more.

We, of course, thought Sabo and the entire Pennsylvania justice system was looking to "execute" justice, but not in the sense that they viewed the matter. We had packaged Mumia's case as a visible referendum on the justice system, and his execution would signify the killing of justice in America. Entering into Judge Sabo's courtroom with that attitude, we couldn't help but look upon him with the same enmity that he did us.

Even with the order from the state's highest court, Judge Sabo resisted reopening the hearing, adopting the prosecutor's argument that we first had to prove that we couldn't have located Jones before or during the 1995 proceedings. The argument was completely nonsensical and duplicitous inasmuch as we had urged Judge Sabo in 1995 to order the district attorney's office to disclose Jones's address so that she could have been located back then. Judge Sabo, who was now throwing up a roadblock to our effort to put Jones on the stand, had in '95 refused to order that disclosure.

He ordered us back into court on October 1, at which point we were given the green light to put Jones on the stand. We had had to go back to the Pennsylvania Supreme Court to secure another order to prod Judge Sabo along. This time the high court was quite blunt, ordering Judge Sabo to conduct an evidentiary hearing that would allow for the development of a "full factual record" concerning Veronica Jones.

No sooner had Jones taken the oath and sat down in the witness chair than Judge Sabo interjected: "I have a few questions I have to ask this witness. Have they, as your attorney, advised you, that if you say something now which is different from what you said at the trial, you could be charged with perjury?" Jones was visibly nervous. She looked toward me and Rachel for guidance, because we were the ones who had forged a relationship with her. Judge Sabo continued: "Did your attorney tell you how much time you could serve if you are convicted?" Needless to say, Judge Sabo had never bothered to take such a concern with any other witness. There was only one purpose behind the questioning: intimidation.

I thought, sitting there watching the judge trying to unnerve a vulnerable witness, that this would end the proceedings. Jones had told me the night before that she was afraid to testify in a crowded courtroom filled with reporters and go back over a time in her life that she deeply regretted. She knew she was going to be attacked; I as much as told her so, and I did my best to teach her how to stay calm on the witness stand—stay focused on your breathing, keep your answers short, ask the prosecutor to repeat the question to control the pacing, etc. I told her it was okay to be afraid; that I too was afraid, always afraid when I enter a courtroom with so much at stake. The question is not whether you are afraid but what you allow your fear to do to you as a person.

Len was furious at Sabo's blatant intimidation, but, true to form, he kept his cool to conduct the questioning, and he wisely didn't waste any time getting into the crux of the matter. "Do you recall in what respect the testimony that you gave in 1982 was untruthful?"

Jones leaned forward toward the microphone. "I told them that I didn't see two men leave the, umm, run away, leave the scene."

Len has an avuncular courtroom style, blending a gentle touch with an understated command of the situation. He spoke softly as he pressed on in the questioning. "And Miss Jones, in fact, did you see two people run from the scene?"

That was the key question, and it was a question Jackson had repeatedly and desperately put to her over fourteen years earlier. He had expected her to acknowledge that she had seen two people run from the scene. After all, he had that police report memorializing her statement to the detectives, which indicated as much. It was a mystery as to why she absolutely denied seeing flight from the scene back in 1982, and we were now going to unravel it. Jones nodded to Len, cautious, as if thinking about Judge Sabo's perjury warning. She then answered simply, "Yes, I did."

Jones had no motive to invent the story of the running men back on December 15, 1981. Nor did she have the means to concoct a story of flight that comported with the observations of others in terms of the location and the direction of that flight, as she had no way of knowing what others had told police. Jones also had no personal bias in Mumia's favor. On the contrary, she had been befriended by Officer Faulkner on two occasions—once saving her from being robbed and once from being assaulted.

Jones explained that, at the time she testified in 1982, she was in jail on serious felony robbery and gun charges for which she had been arrested a few weeks earlier. A few days before she took the stand, while in jail, Jones received a visit from two detectives. She thought that she was being visited by her court-appointed lawyers, but quickly realized her visitors were detectives with an agenda.

Len asked, "Did you have a conversation with them?"

Jones replied, "I did a little talking but I did a lot of listening." It was in her interest to listen as the detectives talked.

Using the threat of years in prison, and a promise to drop the charges if she helped the prosecution, the detectives pressed Jones to identify Mumia as the shooter. The detectives said "they could help me off those charges if I helped them." The detectives repeatedly stressed that Jones faced up to ten years in prison and the loss of her children if she was convicted of the charges. They repeatedly reassured Jones that her charges would be dropped if she helped the prosecution. Jones was a young twenty-year-old woman, the mother of three small children. "It was a big decision to make," Jones explained, "but this is five or ten years away from my kids."

Jones never pretended to be a model mother. "It was bad enough the fact that my mother had to watch over them while I was in the street," Jones stated, genuinely regretful. "But let alone being taken away from them for all those years. They didn't deserve both." Small puddles of tears rested in her eyes. She quickly added, "I never missed a birthday or a holiday." Sitting in a jail cell, she felt trapped. The detectives then put the terms on the table: "I was to name Mr. Jamal as the shooter, you know," she said, pointing toward Mumia. "And if I was to do that, I was supposed to do something like this girl named Lucky White. They said we made a deal with her and it was going to work out for her so they could make it work out for me. All they kept expressing was don't forget five to ten years . . . that's a long time." Jones removed a tissue from her purse and dabbed her eyes. "They kept expressing that point. . . . The gun charges were supposed to be removed if I went with them."

Jones entered Courtroom 253 back in 1982 to testify, unsure what she would do. In fact, when she was brought to court to testify she thought she was being taken to a hearing on her own charges. When she walked into the courtroom she was very surprised to learn that she was appearing in the Jamal case. As Jones explained, "I was scared and I didn't know what was going on. . . . It was a big surprise." In the courtroom, she saw a crowd of police officers, including the two detectives who had previously visited her and pressured her in jail. She couldn't bring herself to point the finger at Mumia as the shooter; her own internal moral barometer would not allow her to go that far. But her failure of nerve didn't prevent her from giving the prosecution half a loaf. "I told them I didn't see two men run away. . . . I denied seeing anything." That was a lie, she admitted.

As for Jones's angry claim at the trial that she was "a nickel bag high," the interviewing detective who took Jones's December 15 statement, Daniel Bennett, flatly refuted the notion, testifying that Jones was too lucid to be high. Jones, too, admitted that she was clearheaded when she gave the December 15 statement.

Inside, Jones was embittered and ashamed. She saw the dismay in Jackson's face when she lied to him about seeing flight from the crime scene. She saw him scrambling to resuscitate his failed examination. Whether it was her natural inclination to protest or her inexpressible sympathy for a floundering lawyer, Jones spontaneously spoke out about her first encounter with law enforcement officers in regard to the Faulkner shooting investigation. She blurted out that cops, in January or February of 1982, had tried to get her to say what Lucky (aka Cynthia White) had said. She remembered how Judge Sabo—this same judge, who didn't seem to change at all over the years—kept her under wraps when she mentioned this earlier attempted police manipulation.

Len brought her back to that time in January or February 1982. "When the police mentioned Lucky to you, did they say anything about your testimony as compared to what Lucky would do?" Jones explained, as she tried to do back at the original trial, "They just told me I would be able to work, I wouldn't have to worry about my charges, I could work the streets."

Len wanted her to be more explicit. "And did they say what you would have to do in order for you to be able to work?"

"Just name Mr. Jamal as the shooter."

Jones didn't exactly fulfill the terms of the agreement with the visiting detectives. She didn't implicate Mumia; but then again, she didn't tell the jury that she saw flight from the crime scene. Apparently, it was enough for the detectives. Jones never went to prison on the four serious weapons and robbery charges lodged against her. She received probation—a virtual slap on the wrist.

Jones's decision to step forward in 1996 was not without its price. She knew she would have to face stiff cross-examination and her name and picture would be splashed on the front pages of newspapers and displayed on television. She knew that her grown children—all three of whom were now solid citizens and two with families of their own— would again be reminded of her past life as a drug-abusing prostitute. The price was heavy, indeed, and she had wondered why she was doing this. It would be so much easier, she thought, just to stay out of this whole mess. But she went ahead and did it: she testified, and now the prosecutor, Arlene Fisk, was fiddling with some documents, preparing to hurl questions at her.

But it wouldn't feel like questions. It was more like a steady stream of aspersions, tiny pointed arrows, whizzing toward her. Yes, I had sold my body for money; yes, I got high almost every day; yes, I neglected my kids; yes, I am ashamed. The pointed arrows struck the same psychic scars, eventually reopening the wounds and unleashing the pent-up memories and emotions tucked away deep in the caverns of her consciousness.

Through it all, Jones stayed remarkably focused. Fisk couldn't shake her from the detailed testimony she had given on direct examination. But Fisk had one particularly nasty arrow in her quiver, and she saved it for last. She gave a nod to one of her assistants, who in turn signaled to the back of the courtroom. I looked back and saw two uniformed troopers, decked out in calf-high boots, enter the courtroom.

Fisk picked up the pace of her questioning. "Let me call your attention specifically to July the fourteenth, 1992. Do you remember being arrested and charged with attempting to pass a bad check?"

Jones acknowledged that she had been "picked up for a bad check."

Fisk then asked her if she had missed any court dates for that charge. Jones denied that she had. At that point, the last arrow was put in the bow. One of the troopers stepped toward the well of the courtroom.

Len stood up, recognizing what was about to happen. "Your Honor, I object to this procedure. There is no reason for this. What is counsel attempting to demonstrate here?"

Fisk was happy to elucidate: "There is an active, open bench warrant for this witness and she has to be taken into custody with regard to this."

Arrested right from the witness stand! Jones had not expected this; neither did we at the defense table. I had never seen such a thing, either in real life or in the movies. But as shocking an exhibition as it was, in retrospect, it seemed a fitting culmination to the way Sabo handled the case, stretching back to 1982. Len appropriately expressed that point to Judge Sabo: "Well, this is the usual form of intimidation. It is a continuation—"

Len couldn't complete the sentence because Jones interrupted him. "This is not going to change my testimony!" she announced, tears gushing down her face. The shamelessness of the prosecution in bringing up a stale and trivial unresolved bad-check charge, in which the New Jersey authorities had never expressed an interest, apparently emboldened Jones. Her eyes came alive. The timidity that pervaded her demeanor all morning disappeared. Her drooping shoulders were now pulled back, giving her a more youthful, infrangible look. It was as if she now fully appreciated the justness in her decision to step forward, and that she was actually grateful to bear her cross for the years of withholding the truth. In a strange way, she seemingly welcomed the arrest.

Len continued the protest. "I ask the court not to now effect the ultimate coercion and intimidation of a witness, namely, denying her freedom and taking her into custody. You could control that and I ask you not to do this." Judge Sabo shook his head, bemused by the spectacle. "You have control over the courtroom," Len pointed out.

"I don't have any control over them," Judge Sabo replied, referring to the New Jersey troopers.

Len quickly noted that this display of force by the district attorney's office explained why Billy Cook remained in hiding, surfacing for short periods of time and then retreating into some lost world. He had not arrived at that place where Veronica Jones now was: willing to pay the price to unburden himself of the truth. If the prosecution was willing to pull this sort of cheap tactic on Jones, what would they do to Mumia's brother? Cook probably didn't want to find out.

Jones was handcuffed and whisked away straight from the witness stand to a jail cell.

Courtroom reporters were outraged by Judge Sabo's conduct. The *Philadelphia Daily News* reported: "Such heavy-handed tactics can only confirm suspicions that the court is incapable of giving Abu-Jamal a fair hearing. Sabo has long since abandoned any pretense of fairness." The drama of good versus evil had traveled a long distance, ending with Sabo himself, in league with the prosecution team, playing the villain.

Certain questions are put to human beings not so much that they should answer them but that they should spend their lives wrestling with them.

LEO TOLSTOY

18. AMBIGUITY REVISITED

A legal case, I stress throughout this book, is never about "the law" as most people would instinctively interpret that term. The law is not simply a system of rules to govern conduct. The law consists of rules and regulations that structure a network of *stories* spawned from human conflicts. Litigation starts with a story told to a lawyer, which then gets molded into legal categories that define how the story will be told, evaluated, and then adjudicated within a courtroom. Some of those stories will be enshrined in published appellate decisions, and hence achieve the august title of *precedent*, that blessed weapon for lawyers brandished in the battle to validate new stories within our legal institutions. No matter how judges, law professors, and appellate lawyers may ultimately squeeze out the lifeblood of a legal case to reduce it to a black-letter rule—to "law"—there is always a drama lurking inside. "Man is in his actions and practice," the philosopher Alasdair MacIntyre observes, "essentially a storytelling animal." We aspire to Truth through the stories we tell. Genuine trial lawyers know this well.

The case of Mumia Abu-Jamal may never become an important legal precedent—or it might. But that is unimportant, in my view. The story of his trial, and of the subsequent courtroom battles, tell us more about the law than do the legal principles that might emanate from his case. Such is the case with all great political trials. Few of the truly great legal battles are remembered within our culture as important legal precedent. Rarely do lawyers cite the trial of Socrates, of Jesus, of Galileo, of Scopes, of the Rosenbergs, of the Chicago Seven, of Sacco and Vanzetti, or other such notable political cases, as precedent in legal briefs, other than, perhaps, as *cultural* references. Yet, more than the multitude of cases printed in law books for lawyers to mine like precious gold in the service of their clients, such cases expose dilemmas within our society just as they define our understanding of justice, of freedom, of community, and of virtually all things that give life true meaning. Such cases tell us who we are. The story of the case of Mumia Abu-Jamal lies within this tradition, regardless of one's view of his guilt or innocence.

In fact, there is no one story of Mumia's case, as there is no one story that exhausts the interpretive possibilities of any human event. Life permits a multiplicity of perspectives; and I suppose if a God exists, God would have the ability to see things from an infinite number of perspectives—an ability that I take to be the sine qua non of Truth with a capital *T*. The fact that, as human beings, we are nowhere near being capable of comprehending infinite perspectives signifies how ambiguous life necessarily is and how important humility is in our effort to achieve more justice in our communal existence. Perhaps that is what is meant when the great prophets preach that Love, the ultimate in humble surrendering to life's mysteries, is the answer.

I have tried in this book to explore the prosecution's perspective in the case, which is to say, it's story line characterizing Mumia as a cold-blooded cop killer. I then provide the defense's challenge to that perspective—our counternarrative, if you will. Ironically, the more I have thought about this case—not from a lawyer's perspective, which I regard as a deeply impoverished way to look at a problem and at human conflict generally—the more I marvel at just how much the hard-line anti-Mumia forces and the hard-line pro-Mumia forces have in common. It strikes me that both continue to pursue story lines of good versus evil that are profoundly ideologically driven.

McGill, the one who first gave voice to the hard-line anti-Mumia perspective, had no interest in learning about Mumia's life to gain insight into his political and moral beliefs. He simply extracted from a 1970 newspaper article a Mao quote that was fashionable among Black Panther members at the time and wove a story around it. Mumia's affiliation with the Black Panther Party and his attraction to MOVE symbolized his renunciation of law and order, which is nothing more than a lazy slogan for preserving the status quo and all of the values that support it. Whether Mumia killed Officer Faulkner or not became secondary inasmuch as it was taken as a *starting point* for McGill. The trial, from the prosecution's perspective, was not so much about *proving* Mumia's guilt as it was about *explaining* it. McGill's success in positing a compelling explanation for the killing—leaving aside whether the explanation was right or wrong—propelled the case toward its ultimate death verdict. That success still drives the anti-Mumia rhetoric.

The hard-line pro-Mumia perspective has its own prepackaged good-versus-evil narrative. I want to be careful to say that the pro-Mumia side of the debate is much more diverse than its counterpart. Most people on the pro-Mumia side take an agnostic view of the guilt-innocence question, or perhaps adopt a strong suspicion that he is innocent. My discussion for the moment concerns the narrower wing of the movement that simply accepts as an article of faith that Mumia is innocent and finds it abominable for anyone to think otherwise.

Under the extremist pro-Mumia perspective, Mumia, an articulate and passionate revolutionary, can do no wrong. In their view, law enforcement comprises, by definition, forces of repression that will stop at nothing to eradicate the budding seeds of change in society. Neither proposition, in unadulterated form, is defensible. Mumia himself objects to being sanctified, often reminding us that he, like you and me, is just a human being. As for law enforcement, historical evidence powerfully documents the frequent use of the "law" to thwart people's movements and prevent genuine social change. Indeed, one need only look to Rizzo's Philadelphia and Hoover's FBI to see that precise phenomenon. Evidence that we have been able to present in this case certainly gives substance to the claim that Mumia was a victim of manipulated and fabricated evidence, and it is no stretch to say that this victimization was a product of political forces that found sustenance in Philadelphia's particular climate of racial dissension. But it would be wrong to dismiss the evidence against Mumia with a glib reference to racism and police corruption. The bottom line is that the extreme pro-Mumia forces, like McGill and the extreme anti-Mumia forces, have propagated claims that deflect attention away from the genuine controversy that arises from the case.

For example, anti-Mumia forces, to this very day, often publicly state that at least five eyewitnesses actually identify Mumia as the shooter. This claim, as we have seen, is manifestly wrong. Only Cynthia White and Robert Chobert ever went on record as being able to make such an identification. Pro-Mumia forces, to this very day, often assert that definitive proof of Mumia's innocence exists, notably in the form of a ballistics finding that the fatal bullet was a .44 caliber, thus excluding Mumia's .38 caliber pistol. Our own ballistics expert refutes this claim and we have never been able to establish, in fact, that Faulkner was killed with a non-.38 caliber bullet. Anti-Mumia forces cling to Cynthia White's account, despite compelling proof that it is a concoction. They even insist that Robert Harkins actually supports the prosecution's theory of what happened at Thirteenth and Locust, when, in fact, it reveals it to be false. They don't even attempt to reconcile White's account with that of Harkins— with good reason, because it is plainly impossible. Hard-line pro-Mumia forces have insisted that William Singletary provides a reliable account of what actually happened on Thirteenth and Locust, even though Len and I have gone on record, in oral statements in court and in court documents, to state exactly the opposite. Regrettably, even Maureen Faulkner has joined in the demonization effort, claiming that Mumia flashed a smile at her during the 1982 trial when her husband's bloody shirt was unfurled from the evidence bag. The court transcripts reveal that Mumia had been banished from the courtroom when that supposedly occurred. Equally regrettable, there have been public statements from the extreme pro-Mumia camp slandering Faulkner as either a corrupt cop involved in prostitution-ring corruption or a "rat" who was killed by the Philadelphia police department to conceal corruption. It all simply becomes mind-boggling.

The upshot to all of this is that both sides enter into the debate with ideological outlooks that render them susceptible to enunciating, or at least believing, insupportable (and sometimes outlandish) claims. Both sides have been able to engineer favorable media coverage for their respective positions, filled with half-truths and distortions. I wonder sometimes whether this sort of thing is just unavoidable whenever heated issues or controversies are debated through slogans and rallies. I no longer wonder whether either side is well served by it. It is my hope that it will remind fair-minded people of how important is an impartial system of justice. The creation of a judicial system ought to reflect our humble recognition that no one individual or group has a monopoly on the truth. A process must be in place, with appropriate checks and balances, that genuinely serves as a forum for disentangling contested stories. I, for one, much prefer to debate over whether such a process is in place than to argue in a public forum whether a particular individual is guilty or innocent. The controversy should center on whether the judicial process worked in a manner that just and compassionate people would find acceptable.

■ After we completed our attack on the prosecution's "open-and-shut case," Joseph McGill (now in private practice) and leaders of the Fraternal Order of Police took to the public airwaves to defend the verdict and death sentence. They insisted that we had done nothing in the 1995 hearings (or since) to undermine the reliability of the 1982 verdict.

Sure, there were discrepancies and inconsistencies, they argued, but they amounted to nothing more than trivial mistakes and innocuous coincidences that supporters of Mumia were prone to exaggerate.

Mistakes? Was it simply a mistake

- that Cynthia White described the shooter as "short"—shorter than five feet eight whereas Mumia is six feet one inches?
- that White testified that Officer Faulkner was shot in the back while standing and then "grabbed for something" as he was falling, while Robert Harkins reported seeing the shooter, a heavyset man, physically scuffle with the officer and then shoot him in the back while the officer was on his hands and knees struggling to regain his balance?
- that Robert Chobert described the shooter to be up to fifty-five pounds heavier than Mumia and wearing jeans and a light tan shirt, whereas Mumia was wearing a brightly colored red-and-blue ski jacket and flowing khaki "Arab" pants, and claimed that the shooter "ran away" in the direction of the alleyway?
- that Michael Scanlan (the prosecution's most reliable fact witness) stated that he was "certain" that the shooter had an "Afro hairstyle," while Mumia had distinctive dreadlocks (perhaps his most distinctive physical attribute)?
- that Veronica Jones told investigating detectives that she saw two men run from the scene?
- that Dessie Hightower also saw someone flee toward the alleyway?
- that Debbie Kordansky came down from her hotel room to tell investigators that she saw someone run from the crime scene in the same direction as described by Chobert, Jones, and Hightower?
- that, of the fifteen to twenty police officers who were surrounding Mumia at the time he supposedly shouted out a confession, none of them, except for Officers Bell and Wakshul, reported it?

- that Bell and Wakshul neglected to report the confession for over two months, even when questioned about it?
- that hospital security guard Priscilla Durham, a woman who wanted to be a cop, never mentioned the confession to law enforcement until a month after Bell and Wakshul had done so?
- that Wakshul signed a police report within two hours of that supposed confession containing the statement, "the Negro male made no comments"?
- that Wakshul's partner, Stephen Trombetta, signed a police report within an hour of the putative confession stating affirmatively that Mumia said nothing?

Innocuous coincidences? Was it a coincidence

- that the slain officer had in his front pants pocket a driver's license application form (usable as a temporary license) that belonged to a third person?
- that Chobert recanted his assertion to crime scene investigators that he saw the shooter "run away"?
- that Jones recanted her "flight" statement also?
- that, in a homicide investigation that generated reams of police reports, not a single one indicated that Mumia confessed (the reports pointed to the opposite conclusion), and yet investigators generated a highly detailed report regarding William Singletary (the man who graphically described police coercion) solely to establish that he saw nothing?
- that no one within the entire crime scene crew—which included the most senior investigators within the Philadelphia police force—allegedly ever thought of testing the supposed murder weapon for recent discharge, or testing Mumia's hands, face, and body for evidence that he had recently fired a handgun?

What particularly troubles me, even beyond the sheer number of so-called mistakes and coincidences that raise questions about the verdict, is McGill's apparent willingness to choose one of two scenarios based upon nothing more than a calculation of which best enhanced the chance for a conviction. McGill opted for Cynthia White and dispensed with Robert Harkins simply because the former provided an inculpatory account that seemingly explained how Mumia was shot. White's account, as we have seen, involved Mumia running across the street, shooting the officer in the back, and then pursuing him as the officer staggered and fell to the ground. Critical for the prosecution was White's trial testimony that Officer Faulkner "grabbed for something" as he was falling. That sliver of information was enough for McGill to confidently insist that Faulkner shot Mumia as the officer was falling toward the pavement.

Harkins, by contrast, affirmatively refutes the claim that the shooter fired into the officer's back while Faulkner was standing. Rather, the shooter grabbed onto the officer and twirled him around, causing the officer to fall onto all fours. It was then that the shooter fired into the officer's back at close range. This particular account fit the physical evidence, as the ballistics analysis established that the gunshot to the back was done at very close range, and the autopsy established that the bullet exited through the throat, knocking off Faulkner's clip-on tie. Upon being hit in the back, the officer lost his balance completely and fell to the ground. At that point, just as all the other witnesses claimed, the shooter then fired several shots at him. Harkins's detailed account, derived from the most advantageous vantage point of all the eyewitnesses, simply refutes the notion that Mumia was shot during the course of an entanglement with Officer Faulkner.

When did Mumia receive that gunshot wound to the chest, if not at the time suggested by Cynthia White? No doubt Mumia ran to the scene at a time when Officer Faulkner was having difficulty with Billy Cook. As Mumia approached, running, the officer may have panicked, fearing that this black man, with "MOVE-type hair"—and thus, from Faulkner's probable point of view, with MOVE-type anger—was intent on interfering in his struggle with the driver. The trajectory of the bullet is indisputably downward; the likely positioning of Mumia's torso as he is running toward the scene is slightly bent forward (typical for a runner). Faulkner fires from a slight elevation above the street by virtue of being on the curb. A bullet striking Mumia in the chest would thus enter and travel through his torso in a downward trajectory.

Hit first with a bullet, Mumia falls to the ground, *before* the attention of any witnesses is drawn to the scene. The actual shooter, highly likely to be the passenger in the Volkswagen, quickly steps out and engages the officer in the manner described by Harkins. Scanlan, having briefly noticed Mumia run across the street but not focusing on the scene before the first eruption of gunfire, understandably—and even plausibly—assumes that it was this runner who shot the officer, unaware that the runner had been felled by a bullet before attention was drawn to the scene. Significantly, it was Scanlan who candidly admitted at trial that his observations were stitched together with "assumptions."

The actual shooter, sporting an "Afro hairstyle" (Scanlan), shorter than five eight (White) and approximately 225 pounds (Chobert) "ran away," according to Chobert's initial report to police, and confirmed by several others. Crucially, however, Chobert assumes that the man who shot the officer was apprehended while fleeing, as he believed that the man in the police van, Mumia, was the one he saw firing into Officer Faulkner. Yet it is undisputed that Mumia did not, and could not, "run away." Moreover, Chobert's own actions at the scene of the crime confirm that he actually saw the shooter run away, as he stepped out of his cab and walked toward the felled officer. He certainly would not have done so if, as he maintained at trial, the actual assassin remained at the scene, poised to kill others. For Chobert to be a genuinely favorable prosecution witness, he would have to retract his claim to seeing the shooter "run away"—which he in fact did at the trial.

This was the scenario that the jury never considered. It is a scenario that fit the physical and medical evidence, and is rooted in an account provided by an eyewitness who was far less malleable and vulnerable than Cynthia White. No doubt, even with this scenario presented to it, the jury would still be moved by the fact that Mumia carried a gun in a holster, and that gun had five empty rounds when it was found. But circumstantial evidence that cannot fit the physical and medical facts in a case, and that is undercut by eyewitness testimony, cannot be a basis for a conviction. More importantly, the question of whether Mumia actually fired his gun could easily have been answered, not only by seasoned crime scene investigators but by the first spate of officers who arrived at the crime scene within a minute or two of the shooting. Those initial arriving officers, surely experienced enough to know this, could have felt the small-barreled gun and smelled it. If it had been fired five times in relatively rapid succession, it would be warm (if not hot) and the smell of burnt gunpowder still distinctive. Significantly, none of the officers who arrived at the scene were willing to step forward and provide that damning evidence.

No doubt people may say that all this is conjecture. My answer is that it is a marshaling of evidence rooted in Harkins's eyewitness account that McGill chose to ignore for no apparent reason other than that he just didn't like what this witness said. My point here, however, is not to convince anyone of Mumia's innocence but only to raise questions. This or any other scenario should be robustly challenged in a courtroom. But the point remains: after a while, the questions and perplexing unresolved issues in a case suggest that law enforcement and prosecutors were more interested in making an immediate arrest, and were comfortable with a particular theory of an event, because it accorded with their own investigative bias. This is not unusual; it is, in fact, symptomatic of mistaken arrests and wrongful convictions in our criminal justice system. At a minimum, any genuinely fair presentation of evidence would have included Harkins's testimony to amplify the eyewitness aspect of the case, and that of Wakshul to amplify the confession aspect.

■ Several weeks after we completed our evidentiary presentation in the PCRA hearings, we appeared in Judge Sabo's courtroom for oral argument. Everyone knew, prosecutors included, that it was a pointless exercise. Sabo was giving us the opportunity to argue our respective positions solely to create the impression that we were receiving a full and fair consideration of our claims. Three days after the arguments, the judge issued his 154-page decision—a virtual verbatim adoption of the brief submitted by the prosecutors. Every single claim we raised was denied. All of the witnesses who provided favorable evidence were deemed "not credible." Robert Chobert's secret colloquy with Joseph McGill was incidental because, as Sabo saw it, Chobert's claim at trial disavowing that he had seen the shooter "run away" did not actually contradict his pretrial statement to police that he saw the shooter run away. The absence of Wakshul from the 1982 trial was actually a blessing for the defense, he concluded, because his testimony would have further corroborated the confession claim. The mitigation evidence, the judge ruled, would not have influenced a Philadelphia jury to impose a sentence other than death. Use of Mumia's Black Panther Party affiliation and the Mao quote was appropriate, notwithstanding the *Dawson v. Delaware* decision. McGill's jury selection practice of eliminating blacks from the panel did not indicate that race was a motivating factor. And on and on.

After Sabo's decision was issued, thousands of people (estimated at four thousand), including the mayor and the police commissioner, appeared at a three-hour anti-Mumia rally. Maureen Faulkner was the highlight as the throng cheered her loudly. "Danny and I were very, very much in love," she told the crowd. "We had our whole lives to live together. The last moment of his life, he was not looking into loving eyes. He was looking into the barrel of a gun." Mayor Rendell, the district attorney at the time of Mumia's trial, told the crowd that the decision to seek the death penalty against Mumia was an easy call. "The evidence in this case was overwhelming. The action in this case dictated the death penalty."

Jesse Jackson, speaking for many who were devastated by Sabo's decision, stated in a radio program: "The people in Philadelphia cannot stand idly by and be unaware of the ramifications of this decision. Because if Mumia Abu-Jamal can be killed in this situation, you've got to realize you may be next."

In late 1998, the Pennsylvania Supreme Court, including Justice Ronald Castille who was the district attorney advocating that Mumia's death sentence should be carried out in the 1989 appeal and who sponsored the McMahon training session, rubber-stamped Judge Sabo's decision. In the spring of 1999, we petitioned the Supreme Court, for the third time, to accept Mumia's case for review. In September of that year, we received notification that, once again, the high court would not take his case.

The legal team, at that point, boiled down to me and Len. We were heading for federal court, the venue that we had always viewed as our only hope to secure Mumia a new trial. It was fitting, in my view, that the PDC contingent left the team that August, because we couldn't afford to engage in ideological grandstanding in federal court. The litigation would be extremely intense. I spent September and the first half of October drafting our federal Petition for Habeas Corpus Relief. We filed it, amidst much fanfare and with renewed hope, on October 15, 1999, in the United States District Court in Philadelphia. As of this writing, that is where Mumia's case presently sits.

The Great Writ, as habeas corpus is known, empowers a judge to "inquire into the legitimacy of any form of loss of personal liberty."[1] Scholars still debate the historical roots of the Great Writ. Judges, when prompted to show off their scholarly bent, often allude to section 39 of the Magna Carta, which came into being in 1215, as the historical source. Modern understanding of habeas corpus, as a device to challenge an unjust conviction, begins with the Habeas Corpus Act of 1679. The colonists treasured the notion of habeas corpus, so it is no surprise that Article I, section 9, of the United States Constitution guaranteed that it would never be suspended "unless when in Cases of Rebellion or Invasion the public Safety may require it." The very first statute enacted by the First Congress, the Judiciary Act of 1789, empowered all federal courts to "grant writs of habeas corpus for the purpose of an inquiry into the cause of commitment." In *The Federalist Papers,* Alexander Hamilton warned against any retrenchment on habeas corpus, arguing it should be "provided for in the most ample manner" as a bulwark against "arbitrary methods of prosecuting pretended offenses, and arbitrary punishment upon arbitrary convictions." Although James Madison didn't remark on habeas corpus (perhaps because he wasn't a lawyer), and said little on the subject of capital punishment, he did express skepticism toward a jury's ability to impose it fairly. He thus told Jefferson, when critiquing one of his legal reforms for Virginia, that safeguards were needed to ensure that only the deserving were executed.[2] In 1867, Congress passed the Habeas Act, which empowered state prisoners to obtain federal review of alleged violations of federal constitutional rights.

Habeas corpus proved to be a powerful device for justice. Between 40 to 60 percent of all capital cases presented for habeas review in federal courts before 1996 resulted in an overturning of the death sentence. States deeply resented this sort of federal intrusion into the state judicial systems. Plus, federal judges grew weary over the years of handling wagon-loads of habeas petitions. Mumblings in Congress could be heard in the late '80s and early '90s about the inordinate delays in carrying out executions and the clogging of the federal courts with frivolous habeas corpus petitions by desperate death row inmates. Reagan appointees on the federal bench began to take their judicial whacks at the habeas corpus statute.

And then came the Oklahoma City bombing.

Responding to the national outrage over the bombing, Congress seized the moment and quickly passed a bill severely restricting the ability of federal judges to grant habeas corpus relief. President Clinton, a constitutional law instructor at one time but a politician on this occasion, signed the bill into law on April 24, 1996. By signing the Anti-Terrorism and Effective Death Penalty Act (AEDPA), President Clinton "imposed the most rigorous constraints on the constitutional right to seek Federal review of convictions since Lincoln suspended the writ of habeas corpus in the Civil War"—so said the *New York*

Times correspondent Stephen Labaton. President Clinton sought to assuage the fears of civil rights activists and constitutional scholars that the AEDPA eviscerated habeas corpus, announcing that federal judges retained the authority to review petitions from inmates for federal constitutional violations. How Mumia's case is handled by a federal judge will tell us much about the continued vibrancy of the Great Writ.

■ The support for Mumia has grown over the past few years as his case enters this most important phase. His face has become the "new face of the death penalty in the United States," according to a May 21, 2000 piece in the Sunday *New York Times* "Week in Review" section. On May 7, 2000, six thousand people packed the Madison Square Garden Theater in Manhattan for a teach-in on Mumia's case. Similar events were held in other cities around the world. A few years ago, Mayor Willie Brown of San Francisco, backed by the city council, declared one day in August Mumia Abu-Jamal Day. In a similar vein, the Central District of Copenhagen (Norrebro), Denmark, and Palermo, Italy, anointed Mumia an honorary citizen. On October 15, 1999, Representatives Chaka Fattah and John Conyers, speaking on behalf of the entire thirty-eight-member Congressional Black Caucus, called for a new trial. "The only thing we know for sure is that he has not been given due process and that alone is enough for a new trial," Representative Fattah announced. The European Parliament and thirty-eight members of the Japanese Diet have raised deep concerns over Mumia's case.

Some have dismissed the "Free Mumia" clamor as a manifestation of a new Internet culture. A Brandeis University expert on conspiracy theory, Jacob Cohen, argues that the "Mumia phenomenon" is rooted in a "group lie" that flourishes because he is the first so-called political prisoner in the Internet era. "The culture is more and more tolerant of these performances—a group lie that they agree to tell in order to be with one another," he contends. "The Internet is just a nest of these conspiracies of group myth-making."

On November 24, 1997, Amnesty International's secretary general Pierre Sane visited Pennsylvania's death row at the State Correctional

Institute in Greene County. He met with Mumia. Sane characterized Pennsylvania's death penalty as "one of the most racist and unfair in the United States. Worse than Georgia, worse than Mississippi, worse than Alabama." He called upon Pennsylvania's governor to "initiate a full investigation into the racist and unfair application of the death penalty in the state, and to call for a moratorium on all executions." A day after Sane's visit, the Philadelphia Bar Association adopted a resolution calling for a moratorium on executions. Three weeks earlier, the Pennsylvania Bar Association also called for a moratorium. On February 10, 2000, the Philadelphia City Council voted for a moratorium resolution. That same month, Amnesty International issued a detailed report denouncing Mumia's trial as a travesty of fairness. Governor Ridge, who has signed over a hundred ninety death warrants, opposes a moratorium, still insisting that Pennsylvania's death penalty system has always been fair. To date, there has been no investigation and no moratorium.

■ As in all death penalty cases, those siding with the forces who are pushing for Mumia's execution, at bottom, insist that it will bring closure to a breach in the social order. McGill's closing argument wove a classic pro-death penalty narrative that still resonates: a brutal, senseless killing of a blameless victim; a rupture of that delicate social fabric stitched together by "law and order"; the onset of fear and anger rooted in our instinctive aversion to chaos and irrationality; a manipulation of that fear with an invocation of our culture's particular outlook on "the jungle" as the nemesis to social order; and the proffer of a solution—execution.

The narratives *for* Mumia are more varied and more complex. Some focus on the trial process, reserving judgment on the issue of innocence; some feel no need to be squeamish on the guilt-innocence question, demanding that Mumia should be freed immediately. Some view the unfairness in Mumia's case as an anomaly in the system; some say it is symptomatic of the discriminatory and arbitrary nature of capital punishment. Some liken Mumia to others on death row, downplaying his unique intellectual and vocal gifts; some highlight those gifts, wrap them up in ideological garb, and argue that he was framed because he threatened the social order.

Whatever the viewpoint, in a crucial respect, those who advocate that Mumia deserves a new trial, including those who are convinced that he is innocent, possess in their narratives a shared foundation with the anti-Mumia forces: a belief that there has been a breach in the social order and a call for a rectification of that breach. While the anti-Mumia forces point to the killing as the breach and an execution as a healing of that breach, those on the pro-Mumia side point to the trial itself as the breach and a new trial that comports with due process as the remedy. Whatever the rhetorical posture, the implicit narrative goal is the same: imposition of order over chaos. That is why both sides call for justice and yet want a very different outcome.

To me, the notion of ambiguity sits silently underneath the debate over this case *and* in the debate over the death penalty itself. Progressives struggling for social change do well to remind themselves that definitive answers to social problems and dilemmas do not exist. There is no social system that will fully conquer the vagaries of human existence. Chaos is never conquered. To believe otherwise is to share a dangerous premise that lies at the heart of capital punishment, because the death penalty stands as a testament to our innate reluctance to accept that life itself is ambiguous. The death penalty exists because politicians, greedy for votes, offer it to us to palliate our desire for order and to dampen our fear over chaos. It symbolizes a rejection of the idea that no one can be defined simply by their best or their worst acts as human beings.

Imposing the death penalty is the apex of human arrogance. It suggests we are entitled to pass judgment on another's entitlement to live when life itself, as precious as it is, is an impenetrable mystery. Because arrogance and absolutism comfort us, because these attitudes mask our fears with a fraudulent sense of security, we gravitate toward them as toward the shiny apple hanging in the Garden of Eden. I like to think that Nikos Kazantzakis in his book *The Last Temptation of Christ* had it right when he portrayed Jesus, himself a victim of capital punishment and the presumed embodiment of absolute good, struggling on the cross with his own material desires, afflicted with the pangs of ambivalence.

The centrality of ambiguity in human affairs is not a recipe for lethargy or hopelessness. It only signifies that it is the *struggle* for justice that matters. If anyone has an excuse to be hopeless and lethargic, it is a death row inmate. As Mumia writes, the "conditions of most of America's death rows" consists of this:

> [S]olitary confinement, around-the-clock lock-in, no-contact visits, no prison jobs, no educational programs by which to grow, psychiatric "treatment" facilities designed only to drug you into a coma; ladle in hostile, overtly racist prison guards and staff; add the weight of the falling away of family ties; and you have all the fixings for a stressful psychic stew designed to deteriorate, to erode, one's humanity.

Yet, living in this hell, Mumia forges on—even, in an odd way, thrives. His intellect is as sharp as ever and his soul as intact as any evolved human being. He struggles still for social justice, raising his Promethean fist in defiance of Fate. Whatever may happen to Mumia Abu-Jamal, he will always stand for the proposition that the struggle for justice matters.

APPENDIX

EXCERPTS FROM
ALL THINGS CENSORED
by Mumia Abu-Jamal

EDITED BY NOELLE HANRAHAN

SEVEN STORIES PRESS, NEW YORK
2000

EXCERPT FROM
"FROM AN ECHO IN DARKNESS, A STEP INTO LIGHT"

v. Control

It is from Pennsylvania's largest death row at the State Correctional Institute at Huntingdon, in rural south-central Pennsylvania, that I write. In the Commonwealth I am but one of 123 persons who await death.* I have lived in this barren domain of death since 1983. For several years now I have been assigned DC (disciplinary custody) status for daring to abide by my faith, the teachings of John Africa, and in particular for refusing to cut my hair.

---

*This essay was written in 1991. Currently 223 men and women (69.95 percent people of color) await execution on Pennsylvania's death row.

For this I have been denied family phone calls, and on occasion I have been shackled for refusing to violate my beliefs.

Life here oscillates between the banal and the bizarre.

Unlike other prisoners, death row inmates are not "doing time." Freedom does not shine at the end of the tunnel. Rather, the end of the tunnel brings extinction. Thus, for many here there is no hope.

As in any massive, quasi-military organization, reality on the row is regimented by rule and regulation. As against any regime imposed on human personality, there is resistance, but far less than one might expect. For the most part, death row prisoners are the best behaved and least disruptive of all inmates. It also is true, however, that we have little opportunity to be otherwise, given that many death units operate on the "22 + 2" system: twenty-two hours locked in cell, followed by two hours of recreation out of cell. Outdoor recreation takes place in a cage, ringed with double-edged razor wire—the "dog pen."

All death rows share a central goal: human storage in an austere world, in which condemned prisoners are treated as bodies kept alive to be killed. Pennsylvania's death row regime is one of America's most restrictive, rivaling the infamous San Quentin death unit for the intensity and duration of restriction. A few states allow four, six, or even eight hours out of cell, prison employment, or even access to educational programs. Not so in the Keystone State.

Here one has little or no psychological life. Here many escape death's omnipresent specter only by way of common diversions—television, radio, or sports. TVs are allowed, but not typewriters: one's energies may be expended freely on entertainment, but a tool essential for one's liberation through the judicial process is deemed a security risk.

One inmate, more interested in his life than his entertainment, argued forcefully with prison administrators for permission to buy a nonimpact, nonmetallic, battery-operated typewriter. Predictably, permission was denied for security reasons. "Well, what do y'all consider a thirteen-inch piece of glass?" the prisoner asked, "ain't that a security risk?"

"Where do you think you'll get that from?" the prison official demanded.

"From my TV!"

Request for the typewriter denied.

TV is more than a powerful diversion from a terrible fate. It is a psychic club used to threaten those who resist the dehumanizing isolation of life on the row. To be found guilty of an institutional infraction means that one must relinquish TV.

After months or years of noncontact visits, few phone calls, and ever decreasing communication with one's family and others, many inmates use TV as an umbilical cord, a psychological connection to the world they have lost. They depend on it, in the way that lonely people turn to TV for the illusion of companionship, and they dread separation from it. For many, loss of TV is too high a price to pay for any show of resistance.

A BRIGHT, SHINING HELL

IMAGINE.

Imagine living, eating, sleeping, relieving oneself, daydreaming, weeping—but mostly waiting, in a room about the size of your bathroom.

Now imagine doing all those things—but mostly waiting, for the rest of your life.

Imagine waiting—waiting—waiting—to die.

I don't have to imagine.

I "live" in one of those rooms, like about 3,000 other men and women in thirty-eight states across the United States.

It's called "death row."

I call it "hell."

Welcome to "hell."

Each of the states that have death rows have a different system for their "execution cases," varying from the relatively open to the severely restrictive.

Some states, like California and Texas, allow their execution cases work, education, and or religious service opportunities, for out of cell time up to eight hours daily.

Pennsylvania locks its "execution cases" down twenty-three hours a day, five days a week; twenty-four hours the other two days.

At the risk of quoting Mephistopheles, I repeat:

Welcome to hell.

A hell erected and maintained by human governments, and blessed by black-robed judges.

A hell that allows you to see your loved ones, but not to touch them.

A hell situated in America's boondocks, hundreds of miles away from most families.

A white, rural Hell, where most of the caged captives are black and urban.

It is an American way of death.

Contrary to what one might suppose, this hell is the easiest one to enter in a generally hellish criminal justice system. Why? Because, unlike any other case, those deemed potential capital cases are severely restricted during the jury selection phase, as any juror who admits opposition to the death penalty is immediately removed, leaving only those who are fervent death penalty supporters in the pool of eligible jurors.

When it was argued that to exclude those who opposed death, and to include only those who supported death, was fundamentally unfair, as the latter were more "conviction-prone," the U.S. Supreme Court, in a case titled *Lockhart v. McCree*, said such a claim was of no constitutional significance.

Once upon a time, politicians promised jobs and benefits to constituents, like "a chicken in every pot," to get elected. It was a surefire vote getter.

No longer. Today the lowest-level politico up to the president uses another surefire gimmick to guarantee victory:

Death. Promise death, and the election is yours.

Guaranteed. *Vraiment.*

A "Vote for hell" in the "Land of liberty," with its over 1 million prisoners, is the ticket to victory.

From death row, this is Mumia Abu-Jamal.

LIVE FROM DEATH ROW

Don't tell me about the valley of the shadow of death. I live there. In south-central Pennsylvania's Huntingdon County, a hundred-year-old prison stands,* its gothic towers projecting an air of foreboding, evoking a gloomy mood of the dark ages. I, and some forty-five other men, spend about twenty-two hours a day in six-by-ten-foot cells. The additional two hours may be spent outdoors in a chain-link-fenced box, ringed by concertina razor wire, under the gaze of gun turrets.

Welcome to Pennsylvania's death row.

I'm a bit stunned. Several days ago, Pennsylvania's Supreme Court affirmed my conviction and sentence of death by a vote of four justices, three did not participate.

As a black journalist who was a Panther way back in my young teens, I've often studied America's long history of legal lynchings of Africans. I remember a front page of the Black Panther newspaper bearing the quote, "A black man has no rights that a white man is bound to respect," attributed to U.S. Supreme Court chief justice Roger B. Taney of the infamous *Dred Scott* case, where America's highest court held that "neither Africans, nor their free descendants, are entitled to the rights of the Constitution."† Deep, huh?

Perhaps I'm naive, or maybe I'm just stupid, but I really thought the law would be followed in my case, and the conviction reversed. Really.

Even in the face of the brutal Philadelphia MOVE massacre on May 13, Ramona Africa's frame-up, Eleanor Bumpers, Michael Stewart, Clement Lloyd, Allan Blanchard, in countless police slaughters of blacks from New York to Miami, with impunity, my *faith* remained. *Even* in the face of this relentless wave of antiblack state terror, I thought my appeals would be successful.

Even with all I knew, I still harbored a belief in U.S. law, and the realization that my appeal has been denied is a shocker.

Now, I could intellectually understand that American courts are reservoirs of racist sentiment and have been historically hostile to black de-

---

*The Pennsylvania Department of Corrections death row unit at Huntingdon State Prison, described here by Jamal in the 1980s. On January 13, 1995, Jamal was transferred to the State Correctional Institute at Greene, a new supermaximum security control unit that now houses the vast majority of Pennsylvania's death row inmates, and has significantly worse conditions.
†*Dred Scott v. Sanford*, 19 U.S. (How.) 393, 407, 15 L.Ed 691 (1857).

fendants, but a lifetime of propaganda about American "justice" is hard to shrug off.

I need but look across the nation, where as of October 1986 blacks constituted some 40 percent of men on death row, or across Pennsylvania, where as of August 1988, 61 out of 113 men—some 50 percent—are black,* to see the truth, a truth hidden under black robes and promises of equal rights.

Blacks are just 9 percent of Pennsylvania's population, just under 11 percent of America's.** As I said, it's hard to shrug off, but maybe we can try this together. How? Try out this quote I saw in a 1982 law book by a prominent Philadelphia lawyer named David Kairys: "Law is simply politics by other means."†

Such a line goes far to explain how courts really function, whether today, or 130 years ago in the Scott case. It ain't about law, it's about politics by other means.

Now ain't that the truth.

As time passes, I intend to share with you some truths in this column. I continue to fight against this unjust sentence and conviction. Perhaps we can shrug off and shred some of the dangerous myths laid on our minds like a second skin, such as the "right" to a fair and impartial jury of our peers, the "right" to represent oneself, the "right" to a fair trial even.

They're not rights.

They're privileges of the powerful and the rich. For the powerless and the poor, they are chimeras that vanish once one reaches out to claim them as something real or substantial. Don't expect the big networks or megachains of "Big Mac" media to tell you. Because of the incestuousness between the media and government, and big business—which they both serve—they can't.

---

* As of September 1, 1999, there are 3,625 men and women on death row in thirty-nine states and jurisdictions: 43 percent are black. In Pennsylvania, of the 223 men and women on death row, 62.7 percent are black. Source: Death Penalty Information Center and NAACP Legal Defense and Education Fund.

**Census Profile Race and Hispanic Origin, Profile No. 2, June 1991, U.S. Census Bureau, U.S. Department of Commerce, Washington, D.C.

†David Kairys, *Legal Reasoning in Politics of Law*, (1982) 24: 16–17. Citing M. A. Foley, "Critical Legal Studies," *Dickinson Law Review* 91 (Winter 1986): 473.

I can.

Even if I must do so from the valley of the shadow of death, I will.

From death row, this is Mumia Abu-Jamal.

All excerpts from
All Things Censored *by Mumia Abu-Jamal*
Edited by Noelle Hanrahan
(Seven Stories Press, New York, 2000)

ACKNOWLEDGMENTS

I engage in all meaningful activity with the thought of writing about it. The deeper I immersed myself into the extraordinary case of *Commonwealth of Pennsylvania v. Mumia Abu-Jamal*, the more I realized that I had to at least attempt setting out one perspective on the story. Len Weinglass, I, and others have conducted many interviews over the past eight years, which have provided much of the material for this book, as did media accounts of the case. Among those interviewed, Anthony Jackson deserves special mention for his openness and generosity in providing his own account of the experience of handling Mumia's case. He did so knowing that his actions would be the subject of scrutiny, criticism, and even ridicule. I have yet to meet a human being who approached such a situation with similar equanimity. I would never have been in the position to write this book if it weren't for Len Weinglass, a truly fine mentor and friend. I am indebted to Len in ways that I can never express. Political activist and ardent Mumia supporter Clark Kissinger has always been generous with his time and his astute insights. I owe thanks to Gerald Nicosia, a San Francisco writer with whom I have spent many hours reflecting upon this case. Those discussions have helped to clarify my own thinking about the events discussed in the book. I also wish to thank Gerry Spence and other faculty and students at his Trial Lawyer's College, which I attended as both a student and instructor. Through my association with Gerry and the college I have gained a deeper appreciation of the magic associated with representing people in need.

I must add that Mumia Abu-Jamal knew I was writing this book but never asked that he see it before publication. I kept the manuscript from him to avoid even the insinuation that he had a hand in it. Mumia is a client no law school curriculum can prepare a lawyer for. Some have wondered whether Mumia could have attained the notoriety he has gained as the cause celebre of death row if he had continued to pursue a journalism career. I'm convinced that he has an enormous capacity to communicate and would have been a major player in journalism at this point in his life had the events of December 9, 1981, not occurred. But there is something inscrutable in Mumia's character that expunges lament or sadness. I'll probably spend a good part of my life joyously pondering what makes him tick. It is truly a lawyer of good fortune who has that kind of client.

Although this book was written without any involvement of the vast support network for Mumia, I would like to acknowledge my appreciation for the efforts of the many people and organizations who have brought this case to the attention of all those who would listen. Most notably, I stand in awe of the tireless efforts of Pam Africa, who for two decades has worked to support Mumia with single-minded devotion. He may very well have been executed by now had it not been for her.

My sister, Lisa Williams, read the manuscript with a keen eye and a humane sensibility. But most important, she was always supportive, even as she prompted me to do better. My wife, Lisa D'Eufemia Williams, and a fine trial lawyer for the poor in her own right, has been heroic over the years in giving me a "room of my own" to work not only on this book but on the case itself. Her words, "Daddy's working," undoubtedly reverberate constantly in my young daughter's head.

Finally, I'd like to thank my agent, Noah Lukeman, my editor, Diane Higgins, her terrific assistant, Nichole Argyres, and my copy editor, Deborah Miller.

■
NOTES

3. THE SOURCE OF GOOD AND EVIL

1. David Garrow, *The FBI and Dr. Martin Luther King, Jr.* (New York: Penguin Books, 1981).

2. Ward Churchill and Jim Vander Wall, ed., *The COINTELPRO Papers* (Boston: South End Press, 1990).

3. Churchill, p. 123.

4. Manning Marable, *Race, Reform and Rebellion: The Second Reconstruction in Black America, 1945–1982* (Mississippi: University of Mississippi Press, 1984), p. 122.

5. Churchill, p. 125.

6. Ibid., p. 164.

7. James Miller, *Democracy Is in the Streets* (New York: Simon & Schuster, 1987), p. 307.

8. Churchill, p. 164.

9. Memorandum from FBI headquarters to Chicago and seven other field offices, dated May 15, 1970, cited in Churchill, p. 159–60.

10. Memorandum from the Special Agent in Charge, New York, to Hoover, dated August 19, 1970, cited in Churchill, p. 160.

11. Mumia Abu-Jamal, *Death Blossoms* (Farmington, Pennsylvania: The Plough Publishing House, 1997), pp. 132–33.

12. John Anderson and Hilary Hevenor, *Burning Down the House* (New York: W. W. Norton & Co., 1978), p. 11.

13. Ibid., p. 14.

5. THE STRUGGLE FOR MONEY

1. American Bar Association, *Toward a More Just and Effective System of Review in State Death Penalty Cases,* 40 Am. U. L. Rev. 1, 79–92 (1990).

2. Stephen Bright, "Counsel for the Poor: The Death Sentence not for the Worst Crime but for the Worst Lawyer," in *The Death Penalty in America* (ed. Hugo Adam Bedau) (New York: Oxford University Press, 1997), p. 281.

7. JURY SELECTION

1. *Gamble v. Georgia*, 357 S.E.2d 792 (Ga. 1987).

2. *Ford v. Georgia*, 423 S.E.2d 245 (Ga. 1992).

3. *Scott v. Alabama*, 599 So.2d 1222 (Ala. Crim. App. 1992).

4. Transcript of Postconviction Rec., pp. 39–56, *Jefferson v. Alabama,* CC-8-77 (Chambers County Cir. Ct. 1989).

5. *Roundtree v. State,* 546 So.2d 1042 (Fla. 1989).

6. *Berger v. United States*, 295 U.S. 78, 88 (1935).

7. *J.E.B. v. Alabama*, 511 U.S. 127, 137 n.8 (1994).

8. RACE AND THE DEATH PENALTY

1. *Callins v. Collins,* 510 U.S. 1141 (1994).

2. Memorandum from Justice A. Scalia to the Conference of the Justices, U.S. Supreme Court, on file with the Library of Congress.

3. John C. Jeffries, *Justice Lewis F. Powell, Jr.: A Biography* (New York: Macmillan Library, 1994), p. 451.

4. "The Death Penalty in Black and White: Who Lives, Who Dies, Who Decides," Death Penalty Information Center (June 1998).

12. DECIDING ON DEATH

1. Margaret Vandiver, "Capital Juror Interviews," in *The Machinery of Death,* ed. by Enid Harlow, David Matos, and Jane Rocamora (New York: AIUSA, 1995), p. 128.

13. A NEW TEAM, A NEW PORTRAIT, AND AN OLD JUDGE

1. "Did Abu-Jamal Want the Jury to Find Him Guilty?" Marc Kaufman, *Philadelphia Inquirer,* 11 July 1982, p. 1.

2. Juror interview by defense team.

3. T. Rosenberg, "The Deadliest DA," *The New York Times Magazine,* 16 July 1995, p. 22.

4. *Mumia Abu-Jamal v. Price,* 1996 U.S. Dist. LEXIS 8570 (W.D. Penn. 1996).

18. AMBIGUITY REVISITED

1. David Fellman, "Habeas Corpus," in Kermit L. Hall, ed. *The Oxford Companion to the Supreme Court of the United States* (New York: Oxford University Press, 1992), pp. 357–58.

2. Gaillard Hunt, ed., "Observations on the 'Draught of a Constitution for Virginia,'" in *The Writings of James Madison, 1787–1790* (New York: Prometheus Books, 1992), pp. 284–89.

INDEX